Discovering the American Past

SEVENTH EDITION

Discovering the American Past

A Look at the Evidence

VOLUME I: TO 1877

William Bruce Wheeler
University of Tennessee

Susan D. Becker
University of Tennessee, Emerita

Lorri Glover
St. Louis University

WADSWORTH
CENGAGE Learning

Australia • Brazil • Japan • Korea • Mexico • Singapore • Spain • United Kingdom • United States

WADSWORTH
CENGAGE Learning

Discovering the American Past: A Look at the Evidence, Volume I: To 1877, Seventh Edition
William Bruce Wheeler, Susan D. Becker, and Lorri Glover

Senior Publisher: Suzanne Jeans

Senior Sponsoring Editor: Ann West

Development Editor: Kirsten Guidero

Assistant Editor: Megan Chrisman

Senior Marketing Manager: Katherine Bates

Marketing Coordinator: Lorreen Pelletier

Executive Marketing Communications Manager: Talia Wise

Associate Content Project Manager: Anne Finley

Senior Art Director: Cate Rickard Barr

Senior Print Buyer: Judy Inouye

Senior Rights Acquisition Specialist, Text: Katie Huha

Senior Image Rights Acquisition Specialist: Jennifer Meyer Dare

Production Service: MPS Limited, A Macmillan Company

Cover Designer: Walter Kopec, Boston

Cover Image: Les Polders/Alamy Images

Compositor: MPS Limited, A Macmillan Company

For product information and technology assistance, contact us at **Cengage Learning Customer & Sales Support, 1-800-354-9706**

For permission to use material from this text or product, submit all requests online at www.**cengage.com/permissions**. Further permissions questions can be emailed to **permissionrequest@cengage.com**.

Library of Congress Control Number: 2001012345

ISBN-13: 978-0-495-79984-9

ISBN-10: 0-495-79984-X

Wadsworth
20 Channel Center Street
Boston, MA 02210
USA

Cengage Learning is a leading provider of customized learning solutions with office locations around the globe, including Singapore, the United Kingdom, Australia, Mexico, Brazil, and Japan. Locate your local office at **international.cengage.com/region**

Cengage Learning products are represented in Canada by Nelson Education, Ltd.

For your course and learning solutions, visit **www.cengage.com**

Purchase any of our products at your local college store or at our preferred online store **www.cengagebrain.com.**

Printed in the United States of America
1 2 3 4 5 6 7 14 13 12 11 10

Contents

CHAPTER **6**

Church, State, and Democracy:
The Sunday Mail Controversy, 1827–1831

CHAPTER **7**

Land, Growth, and Justice:
The Removal of the Cherokees

CHAPTER **8**

Women's Equality

CHAPTER **9**

The "Peculiar Institution": Slaves Tell Their Own Story

Preface

In his 1990 State of the Union Address, President George Herbert Walker Bush set forth a set of National Education Goals, one of which was the objective that by the year 2000 "American students will leave grades four, eight, and twelve having demonstrated competency in ... English, mathematics, science, history, and geography."[1]

Almost immediately large committees were established in each of the above disciplines, including the National Council for History Standards, composed of history professors, pre-college teachers, members of numerous organizations, educators, and parents. For two years the Council worked to draft a voluntary set of National History Standards that would provide teachers, parents, and American history textbook publishers with guidelines regarding what students ought to know about the United States' past.

Yet before the Standards even were released to the general public, a storm of controversy arose, in which the Council was accused of a "great hatred of traditional history," of giving in to "political correctness," and of jettisoning the Founding Fathers, the Constitution, and people and events that have made the nation great in favor of individuals and events that portrayed the United States in a less complimentary light. Finally, in January 1995, the U.S. Senate, by a vote of 99-1, approved a "sense-of-the-Senate" resolution condemning the standards developed by the National Council for History Standards and urging that any future guidelines for history should not be based on them.[2]

This was not the first time that American history standards and textbooks had been the sources of bitter controversy. In the late nineteenth century, northern and southern whites had radically different ideas about the Civil War and Reconstruction and demanded that public school textbooks reflect those notions. As a result, publishers created separate chapters on these periods for northern and southern schools. At the same time, Roman Catholic

1. Transcript, State of the Union Address, January 31, 1990, in C-SPAN.org/Transcripts/SOTU-1990.aspx. See also U.S. Department of Education, *National Goals for Education* (Washington: Dept. of Education, 1990), p. 1.
2. The Senate proceedings are summarized in Gary B. Nash, Charlotte Crabtree, and Ross E. Dunn, *History on Trial: Culture Wars and the Teaching of the Past* (New York: Alfred A. Knopf, 1997), pp. 231–235. The lone Senator who voted against the resolution was Bennett Johnston of Louisiana.

leaders in the United States complained about the Protestant control of public education and of the history textbooks, resulting in Catholics writing their own textbooks for their parochial schools.[3]

Then, in the 1940s, the popular American history textbooks of Professor Harold Rugg of Columbia University were assaulted as being too radical, mainly because Rugg had discussed subjects such as economic classes, inequality, and what he called the apparent failure of laissez-faire economics. By 1944, sales of his public school textbooks had dropped 90 percent, and by 1951 they had totally disappeared from American classrooms. The Cold War and the fear of communism extended this controversy and led to the removal from most textbooks of the sensitive subjects that had gotten Rugg into so much trouble.[4]

By the 1960s, scholars in many American colleges and universities had begun to view the nation's past in decidedly different ways, due in part to the gradual inclusion of African Americans, women, Native Americans, laborers, immigrants, and the "common folk" in the story of America's past. As these individuals took their places alongside the nation's founders, presidents, generals, corporate leaders, and intellectuals (almost all male and white), the texture and shape of American history began to change. At the same time, the Vietnam War prompted some scholars to look at the United States' overseas record in new, less laudable ways.[5]

By the 1980s, this "new history" began to be included in pre-college American history textbooks. Since the nineteenth century, America's public schools have relied heavily on textbooks, in part as "substitutes for well-trained teachers." But as the quality of teachers improved, most of them continued to rely on textbooks that were dramatically larger, more inclusive, and generally more interesting to students. At the same time, however, both teachers and students came to realize that any American history textbook inevitably reflects the views of the author(s) and is not a completely objective, unbiased view of the past. Indeed, many understood what George Orwell meant when he wrote (in *1984*), "He who controls the past controls the

---

3. Joseph Moreau, *Schoolbook Nation: Conflicts over American History Textbooks from the Civil War to the Present* (Ann Arbor: University of Michigan Press, 2003), pp. 15–20.
4. *Ibid.,* pp. 219–221; Frances Fitzgerald, *America Revised: History Schoolbooks in the Twentieth Century* (Boston: Atlantic Monthly Press, 1979), pp. 36–37. For one attack on textbooks, see E. Merrill Root, *Brainwashing in the High Schools: An Examination of Eleven American History Textbooks* (New York: The Devin-Adair Co., 1958).
5. On the "inclusion" movements of the 1960s and 1970s, see Joyce Appleby, Lynn Hunt, and Margaret Jacob, *Telling the Truth About History* (New York: W.W. Norton, 1994), pp. 147–198.

future." Hence, conflicts over textbooks (see Chapter 11 in Volume 2) are not only warm but inevitable.[6]

How can students hope to come to *their own* understanding of America's past? One way to do this is to go directly to the sources themselves, the "raw material" of history. In *Discovering the American Past*, we have included an engaging and at the same time challenging mixture of types of evidence, ranging from more traditional sources such as letters, newspapers, public documents, speeches, and oral reminiscences to more innovative evidence such as photographs, art, statistics, cartoons, films, interviews, and so forth. In each chapter students will use these as evidence to solve the problem or answer the central question that each chapter poses. Soon they will understand that the historian operates in much the same way as a detective in novels, films, or television programs does when solving a crime.[7]

As much as possible, we have tried to "let the evidence speak for itself" and have avoided (we hope) leading students toward one particular interpretation or another. *Discovering the American Past*, then, is a sort of historical sampler that we believe will help students learn the methods and skills all educated people must be able to master, as well as help them learn the historical content. In the words of an old West African saying, "However far the stream flows, it never forgets its source." Nor, we trust, will you.[8]

◆

Format of the Book

Each chapter is divided into six parts: The Problem, Background, The Method, The Evidence, Questions to Consider, and Epilogue. Each part builds upon the others, creating a uniquely integrated chapter structure that helps guide the reader through the analytical process. The Problem section begins with a brief discussion of the central issues of the chapter and then states the questions students will explore. A Background section follows, designed to help students understand the historical context of the problem. The Method section gives students suggestions for studying and analyzing the evidence. The Evidence section is the heart of the chapter, providing a variety of primary source material

6. On the heavy reliance on textbooks, see Fitzgerald, *America Revised*, p. 19. Subjectivity was understood early by college professors. See Charles A. Beard, "Written History as an Act of Faith," in *American Historical Review*, vol. 39 (1933), pp. 219–231; Robert Allen Skotheim, ed., *The Historian and the Climate of Opinion* (Reading, MA: Addison-Wesley, 1969).
7. See the exciting Robin W. Winks, ed., *The Historian as Detective: Essays on Evidence* (New York: Harper & Row, 1968), esp. pp. xiii–xxiv.
8. For the saying, see Nash, *History on Trial*, p. 8.

on the particular historical event or issue described in the chapter's Problem section. Questions to Consider, the section that follows, focuses students' attention on specific evidence and on linkages among different evidence material. The Epilogue section gives the aftermath or the historical outcome of the evidence—what happened to the people involved, who won an election, how a debate ended, and so on.

◆

Changes in the Seventh Edition

Each chapter in this edition has had to pass three important screening groups: (1) the authors (and some of our graduate students) who used the chapters to teach our students, (2) student evaluators who used *Discovering the American Past* in class, and (3) instructors who either used the book or read and assessed the new and revised chapters. With advice from our screeners, we have made the following alterations that we believe will make this edition of *Discovering the American Past* even more useful and contemporary.

Volume I contains six entirely new chapters: Chapter 1, "A History Mystery: What Happened at Roanoke?"; Chapter 3, "Colonies, Commerce, and Empire: The British Plantation System in the Chesapeake and Caribbean"; Chapter 5, "The Evolution of American Citizenship: The Louisiana Purchase, 1803–1812"; Chapter 6, "Church, State, and Democracy: The Sunday Mail Controversy, 1827–1831"; Chapter 8, "Women's Equality"; and Chapter 10, "Civil Liberties in Time of War: The Case of Clement Vallandigham." In addition, Chapter 4 includes more evidence from the 1770 trial of Captain Thomas Preston. Chapter 7 has incorporated more Native American voices. Chapter 9 has added more reminiscences of former slaves. Finally, Chapter 11, "Reconstructing Reconstruction," appeared in earlier editions of *Discovering the American Past*, and has been brought back by student and instructor requests.

Volume II offers four completely new chapters: Chapter 3, "Selling Consumption, 1890–1930" (on department stores); Chapter 8, "The American Judicial System and Japanese American Internment During World War II"; Chapter 9, "The 1960 Student Campaign for Civil Rights"; and Chapter 11, "Who Owns History? The Texas Textbook Controversy." More evidence has been added to Chapters 5 and 6, and Chapter 7 contains some dramatically different evidence that makes it virtually a new chapter.

In all, we have paid close attention to students, fellow instructors, and reviewers in our efforts to keep *Discovering the American Past* fresh, challenging, and relevant. Earlier editions have shown clearly students' positive responses to the challenge of being, as Robin Winks put it, "historical detectives" who use historical evidence to reach their own conclusions.

Instructor's Resource Manual

Because we value the teaching of American history and yet fully understand how difficult it is to do well, we have written our own Instructor's Resource Manual to accompany *Discovering the American Past*. In this manual, we explain our specific content and skills objectives for each chapter. In addition, we include an expanded discussion of the Method and Evidence sections. We also answer some of our students' frequently asked questions about the material in each problem. Our suggestions for teaching and evaluating student learning draw not only upon our own experiences but also upon the experiences of those of you who have shared your classroom ideas with us. Finally, we wrote updated bibliographic essays for each problem.

Acknowledgments

We would like to thank all the students and instructors who have helped us in developing and refining our ideas for this edition. Also, Bruce and Susan would like to welcome to our team Dr. Lorri Glover, Professor of History at Saint Louis University. She has brought fresh ideas and new insights to this edition. All three of us extend deep thanks to those reviewers who evaluated the sixth edition and gave us candid feedback for preparing this new edition to be even more comprehensive and impactful: Carl Guarneri, Saint Mary's College of California; Juan Garcia, The University of Arizona; Molly Ladd-Taylor, York University; Earl Mulderink, Southern Utah University; Sean Taylor, Minnesota State University—Moorhead; Michael Sherfy, Western Illinois University; Zachery Williams, University of Akron; and Allan Winkler, Miami University.

   All three of us would also like to thank the members of the publishing team who worked together to make this edition a reality. We thank Suzanne Jeans and Ann West for handling the big-picture details of the project; Kirsten Guidero and Megan Chrisman for shepherding the book through development;

Anne Finley and Lauren MacLachlan for managing all the little details and pulling things together; Cate Rickard Barr for handling the art; Katie Huha and Jennifer Meyer Dare for running the complex permissions processes for art and print; Judy Inouye and Marcia Locke for their production work; and Katherine Bates and Talia Wise for their excellent marketing management.

A History Mystery: What Happened at Roanoke?

◆

The Problem

Two decades before Christopher Newport and John Smith helped the English found their first permanent North American colony at Jamestown, another group of English adventurers cast their lot in what Europeans called the "New World." In the spring of 1584, the handsome, daring courtier Walter Ralegh convinced Queen Elizabeth to grant him an exclusive charter to establish a colony on the North American coast. Within a month, he hired Philip Amadas and Arthur Barlowe to lead an exploratory voyage to the land that would be named, in honor of their reputedly chaste queen, Virginia. The results of that brief journey to the coast of what is today North Carolina proved so promising that Ralegh sent out the first group of settlers the following year. These colonists were assured they would find on Roanoke Island a new Eden, a land overflowing with bounty. Amadas and Barlowe insisted, "in all the world the like abundance is not to be found." The Native Americans who lived nearby were, the captains maintained, ideal neighbors. The men and women Amadas and Barlowe met

during their brief foray seemed "very handsome and goodly people, and in their behavior as mannerly and civil as any of Europe." What could possibly go wrong?

Within a year, the Roanoke colonists had grown so weary of the deprivation and violence that plagued the settlement that they abandoned America. In June 1586, they caught a ride home with a visiting fleet commanded by the famous privateer, Francis Drake. Despite this devastating setback, Ralegh (who incidentally never made an Atlantic crossing) refused to give up on his American enterprise. In July of 1587, another group of settlers, under the command of Governor John White, made their way to the Outer Banks. The governor soon decided to undertake what he imagined would be a quick trip to England.

By the time John White finally made his way back to Roanoke—in 1590—he found the settlement deserted, and no sign of the 110 men and women he had left there, including his own daughter and grandchild. The only clue White unearthed as to the fate of his countrymen was that, on a large post just to the right side of the entrance to the fort, "in fair Capital letters was graven CROATOAN." What happened to the "lost colonists" at Roanoke has been the source of rumor and intrigue for over four hundred years. No definitive answer has ever been produced. The larger question, though, is how did things go so wrong so quickly in Roanoke? Why did Ralegh and his contemporaries so badly misjudge their prospects in the New World? Why did an enterprise of such promising origins fail so spectacularly?

◆

Background

The English were latecomers to colonizing in the west. The Spanish, Portuguese, French, and Dutch had already established their imperial presence in the New World when England made its first forays into the Atlantic. As Englishmen began to conceive of staking a claim in the Americas, they saw Spain as their principal rival. The longstanding and bitter tension between the two countries was rooted in nationalism and religion. England coveted the wealth and power Spain derived from its American empire; and English Protestants reviled the Catholic faith of Spaniards and their efforts at spreading Catholicism among Native Americans.

The envy was perhaps understandable. Spain's funding of the voyages of Christopher Columbus in the closing decade of the fifteenth century marked the beginning of sustained contact between Europe and the Americas. During the early sixteenth century, conquistadores—aided in no small measure by diseases—overthrew indigenous governments and asserted imperial authority. Hernán Cortés's siege of Tenochtitlán in 1519 marked the beginning of the conquest of Mexico. That was followed in the 1530s by Francisco Pizarro's triumph over the Incan empire. By the 1550s, Spain's domination had spread deep into Central and South America. New Spain was, by that time, ten times larger than Spain itself, and the colonizers claimed for King Philip II some 20 million New World subjects. This vast Spanish empire produced spectacular wealth, because the colonizers used enslaved Indians (and later Africans) to mine precious metals in Mexico and Peru. In just over a century, they shipped 16,000 tons of silver from America to Europe, 20 percent of which went to the crown as taxes. By the last third of the sixteenth century, King Philip II of Spain presided over a global empire that could rightly claim to be a latter-day Rome.

Everywhere the conquistadores went, Catholic priests followed, seeking to convert native peoples to their Christian faith. Many English Protestants were horrified by this evangelicalism, as they saw the Roman faith as a heresy. The most strident Protestants condemned the "popish" teachings of the Catholic church as not simply wrongheaded but diabolical.

The power that Philip II enjoyed as a consequence of his global empire deeply concerned England's Protestant queen,

Elizabeth. But neither she nor the Anglican Church had the resources to subsidize English colonizing efforts—at least nothing on a scale to threaten Spain. So, during the 1580s, she encouraged mariners such as Francis Drake to raid Spanish ships travelling through the Caribbean. This "privateering" was really state-sponsored piracy. Small groups of English sailors, led by the likes of Drake, would attack Spanish vessels carrying gold and silver from the American mainland to Spain and steal their cargo. Queen Elizabeth took a cut of Drake and other privateers' profits. In addition to producing revenue, these raids disrupted Spanish shipping. It cost a lot of money and many men's lives to provide military defense for Spanish vessels and seaports, all of which distressed the Spanish monarch.

Between attacks, English ship captains explored the Atlantic and Pacific Oceans. Drake, for example, circumnavigated the globe in 1577–80. Others, such as Humphrey Gilbert, probed the North Atlantic, looking for the elusive Northwest Passage to Asia. The desire to find a short, safe route to the Far East, particularly to the lucrative commodities markets in China, had been a principal animating factor in European exploration since the days of Columbus. He, after all, was looking for a passage east. Spanish and English mariners headed west to get east because the known routes were controlled by the Ottoman Empire. The Muslim realm spread from North Africa, across the southern Mediterranean, to Central and Southeast Asia. Christian Europeans resented paying Turkish taxes and high prices to Muslim merchants. They wanted to arrest the territorial, cultural, and religious expansion of their Muslim rivals. Breaking the Islamic monopoly of the most lucrative trading routes would, European leaders concluded, go a long way toward deciding this contest between the world's two great expansionist religions. A century of failing to find a quick route from the Americas to Asia did remarkably little to temper that hope. Both the Roanoke and Jamestown colonists searched in vain for the "other sea."

This seafaring life was extraordinarily risky. Besides the perils of engaging the Spanish military, ships could be destroyed by frequent Atlantic storms. Dead calm might strand a ship for weeks at a time, so that provisions ran out. Being deprived of fresh water while stuck in the middle of a vast ocean would have been a special kind of torment for mariners. Sailors sometimes fomented mutinies, taking over their ships and even murdering their commanding officers. Many of the leading explorers of the age lost their lives to their ocean exploits. Humphrey Gilbert never made it home from his explorations in Newfoundland; he perished at sea in 1583. During a misguided effort to find the Northwest Passage over the top of the world, Henry Hudson was left by his rebellious crew in a small boat in the ice-packed North Atlantic to suffer a frigid death. Undeterred, mariners continued to wager their lives that such perils could be avoided, and adventure, prominence, and wealth found on the high seas.

Wealthy and well-connected men in England, meanwhile, risked their fortunes. And no one in late sixteenth-century England proved a more resolute promoter of overseas adventuring than Sir Walter Ralegh. Ralegh was the half-brother of Humphrey Gilbert, a patron of Francis Drake, and a favorite courtier of Queen Elizabeth. Ralegh, along with Gilbert, Drake, and Richard Grenville, comprised a powerful group of entrepreneurial adventurers known as the "West Country men." They were key players in the sixteenth-century conquest of Ireland. Ralegh personally participated in the occupation, and Arthur Barlowe (whom he later hired to launch the exploration of Roanoke) served under his command in 1580–1581. Convinced of their superiority, the English were shocked when the Irish did not welcome their dispossession and refused to submit. In response the English lowered the threshold of acceptable violence. For example, Humphrey Gilbert, a commander of English forces in Ireland, lined the path to his post with human heads. "Nothing but fear and force," the colonizers decided, "can teach duty and obedience to such rebellious people." Brutal and systematic violence became the method of seizing Irish lands and subjecting Irish people to colonial rule. Emboldened by their experiences in Ireland, the West Country men soon set their sights on America.

On March 25, 1584, Ralegh secured from Queen Elizabeth a patent which granted him the exclusive right to establish a colony in "remote and heathen barbarous lands, countries and territories not actually possessed of any Christian prince and inhabited by Christian people." He enjoyed the widest latitude in managing his settlement. As long as his laws did not violate those of England and upheld the "true Christian faith . . . professed in the

Church of England," he could govern as he saw fit. His domain would extend six hundred miles north and south of the settlement. He would own the land forever, provided he give Queen Elizabeth 20 percent of all precious minerals.

As a first step toward pursuing his grand ambitions in America, Ralegh commissioned Arthur Barlowe and Philip Amadas to scout a location for the settlement. They left Plymouth in late April—just a month after Ralegh received his patent—and by mid-July they had passed Florida and were heading toward the Outer Banks. The captains first went ashore at Hatarask Island, then Roanoke Island, and found the region exceedingly promising. Encouraging too were the initial encounters with the Roanoke Indians. Wingina, the principal chief, had been wounded in a recent skirmish with his neighbors, the Secotans. But his brother, Granganimeo, ensured that the first encounters with these Englishmen would be peaceful and profitable. In his report to Ralegh, Barlowe declared, "We were entertained with all love and kindness, and with as much bounty (after their manner) as they could possibly devise. We found the people most gentle, loving, and faithful, void of all guile and treason." Barlowe and Amadas also brought home promising bounty from their voyage, including a bag of pearls. Making the crossing with them came two Native American men: Manteo and Wanchese.

While Amadas and Barlowe explored the coast of North America, Ralegh busied himself promoting his enterprise. He was aided in that endeavor by Richard Hakluyt, a prominent scholar and ambassador. In 1585, Hakluyt wrote an influential essay extolling the many benefits of English colonization in what was then called Virginia but is today part of North Carolina. Hakluyt promised a wide range of advantages that England would achieve as a consequence of the undertaking; the essay summarized the dreams that had long animated the English in their quest to challenge Spain's domination of the New World.

Emboldened by the excellent news that Barlowe and Amadas brought home, Ralegh sped up his effort at launching a colony. As Ralegh readied his fleet, Manteo and Wanchese learned English, and they taught the Algonquian language to Thomas Hariot, a recent Oxford graduate and protégé of Ralegh. When the convoy of seven ships and 600 men—mostly sailors and soldiers—headed to America in the summer of 1585, Manteo, Wanchese, and Hariot all went. Under the command of Richard Grenville, one of the West Country men, the fleet departed in April 1585. Also making the trip was John White, a painter who, along with Hariot, was charged with chronicling the people and environment of Roanoke.

Life in the New World soon proved more complicated than first impressions had predicted, as is made clear in the documents that follow. A portent of the troubles that might beset the settlers came before they even disembarked. Simon Fernandes, an Azorean, was chosen to captain the flagship in the fleet because of his extensive knowledge of the Atlantic. But he was not terrifically successful when he reached the coast of America. He ran the *Tyger* aground a sand bar, which caused many of the colonists' essential supplies to be flooded in the ship's hold. Without adequate supplies for the 600 voyagers, Grenville and the soldiers and sailors soon departed, leaving some 100 men under the leadership of Governor Ralph Lane. Manteo and Wanchese provided the colonists invaluable help in understanding their new neighbors and in exploring the interior of North Carolina, but confusions arose and often devolved into conflict. While maintaining that the Roanoke Indians were peaceful people eager to trade, colonists nonetheless went about carefully fortifying their settlement. Certainly the strong military presence among colonial leaders played a role in this decision, as did the very legitimate fear of a Spanish invasion. Roanoke was chosen because it offered protection from Spanish assault. At the same time, it was used as a base for launching raids on Spanish ships. Everyone involved understood that Philip II would see the Roanoke colony as a gross encroachment on his territory. But in addition to anxiety about Spain, fear of an Indian attack— if not from the Roanoke, Indians, then perhaps neighboring nations—was also a very real concern to the men who populated the colony.

As the Roanoke settlers struggled to maintain their small outpost, tensions between Spain and England deepened. Between 1585 and 1588, Philip II grew increasingly exasperated by English privateers raiding his ships. Moreover, English Protestants were abetting a rebellion in the Netherlands, which prolonged Spanish military action there. Philip had long wanted Elizabeth dethroned, if not dead. The Pope had excommunicated Elizabeth in 1571 and freed all Catholics in her realm from allegiance to her. As a result numerous attempts were made on her life, which aggravated tensions between Catholics and Protestants in England and further poisoned relations between Spain and England. Philip believed that if Elizabeth were somehow removed, her Catholic kinswoman, Mary, Queen of Scots, might ascend. Mary would return England to the Roman faith and bring England under Spain's influence. Elizabeth, meanwhile, continued to promote an independent Anglican church, and she went so far in pursuit of the Protestant agenda as to send troops to the Netherlands to fight that territorial and religious war against Spain. Hostilities escalated at exactly the same time as the launch of the Roanoke voyages. Privateers now enjoyed a permanent base for their predations. And Elizabeth, who had imprisoned Mary for several years, ordered her execution in 1587. The following year, Philip sent the Spanish Armada, some 130 warships carrying 22,000 soldiers and sailors, to seize control of the English Channel and commence an invasion of England. When the assault failed—in part because of weather—English men and women read that remarkable chain of events as evidence of providential intervention. God, they believed, stood on the side of Protestant England. In the meantime, though, fears of the conflict with Spain pushed aside all thoughts of North America.

By the time Ralegh and his countrymen turned their attention back to their American colony, things in Roanoke had gone terribly wrong.

✦

The Method

In this chapter you will be working with two distinct types of evidence: (1) written accounts and (2) artistic representations. The written accounts take several different forms. Understanding the context of these writings—the author's purpose, the intended audience, the form these documents take, and the timing of their creation—is essential. Not all documents can or should be read the same way. In order to thoughtfully evaluate the ideas in the documents, you will have to think about all these issues and read between the lines.

The first document is a piece of promotional literature. Hakluyt wrote his "Inducements" expressly for the purpose of encouraging support for Ralegh's colony. He intended the document to represent a wide range of interests and to appeal to many different people. While he knew a great deal about English ambitions for a New World colony, Hakluyt never saw Roanoke. Consequently, his piece tells us more about English values than about colonial experiences. "Inducements" differs in many important ways from the subsequent texts, which are first-hand accounts written by men who travelled to Roanoke. The second document, for example, was presented to Ralegh by Amadas and Barlowe following their exploratory voyage. As you read this text, compare it to Hakluyt's piece. Think about the differences between the two documents. Compare the merits of each as well as their limitations. Also, think about their connections, particularly the ways in which the intentions of colonial promoters might have shaped the reporting of the explorers. How might the fact that Amadas and Barlowe were in Ralegh's employ influence what they wrote? What about the length of time they spent in North America?

As you read through the various first-person accounts, you will notice that the content and tone of the documents changes over time. Ralph Lane's description of the evacuation of the settlement in the spring of 1586, for example, affords a very different perspective on Roanoke than does his optimistic letter from the fall of 1585. How did English perceptions and experiences change over time?

The sixteenth century was profoundly different from our own world in a myriad of ways, and sixteenth-century English varies significantly from modern usage. Spelling has been modernized in the longer passages, but major disparities in structure and tone remain. As you read these documents, think about what the form of writing tells us about that age. How did subordinates write to superiors? How did they depict Native Americans? How did they conceive of their environment?

There are no surviving documents from the Roanoke Indians or, for that matter, any of the neighboring nations. North American Indians of the North did not have written languages before contact, so most of what we can know about their culture and experiences must be interpreted through texts created by whites. As you read the English sources, consider how the Indians might have perceived the situation. How might they have interpreted the newcomers? And how might the newcomers have misunderstood Indian intentions? This is all part of reading between the lines of these documents.

The second kind of evidence, artistic works, must be carefully "read" as well. Think of art as words made into pictures, and you will see that you can approach this type of evidence as you do the written accounts. John White's drawings of Indians and their communities are the closest we are able to come to seeing Native American life before European influences. As such, his pictures are, as they say, worth a thousand words. What can we learn about Native American culture and values from his drawings? What can we learn about his perceptions of Native Americans? How do White's drawings compare to the portraits of Walter Ralegh and Queen Elizabeth? What can we learn about English culture and values from these paintings? What, for example, might we infer from the positioning of the globe in both their portraits?

Finally, think about the limitations of each kind of evidence. Sometimes images and documents obscure as much as they reveal. What is not said or depicted in these sources? How might the audience and intention of each source potentially mask the reality of events?

As you analyze the evidence in this chapter, keep two central questions in mind. First, how did the initial expectations for Roanoke differ from the reality of life there? And second, why did things go so wrong for the colony?

✦

The Evidence

Source 1 from Richard Hakluyt the Elder, "Inducements to the Liking of the
Voyage intended Towards Virginia in 40. And 42. Degrees," in David B. Quinn, ed.,
New American World: A Documentary History of North America to 1612 5 Volumes
(New York: Arno Press, 1979) Vol. 3: 64.

1. An excerpt from a 1584 pamphlet written by Richard Hakluyt to support the colony planned by his friend Walter Ralegh.

1. The glory of God by planting of religion among those infidels.
2. The increase of the force of the Christians.
3. The possibilitie of the inlarging of the dominions of the Queenes most excellent Maiestie, and consequently of her honour, revenues, and of her power by this enterprise.
4. An ample vent in time to come of the Woollen clothes of England, especially those of the coursest sorts, to the maintenance of our poore, that els sterve or become burdensome to the realme: and vent also of sundry our commodities upon the tract of that firme land, and possibly in other regions from the Northerne side of that maine.
5. A great possibilitie of further discoveries of other regions from the North part of the same land by sea, and of unspeakable honor and benefit that may rise upon the same, by the trades to ensue in Iapan, China, and Cathay, &c.
6. By returne thence, this realme shall receive (by reason of the situation of the climate, and by reason of the excellent soile) Oade, Oile, Wines, Hops, Salt, and most or all the commodities that we receive from the best parts of Europe, and we shall receive the same better cheape, than now we receive them, as we may use the matter.
7. Receiving the same thence, the navie, the humane strength of this realme, our merchants and their goods shal not be subiect to arrest of ancient enemies & doubtfull friends, as of late yeeres they have beene.
8. If our nation do not make any conquest there, but only use trafficke and change of commodities, yet by meane the countrey is not very mightie, but divided into pety kingdoms, they shall not dare to offer us any great annoy, but such as we may easily revenge with sufficient chastisement to the unarmed people there.
9. Whatsoever commodities we receive by the Steelyard merchants, or by our owne merchants from Eastland, be it Flaxe, Hempe, Pitch, Tarre,

Masts, Clap-boord, Wainscot, or such like; the like good may we receive from the North and Northeast part of that countrey neere unto Cape Briton, in returne for our course Woollen clothes, Flanels and Rugges fit for those colder regions.

10. The passage to and fro, is thorow the maine Ocean sea, so as we are not in danger of any enemies coast.

Source 2: Arthur Barlowe, "The first voyage made to the coasts of America, with two barks, where in were Captains M. Philip Amadas, and M. Arthur Barlowe, who discovered part of the Country now called Virginia, Anno 1584. Written by one of the said Captains, and sent to Sir Walter Raleigh knight, at whose charge and direction, the said voyage was set forth," transcribed and modernized at http://www.virtualjamestown.org. Copyright © Virginia Center for Digital History. Reproduced by permission.

2. Arthur Barlowe's report on his exploratory voyage, 1584.

[Barlowe and Amadas led the exploratory voyage to "Virginia" in 1584. Barlowe's report to Ralegh indicated that they found much that Hakluyt had promised in his pamphlet. They also had a very promising meeting with Granganimeo, the brother of Wingina, and the Roanoke Indians. While the colonists and Indians struggled to understand one another, Granganimeo and his people appeared to Barlowe as open, generous trading partners. From Granganimeo the explorers learn about other native nations further inland and begin to get drawn into politics and competition in Indian country.]

The second of July, we found shoal water, where we smelled so sweet, and so strong a smell, as if we had been in the midst of some delicate garden abounding with all kind of odoriferous flowers, by which we were assured, that the land could not be far distant: and keeping good watch, and bearing but slack sail, the fourth of the same month we arrived upon the coast, which we supposed to be a continent and firm land, and we sailed along the same a hundred and twenty English miles before we could find any entrance, or river issuing into the Sea. The first that appeared unto us, we entered, though not without some difficulty, & cast anchor . . . and after thanks given to God for our safe arrival thither, we manned our boats, and went to view the land next adjoining, and to take possession of the same, in the right of the Queen's most excellent Majesty, as rightful Queen, and Princess of the same, and after delivered the same over to your use, according to her Majesty's grant, and letters patents, under her Highness great Seale. Which being performed, according to the ceremonies used in such enterprises, we viewed the land about us, being, whereas we first landed, very sandy and low towards the waters side, but so full of grapes, as the very beating and surge of the Sea overflowed them, of which we found such plenty, as well there as in all places else, both on the sand and on the green soil on the hills, as in the plains, as well on every little shrub, as also climbing towards the tops of high Cedars, that I think in all the world the like abundance is not to be found: and my self having seen those parts of Europe that most abound, find such difference as were incredible to be written. . . .

. . . This Island had many goodly woods full of Deer, Conies, Hares, and Fowl, even in the midst of Summer in incredible abundance. The woods are not such as you find in Bohemia, Muscovia, or Hercynia, barren and fruitless, but the highest and reddest Cedars of the world, far bettering the Cedars of the Azores, of the Indies, or Lybanus, Pines, Cypress, Sassafras. . . . We remained by the side of this Island two whole days before we saw any people of the Country: the third day we spied one small boat rowing towards us having in it three persons: this boat came to the Island side, four harquebuz-shot from our ships, and there two of the people remaining, the third came along the shoreside towards us, and we being then all within board, he walked up and down upon the point of the land next unto us: then the Master and the Pilot of the Admiral, Simon Fernandino, and the Captain Philip Amadas, my self, and others rowed to the land, whose coming this fellow attended, never making any show of fear or doubt. And after he had spoken of many things not understood by us, we brought him with his own good liking, aboard the ships, and gave him a shirt, a hat & some other things, and made him taste of our wine, and our meat, which he liked very well: and after having viewed both barks, he departed, and went to his own boat again, which he had left in a little Cove or Creek adjoining: as soon as he was two bow shoot into the water, he fell to fishing, and in less then half an hour, he had laden his boat as deep, as it could swim, with which he came again to the point of the land, and there he divided his fish into two parts, pointing one part to the ship, and the other to the pinnesse: which, after he had (as much as he might) requited the former benefits received, departed out of our sight.

The next day there came unto us diverse boats, and in one of them the Kings brother, accompanied with forty or fifty men, very handsome and goodly people, and in their behavior as mannerly and civil as any of Europe. His name was Granganimeo, and the king is called Wingina, the country Wingandacoa, and now by her Majesty Virginia. The manner of his coming was in this sort: he left his boats altogether as the first man did a little from the ships by the shore, and came along to the place over against the ships, follow-ed with forty men. When he came to the place over against the ships, followed with forty men. When he came to the place, his servants spread a long mat upon the ground, on which he sat down, and at the other end of the mat four others of his company did the like, the rest of his men stood round about him, somewhat a far off: when we came to the shore to him with our weapons, he never moved from his place, nor any of the other four, nor never mistrusted any harm to be offered from us, but sitting still he beckoned us to come and sit by him, which we performed: and being set he made all signs of joy and welcome, striking on his head and his breast and afterwards on ours, to show we were all one, smiling and making show the best he could of all love, and familiarity. After he had made a long speech unto us, we presented him with diverse things, which he received very joyfully, and thankfully. None of the company dared speak one word all the time: only the four which were at the other end, spoke one in the others ear very softly. . . .

. . . After we had presented this his brother with such things as we thought he liked, we likewise gave somewhat to the other that sat with him on the mat: but presently he arose and took all from them and put it into his own basket, making signs and tokens, that all things ought to be delivered unto him, and the rest were but his servants, and followers. A day or two after this we fell to trading with them, exchanging some things that we had, for Chamois, Buffe, and Deer skins: when we showed him all our packet of merchandise, of all things that he saw, a bright tin dish most pleased him, which he presently took up and clapped it before his breast, and after made a hole in the brim thereof and hung it about his neck, making signs that it would defend him against his enemies arrows: for those people maintain a deadly and terrible war, with the people and King adjoining. We exchanged our tin dish for twenty skins, worth twenty Crowns, or twenty Nobles: and a copper kettle for fifty skins worth fifty Crowns. They offered us good exchange for our hatchets, and axes, and for knives, and would have given any thing for swords: but we would not depart with any. After two or three days the Kings brother came aboard the ships, and drank wine, and eat of our meat and of our bread, and liked exceedingly thereof: and after a few days overpassed, he brought his wife with him to the ships, his daughter and two or three children: his wife was very well favored, of mean stature and very bashful: she had on her back a long cloak of leather, with the fur side next to her body, and before her a piece of the same: about her forehead she had a band of white Coral, and so had her husband many times: in her ears she had bracelets of pearls hanging down to her middle, (whereof we delivered your worship a little bracelet) and those were of the bigness of good peas. The rest of her women of the better sort had pendants of copper hanging in either ear, and some of the children of the kings brother and other noble men, have five or six in either ear: he himself had upon his head a broad plate of gold, or copper for being unpolished we knew not what metal it should be, neither would he by any means suffer us to take it off his head, but feeling it, would bow very easily. His apparel was as his wives, only the women wear their hair long on both sides, and the men but on one. They are of color yellowish, and their hair black for the most part, and yet we saw children that had very fine auburn, and chestnut colored hair. . . .

. . . [Granganimeo] was very just of his promise: for many times we delivered him merchandise upon his word, but ever he came within the day and performed his promise. He sent us every day a brace or two of fat Bucks, Conies, Hares, Fish, the best of the world. He sent us diverse kinds of fruits, Melons, Walnuts, Cucumbers, Gourds, Peas, and diverse roots, and fruits very excellent good, and of their Country corn, which is very white, fair, and well tasted, and grows three times in five months: in May they sow, in July they reap, in June they sow, in August they reap: in July they sow, in September they reap: only they cast the corn into the ground breaking a little of the soft turf with a wooden mattock, or pickaxe: our selves proved the soil, and put some of our Peas in the ground, and in ten days they were of fourteen inches high: they have also Beans very fair of diverse colors and wonderful plenty: some growing naturally, and some in their gardens, and so have they both wheat and oats. . . .

The soil is the most plentiful, sweet, fruitful, and wholesome of all the world: there are above fourteen several sweet smelling timber trees, and the most part of their underwoods are Bayes and such like: they have those Oaks that we have, but far greater and better. After they had been diverse times aboard our ships, my self, with seven more went twenty mile into the River, that runs toward the City of Skicoak, which River they call Occam: and the evening following, we came to an island, which they call Raonoak, distant from the harbor by which we entered, seven leagues: and at the North end thereof was a village of nine houses, built of Cedar, and fortified round about with sharp trees, to keep out their enemies, and the entrance into it made like a turnpike very artificially; when we came towards it, standing near unto the waters side, the wife of Granganimo the kings brother came running out to meet us very cheerfully and friendly, her husband was not then in the village; some of her people she commanded to draw our boat on shore for the beating of the billoe: others she appointed to carry us on their backs to the dry ground, and others to bring our oars into the house for fear of stealing. When we were come into the other room, having five rooms in her house, she caused us to sit down by a great fire, and after took off our clothes and washed them, and dried them again: some of the women plucked off our stockings and washed them, some washed our feet in warm water, and she her self took great pains to see all things ordered in the best manner she could, making great haste to dress some meat for us to eat. . . .

. . . We were entertained with all love and kindness, and with as much bounty (after their manner) as they could possibly devise. We found the people most gentle, loving, and faithful, void of all guile and treason, and such as live after the manner of the golden age. The people only care how to defend themselves from the cold in their short winter, and to feed themselves with such meat as the soil affords: their meat is very well sodden and they make broth very sweet and savory: their vessels are earthen pots, very large, white, and sweet, their dishes are wooden platters of sweet timber: within the place where they feed was their lodging, and within that their Idol, which they worship, of whom they speak incredible things. . . .

. . . Beyond this Island there is the main land, and over against this Island falls into this spacious water, the great river called Occam by the inhabitants on which stands a town called Pomeiock, & six days journey from the same is situated their greatest city called Skicoak, which this people affirm to be very great. . . .

Into this river falls another great river, called Cipo, in which there is found great store of Mussels in which there are pearls: likewise there descends into this Occam, another river, called Nomopana, on the one side whereof stands a great town called Chawanook, and the Lord of that town and country is called Pooneno: this Poomeno is not subject to the king of Wingandacoa, but is a free Lord: beyond this country is there another king, whom they call Menatonon, and these three kings are in league with each other. Towards the Southwest, four days journey is situated a town called Sequotan, which is the Southernmost town of Wingandacoa, near unto which, six and twenty years past there was a ship cast away, whereof some of the people were saved, and those were white people, whome the country people preserved. . .

Adjoining to this country aforesaid called Secotan begins a country called Pomovik, belonging to another king whom they call Piamacum, and this king is in league with the next king adjoining towards the setting of the Sun, and the country Newsiok, situated upon a goodly river called Neus: these kings have mortal war with Wingina king of Wingandacoa: but about two years past there was a peace made between the King Piemacum, and the Lord of Secotan, as these men which we have brought with us to England, have given us to understand: but there remains a mortal malice in the Secotanes, for many injuries and slaughters done upon them by this Piemacum. They invited diverse men, and thirty women of the best of his country to their town to a feast: and when they were altogether merry, & praying before their Idol, (which is nothing else but a mere illusion of the devil) the captain or Lord of the town came suddenly upon them, and slew them every one, reserving the women and children: and these two have often times since persuaded us to surprise Piemacum [in] his town, having promised and assured us, that there will be found in it great store of commodities. But whether their persuasion be to the end they may be revenged of their enemies, or for the love of they bear to us, we leave that to the trial hereafter.

Source 3 from Ralph Lane to Richard Hakluyt the Elder, 3 September 1585, in David B. Quinn, ed., *New American World: A Documentary History of North America to 1612* 5 volumes (New York: Arno Press, 1979) vol. 3: 293.

3. Ralph Lane's description of Roanoke, 1585.

[When Grenville and his men left the settlement, leadership of the Roanoke colony fell to Ralph Lane. He undertook an exploration of the mainland with the aid of Wachese and Manteo and happily reported his discoveries to Richard Hakluyt.]

. . . In the meane while you shall understand that since sir Richard Greenvils departure from us, as also before, we have discovered the maine to bee the goodliest soile under the cope of heaven, so abounding with sweete trees, that bring such sundry rich and most pleasant gummes, grapes of such greatnes, yet wild, as France, Spaine, nor Italy hath no greater, so many sortes of Apothecarie drugs, such severall kindes of flaxe, and one kind like silke, the same gathered of a grasse, as common there as grasse is here. And now within these few dayes we have found here a Guinie wheate, whose eare yeeldeth corne for bread, 400. Upon one eare, and the Cane maketh very good and perfect sugar, also Terra Samia, otherwise Terra sigillata. Besides that, it is the goodliest and most pleasing territorie of the world (for the soile is of an huge unknowen greatnesse, and very wel peopled and towned, though savagelie) and the climate so wholesome, that we have not had one sicke, since we touched land here. To conclude, if Virginia had but Horses and Kine in some reasonable proportion, I dare assure my selfe being inhabited with English, no realme in Christendome were comparable to it. For this alreadie we find, that what commodities soever Spaine, France, Italy, or the East parts do yeeld unto us in wines of all sortes, in oiles, in flaxe, in rosens, pitch, frankenscence, currans, sugers, & such like, these parts do abound with ye growth of them all, but being Savages that possesse the land, they know no use of the same. And sundry other rich commodities, that no parts of the world, be they West or East Indies, have, here we finde great abundance of. The people naturally most curteous, & very desirous to have clothes, but especially of course cloth rather than silke. . .

Sources 4 through 9 from John White, 1585–1586. Watercolor over graphite sketches (British Museum).

4. White, Indian Elder or Chief.

5. **White, Indian Woman of Secotan.**

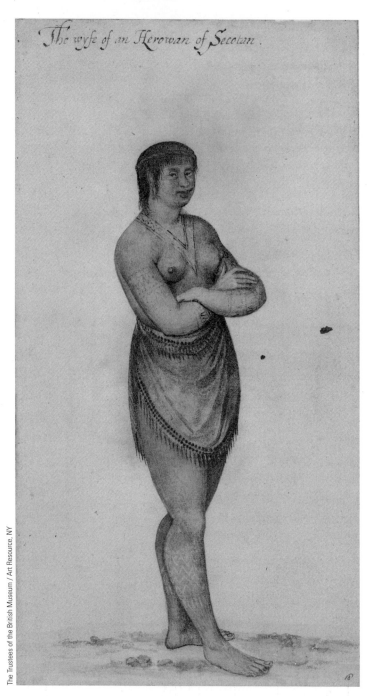

6. White, Indians Fishing.

7. White, Indians Dancing.

8. White, Indian Village of Secotan.

9. White, Indian Village of Pomeiooc.

Source 10: Ralph Lane, "An account of the particularities of the employments of the English men left in Virginia by Sir Richard Greenevill under the charge of Master Ralph Lane General of the same, from the 17. of August 1585. until the 18. of June 1586. at which time they departed the Country: sent and directed to Sir Walter Ralegh," transcribed and modernized at http://www.virtualjamestown.org. Copyright © Virginia Center for Digital History. Reproduced by permission.

10. Ralph Lane's account of events in Roanoke, 1586.

[The longer Lane remained in Roanoke, the more complicated things seemed to become. As he continued to explore, he found neither gold nor a quick route to the "other sea" and eastern markets. Relations with Wingina (also known as Pemisapan) deteriorated when it became clear that the colonists would not feed themselves and insisted on staying in his country. As a professional soldier, Lane tended to fall back on force instead of pursuing diplomacy, which proved a counterproductive way of dealing with Wingina. Lane became suspicious that Wingina/Pemisapan was

spreading rumors with other Native American leaders in order to foment an attack on the English. His preemptive strike is detailed below, and the excerpt reveals how much difference a few months in North Carolina made for Lane and the colonists.]

. . . whereupon I sent to Pemisapan to put suspicion out of his head, that I meant presently to go to Croatoan,[1] for that I had heard of the arrival of our fleet, (though I in truth had neither heard nor hoped for so good adventure,) and that I meant to come by him, to borrow of his men to fish for my company, & to hunt for me at Croatoan, as also to buy some four days provision to serve for my voyage.

He sent me word that he would himself come over to Roanoke, but from day to day he deferred, only to bring the Weopomeioks with him & the Mandoags, whose time appointed was within eight days after. It was the last of May 1586 when all his own Savages began to make their assembly at Roanoke, at his commandment sent abroad unto them, and I resolved not to stay longer upon his coming over, since he meant to come with so good company, but thought good to go and visit him with such as I had, which I resolved to do the next day: but that night I meant by the way to give them in the Island a sudden attack, and at the instant to seize upon all the canoes about the Island, to keep him from advertisements.

But the town took the alarm before I meant it to them: the occasion was this. I had sent the Master of the light horseman, with a few with him, to gather up all the canoes in the setting of the Sun, & to take as many as were going from us to Dasamonquepeio, but to suffer any that came from thence, to land. He met with a Canoe going from the shore, and overthrew the Canoe, and cut off two Savages heads: this was not done so secretly but he was discovered from the shore; whereupon the cry arose: for in truth they, privy to their own villainous purposes against us, held as good spy upon us, both day and night, as we did upon them.

The alarm given, they took themselves to their bows, and we to our arms: some three or four of them at the first were slain with our shot: the rest fled into the woods. The next morning with the light horsemen & one Canoe taking 25 with the Colonel of the Chesepians, and the Sergeant major, I went to Dasamonquepeio: and being landed, sent Pemisapan word by one of his own Savages that met me at the shore, that I was going to Croatoan, and meant to take him in the way to complain unto him of Osocon, who the night past was conveying away my prisoner, whom I had there present tied in an handlock. Hereupon the king did abide my coming to him, and finding my self amidst seven or eight of his principal Weroances and followers, (not regarding

---

1. Croatoan was a nearby town which would play a critical role in the "lost colonists" story.

any of the common sort) I gave the watch-word agreed upon, (which was, Christ our victory) and immediately those his chief men and himself had by the mercy of God for our deliverance, that which they had purposed for us. The king himself being shot thorow by the Colonel with a pistol, lying on the ground for dead, & I looking as watchfully for the saving of Manteos friends, as others were busy that none of the rest should escape, suddenly he started up, and ran away as though he had not been touched, insomuch as he overran all the company, being by the way shot through the buttocks by mine Irish boy with my petronell. In the end an Irish man serving me, one Nugent, and the deputy provost, undertook him; and following him in the woods, overtook him: and I in some doubt least we had lost both the king & my man by our own negligence to have been intercepted by the Savages, we met him returning out of the woods with Pemisapans head in his hand. . . .

[Lane quickly decided it was in his best interest to vacate the settlement. The following week, Francis Drake arrived from raiding Spanish ships in the Caribbean. Drake briefly convinced Lane to stick it out by offering him supplies and several ships. But when a storm struck on June 13 and scattered the fleet and destroyed many of the provisions, Lane refused to stay any longer. He loaded all his settlers aboard the remains of Drake's fleet and headed home.]

Source 11: "The fourth Voyage made to Virginia with three ships, in the year 1587," transcribed and modernized at http://www.virtualjamestown.org. Copyright © Virginia Center for Digital History. Reproduced by permission.

11. 1587 account of the second effort to launch a colony at Roanoke.

[Chastened, if undeterred, by Lane's abandonment of Roanoke, Ralegh set about organizing a second colonizing effort, this time to be peopled by families. Meanwhile Grenville arrived at Roanoke just a few weeks after Lane left. Finding the settlement deserted, he posted fifteen men there while he headed to the Caribbean. Ralegh subsequently decided that the Outer Banks had been a bad location for his colony; it lacked a deep water port and good soil for growing crops. He set his sights further north, in the Chesapeake Bay. When the colonists, headed by John White, arrived in North America in July 1587, they had been instructed to make a quick stop at Roanoke to collect Grenville's men, then to head on to stake a new settlement in the Chesapeake Bay. Captain Simon Fernandes, however, was eager to get to his privateering in the Caribbean and had had enough of ferrying White's company.]

. . . The two and twentieth of July we arrived safe at Hatorask, where our ship and pinnesse anchored: the Governor went aboard the pinnesse, accompanied with forty of his best men, intending to pass up to Roanoke forthwith, hoping there to find those fifteen Englishmen, which Sir Richard Grinvile had left there the year before, with whom he meant to have conference, concerning the state of the Country, and Savages, meaning after he had done so, to return again to the fleet, all pass along the coast, to the Bay of Chesapeake, where we intended to make our seat and fort, according to the charge given us among other directions in writing under the hand of Sir Walter Ralegh: but as soon as we were put with our pinnesse from the ship, a Gentleman by the means of Ferdinando,[2] who was appointed to return for England, called to the sailors in the pinnesse, charging them not to bring any of the planters back again, but to leave them in the Island, except the Governor, & two or three such as he approved, saying that the Summer was far spent, wherefore he would land all the planters in no other place. . . .

. . . The three and twentieth of July the Governor with diverse of his company, walked to the North end of the Island, where Master Ralfe Lane had his fort, with sundry necessary and decent dwelling houses, made by his men about it the year before, where we hoped to find some signs, or certain knowledge of our fifteen men. When we came thither, we found the fort razed down, but all the houses standing unhurt, saving that the nether rooms of them, and also of the fort, were overgrown with Melons of diverse sorts, and Deer within them, feeding on those Melons: so we returned to our company, without hope of ever seeing any of the fifteen men living. . . .

[Doubtless demoralized by being left in the wrong location, the colonists soon confronted more confusion and violence in dealing with the Indians. Manteo was of great aid in some situations, but could not help forestall others.]

. . . On the thirtieth of July Master Stafford and twenty of our men passed by water to the Island of Croatoan, with Manteo, who had his mother, and many of his kindred dwelling in that island, of whom we hoped to understand some news of our fifteen men, but especially to learn the disposition of the people of the country towards us, and to renew our old friendship with them. At our first landing they seemed as though they would fight with us: but perceiving us begin to march with our shot towards them, they turned their backs, and fled. Then Manteo their country man called to them in their own language, whom, as soon as they heard, they returned, and threw away their bows and arrows, and some of them came unto us, embracing us and entertaining us friendly, desiring us not to gather or spill any of their corn, for that they had but little. We answered them, that neither their corn, nor any other thing of theirs should be diminished by any of us, and that our coming was only to renew the old love, that was between us and them at the first, and to live with them as brethren and friends: which answer seemed to please them well . . . They told us further, that for . . . diverse of them were hurt the year before,

2. Captain Simon Fernandes.

being found out of the Island by Master Lane his company, where of they showed us one, which at that very instant lay lame, and had lain of that hurt ever since: but they said, they knew our men mistook them, and hurt them in stead of Winginos men, wherefore they held us excused. . . .

. . . The next day we had conference further with them, concerning the people of Secotan, Aquascogoc, & Pomeiok, willing them of Croatoan to certify the people of those towns, that if they would accept our friendship, we would willingly receive them again, and that all unfriendly dealings past on both parts, should be utterly forgiven and forgotten. To this the chief men of Croatoan answered, that they would gladly do the best they could, and within seven days, bring the Wiroances and chief Governors of those towns with them, to our Governor at Roanoke, or their answer . . . . we understood by them of Croatoan, how that the 15 Englishmen left at Roanoke the year before, by Sir Richard Grinvile, were suddenly set upon, by 30 of the men of Secota, Aquascogoc, and Dasamonguepek, in manner following. They conveyed themselves secretly behind the trees, near the houses where our men carelessly lived: and having perceived that of those fifteen they could see but eleven only, two of those Savages appeared to the 11 Englishmen, calling to them by friendly signs, that but two of their chiefest men should come unarmed to speak with those two Savages, who seemed also to be unarmed. Wherefore two of the chiefest of our Englishmen went gladly to them: but while one of those Savages traitorously embraced one of our men, the other with his sword of wood, which he had secretly hidden under his mantle, struck him on the head and slew him, and presently the other eight and twenty Savages showed them selves: the other Englishman perceiving this, fled to his company, whom the Savages pursued with their bows, and arrows, so fast, that the Englishmen were forced to take the house, wherein all their victuals, and weapons were: but the Savages, forthwith set the same on fire: by means whereof our men were forced to take up such weapons as came first to hand, and without order to run forth among the Savages, with whom they skirmished above an hour. In this skirmish another of our men was shot into the mouth with an arrow, where he died: and also one of the Savages was shot into the side by one of our men, with a wild fire arrow, whereof he died presently. The place where they fought was of great advantage to the Savages, by means of the thick trees, behind which the Savages through their nimbleness, defended themselves, and so offended our men with their arrows, that our men being some of them hurt, retired fighting to the water side, where their boat lay, with which they fled towards Hatorask. By that time they had rowed but a quarter of a mile, they spied their four fellows coming from a creek thereby, where they had been to fetch Oysters: these four they received into their boat, leaving Roanoke, and landed on a little Island on the right hand of our entrance into the harbor of Hatorask, where they remained a while, but afterward departed, whither as yet we know not. . . .

[With the colonists facing a dire situation of inadequate supplies and heightened anxieties over conflicts with the Native Americans, Lane was (at least in his account of events) reluctantly cajoled into going back to England to secure desperately needed provisions.]

. . . . The next day the 22 of August, the whole company both of the Assistants and planters came to the Governor, and with one voice requested him to return himself into England, for the better and sooner obtaining of supplies, and other necessaries for them: but he refused it, and alleged many sufficient causes, why he would not: the one was, that he could not so suddenly return back again without his great discredit, leaving the action, and so many whom he partly had procured through his persuasions, to leave their native country, and undertake that voyage, and that some enemies to him and the action at his return into England would not spare to slander falsely both him and the action, by saying, he went to Virginia, but politically, and to no other end but to leade so many into a country, in which he never meant to stay himself, and there to leave them behind him. Also he alleged, that seeing they intended to remove 50 miles further up into the main presently, he being then absent, his stuff and goods might be both spoiled, & most of them pilfered away in the carriage, so that at his return he should be either forced to provide himself of all such things again, or else at his coming again to Virginia find himself utterly unfurnished, whereof already he had found some proof, being but once from them three days. Wherefore he concluded that he would not go himself.

The next day, not only the Assistants but diverse others, as well women as men, began to renew their requests to the Governor again, to take upon him to return into England for the supply, and dispatch of all such things as there were to be done, promising to make him their bond under all their hands and seals for the safe preserving of all his goods for him at his return to Virginia, so that if any part thereof were spoiled or lost, they would see it restored to him, or his Assignees, whensoever the same should be missed and demanded: which bond, with a testimony under their hands and seals, they forthwith made, and delivered into his hands. The copy of the testimony I thought good to set down.

May it please you, her Majesty's subjects of England, we your friends and country - men, the planters in Virginia, do by these presents let you and every of you to understand, that for the present and speedy supply of certain our known and apparent lacks and needs, most requisite and necessary for the good and happy planting of us, or any other in this land of Virginia, we all of one mind & consent, have most earnestly entreated, and incessantly requested John White, Governor of the planters in Virginia, to pass into England, for the better and more assured help, and setting forward of the foresaid supplies: and knowing assuredly that he both can best, and will labor and take pains in that behalf for us all, and he not once, but often refusing it, for our sakes, and for the honor and maintenance of the action, hath at last, though much against his will, through our importuning, yielded to leave his government, and all his goods among us, and himself in all our behalfs to pass into England, of whose knowledge and fidelity in handling this matter, as all others, we do assure ourselves by these presents, and will you to give all credit thereunto, the 25 of August 1587. . . .

Source 12: John White, "The fifth voyage of M. John White into the West Indies and parts of America called Virginia, in the year 1590," transcribed and modernized at http://www.virtualjamestown.org. Copyright © Virginia Center for Digital History. Reproduced by permission.

12. John White's account of his return to Roanoke, 1590.

[White did not make it back to Roanoke until August 1590, three years after his departure. The following excerpts differ sharply from Arthur Barlowe's report five years earlier. The difficulty of making land is a fitting metaphor for the whole Roanoke enterprise.]

. . . On the first of August the wind scanted, and from thence forward we had very foul weather with much rain, thundering, and great spouts, which fell round about us nigh unto our ships.

The 3 we stood again in for the shore, and at midday we took the height of the same. The height of that place we found to be 34 degrees of latitude. Towards night we were within three leagues of the Low sandy Islands West of Wokokon. But the weather continued so exceeding foul, that we could not come to an anchor near the coast: wherefore we stood off again to Sea until Monday the 9 of August.

On Monday the storm ceased, and we had very great likelihood of fair weather: therefore we stood in again for the shore: & came to an anchor at 11 fathoms in 35 degrees of latitude, within a mile of the shore, where we went on land on the narrow sandy Island, being one of the Islands West of Wokokon: in this Island we took in some fresh water and caught great store of fish in the shallow water. Betweene the main (as we supposed) and that Island it was but a mile over and three or four feet deep in most places. . . .

. . . The 15 of August towards evening we came to an anchor at Hatorask, in 36 degr. and one third, in five fathom water, three leagues from the shore. At our first coming to anchor on this shore we saw a great smoke rise in the

Isle Roanoke near the place where I left our Colony in the year 1587, which smoake put us in good hope that some of the colony were there expecting my return out of England.

The 16 and next morning our two boats went a shore & Captain Cooke, & Cap. Spicer, & their company with me, with intent to pass to the place at Roanoke, where our countrymen were left. At our putting from the ship we commanded our Master gunner to make ready two Minions and a Falkon well loaded, and to shoot them off with reasonable space between every shot, to the end that their reports might be heard to the place where we hoped to find some of our people. This was accordingly performed, & our two boats put off unto the shore, in the Admirals boat we sounded all the way and found from our ship until we came within a mile of the shore nine, eight, and seven fathoms: but before we were half way between our ships and the shore we saw another great smoke to the Southwest of Kindrikers mountains: we therefore thought good to go to the second smoke first: but it was much further from the harbor where we landed, then we supposed it to be, so that we were very sore tired before we came to the smoke. But that which grieved us more was that when we came to the smoke, we found no man nor sign that any had been there lately, nor yet any fresh water in all this way to drink. Being thus wearied with this journey we returned to the harbor where we left our boats, who in our absence had brought their cask a shore for fresh water, so we deferred our going to Roanoke until the next morning, and caused some of those sailors to dig in those sandy hills for fresh water whereof we found very sufficient. That night we returned aboard with our boats and our whole company in safety.

[As the mariners attempted to go ashore, one of the small boats capsized, killing seven men.]

. . . Our boats and all things fitted again, we put off from Hatorask, being the number of 19 persons in both boats: but before we could get to the place, where our planters were left, it was so exceeding dark, that we overshot the place a quarter of a mile: there we spied towards the North end of the Island the light of a great fire through the woods, to the which we presently rowed: when we came right over against it, we let fall our Grapnel near the shore, & sounded with a trumpet a Call, & afterwards many familiar English tunes of Songs, and called to them friendly; but we had no answer, we therefore landed at day-break, and coming to the fire, we found the grass & sundry rotten trees burning about the place. From hence we went through the woods to that part of the Island directly over against Dasamongwepeuk, & from thence we returned by the water side, round about the North point of the

Island, until we came to the place where I left our Colony in the year 1586. In all this way we saw in the sand the print of the Savages feet of 2 or 3 sorts trodden the night, and as we entered up the sandy bank upon a tree, in the very brow thereof were curiously carved these fair Roman letters C R O: which letters presently we knew to signify the place, where I should find the planters seated, according to a secret token agreed upon between them & me at my last departure from them, which was, that in any ways they should not fail to write or carve on the trees or posts of the doors the name of the place where they should be seated; for at my coming away they were prepared to remove from Roanoke 50 miles into the main. Therefore at my departure from them in An. 1587 I willed them, that if they should happen to be distressed in any of those places, that then they should carve over the letters or name, a cross + in this form, but we found no such sign of distress. And having well considered of this, we passed toward the place where they were left in sundry houses, but we found the houses taken down, and the place very strongly enclosed with a high pallisade of great trees, with cortynes and flankers very Fort-like, and one of the chief trees or posts at the right side of the entrance had the bark taken off, and 5 feet from the ground in fair Capital letters was graven CROATOAN without any cross or sign of distress; this done, we entered into the pallisade, where we found many bars of Iron, two pigs of Lead, four iron fowlers, Iron sacker-shot, and such like heavy things, thrown here and there, almost overgrown with grass and weeds. From thence we went along by the water side, towards the point of the Creek to see if we could find any of their boats or Pinnisse, but we could perceive no sign of them, nor any of the last Falcons and small Ordinance which were left with them, at my departure from them. At our return from the Creek, some of our Sailors meeting us, told that they had found where diverse chests had been hidden, and long since digged up again and broken up, and much of the goods in them spoiled and scattered about, but nothing left, of such things as the Savages knew any use of, undefaced. Presently Captain Cooke and I went to the place, which was in the end of an old trench, made two years past by Captain Amadas: where we found five Chests, that had been carefully hidden of the Planters, and of the same chests three were my own, and about the place many of my things spoiled and broken, and my books torn from the covers, the frames of some of my pictures and Maps rotten and spoiled with rain, and my armor almost eaten through with rust; this could be no other but the deed of the Savages our enemies at Dasamongwepeuk, who had watched the departure of our men to Croatoan; and as soon as they were departed, digged up every place where they suspected any thing to be buried: but although it much grieved me to see such spoil of my goods, yet on the other side I greatly joyed that I had safely found a certain token of their safe being at Croatoan, which is the place where Manteo was born, and the Savages of the Island our friends.

When we had seen in this place so much as we could, we returned to our Boats, and departed from the shore towards our Ships, with as much speed as we could: For the weather began to overcast, and very likely that a foul and stormy night would ensue. Therefore the same Evening with much danger and labor, we got our selves aboard, by which time the wind and seas were so greatly risen, that we doubted our Cables and Anchors would scarcely holde until Morning: wherefore the Captain caused the Boat to be manned with five lusty men, who could swim all well, and sent them to the little Island on the right hand of the Harbor, to bring aboard six of our men, who had filled our cask with fresh water: the Boat the same night returned aboard with our men, but all our Cask ready filled they left behind, impossible to be had aboard without danger of casting away both men and Boats: for this night proved very stormy and foul.

The next Morning it was agreed by the Captain and my self, with the Master and others, to weigh anchor, and go for the place at Croatoan, where our planters were for that then the wind was good for that place, and also to leave that Cask with fresh water on shore in the Island until our return. So then they brought the cable to the Capston, but when the anchor was almost aboard, the Cable broke, by means whereof we lost another Anchor, wherewith we drove so fast into the shore, that we were forced to let fall a third Anchor . . . for we had but one Cable and Anchor left us of four, and the weather grew to be fouler and fouler; our victuals scarce, and our cask and fresh water lost: it was therefore determined that we should go for Saint John or some other Island to the Southward for fresh water. And it was further purposed, that if we could any ways supply our wants of victuals and other necessaries, either at Hispaniola, Saint John, or Trinidad, that then we should continue in the Indies all the Winter following, with hope to make 2 rich voyages of one, and at our return to visit our countrymen at Virginia. . . .

Source 13 from Edmund Lodge, *Portraits of Illustrious Personages of Great Britain* (London: Harding and Lepard, 1835). Engraving from painting by Federigo Zucchero.

13. Portrait of Sir Walter Ralegh.

Ken Welsh / The Bridgeman Art Library International

Source 14 from George Gower, 1588, Armada Portrait. Oil paint on oak paneling (Woburn Abbey, England).

14. Portrait of Queen Elizabeth I.

The Bridgeman Art Library International

Questions to Consider

As you read the various sources, it should be apparent that Ralegh, Hakluyt, and their associates held extraordinarily grand expectations for what could be achieved in Roanoke. Think about categories of ambition: religious, social, economic, and political. Remember that the Roanoke colony was located in territory King Philip II of Spain insisted belonged to him, that it was used by privateers raiding Spanish ships, and that it was promoted as a means of breaking Spanish domination in the New World. Remember as well the close connections between international rivalry and religious competition. Consider the ways in which Protestant faith factored into the ambitions for the colony. Finally, think about how colonial promoters expected the colony to remedy problems internal to England. What did the architects of the Roanoke colony expect to achieve there? What did they in fact do to turn those hopes into reality?

The Indians in Virginia had an entirely different set of values, ambitions, and

[31]

traditions than the newcomers, and not surprisingly, they did not hew to plans laid out by English colonists. What were the most important differences between Indians and English? Using the White drawings in particular, try to imagine the culture and values of the Roanoke Indians. How did their society seem to be organized? What did they prize? How do you think the Roanoke Indians and other Native American nations would have perceived the colonists? How did those perceptions differ and how did they change over time? How did interactions with the Indians differ from English expectations? How did confusion exacerbate tensions? Remember as well that many of the leading figures in the Roanoke colony had participated in the conquest of Ireland. How might that experience have shaped their encounters with Indians? Consider as well the images of Ralegh and Queen Elizabeth. Contrast their portraits with the White drawings. Overall, think about the underlying assumptions—of the colony's architects, of the colonists, of the Indians they encountered. How did context and culture shape actions?

As best you can tell, what happened in Roanoke between 1585, when the first colonists arrived, and 1587, when John White left the settlement? Make a list of the problems settlers encountered and the mistakes they made. Make a second list of factors that fell beyond the control of the colonists. How did events in Indian country, in England, and in the larger Atlantic world affect their lives in America? Were the biggest obstacles to the success of Roanoke caused in the colony itself, or did the settlers' difficulties derive from issues beyond their control? Are there additional clues to be found in White's report of his trip to Roanoke in 1590? How did this final account of Roanoke compare to what you know happened between 1585–1587?

While we may never know exactly what happened to the "lost colonists," we can reach reasonable conclusions about the larger matter of the colony's collapse. Considering all the evidence, why do you think Roanoke failed?

◆

Epilogue

John White did not spend the winter of 1590–1591 in the Caribbean. Instead, another storm changed his plans again, and he was forced to make for the Azores and then England. He arrived home in late October 1590. White never returned to America. In a 1593 letter to Richard Hakluyt, he conceded that he had committed the Roanoke colonists "to the merciful help of the Almighty, whom I most humbly beseech to helpe and comfort them." But the English refused to give up on their search for their lost countrymen. Several efforts were made during the 1590s, but no sign that they survived was ever found. No bodies, no bones, no graves were ever located, either.

Rumors filled the void left by solid evidence. When George Percy arrived with the first Jamestown colonists in 1607, he wrote home that he heard from the local Native Americans about a "savage boy . . . who had a head of haire of perfect yellow and a reasonable white skinne." Search parties sent out by the Jamestown colonists claimed they found "crosses and letters, of characters and assured testimonies of Christians" in the forests near Jamestown Island. John Smith said that Powhatan, the principal chief of a Confederation of some 20,000 Algonquian people living in the Chesapeake Bay, told him that the Roanoke colonists had made their way to his country and that he had ordered them killed. Still, rumors continued. As late as the early nineteenth century, President Thomas Jefferson instructed Lewis and Clark to "keep an eye out for errant bands" of "white Indians"—possible descendents of the Roanoke colonists. Four hundred years of historical and archaeological research has yet produced no definitive answer to the question: what happened to the lost colonists? Most likely, the story told by Powhatan was true. The colonists left in Roanoke had never intended to live there. They knew about the town of Croatoan, and they had promised White that if they left Roanoke they would "not fail to write or carve on the trees or posts of the doors the name of the place where they should be seated." If things went poorly at Croatoan, the colonists would have been inclined to try and make their way to the intended location of their settlement, the Chesapeake Bay. This logical plan would have carried them into the heart of Powhatan country.

Whatever the precise fate of these men, women, and children, their story reveals a great deal about English ambitions for, and misunderstanding of,

the New World. Although they knew the story well and in fact were repeatedly instructed to search for their countrymen—the Jamestown colonists appeared to learn little from their Roanoke predecessors' dearly bought experience. The first fleet brought only men, and with a heavy military presence, to Virginia. The settlement antagonized the Spanish and fairly quickly alienated the Indians. Powhatan, like Wingina before him, initially traded with the English, but soon grew weary of their unceasing needs and determined to rid himself of the unwelcome newcomers by confining them to their fort and refusing them food. The result was the "starving time" of 1609–1610, the winter when the great majority of the Jamestown settlers died. Some survivors resorted to cannibalism, raiding the graves of their fallen countrymen and Indians they had killed in battle.

Despite the failure in Roanoke and the abysmal situation in Virginia, the architects of English overseas adventuring refused to give up on their American dreams. They did, however, begin to define more modest goals to balance the elusive search for gold and silver and a quick passage to the Far East: growing corn and tobacco, harvesting timber, and engaging in commercial fishing. The founding of a second colony, located in the middle of the hotly contested Atlantic, also helped the English to persist on the mainland of North America. Bermuda was an uninhabited island when a hurricane stranded 140 Jamestown-bound English men and women there in the summer of 1609. Bermuda, England's second permanent New World colony, was, unlike its mainland counterpart, safe, fertile, and healthful. Most importantly, it was the entrée into the Spanish-dominated Caribbean that Roanoke and Jamestown failed to create. Subsequent colonies, in Plymouth, Massachusetts, Barbados, Antigua, Jamaica, and Maryland, followed. Neither the Anglican Church nor the crown possessed the wealth to fund these efforts, so it fell to individuals and companies to oversee England's Atlantic enterprises. The ambitions for these seventeenth-century colonies varied wildly, as did the experiences of the men and women who migrated. There would be other false starts. For example, the English had to abandon Providence Island, a colony launched in the heart of Spanish territory. But English men and women continued to be inspired by the "inducements" laid out by Richard Hakluyt in the 1580s, and, over the course of the seventeenth century, gradually made their country a permanent and formidable force in the New World.

2

The Threat of Anne Hutchinson

The Problem

On the first day of April, 1638, Anne Hutchinson, accompanied by nine of her children and three grandchildren, fled the Puritan colony of Massachusetts Bay. She joined her husband, William, and a small band of their friends in Rhode Island. Just a year before, Anne and William had been respected members of the First Church of Boston. But in November 1637, she was tried by the Massachusetts Bay General Court and banished from the colony; she was kept under house arrest that winter, awaiting a separate church trial that would result in her excommunication and final exile.

What had Anne Hutchinson done? Why did Massachusetts leaders find her "a woman not fit for our society"? Why was she too dangerous to remain in the Puritan colony? You will be reading part of a transcript from her civil trial in 1637 to find the answers to these questions.

Background

Anne and William Hutchinson left their home in England as part of the "Great Migration" of the 1630s. During that decade some 14,000 Puritans moved to the New World, principally to New England. These colonists sought, as did Anne, a place to practice what they believed was "true" Christianity, purified of the corruptions they saw running amok in the Church of England.

"Puritan" was, in fact, a disparaging term in the early seventeenth century.

Leaders of the Church of England (Anglican Church) used the word to dismiss reformers who objected to the course the established church was pursuing. Nevertheless, it remains a term that historians (intending no judgment at all) nearly universally use to designate the English Protestant migrants who came to colonial New England.

Puritans in England in the early 1600s generally believed that the Protestant Reformation had not gone far enough in their country; too many Roman Catholic influences remained. Puritans did not, for example, approve of high church liturgy, and they rejected priests' authority to administer sacraments. Ceremonialism within the Church of England seemed too similar to Catholicism, which Puritans viewed as heresy. Any Roman influences in the architecture and rituals of the Church of England the Puritans labeled "popery." The Puritans believed that "popery" actually obstructed the ties between God and humankind and had to be eliminated.

The contempt that Puritans felt for the Roman Church is hard to overestimate. Puritans believed "papists" were deluded, if not actually in league with the devil. Puritans often referred to the Roman Church as the "Great Whore of Babylon." And while the Church of England differed in many and profound ways from the Roman Church, Puritans did not necessarily see it that way.

In addition to the outward appearances and practices of the established church, Puritans held theological differences with the leaders of the Anglican Church, particularly on the nature of salvation. Ever since the ascension of King James in 1606, Puritans had worried about the Anglican Church drifting toward a theology known as Arminianism. Arminianism was the belief that individuals, through their own will and works, could achieve salvation. Puritans, however, embraced Calvinist theology, which maintained that God alone, through his grace, saved men and women. According to Calvinist and Puritan beliefs, there was nothing any human being could do to influence God's will. Salvation came through a "covenant of grace"—God predestined some individuals (known as the elect) for salvation and endowed them with faith to fulfill the covenant. Arminianism, with its promise that through good works men and women could earn salvation, advanced a false "covenant of works." This, in the eyes of Puritans, was not much better than the heretical "popery" of the Roman Church.

Despite these important disagreements, during the reign of King James (whose famous commission of an English Bible remains extraordinarily influential among modern-day evangelical Christians), Anglicans and Puritans tolerated one another without too much open conflict. Puritan ministers led many nominally Anglican parishes, and the Church of England relaxed some of its ceremonial practices.

The accession of King Charles in 1625 ended all of that. Charles restored the ceremonialism his father, James, had allowed to erode. In 1628, he installed as the Bishop of London William Laud, a strong advocate of high church ritual. In 1633, he promoted Laud to Archbishop of the Church of England. By that time, Puritan ministers were being fired from their church positions, and church courts were prosecuting Puritans who refused to renounce their beliefs.

Puritans had at first sought relief from Parliament. But when, in 1629, the House of Commons passed a resolution making "popery" or Arminianism a capital offense, King Charles had Parliament dissolved. By then, a growing number of Puritans believed their country and their souls were in such peril that they made the radical decision to leave England entirely.

Deciding it was impossible to affect their reforms in England, some Puritans sought "voluntary banishment," as one of them called it, to the New World. There they would build a model godly community, based solely on the laws of God and his commandments. "We shall be as a city upon a hill," proclaimed Puritan leader and colonial governor John Winthrop, "the eyes of all people are upon us." The earliest migrants to Massachusetts Bay intended to create an example of Christian goodness so compelling that their countrymen in England would be inspired to reform. The Puritans would save the Church of England from diabolical "popish" influences by living in that model community. The stakes for the colonists, then, were extraordinarily high. Puritan leaders expected every man and woman in the settlement to focus on making this vision of the Massachusetts Bay colony a reality.

Anne and William Hutchinson remained in England until 1634. William was a wealthy merchant, and Anne the mother of twelve children; a perilous Atlantic crossing was not to be undertaken lightly. Besides, even in the early 1630s, despite the crackdown on Puritan dissenters, the Hutchinsons were still able to attend church services led by two Puritan ministers they greatly admired: the Reverend John Cotton and the Reverend John Wheelwright, the latter the husband of William Hutchinson's youngest sister, Mary. But, in 1633, Cotton's unorthodoxy caught the attention of Archbishop Laud. Summoned to London to answer for his behavior, Cotton fled to Massachusetts Bay instead. Wheelwright was banned from preaching around the same time,

and Anne concluded "there was none in England that I durst heare." She and William departed for New England with eleven children in 1634.

William, Anne, and their family, along with some two hundred other passengers, arrived in Boston on September 18. John Cotton had been there nearly a year, and in that time had acquired a reputation for excellent preaching; Governor John Winthrop numbered among his admirers. Anne quickly reconnected with John Cotton. She was particularly drawn to his very strong defense of the "covenant of grace."

While all New England Puritans believed that salvation came through God's grace alone, divisions were already appearing in the early 1630s about how exactly to live that theology. Some ministers stressed to their congregations the importance of preparing to receive God's grace—of living just, ordered lives so as to be ready should God decide to grant them faith and salvation. And many Puritans read events in this world—productive crops, respectful children, ordered communities—as signs of their election. God, after all, smiled on his chosen people. John Cotton and his protégé Anne Hutchinson roundly rejected all of this. From the pulpit Cotton condemned this drift toward Arminianism and embracing a covenant of works. Hutchinson, who was extraordinarily intelligent and deeply pious, expanded on these ideas in meetings she hosted at her home.

In addition to being highly regarded as a devout Christian, Anne Hutchinson gained respect in Boston for her skills as a midwife. In the early seventeenth century, caring for pregnant women and delivering infants was totally female centered. Midwives like Anne were also healers of a sort, greatly needed and therefore esteemed by women. Anne's skills gave her special authority within the female world of Massachusetts Bay. Men in the community respected her talents as well—they did not know what she knew and could not do what she did. It was from that valued position as a midwife that Anne began to conduct religious discussions in her home. Her concerns in these meetings echoed those of her spiritual advisor, Reverend Cotton: particularly the tendency of Bostonians to slide into Arminianism when they should focus instead on the omnipotence of God. While not a theologian, Hutchinson was extremely learned and able to hold her own with leading ministers in Massachusetts.

Debates of the sort that engaged Cotton and Hutchinson during the mid-1630s were not uncommon in Massachusetts Bay. Religious squabbles often arose over biblical interpretation, the theological correctness of one minister or another, and the behavior of fellow colonists. To a limited extent, Puritan leaders accepted these discussions because they seemed to demonstrate that religion was a vital aspect of colonists' lives. However, there were very strict limits to what kinds of religious disputes were acceptable. It was one thing for members of a church to contend over a particular Bible passage or discuss how Christians should live in community. But dissent from Puritan tenets and social disruptions that threatened the mission of building their "city upon a hill" simply was [agrees with "dissent" – dissent was not tolerated] not tolerated.

Contemporary Americans like to believe that the Puritans came to the New World in order to build a colony (and nation) dedicated to freedom of religion. In point of fact, the Puritans did want to be free from Anglican interference to practice their faith as they saw fit. But they most assuredly did not believe in freedom of religion. Seeing themselves as the modern version of the ancient Israelites, Puritans believed that God had entered into a special covenant with them. As John Winthrop explained, "Thus stands the cause between God and us: we are entered into covenant with Him. . . . The God of Israel is among us." To Puritans, this covenant meant that the entire community had to follow God's laws as interpreted by Puritan leaders. If they did, God would reward them; if they did not, the whole community would be severely punished. Therefore, community solidarity was essential, and individual desires and thoughts always were subjugated to the needs of the larger society. "We must be knit together in this work as one man," Winthrop insisted. Discord would lead to the breakdown of community cohesion, violation of the covenant, and God's wrath. Therefore, individuals following other Christian faiths—Baptists and Quakers, for example—were fined, imprisoned, "warned out" (expelled from the colony), and even executed if they refused to repent. Drawing on Old Testament laws, Puritan leaders made adultery, blasphemy, sodomy, and witchcraft capital offenses, deserving of the same punishment as murder and treason. God's law was strictly enforced in Puritan New England. As Anne Hutchinson learned, violating the Fifth Commandment was a civil offense.

The need for Puritans to be "knit together in this work" meant that every part of an individual's life was subject to community oversight, starting with his or her religious faith. New England Puritans placed tremendous emphasis on having a publicly validated conversion experience. Only a confirmed conversion would admit a person into full church membership; men who were not full members of a church could not vote or hold public office. To become a confirmed "saint"—a person whose conversion was validated by the community—one had to be examined by a church committee and demonstrate that he or she had experienced the presence of God and the Holy Spirit. There was no universal agreement among ministers about the exact nature of this revelation. For most it was closely connected with studying the Bible; God communicated with believers not in direct, immediate revelations, but rather through His word. A few ministers described hearing the voice of God; however, this was quite controversial. And, as you will see in Anne Hutchinson's trial, a lay person claiming so direct a revelation—to say nothing of a woman's doing so—was especially shocking.

Family life was another essential element of the community order Puritan leaders demanded. Anne Hutchinson's testimony cannot be fully understood without some knowledge of how families were organized in the seventeenth century, and how men and women were supposed to interact. Husbands were to lead their families, just as Christ was head of the church. Wives and children were to defer to that patriarchal authority. While women could become confirmed saints in their churches, as Anne Hutchinson had done, they had no separate economic or political identity. According to the legal doctrine of coverture, women were subsumed under the law first by their fathers and then by their husbands. Women rarely owned property; they certainly could not vote and they were forbidden from speaking at public gatherings that men attended. They did not even have a right to custody of their children should a divorce occur. Signifying the importance of family duty and submission in their lives, Puritan wives were often referred to not by their own names but rather as "Goodwife" Smith or "Goody" Jones.

The same kind of hierarchy that prevailed in family life underlay both the colony's churches and its government. Within this hierarchy, ministers played a very important role. Expected to be highly educated and articulate, the minister of each Puritan church was to be the teacher and leader of his congregation. Of course, the civil officials of Massachusetts Bay, such as the governor and his council, were good Puritans and full members of their churches. The political leaders' job was to ensure that the laws and practices of civil government were in accord with the requirements of living in a godly community. Civil authorities, then, were expected to support religious authorities, and vice versa. Good Puritans honored both. It is in this light that you should consider the Reverend Hugh Peter's charge that Anne Hutchinson had "stepped out of place" and that she "had rather been a husband than a wife; and a preacher than a hearer; and a magistrate than a subject."

By the summer of 1636, Massachusetts Bay was embroiled in a controversy that threatened all these values—the covenant with God, the city upon a hill that would redeem England, the community ethic on which that mission was built, and souls of the true believers. Some Puritans, including Anne's brother-in-law, John Wheelwright, had begun to espouse an extreme version of the covenant of grace: they believed that, having been assured of salvation, an individual was virtually freed from the manmade laws of both church and state, taking commands only from God, who communicated his wishes to the saints. Called Antinomians (from *anti,* "against," and *nomos,* "law"), these Puritan extremists attacked what one of them called the "deadness" of religious services and charged that several ministers were preaching the covenant of works. This accusation was extremely offensive to these orthodox ministers, who did not at all believe they were teaching salvation through good behavior but rather preparation for the possibility of God's grace. The Antinomians countered that "sanctification"—living a good life—was no evidence of "justification"—numbering among the elect. In other words, what one did in this world had nothing to do with his or her fate in the next.

Carried to its logical extension, Antinomianism threatened to overthrow the authority of the ministers and even the colonial government itself. Growing in number and intensity, the Antinomians in 1636 were able to elect one of their own, Francis Vane, to replace Winthrop as colonial governor. Vane lodged with Reverend Cotton and attended Anne Hutchinson's meetings. Although Winthrop managed to return to office the next year, he and many of the leading men of Massachusetts Bay understood perfectly the threat the Antinomian crisis posed to everything they were trying to build in Massachusetts.

The meetings Anne Hutchinson led at her home thus became the source of increasing distress to Governor Winthrop. Initially she had used these sessions to discuss the previous Sunday's sermon. Then she began to expound on her own religious ideas. At first she had drawn only a few women. Then scores came, joined by men, wealthy merchants, and political elites, including some, like Francis Vane, who seized civil power. So many people attended that by 1636 Anne began offering two sessions each week. Governor Winthrop saw it all, for he lived across the road from the Hutchinsons in Boston.

In November 1637, Anne's brother-in-law, Reverend Wheelwright, was banished from the colony because of his radical sermons. Then the General Court sent for Anne. With Governor Winthrop presiding, the court met to decide her fate. Privately, Winthrop called Hutchinson "a woman of ready wit and bold spirit," which was not a compliment in seventeenth-century Massachusetts. But no matter what he thought of Hutchinson personally, the governor was determined to be rid of her.

Why were Winthrop and other orthodox Puritans so opposed to Hutchinson? Some of Wheelwright's followers had been punished for having signed a petition supporting him, but Hutchinson had not signed it. Many other Puritans had held religious discussions in their homes, and more than a few had opposed the views of their ministers, but they were not singled out by the General Court. Technically, in fact, Hutchinson had broken no law. Why, then, was she considered such a threat that she was brought to trial and ultimately banished from the colony?

◆

The Method

For two days, Anne Hutchinson stood before the General Court, presided over by Governor John Winthrop. Forty magistrates filled the meetinghouse, along with six ministers who had offered testimony against Anne. Nearly a dozen judges interrogated the forty-six-year-old mother of twelve living children.

Fortunately, a fairly complete transcript of the proceedings has been preserved. That transcript holds the clues that you, as the historian-detective, will need to answer the questions previously posed. Although spelling and punctuation have been modernized in most cases, the portions of the transcript you are about to read are reproduced verbatim. At first some of the seventeenth-century phraseology might seem a bit strange. As are most spoken languages, English is constantly changing (think of how much English has changed since Chaucer's day). Yet if you read slowly and carefully, the transcript should give you no problem.

Before you begin studying the transcript, keep in mind two additional instructions:

1. Be careful to not lose sight of the central question: Why was Anne Hutchinson such a threat to the Massachusetts Bay colony? The transcript raises several other questions, some of them so interesting that they might pull you off the main track. As you read through the transcript, make a list of the various ways you think Hutchinson might have threatened Massachusetts Bay.

2. Be willing to read between the lines. As you read the transcript, don't just ask yourself what is being said; try to deduce what is actually meant by what is being said in the context of the early 1600s. Sometimes people say exactly what they mean, but often they do not. They might intentionally or unintentionally disguise the real meaning of what they are saying, but the real meaning can usually be found. In face-to-face conversation with a person, voice inflection, body language, and other visual clues often provide the real meaning to what is being said. In this case, where personal observation is impossible, you must use both logic and imagination to read between the lines. Always keep the context—the nature of Puritan society—in mind. Consider, for example, the significance of and likely reaction to the first words Anne Hutchinson spoke in court: "I am called here to answer before you but I hear no things laid to my charge."

◆

The Evidence

Source 1: Reprinted by permission of the publisher from "The Examination of Mrs. Anne Hutchinson at the Court of Newton, November 1637," in *The History of the Colony and Province of Massachusetts-Bay:* Volume II by Thomas Hutchinson, edited by Lawrence Shaw Mayo, pp. 336–391, Cambridge, Mass.: Harvard University Press, Copyright © 1936 by the President and Fellows of Harvard College. Copyright © renewed 1964 by Lawrence Shaw Mayo.

1. The Examination of Mrs. Anne Hutchinson at the Court of Newton, November 1637.[1]

CHARACTERS

Mrs. Anne Hutchinson, the accused

General Court, consisting of the governor, deputy governor, assistants, and deputies

Governor, John Winthrop, chair of the court

Deputy Governor, Thomas Dudley

Assistants, Mr. Bradstreet, Mr. Nowel, Mr. Endicott, Mr. Harlakenden, Mr. Stoughton

Deputies, Mr. Coggeshall, Mr. Bartholomew, Mr. Jennison, Mr. Coddington, Mr. Colborn

Clergymen and Ruling Elders:

Mr. Peters, minister in Salem

Mr. Leveret, a ruling elder in a Boston church

Mr. Cotton, minister in Boston

Mr. Wilson, minister in Boston, who supposedly made notes of a previous meeting between Anne Hutchinson, Cotton, and the other ministers

Mr. Sims, minister in Charlestown

MR. WINTHROP, GOVERNOR. Mrs. Hutchinson, you are called here as one of those that have troubled the peace of the commonwealth and the churches here; you are known to be a woman that hath had a great share in the promoting and divulging of those opinions that are causes of this trouble, and to be nearly joined not only in affinity and affection with some of those the court had taken notice of and passed censure upon, but you have spoken

1. Normally the trial would have been held in Boston, but Anne Hutchinson had numerous supporters in that city, so the proceedings were moved to the small town of Newton, where she had few allies.

divers things as we have been informed very prejudicial to the honour of the churches and ministers thereof, and you have maintained a meeting and an assembly in your house that hath been condemned by the general assembly as a thing not tolerable nor comely in the sight of God nor fitting for your sex, and notwithstanding that was cried down you have continued the same. Therefore we have thought good to send for you to understand how things are, that if you be in an erroneous way we may reduce you so that you may become a profitable member here among us. Otherwise if you be obstinate in your course that then the court may take such course that you may trouble us no further. Therefore I would intreat you to express whether you do assent and hold in practice to those opinions and factions that have been handled in court already, that is to say, whether you do not justify Mr. Wheelwright's sermon and the petition.

MRS. HUTCHINSON. I am called here to answer before you but I hear no things laid to my charge.

GOV. I have told you some already and more I can tell you.

MRS. H. Name one, Sir.

GOV. Have I not named some already?

MRS. H. What have I said or done?

[Here, in a portion of the transcript not reproduced, Winthrop accused Hutchinson of harboring and giving comfort to a faction that was dangerous to the colony.]

MRS. H. Must not I then entertain the saints because I must keep my conscience?

GOV. Say that one brother should commit felony or treason and come to his brother's house. If he knows him guilty and conceals him he is guilty of the same. It is his conscience to entertain him, but if his conscience comes into act in giving countenance and entertainment to him that hath broken the law he is guilty too. So if you do countenance those that are transgressors of the law you are in the same fact.

MRS. H. What law do they transgress?

GOV. The law of God and of the state.

MRS. H. In what particular?

GOV. Why in this among the rest, whereas the Lord doth say honour thy father and thy mother.[2]

MRS. H. Ey, Sir, in the Lord.

GOV. This honour you have broke in giving countenance to them.

---

2. Exodus 20:12. Anne Hutchinson's natural father was in England and her natural mother was dead. To what, then, was Winthrop referring?

MRS. H. In entertaining those did I entertain them against any act (for there is the thing) or what God hath appointed?

GOV. You knew that Mr. Wheelwright did preach this sermon and those that countenance him in this do break a law?

MRS. H. What law have I broken?

GOV. Why the fifth commandment.[3]

MRS. H. I deny that for he [Wheelwright] saith in the Lord.

GOV. You have joined with them in the faction.

MRS. H. In what faction have I joined with them?

GOV. In presenting the petition.

MRS. H. Suppose I had set my hand to the petition. What then?

GOV. You saw that case tried before.

MRS. H. But I had not my hand to the petition.

GOV. You have councelled them.

MRS. H. Wherein?

GOV. Why in entertaining them.

MRS. H. What breach of law is that, Sir?

GOV. Why dishonouring of parents.

MRS. H. But put the case, Sir, that I do fear the Lord and my parents. May not I entertain them that fear the Lord because my parents will not give me leave?

GOV. If they be the fathers of the commonwealth, and they of another religion, if you entertain them then you dishonour your parents and are justly punishable.

MRS. H. If I entertain them, as they have dishonoured their parents I do.

GOV. No but you by countenancing them above others put honour upon them.

MRS. H. I may put honour upon them as the children of God and as they do honour the Lord.

GOV. We do not mean to discourse with those of your sex but only this: you do adhere unto them and do endeavour to set forward this faction and so you do dishonour us.

MRS. H. I do acknowledge no such thing. Neither do I think that I ever put any dishonour upon you.

GOV. Why do you keep such a meeting at your house as you do every week upon a set day?...

MRS. H. It is lawful for me so to do, as it is all your practices, and can you find a warrant for yourself and condemn me for the same thing? The ground of my taking it up was, when I first came to this land because I did not go to such meetings as those were, it was presently reported that I did not allow

3. "Honour thy father and thy mother: that thy days may be long upon the land which the Lord thy God giveth thee." Exodus 20:12.

of such meetings but held them unlawful and therefore in that regard they said I was proud and did despise all ordinances. Upon that a friend came unto me and told me of it and I to prevent such aspersions took it up, but it was in practice before I came. Therefore I was not the first.

GOV. For this, that you appeal to our practice you need no confutation. If your meeting had answered to the former it had not been offensive, but I will say that there was no meeting of women alone, but your meeting is of another sort for there are sometimes men among you.

MRS. H. There was never any man with us.

GOV. Well, admit there was no man at your meeting and that you was sorry for it, there is no warrant for your doings, and by what warrant do you continue such a course?

MRS. H. I conceive there lies a clear rule in Titus[4] that the elder women should instruct the younger and then I must have a time wherein I must do it.

GOV. All this I grant you, I grant you a time for it, but what is this to the purpose that you Mrs. Hutchinson must call a company together from their callings to come to be taught of you?

MRS. H. Will it please you to answer me this and to give me a rule for then I will willingly submit to any truth. If any come to my house to be instructed in the ways of God what rule have I to put them away?

GOV. But suppose that a hundred men come unto you to be instructed. Will you forbear to instruct them?

MRS. H. As far as I conceive I cross a rule in it.

GOV. Very well and do you not so here?

MRS. H. No, Sir, for my ground is they are men.

GOV. Men and women all is one for that, but suppose that a man should come and say, "Mrs. Hutchinson, I hear that you are a woman that God hath given his grace unto and you have knowledge in the word of God. I pray instruct me a little." Ought you not to instruct this man?

MRS. H. I think I may. Do you think it is not lawful for me to teach women and why do you call me to teach the court?

GOV. We do not call you to teach the court but to lay open yourself.

---

4. Here Hutchinson is referencing Titus 2:3–5, which in the New International Version reads, "Likewise, teach the older women to be reverent in the way they live, not to be slanderers or addicted to much wine, but to teach what is good. Then they can train the younger women to love their husbands and children, to be self-controlled and pure, to be busy at home, to be kind, and to be subject to their husbands, so that no one will malign the word of God." The text in the Geneva Bible, which was popular among seventeenth-century Puritans, reads: "The elder women likewise, that they be in such behauiour as becommeth holinesse, not false accusers, not subject to much wine, but teachers of honest things, That they may instruct the yong women to be sober minded, that they loue their husbands, that they loue their children, That they be temperate, chaste, keeping at home, good & subject unto their husbands, that the word of God be not euill spoken of."

[In this portion of the transcript not reproduced, Hutchinson and Winthrop continued to wrangle over specifically what law she had broken.]

GOV. Your course is not to be suffered for. Besides that we find such a course as this to be greatly prejudicial to the state. Besides the occasion that it is to seduce many honest persons that are called to those meetings and your opinions being known to be different from the word of God may seduce many simple souls that resort unto you. Besides that the occasion which hath come of late hath come from none but such as have frequented your meetings, so that now they are flown off from magistrates and ministers and since they have come to you. And besides that it will not well stand with the commonwealth that families should be neglected for so many neighbours and dames and so much time spent. We see no rule of God for this. We see not that any should have authority to set up any other exercises besides what authority hath already set up and so what hurt comes of this you will be guilty of and we for suffering you.

MRS. H. Sir, I do not believe that to be so.

GOV. Well, we see how it is. We must therefore put it away from you or restrain you from maintaining this course.

MRS. H. If you have a rule for it from God's word you may.

GOV. We are your judges, and not you ours and we must compel you to it.

[Here followed a discussion of whether men as well as women attended Hutchinson's meetings. In response to one question, Hutchinson denied that women ever taught at men's meetings.]

DEPUTY GOVERNOR. I would go a little higher with Mrs. Hutchinson. About three years ago we were all in peace. Mrs. Hutchinson from that time she came hath made a disturbance, and some that came over with her in the ship did inform me what she was as soon as she was landed. I being then in place dealt with the pastor and teacher of Boston and desired them to enquire of her, and then I was satisfied that she held nothing different from us. But within half a year after, she had vented divers of her strange opinions and had made parties in the country, and at length it comes that Mr. Cotton and Mr. Vane[5] were of her judgment, but Mr. Cotton had cleared himself that he was not of that mind. But now it appears by this woman's meeting that Mrs. Hutchinson hath so forestalled the minds of many by their resort to her meeting that now she hath a potent party in the country. Now if all these things have endangered us as from

5. Henry Vane, supported by the Antinomians and merchant allies, was elected governor of Massachusetts Bay colony in 1636 and lost that office to Winthrop in 1637.

that foundation and if she in particular hath disparaged all our ministers in the land that they have preached a covenant of works, and only Mr. Cotton a covenant of grace, why this is not to be suffered, and therefore being driven to the foundation and it being found that Mrs. Hutchinson is she that hath depraved all the ministers and hath been the cause of what is falled out, why we must take away the foundation and the building will fall.

MRS. H. I pray, Sir, prove it that I said they preached nothing but a covenant of works.

DEP. GOV. Nothing but a covenant of works. Why a Jesuit[6] may preach truth sometimes.

MRS. H. Did I ever say they preached a covenant of works then?

DEP. GOV. If they do not preach a covenant of grace clearly, then they preach a covenant of works.

MRS. H. No, Sir. One may preach a covenant of grace more clearly than another, so I said.

DEP. GOV. We are not upon that now but upon position.

MRS. H. Prove this then Sir that you say I said.

DEP. GOV. When they do preach a covenant of works do they preach truth?

MRS. H. Yes, Sir. But when they preach a covenant of works for salvation, that is not truth.

DEP. GOV. I do but ask you this: when the ministers do preach a covenant of works do they preach a way of salvation?

MRS. H. I did not come hither to answer to questions of that sort.

DEP. GOV. Because you will deny the thing.

MRS. H. Ey, but that is to be proved first.

DEP. GOV. I will make it plain that you did say that the ministers did preach a covenant of works.

MRS. H. I deny that.

DEP. GOV. And that you said they were not able ministers of the New Testament, but Mr. Cotton only.

MRS. H. If ever I spake that I proved it by God's word.

COURT. Very well, very well.

MRS. H. If one shall come unto me in private, and desire me seriously to tell then what I thought of such an one, I must either speak false or true in my answer.

6. The Society of Jesus (Jesuits) is a Roman Catholic order that places special emphasis on missionary work. The Jesuits were particularly detested by the Puritans for their evangelical efforts in the New World. Jesuits played a prominent role in founding New France, which was just to the north of Massachusetts Bay, and in spreading Catholicism among the Native American nations there. That Catholic, French colony represented both a secular and a sacred rival to the New Englanders.

[In this lengthy section, Hutchinson was accused of having gone to a meeting of ministers and accusing them all—except John Cotton—of preaching a covenant of works rather than a covenant of grace. The accusation, if proved, would have been an extremely serious one. Several of the ministers testified that Hutchinson had made this accusation.]

DEP. GOV. I called these witnesses and you deny them. You see they have proved this and you deny this, but it is clear. You said they preached a covenant of works and that they were not able ministers of the New Testament; now there are two other things that you did affirm which were that the scriptures in the letter of them held forth nothing but a covenant of works and likewise that those that were under a covenant of works cannot be saved.

MRS. H. Prove that I said so.

GOV. Did you say so?

MRS. H. No, Sir. It is your conclusion.

DEP. GOV. What do I do charging of you if you deny what is so fully proved?

GOV. Here are six undeniable ministers who say it is true and yet you deny that you did say that they did preach a covenant of works and that they were not able ministers of the gospel, and it appears plainly that you have spoken it, and whereas you say that it was drawn from you in a way of friendship, you did profess then that it was out of conscience that you spake and said, "The fear of man is a snare. Wherefore shall I be afraid, I will speak plainly and freely."

MRS. H. That I absolutely deny, for the first question was thus answered by me to them: They thought that I did conceive there was a difference between them and Mr. Cotton. At the first I was somewhat reserved. Then said Mr. Peters, "I pray answer the question directly as fully and as plainly as you desire we should tell you our minds. Mrs. Hutchinson we come for plain dealing and telling you our hearts." Then I said I would deal as plainly as I could, and whereas they say I said they were under a covenant of works and in the state of the apostles why these two speeches cross one another. I might say they might preach a covenant of works as did the apostles, but to preach a covenant of works and to be under a covenant of works is another business.

DEP. GOV. There have been six witnesses to prove this and yet you deny it.

MRS. H. I deny that these were the first words that were spoken.

GOV. You make the case worse, for you clearly shew that the ground of your opening your mind was not to satisfy them but to satisfy your own conscience.

[There was a brief argument here about what Hutchinson actually said at the gathering of ministers, after which the court adjourned for the day.]

[The next morning.]

GOV. We proceeded the last night as far as we could in hearing of this cause of Mrs. Hutchinson. There were divers things laid to her charge: her ordinary meetings about religious exercises, her speeches in derogation of the ministers among us, and the weakening of the hands and hearts of the people towards them. Here was sufficient proof made of that which she was accused of in that point concerning the ministers and their ministry, as that they did preach a covenant of works when others did preach a covenant of grace, and that they were not able ministers of the New Testament, and that they had not the seal of the spirit, and this was spoken not as was pretended out of private conference, but out of conscience and warrant from scripture alleged the fear of man is a snare and seeing God had given her a calling to it she would freely speak. Some other speeches she used, as that the letter of the scripture held forth a covenant of works, and this is offered to be proved by probable grounds. If there be any thing else that the court hath to say they may speak.

[At this point, a lengthy argument erupted when Hutchinson demanded that the ministers who testified against her be recalled as witnesses, put under oath, and repeat their accusations. One member of the court said that "the ministers are so well known unto us, that we need not take an oath of them."]

GOV. I see no necessity of an oath in this thing seeing it is true and the substance of the matter confirmed by divers. Yet that all may be satisfied, if the elders will take an oath they shall have it given them. . . .

MRS. H. I will prove by what Mr. Wilson hath written[7] that they [the ministers] never heard me say such a thing.

MR. SIMS. We desire to have the paper and have it read.

MR. HARLAKENDEN. I am persuaded that is the truth that the elders do say and therefore I do not see it necessary now to call them to oath.

GOV. We cannot charge any thing of untruth upon them.

MR. HARLAKENDEN. Besides, Mrs. Hutchinson doth say that they are not able ministers of the New Testament.

MRS. H. They need not swear to that.

DEP. GOV. Will you confess it then?

MRS. H. I will not deny it or say it.

DEP. GOV. You must do one.

7. Wilson had taken notes at the meeting between Hutchinson and the ministers. Hutchinson claimed that these notes would exonerate her. They were never produced and are now lost.

[More on the oath followed.]

DEP. GOV. Let her witnesses be called.

GOV. Who be they?

MRS. H. Mr. Leveret and our teacher and Mr. Coggeshall.

GOV. Mr. Coggeshall was not present.

MR. COGGESHALL. Yes, but I was. Only I desired to be silent till I should be called.

GOV. Will you, Mr. Coggeshall, say that she did not say so?

MR. COGGESHALL. Yes, I dare say that she did not say all that which they lay against her.

MR. PETERS. How dare you look into the court to say such a word?

MR. COGGESHALL. Mr. Peters takes upon him to forbid me. I shall be silent.

MR. STOUGHTON. Ey, but she intended this that they say.

GOV. Well, Mr. Leveret, what were the words? I pray, speak.

MR. LEVERET. To my best remembrance when the elders did send for her, Mr. Peters did with much vehemency and intreaty urge her to tell what difference there was between Mr. Cotton and them, and upon his urging of her she said, "The fear of man is a snare, but they that trust upon the Lord shall be safe." And being asked wherein the difference was, she answered that they did not preach a covenant of grace so clearly as Mr. Cotton did, and she gave this reason of it: because that as the apostles were for a time without the spirit so until they had received the witness of the spirit they could not preach a covenant of grace so clearly.

[Here Hutchinson admitted that she might have said privately that the ministers were not able ministers of the New Testament.]

GOV. Mr. Cotton, the court desires that you declare what you do remember of the conference which was at the time and is now in question.

MR. COTTON. I did not think I should be called to bear witness in this cause and therefore did not labour to call to remembrance what was done; but the greatest passage that took impression upon me was to this purpose. The elders spake that they had heard that she had spoken some condemning words of their ministry, and among other things they did first pray her to answer wherein she thought their ministry did differ from mine. How the comparison sprang I am ignorant, but sorry I was that any comparison should be between me and my brethren and uncomfortable it was. She told them to this purpose that they did not hold forth a covenant of grace as I did. . . . I told her I was very sorry that she put comparisons between my ministry and theirs, for she had said more than I could myself, and rather

I had that she had put us in fellowship with them and not have made the discrepancy. She said she found the difference. . . . And I must say that I did not find her saying they were under a covenant of works, not that she said they did preach a covenant of works.

[Here John Cotton tried to defend Hutchinson, mostly by saying he did not remember most of the events in question.]

MRS. H. If you please to give me leave I shall give you the ground of what I know to be true. Being much troubled to see the falseness of the constitution of the Church of England, I had like to have turned Separatist. Whereupon I kept a day of solemn humiliation and pondering of the thing, the scripture was brought unto me—he that denies Jesus Christ to be come in the flesh is antichrist. This I considered of and in considering found that the papists[8] did not deny him to come in the flesh, nor we did not deny him. Who then was antichrist? Was the Turk antichrist only? The Lord knows that I could not open scripture; he must by his prophetical office open it unto me. So after that being unsatisfied in the thing, the Lord was pleased to bring this scripture out of the Hebrews. He that denies the testament denies the testator, and in this did open unto me and give me to see that those which did not teach the new covenant had the spirit of antichrist, and upon this he did discover the ministry unto me, and ever since, I bless the Lord. He hath let me see which was the clear ministry and which the wrong. Since that time I confess I have been more choice and he hath left me to distinguish between the voice of my beloved and the voice of Moses, the voice of John Baptist and the voice of antichrist, for all those voices are spoken of in scripture. Now if you do condemn me for speaking what in my conscience I know to be truth I must commit myself unto the Lord.

MR. NOWEL. How do you know that that was the spirit?

MRS. H. How did Abraham know that it was God that bid him offer his son, being a breach of the sixth commandment?[9]

DEP. GOV. By an immediate voice.

MRS. H. So to me by an immediate revelation.

DEP. GOV. How! an immediate revelation.

MRS. H. By the voice of his spirit to my soul. . . .

[In spite of the general shock that greeted her claim that she had experienced an immediate revelation from God, Hutchinson went on to state that God had compelled

8. *Papists* is a derisive Protestant term for Roman Catholics, referring to the papacy.
9. The sixth commandment prohibited murder.

her to take the course she had taken and that God had said to her, as He had to Daniel of the Old Testament, that "though I should meet with affliction, yet I am the same God that delivered Daniel out of the lion's den, I will also deliver thee."]

MRS. H. You have power over my body but the Lord Jesus hath power over my body and soul, and assure yourselves thus much: you go on in this course you begin you will bring a curse upon you and your posterity, and the mouth of the Lord hath spoken it.[10]

DEP. GOV. What is the scripture she brings?

MR. STOUGHTON. Behold I turn away from you.

MRS. H. But now having seen him which is invisible I fear not what man can do unto me.

GOV. Daniel was delivered by miracle. Do you think to be deliver'd so too?

MRS. H. I do here speak it before the court. I took that the Lord should deliver me by his providence.

MR. HARLAKENDEN. I may read scripture and the most glorious hypocrite may read them and yet go down to hell.

MRS. H. It may be so.

[Hutchinson's "revelations" were discussed among the stunned court.]

MR. BARTHOLOMEW. I speak as a member of the court. I fear that her revelations will deceive.

[More on Hutchinson's revelations followed.]

DEP. GOV. I desire Mr. Cotton to tell us whether you do approve of Mrs. Hutchinson's revelations as she hath laid them down.

MR. COTTON. I know not whether I do understand her, but this I say: If she doth expect a deliverance in a way of providence, then I cannot deny it.

DEP. GOV. No, sir. We did not speak of that.

MR. COTTON. If it be by way of miracle then I would suspect it.

DEP. GOV Do you believe that her revelations are true?

MR. COTTON. That she may have some special providence of God to help her is a thing that I cannot bear witness against.

DEP. GOV. Good Sir, I do ask whether this revelation be of God or no?

MR. COTTON. I should desire to know whether the sentence of the court will bring her to any calamity, and then I would know of her whether she expects to be delivered from that calamity by a miracle or a providence of God.

---

10. The Bible contains several references to punishing subsequent generations, including Exodus 20: 5, Numbers 14: 18, and Deuteronomy 5: 9.

MRS. H. By a providence of God I say I expect to be delivered from some calamity that shall come to me.

[Hutchinson's revelations were further discussed.]

DEP. GOV. These disturbances that have come among the Germans[11] have been all grounded upon revelations, and so they that have vented them have stirred up their hearers to take up arms against their prince and to cut the throats of one another, and these have been the fruits of them, and whether the devil may inspire the same into their hearts here I know not, for I am fully persuaded that Mrs. Hutchinson is deluded by the devil, because the spirit of God speaks truth in all his servants.

GOV. I am persuaded that the revelation she brings forth is delusion.

[All the court but some two or three ministers cried out, "We all believe—we all believe it." Hutchinson was found guilty. Coddington made a lame attempt to defend Hutchinson but was silenced by Governor Winthrop.]

GOV. The court hath already declared themselves satisfied concerning the things you hear, and concerning the troublesomeness of her spirit and the danger of her course amongst us, which is not to be suffered. Therefore if it be the mind of the court that Mrs. Hutchinson for these things that appear before us is unfit for our society, and if it be the mind of the court that she shall be banished out of our liberties and imprisoned till she be sent away, let them hold up their hands.

[All but three did so.]

GOV. Those that are contrary minded hold up yours.

[Only Mr. Coddington and Mr. Colborn did so.]

MR. JENNISON. I cannot hold up my hand one way or the other, and I shall give my reason if the court require it.

GOV. Mrs. Hutchinson, the sentence of the court you hear is that you are banished from out of our jurisdiction as being a woman not fit for our society, and are to be imprisoned till the court shall send you away.

MRS. H. I desire to know wherefore I am banished?

GOV. Say no more. The court knows wherefore and is satisfied.

---

11. This reference is to the bloody and violent fighting that took place between orthodox Protestants and the followers of the radical Anabaptist John of Leiden in 1534 and 1535.

◆

Questions to Consider

Now that you have examined the evidence, at least one point is clear: the General Court of Massachusetts Bay was determined to get rid of Anne Hutchinson, whether or not she actually had broken any law. They tried to bait her, force admissions of guilt from her, confuse her, browbeat her. Essentially, they had already decided on the verdict before the trial began. So we know that Anne Hutchinson was a threat—and a serious one to the colony.

And yet the colony had dealt quite differently with Roger Williams, a Puritan minister banished in 1635 because of his extreme religious beliefs. Williams was given every chance to mend his ways, Governor Winthrop remained his friend throughout Williams's appearances before the General Court, and it was only with great reluctance that the court finally decided to exile him.

Anne's brother-in-law, Reverend Wheelwright, was banished before her, but his actions were far different from hers. At the close of an afternoon lecture by Reverend Cotton, Wheelwright rose before the crowd to give his own sermon against men who thought living a virtuous life was somehow evidence of their salvation. "The more holy they are," he proclaimed, "the greater enemies they are to Christ." Then he called on the true Christians, the ones who still acknowledged the omnipotence of God, to rise up against these "enemies of Christ"—which, he implied, included most of the ministers in Massachusetts and most of the civil authorities: "We must lay loade upon them, we must kille them with the worde of the

Lorde." He was consequently convicted of sedition. Even then the General Court, under Governor Winthrop's leadership, delayed sentencing and sought reconciliation with Wheelwright for months before reluctantly banishing him.

Why, then, was Anne Hutchinson's case so threatening and her trial such an ordeal? Obviously, she did pose a religious threat. As you look back through the evidence, try to clarify the exact points of difficulty between Hutchinson and the ministers. What was the basis of the argument over covenants of grace and works? What was Hutchinson supposed to have said? Under what circumstances had she allegedly said this? To whom? What was the role of her own minister, John Cotton, in the trial?

Remember that Hutchinson's trial took place in the midst of the divisive Antinomian controversy. What social and political threat did the Antinomians pose to Massachusetts Bay? What threat did it pose to the mission of building a "city upon a hill"? Did Hutchinson say anything in her testimony that would indicate she was an Antinomian? How would you prove whether or not she was?

A pivotal moment in the trial comes when Hutchinson announces that she had received an "immediate revelation" from the voice of God. Why? And why was Anne's likening of herself to Daniel and Abraham so upsetting to the Court? What theological beliefs and what social values did she violate with this revelation?

Hutchinson's role in the community also comes into question during the trial.

What do the questions about the meetings she held in her home reveal? Look beyond what the governor and members of the court are actually saying. Try to imagine what they might have been thinking. How did Hutchinson's meetings pose a threat to the larger community?

Finally, look through the transcript one more time. It provides some clues, often subtle ones, about the roles of and relationships between men and women in colonial Massachusetts. How did Anne's gender factor into her examination? What did it mean when Governor Winthrop said: "We do not mean to discourse with those of your sex"? Would the same thing have happened during the proceedings were Anne a man? Or did the fact that Anne was a woman play a pivotal role in her treatment before the General Court? Did Anne violate Puritan assumptions of how women should behave and how they should relate to men? Why would this be dangerous enough to require her expulsion?

In conclusion, try to put together all you know from the evidence to answer the central question: Why was Anne Hutchinson too dangerous to remain in the Massachusetts Bay colony?

Epilogue

After her civil case concluded, Anne Hutchinson was kept in Roxbury, under house arrest, during the winter of 1637–1638, awaiting trial before a church court. She had been deemed a heretic in the civil trial, so ministers and elders from churches throughout Massachusetts needed to either cleanse her of her sins or, failing that, excommunicate her from the community of saints. That is exactly what happened in March 1638. Expelling a congregant was a public affair, just like confirming a saint. The meetinghouse at Boston was therefore packed when Hutchinson was excommunicated. "I not only pronounce you worthy to be cast out, but I do cast you out," proclaimed one of the ministers who participated in the trial, "And in the name of Jesus Christ, I do deliver you up to Satan."

After the civil trial, John Cotton distanced himself from Hutchinson. As to their two-decade long friendship, he now claimed, "Mistress Hutchinson seldom resorted to me and when she did come to me, it was seldom or never . . . that she tarried long. I rather think she was loathe to resort much to me . . . lest she might seem to learn somewhat from me." He joined the ministers and elders who sat in judgment of her during the church trial. Cotton conceded that when she first came to Massachusetts, Hutchinson had "been an instrument for doing some good." But forced to choose between allying with his fellow ministers and defending his protégé, Cotton succumbed to the pressure. "I do admonish you and charge you," he proclaimed, "in the name of Jesus Christ, in whose place I stand, that you would sadly consider the just hand of God against you, the great hurt you have done to the churches, the great dishonour you have brought to Jesus Christ, and the evil that you have done to many a poor soul."

Most of Anne's supporters had fled Massachusetts or been exiled, disenfranchised, or silenced in the months following her civil trial. A handful of friends stood with her at the church proceedings; many of them joined her in the new settlement in Rhode Island. She and William were reunited, after living six months apart, in mid-April.

John Winthrop kept himself well informed of his vanquished rival's new life in Rhode Island. When a mild earthquake struck the settlement a few weeks after Anne's arrival, he maintained the tremor was proof of "God's continued disquietude against the existence of Anne Hutchinson." And when the forty-six-year-old went into labor with her sixteenth child and suffered a miscarriage, Winthrop—along with Reverend Cotton—publicly proclaimed the "monster" birth proof of Hutchinson's religious heresy.

In 1642, William Hutchinson died, and Anne moved with her six youngest children to the Dutch colony of New Netherland in what is now the Bronx borough of New York City. The next year, she and all but one of her children were killed in an Indian raid. The leading men of Boston rejoiced at her murder. They saw "God's hand" in her death. "The Lord heard our groans in Heaven," concluded one minister, "and freed us from this great and sore affliction."

Six years after Hutchinson died, in March 1649, John Winthrop passed away, having spent nearly twenty years at the center of political power in Massachusetts Bay. Winthrop believed until the end of his life that he had had no choice other than to expel Hutchinson. However, even Winthrop's most sympathetic biographer, historian Edmund S. Morgan, describes the Hutchinson trial and its aftermath as "the least attractive episode" in Winthrop's long public career.

John Winthrop triumphed over Anne Hutchinson, but he was unable to leave to the Massachusetts Bay colony a permanent legacy of religious uniformity. The second and third generations of colonists did not always share their parents' zeal for building a model Christian community. New migrants came, bringing different ideas and building new towns. As the colony's size increased and its population diversified, religious uniformity became more and more difficult. Growth and prosperity seemed to foster an increased interest in individual wealth and a corresponding decline in religious fervor. In the mid-seventeenth century, reports of sleeping during sermons, fewer conversions of young people, blasphemous language, and growing attention to physical pleasures were numerous, as were election disputes, intrachurch squabbling, and community bickering.

For better than a century after its founding, New England continued to reexperience the tensions between drifting toward Arminianism and reasserting strict Calvinism. Jeremiads—sermons that predicted disasters because of declining religious zeal and were especially popular in the 1660s—offer one example of this pattern. The witchcraft trials that wracked Salem in 1692 provide another, as does Jonathan Edwards and the Great Awakening ministers of the 1740s. Although the Puritans' congregational church remained the established church of Massachusetts until 1833—two centuries after the Great Migration—John Winthrop's vision of New Englanders being "knit together in this work" of creating a "city upon a hill" had been altered long before then.

Colonies, Commerce, and Empire: The British Plantation System in the Chesapeake and Caribbean

◆

The Problem

In 1627 James Drax, a young man "of uncertain origins," arrived in Barbados among the first wave of settlers sent by an English merchant-investor to establish a colony that would become a profitable venture. According to legend, Drax once boasted that he would not return to England until he "was able to purchase an estate with an annual income of £ 10,000." Less than thirty years later he was the richest man in the West Indies. Drax left for England in 1654 (he was seen off by the governor of Barbados), was knighted by Oliver Cromwell, and the year after the restoration of the British monarchy in 1660 was made a baronet by King Charles II.[1]

In 1635 John Wise, age 18, was seized by hoodlums and put aboard a ship of indentured servants bound for the fledgling colony of Barbados. Securing his release, he moved to the Eastern Shore of Virginia, became a well-to-do planter, was selected as a church warden of the local Anglican parish in 1662, and by the time of his death in 1695 had been awarded the rank of "colonel."[2]

1. On Drax see Larry Gragg, *Englishmen Transplanted: The English Colonization of Barbados, 1627–1660* (New York: Oxford University Press, 2003), pp. 51–52 and *passim*; Hilary McD Beckles, *A History of Barbados: From Amerindian Settlement to Caribbean*

Single Market (Cambridge: Cambridge University Press, 2006), pp. 28–29; Ronald Tree *A History of Barbados* (New York: Random House, 1972), pp. 17–18. For more on the Drax family see Peter Thompson, "Henry Drax's Instructions of the Management of a Seventeenth-Century Barbadian Sugar Plantation" in *William and Mary Quarterly*, vol. 66 (July 2009), pp. 565–604.

2. On Wise see Jennings Cropper Wise, *Col. John Wise of England and Virginia, 1617–1695* (Richmond: Bell Books, 1918), pp. 29–30; Alison F. Gains, "Opportunity and Mobility in Early Barbados," in Robert L. Paquette and Stanley L. Engerman, eds. *The Lesser Antilles in the Age of European Expansion* (Gainesville: University Press of Florida, 1996), p. 165.

◆ CHAPTER 3

Colonies,
Commerce, and
Empire: The
British Plantation
System in the
Chesapeake and
Caribbean

Drax and Wise were by no means typical British colonists. Yet they are representative of those Englishmen who were able to take advantage of and profit from the emergence of a global economy that profoundly affected nearly every man, woman, and child in the Atlantic world from the 1500s to the 1700s and beyond. Part of this economic transformation involved the establishment of colonies in what Europeans called the "New World;" colonies that could serve as military outposts, extractors of raw materials that could be sent to the mother country for processing, and eventually as markets for England's processed and manufactured goods.

The founding of such colonies, however, was no simple operation. In Virginia, of the 105 original settlers of Jamestown in May 1607, only 38 were still alive by January 1608. Indeed, it took several decades before Britons could feel confident that the fragile settlement would be a permanent one.

Initial settlers on the West Indian island of Barbados fared little better. The island was heavily forested and totally destitute of any edible plants. Some of the earliest settlers lived in caves while others built flimsy huts of palmetto fronds which often fell victim to storms. A visiting soldier of fortune who passed through the settlement a few years later observed

This Island is the dunghill whar our England doth cast forth its rubidg. Rodgs and Hors and such like people

are . . . generally broght heare; . . . a hor if handsome makes a wife for some rich planter.[3]

And yet, by the middle of the eighteenth century the Chesapeake and Caribbean societies had not only grown and matured but also had become among the most opulent and refined of Great Britain's American colonies. By the late 1600s Barbados contained "the wealthiest men in British America" and was described as "that fair jewel of your Majesty's Crown." For its part Virginia and Maryland were on the brink of providing exceptionally talented leadership for Britain's North American colonies as well as for the early nation.[4]

How were these colonial societies able to reach such impressive heights after such inauspicious beginnings? What factors were responsible for these colonies' prosperity and maturity? What parts did Virginia, Maryland, and Barbados play in England's emergence as a major world commercial and economic power?

The evidence you will be using to answer these central questions will be statistics. Analyzing and interpreting statistics is one of the best ways that historians can measure and assess change over time. In this chapter you will be doing precisely that.

---

3. The soldier of fortune was Henry Whistler. See Tree, *History of Barbados*, p. 16. Interestingly, the initial settlements in Virginia and Barbados both were named Jamestown.
4. Gragg, *Englishmen Transplanted*, p. 1.

Background

Although the discoveries of Christopher Columbus (1446?–1506) and the forays by *conquistadores* like Hernando Cortés (1485–1547) and others proved that the so-called "New World" was a place of enormous wealth, it took nearly a century for England to turn its attention to concerted exploration and colonization. This was primarily because of internal instability as well as England's engagement in a series of wars in France, Scotland, and Ireland that kept the English home. Although Henry VII's defeat of Richard III on Bosworth Field in 1485 brought some measure of internal peace to England, it was not until the reign of Elizabeth I (queen from 1558 until her death in 1603) that the emerging nation-state could consider itself comparatively stable. Even so, bitter fighting in Ireland in 1568 (the "Northern Rebellion") and numerous plots on Elizabeth's life (prompted in part by Pope Pius V's excommunication of the English queen and call for her overthrow in 1571 and efforts to replace Elizabeth with the imprisoned Mary Queen of Scots) kept England and its government in an almost constant state of uncertainty. In addition, threats from abroad such as the Spanish Armada (1588) prompted England to keep her forces and ships at home.[5]

At the same time, however, other forces were pushing England toward the sea and colonization. Chief among them was a demographic explosion in the sixteenth century, in which England's population surged from approximately 2.3 million in 1552 to between 4.11 and 5 million by 1600. These figures are especially astounding given that England experienced a horrible influenza epidemic between 1557 and 1559 that resulted in a death toll of almost 15 percent of England's total population in 1551. To be sure, life expectancy was short (roughly 36.23 years in the period from 1551 to 1591), but crude birth rates were very high (12.72 in 1551). For its part, London's population mushroomed during the sixteenth century, from approximately 50,000 people in 1500 (2 percent of the total English population) to about 200,000 by 1600 (5 percent).[6]

England's rapid population increase was accompanied by a dramatic price revolution during the sixteenth century. A doubling of the money supply (due to increased trade and to floods of gold and silver pouring into Europe from Spanish America and elsewhere)

5. Mary was the great-granddaughter of Henry VII and therefore the next lawful heir to the throne after Elizabeth. Roman Catholics often referred to Elizabeth as "Queen of the Heretics." Fearing that the impending attack by Spain might cause a Roman Catholic uprising in Mary's favor, Elizabeth finally had her put to death in 1587.

6. For studies of England's population, see E. A. Wrigley and R. S. Scholfield, *The Population History of England, 1541–1871* (Cambridge: Harvard University Press, 1981), esp. pp. 496–497, 528; R. A. Houston, *The Population History of Britain and Ireland, 1500–1700* (London: Macmillan, 1992); David Coleman and John Salt, *The British Population: Pat-terns, Trends, and Processes* (Oxford University Press, 1992), esp. pp. 20–21, 28.

✦ CHAPTER 3

Colonies,
Commerce, and
Empire: The
British Plantation
System in the
Chesapeake and
Caribbean

combined with the burgeoning population and a failure of agriculture and manufacturing production to keep pace with demand caused an enormous rise in prices. Agricultural prices rose approximately 150 percent between 1510 and the 1550s, as demand for food far outstripped supply. The price of wheat tripled, and throughout the century the prices for all goods in England quadrupled. Because of population increases, wages failed to keep pace with the rise in prices, and real wages slumped from an index of 615 in 1559–1560 to 436 in 1599–1600. General famines due to crop failures in 1586 and 1598 only made a terrible situation even worse.

Seeking to increase their own incomes to keep pace with prices, landowners raised the rents they charged to peasants, driving many off the land entirely. In addition, landlords and wool merchants sought to increase wool production by dividing up the traditional open fields into individual parcels, which forced even more people off the land. Many lived in cottages and barely eked out a living on the "putting out system," whereby a merchant would deliver raw materials (wool, for instance), which would be carded, spun, and woven in the cottages and then picked up by the merchant, who in turn brought more raw materials. Others simply abandoned their cottages and wandered as vagabonds who lived by getting odd jobs, begging, and crime.[7]

For some Englishmen, colonization was one way to remove what they considered an excessively large and increasingly dangerous population. In a extended essay on "western planting" (New World colonization) written by Richard Hakluyt (Hak' loot, 1152?–1616) and given to Queen Elizabeth in October 1584, the author expressed his deep concern about the "multitudes of loiterers and idle vagabonds":

> wee are growen more populous than ever . . . that they can hardly lyve one by another . . . and often fall to pilferinge and thevinge and other lewd-ness, whereby all the prisons of the lande are daily . . . stuffed full of them, where either they pitifully pyne awaye, or els at lengthe are miserably hanged.[8]

In Hakluyt's opinion, this was a strong argument in favor of colonization.

In addition to ridding England of its excess population, Hakluyt offered the queen other reasons why Britain should embark upon a program of colonization. He asserted that Englishmen could bring "the gospel of Christe" to other peoples, stimulate trade to "supply the wantes of all our decayed trades," establish coastal outposts for

---

7. On England's price revolution, see Barry Coward, *Social Change and Continuity in Early Modern England, 1550–1750* (London: Longman, 1988), esp. pp. 31–39, 53–55, 70. On transient labor, see Warren M. Billings, John E. Selby, and Thad W. Tate, *Colonial Virginia: A History* (White Plains, NY: KTO Press, 1986), p. 5.

8. Richard Hakluyt was called Richard Hakluyt the Younger to distinguish him from his cousin, also named Richard Hakluyt and also a proponent of colonization. See Hakluyt the Younger's *Discourse Concerning Western Planting* (1584) in David B. Quinn, ed., *English Plans for North America,* Vol. III of *New American World: A Documentary History of North America to 1612* (New York: Arno Press, 1979), p. 82. The words *colony* and *plantation* began to appear in English in the 1550s. See D. W. Meinig, *The Shaping of America: A Geographical Perspective on 500 Years of History* (New Haven: Yale University Press, 1986), Vol. I, p. 29.

protecting and resupplying the British navy, increase revenue through custom duties, discover the immensely profitable Northwest Passage "to Cathaio and China," and check the expansion of Spain in the New World.[9]

Yet it was easier to advocate planting colonies than actually to plant them. In 1583, Sir Humphrey Gilbert led five ships to Newfoundland, where he planted a colony; but that effort collapsed after Gilbert perished at sea (according to witnesses, his last words were: "We are as neere to heaven by the sea as by lands"). The next year, Gilbert's half-brother, Sir Walter Raleigh, convinced Queen Elizabeth to renew Gilbert's charter in his own name. Raleigh's two attempts at colonization were disastrous, however, especially the "lost colony" of 1587 in which 118 men, women, and children simply vanished into thin air. And another abortive effort, this one at Plymouth, was abandoned after two years of struggling and pain.[10]

Nor did the prospects seem more promising for the Jamestown settlement. In December 1606, the three ships *Susan Constant, Godspeed,* and *Discovery* sailed from England bound for the New World. Earlier that year, King James I had granted a charter to the Virginia Company of London (more familiarly known as the London Company, to distinguish it from the Virginia Company of Plymouth), a private corporation that hoped to imitate Spain's good fortune by finding gold, silver, and precious gems that would enrich the stockholders. On board the three vessels were 144 prospective colonists, the vast majority of them either fortune seekers or salaried company employees (such as goldsmiths, jewelers, and apothecaries[11]). None planned to be permanent settlers.

In spite of meticulous planning by the company, in Virginia things were desperate almost from the start. Only 105 would-be colonists survived the voyage, and a combination of disease, starvation, the eventual hostility of the nearby Native Americans, and conflicts between the settlement's leaders made the situation ever more dire. By the time relief ships sent by the company arrived in January 1608 with provisions and more colonists, only thirty-eight survivors remained at Jamestown.

Nor did the Virginia colony immediately improve. With few colonists skilled in agriculture and clearing land (most colonists had to be taught how to use an axe), the colony depended on food from company relief ships and trading with the Native Americans. Thus, in the winter of 1609 to 1610, Jamestown experienced its horrible "starving time," when only sixty of a fall 1609 population of five hundred survived,

9. Hakluyt, *Discourse Concerning Western Planting,* pp. 71–72.

10. For Gilbert's supposed last words, see William S. Powell, *Paradise Preserved* (Chapel Hill: University of North Carolina Press, 1965), p. 3. For what is probably the definitive history of the "lost colony" of Roanoke Island, see David Beers Quinn, *Set Fair for Roanoke: Voyages and Colonies, 1584–1606* (Chapel Hill: University of North Carolina Press, 1985). For a conspiratorial view of what happened to the Roanoke Island colony, see Lee Miller, *Roanoke: Solving the Mystery of the Lost Colony* (New York: Arcade Publishing, 2000).

11. Apothecary: pharmacist, druggist.

◆ CHAPTER 3

Colonies,
Commerce, and
Empire: The
British Plantation
System in the
Chesapeake and
Caribbean

as they were forced to eat dogs, cats, rats, snakes, and even corpses from the graveyard. As Captain John Smith later wrote:

> And one amongst the rest did kill his wife, powdered her, and had eaten part of her before it was knowne, for which hee was executed, as hee well deserved.[12]

Even after the "starving time," it was by no means clear that Virginia would survive. By 1616, the colony's population hovered at only 380, and a well-coordinated Indian attack in 1622 very nearly wiped out the fledgling settlement.[13] But John Rolfe had experimented with transplanting a variety of West Indian tobacco to the "lusty soyle" of Virginia, where it thrived. In 1614, Virginia shipped four barrels of tobacco to England and by 1617 was exporting 50,000 pounds of tobacco leaves. And in spite of the facts that the London Company initially opposed the cultivation of the "noxious weed" and King James I railed against its importation and use, tobacco ultimately became the colony's salvation.[14]

In the meantime, the company had abandoned its hopes of finding gold and precious gems in Virginia and turned to

12. John Smith, *The Generall Historie of Virginia. . . .* (1624) in James Horn, ed., *Captain John Smith Writings and Other Narratives. . . .* (New York: Literary Classics of the United States, 2007), p. 411. "Powdered" meant "salted."
13. The colonists retaliated against the Native Americans by inviting them to a peace conference at which they killed around 250 of them with poisoned wine.
14. A short excerpt from James's *A Counter-blast to Tobacco* (1604) may be found in Warren M. Billings, John E. Selby, and Thad W. Tate, *Colonial Virginia: A History* (White Plains, N.Y.: KTO Press, 1986), pp. 40–41n.

long-range profits from lumber, hemp, turpentine, and finally tobacco. In order to attract settlers to the colony, in 1618 the company revised its charter to permit individuals to own land—previous to that "greate charter," all land had been owned by the company. Settlers claimed lands touching Chesapeake Bay and the many rivers and streams that fed it (to use the waterways to ship their tobacco). By the time the London Company finally went bankrupt and Virginia became a royal colony (1625), landowners were building homes close to their fields and away from the settlements and stockades. Laborers were found in the form of indentured servants from England who, in exchange for their passage and a land grant after finishing their "indenture" (usually seven years), agreed to work for the landowners. Even so, it was not until around 1675 that Virginia's natural increase and not immigration replenished the colony's population.

Maryland, the other colony on the Chesapeake Bay, was created by King Charles I in 1632 as an immense land grant to George Calvert, a gentleman who had served the Crown in return for a peerage (as Lord Baltimore) and a land grant in America. According to tradition, Calvert himself drew up the document, leaving a blank space for the name of the proposed colony, which Charles I filled in with "Terra Mariae" (Mary's Land, or Maryland) in honor of his wife Queen Henrietta Maria.

The first settlers came ashore in Maryland on March 25, 1634. Avoiding many of the errors made by the early settlers of Virginia, Maryland colonists (led by Cecilius's younger brother) purchased land from the Native Americans, planted food crops as well as tobacco, and laid claim to generous land grants on which Calvert charged low rents ("quit rents"). As was the case later in Virginia, the population was dispersed, living on or near their landholdings and thus breaking the English pattern of village life and discouraging the growth of large towns or cities.

By the mid-1700s, when many of those who would become leaders of Virginia and Maryland societies during the American Revolution were coming of age, the Chesapeake region was dotted with large plantations, fine houses, an educated and cultured gentry class, and enough socioeconomic mobility to give at least the appearance of an open and egalitarian society. Indeed, the Chesapeake region had come a long way from the "starving time" of 1609–1610.

The island of Barbados is the easternmost island in what Europeans named the West Indies. When the original British colonists arrived in 1627, the island was completely uninhabited, although there was considerable evidence that Native American people had once lived there. By 1627, however, they were gone, either taken off by Spanish slave raiders or driven away by other Native Americans.

As noted earlier, Barbados originally was covered with dense vegetation but contained no edible plants. Until later ships arrived with seeds and provisions, the early settlers lived on fish and wild pigs that had been brought to the island decades ago by Portuguese explorers. Equally important, those same ships brought axes and saws that could be used to clear the forests and plant food crops (by 1650, most of the forests had been cut down). Land was

cheap and those who arrived earliest (like James Drax) acquired the best land. By 1635, there were over 1,200 colonists above the age of 14.[15]

Barbados originally was the brainchild of William Courteen, a wealthy merchant who envisioned an agricultural colony that would ship food products to England for sale in the market of inflated prices. Courteen and his brother invested over £200,000 in the Barbados venture, sending several shiploads of settlers and numerous supplies. He encouraged the colonists to grow tobacco (to copy Virginia's success), cotton, ginger, and indigo. He also encouraged them to raise their own food.[16]

Unfortunately for Courteen, he had never secured a royal charter for Barbados. Recognizing the chance to oust Courteen and make a fortune for himself, the Earl of Carlisle convinced James I to grant him ownership of Barbados as a proprietary colony. Settlers sent by the greedy and duplicitous nobleman clashed with the original colonists over land ownership and governance. The earl emerged triumphant and Courteen died in 1636 impoverished and embittered.

Hoping to imitate Virginia's prosperity, Barbados planters embraced tobacco. The climate, however, was too hot and the Barbadian leaf was coarse. As one person who examined

15. Richard S. Dunn, *Sugar and Slaves: The Rise of the Planter Class in the English West Indies, 1624–1713* (Chapel Hill: University of North Carolina Press, 1972), p. 55.
16. Between 1623 and 1625 the price of tobacco on the London market doubled, a sure invitation to Courteen and Barbadian planters. Beckles, *History of Barbados,* p. 16.

◆ CHAPTER 3

Colonies,
Commerce, and
Empire: The
British Plantation
System in the
Chesapeake and
Caribbean

the first Barbadian shipment (in 1628) observed, it was "ill-conditioned, foul, full of stalks, and evil colored" and "the worst that grows in the world." As bad as Barbadian tobacco was, however, its sale drove down the price of all tobacco and the Barbados "tobacco fever" simply collapsed. Once mocked as a colony "wholly built on smoke," Barbados abandoned tobacco cultivation and searched for another cash crop. An effort to flood the London market with Barbadian cotton was only a repeat of the tobacco tragedy (the price of cotton in London plummeted 50% between 1635 and 1641). An experiment with indigo produced the same results in 1643. It was at this point that planter James Drax learned from Dutch merchants how to grow sugar cane and produce sugar. At last, it was hoped, Barbados had found its cash crop . . . and its wealth.[17]

What were the major factors responsible for the evolution of both Chesapeake and Barbados societies? What were the key ingredients of those societies? What part did those two colonies play in England's emergence as a major economic power?

◆

The Method

How can we begin to answer such questions? Even the tiny fraction of Chesapeake and Barbadian colonists who left letters, diaries, account books, and so forth represented only a small fraction of the total population and, moreover, rarely if ever addressed these questions or issues. Indeed, it is not clear that many of those colonists who left written records were even aware of the trends and forces that were acting to shape their lives. And, of course, the vast majority of colonists left no written records at all.

Recently, however, historians have become more imaginative in using the comparatively limited material at their disposal. We know, for instance, that almost every person, even the poorest, left some record that he or she existed. That person's name may appear in any number of places, including church records of baptisms, marriages, and deaths; property-holding and tax records; civil or criminal court records; military records; ship manifests; slave auction records; and cemetery records. Thus, demographic and economic trends can be reconstructed, in some cases allowing us to understand aspects of these people's lives that they may not have perceived themselves.

How is this done? One important way is to use statistics to help reconstruct the past. Today we are bombarded almost daily with statistics—about the stock market, teenage pregnancy, and illegal drug use, for example. In order to function productively and successfully in today's world, we must use those statistics to aid us in shaping our opinions and making decisions.

17. *Ibid.*, p. 17.

Historians have learned to use these same types of statistics and statistical methods and to apply them to the past. Working carefully through those materials that still exist, historians begin to reconstruct the demographic and economic trends and forces that affected a past epoch. Was the population growing, shrinking, or static? Was the source of that population changing? Did the nature of landholding and wealth change over time? Did the source of labor change? To historians, each statistical summary (called a statistical *set* or *aggregate* picture) contains important information that increases our understanding of a community or people being studied. Table 1 shows the types of questions historians ask with regard to several different kinds of records.

Having examined each set of statistics, the historian places the sets in some logical order, which may vary depending on the available evidence, the central questions the historian is attempting to answer, and the historian's own preferences. For this chapter, we have divided the statistics into two major groupings: Chesapeake statistics and Barbados statistics. For each grouping, we have arranged the statistical sets beginning with population, then moving through size of landholding, wealth distribution, crops and prices, types of labor, and so forth. Note that the statistical sets for each colony do not always match perfectly the sets for the other colony.

Up to this point, the historian has 1) collected the statistics and arranged them into sets, 2) examined each set in order to measure trends, tendencies, or changes over time, and 3) arranged the sets in some logical order. Now the historian must begin to ask "why" for each set. For example:

1. Why did the crops being raised in the Chesapeake and Barbados change over time?
2. Why did the type of labor in both colonies change over time?
3. Why did planters in the Chesapeake and Barbados grow richer or poorer?

Table 1

Type of Record	Questions
Census	Was the population growing, shrinking, or static? What were the sources of population growth (immigration, natural increase, slave importation)? Was the composition (race, etc.) of the population changing or stationary?
Land records, wills, probates	Did the prices of land change over time? Was wealth evenly distributed among the adult male population? Were various socioeconomic groups growing wealthier? Poorer? Did landowners employ non-family members? Did the source of that labor change over time?
Trade and custom records	Were agricultural crops being raised change over time? Was production increasing, decreasing, or stationary? Were prices increasing, decreasing, or static? Was the balance of trade (exports over imports) positive? Negative?

◆ CHAPTER 3

Colonies,
Commerce, and
Empire: The
British Plantation
System in the
Chesapeake and
Caribbean

In many cases, the answer to each question (and other "why" questions) is in one of the other statistical sets. That may cause the historian to alter his or her ordering of the sets in order to make the story clearer.

The historian is actually linking the sets to one another to form a chain. When two sets have been linked (because one set answers the "why" question of another set), the historian repeats the process until all the sets have been linked to form one chain of evidence. At that point, the historian can summarize the tendencies that have been discovered and, if desired, can connect those trends or tendencies to other events occurring in the period, perhaps even the American Revolution.

One example of how historians link statistical sets together to answer a "why" question is sufficient. Sources 6 and 21 in the Evidence section showed that between 1654 and 1689 the number of indentured servants shipped from Bristol to Virginia, Maryland, and Barbados declined precipitously. How can we account for this trend? Would the fact that Irish indentured servants revolted against their masters in the 1650s provide an important clue? Look at sources 1, 7, 9, 13, 22, and 23, all of which deal with the slave populations in both the Chesapeake colonies and Barbados. We can clearly conclude that planters in both regions were changing their sources of labor from British indentured servants—who in Virginia and Maryland could acquire land after their terms of service and begin to raise tobacco to compete with their former masters, and in Barbados would have great difficulty becoming landowners

and would either leave the colony or remain as a troublesome population—to permanent slaves from Africa.[18]

Now ask yourself why both Chesapeake and Barbados planters did that. Is the answer to *that* "why" question another statistical set? For other possible answers to that "why" question, consult your instructor.

One thing you will notice almost immediately is that historians never have all the primary sources they need. When dealing with statistics, we know that until the nineteenth century record keeping was haphazard at best. Many of the statistical sets you will be examining and analyzing have been painstakingly compiled by historians from the fragmentary data that has been saved. Also, the lack of air conditioning prior to the mid-twentieth century meant that many historical records in the mainland South and the Caribbean fell victim to a combination of heat and humidity. In some of those historical archives, historians could almost literally smell their valuable sources decomposing. In the Caribbean, some records were destroyed by hurricanes. And in the American South some records perished in the Civil War.

18. In his extremely valuable article "Servant Emigration to the Chesapeake in the Seventeenth Century," historian James Horn has reported that between 1650 and 1680, 70% to 85% of all British migrants to the Chesapeake region were indentured servants, most between the ages of 15 and 24. In Thad W. Tate and David L. Ammerman, eds., *The Chesapeake in the Seventeenth Century: Essays on Anglo-American Society* (Chapel Hill: Univ. of North Carolina Press, 1979), pp. 54, 62. See also Edmund Morgan, *American Slavery, American Freedom: The Ordeal of Colonial Virginia* (New York: W. W. Norton, 1975), pp. 295–299 and *passim*.

Working with historical statistics is not so difficult as it may first appear. Often it is helpful to assemble a small study group with a few of your classmates. As members of the group discuss the problem, each individual can contribute something that possibly the other members of the group did not see, thereby broadening every student's understanding of the problem. Analyzing statistics can be a challenging undertaking, but the results can be immensely satisfying, especially as you come to "see" the *people* the statistics represent.

◆

The Evidence

THE CHESAPEAKE (VIRGINIA & MARYLAND)

Sources 1 and 2 data from the U.S. Bureau of the Census, *Historical Statistics of the United States* (Washington, D.C.: U.S. Government Printing Office, 1975), pt. 2, p. 1168; and Jim Potter, "Demographic Development and Family Structure," in Jack P. Greene and J. R. Pole, eds., *Colonial British America: Essays in the New History of the Early Modern Era* (Baltimore: The Johns Hopkins University Press, 1984), p. 138.

1. Population Growth, Virginia, 1640–1770.

Year	Whites	Increase (%)	Blacks	Increase (%)	Blacks as % of Total Pop.
1640	10,292	—	150	—	1
1650	18,326	78	405	170	—
1660	26,070	42	950	135	—
1670	33,309	28	2,000	111	6
1680	40,596	22	3,000	50	—
1690	43,701	8	9,345	212	—
1700	42,170	−4	16,390	75	28
1710	55,163	31	23,118	41	—
1720	61,198	11	26,559	15	—
1730	84,000	37	30,000	13	26
1740	120,440	43	60,000	100	—
1750	129,581	8	101,452	69	—
1760	199,156	35	140,570	39	41
1770	259,411	30	187,605	33	42

◆ CHAPTER 3

Colonies,
Commerce, and
Empire: The
British Plantation
System in the
Chesapeake and
Caribbean

2. Population Growth, Maryland, 1640–1770.

Year	Whites	Increase (%)	Blacks	Increase (%)	Blacks as % of Total Pop.
1640	563	—	20	—	3
1650	4,204	647	300	1350	—
1660	7,668	82	758	153	—
1670	12,036	57	1,190	57	9
1680	16,293	35	1,611	35	—
1690	21,862	34	2,162	34	—
1700	26,377	21	3,227	49	11
1710	34,796	32	7,945	146	—
1720	53,634	54	12,499	57	—
1730	73,893	38	17,220	38	19
1740	92,062	25	24,031	40	—
1750	97,623	6	43,450	81	—
1760	113,263	16	49,004	13	30
1770	138,781	23	63,818	30	31

Source 3: From *A Place in Time: Middlesex Country, Virginia 1650–1750* by Darrett B. Rutman and Anita H. Rutman, p. 129. Copyright © 1984 by Darrett B. Rutman and Anita H. Rutman. Used by permission of W. W. Norton & Company, Inc.

3. Wealth Distribution in Middlesex County, Virginia: Personal Property of Deceased Adult Males, 1699–1750.

Through 1699

1. The poorest 31.2% of the male population owned 3.6% of the total wealth.
2. The next poorest 28.6% of the male population owned 12.8% of the total wealth.
3. The next poorest 13.9% of the male population owned 11.1% of the total wealth.
4. The next poorest 20.8% of the male population owned 30.9% of the total wealth.
5. The wealthiest 5.6% of the male population owned 41.6% of the total wealth.

1700–1719

1. The poorest 42.5% of the male population owned 3.4% of the total wealth.
2. The next poorest 26% of the male population owned 7.9% of the total wealth.
3. The next poorest 17.8% of the male population owned 12.6% of the total wealth.
4. The next poorest 7.9% of the male population owned 14.7% of the total wealth.
5. The wealthiest 5.8% of the male population owned 61.5% of the total wealth.

1720–1750

1. The poorest 35.3% of the male population owned 3.1% of the total wealth.
2. The next poorest 30.4% of the male population owned 11.2% of the total wealth.
3. The next poorest 26% of the male population owned 31.3% of the total wealth.
4. The next poorest 5.6% of the male population owned 21.3% of the total wealth.
5. The wealthiest 2.7% of the male population owned 33.2% of the total wealth.

Source 4 from Gloria L. Main, *Tobacco Colony: Life in Early Maryland, 1650–1720* (Princeton: Princeton University Press, 1982), p. 54. Data from probate records of six counties, Maryland Hall of Records, Annapolis. © 1982 Princeton University Press. Reprinted by permission of Princeton University Press.

4. Average Gross Personal Wealth of Ranked Strata of Maryland Probated Estates, 1656–1719 (in pounds sterling).

Strata of Estates	1656–1683	1684–1696	1697–1704	1705–1712	1713–1719	% Change 1656–83/ 1713–19
Bottom 30%	£16	£15	£14	£14	£13	−19
Lower-middle 30%	48	49	48	46	42	−12
Upper-middle 30%	142	150	169	146	146	+3
Wealthiest 10%	473	652	719	971	1009	+113

Source 5 data from Social Science Research Council, *The Statistical History of the United States from Colonial Times to the Present* (Stamford, Conn.: Fairfield Publishers, 1965), pp. 765–766; and Census Bureau, *Historical Statistics of the United States*, pt. 2, p. 1198. Slightly different numbers can be found in Elizabeth Boody Schumpeter, *English Overseas Trade Statistics 1697–1808* (Oxford: Clarendon Press, 1960), pp. 52–55.

5. Tobacco Imported by England from Virginia and Maryland (in thousands of pounds) and Maryland Tobacco Prices (in pence sterling/ pound), 1620–1770.

Year	Total (in thousands of pounds)	Tobacco Prices (pence sterling/pound)
1620	119.0	12.00
1630	458.2	4.00
1640	1,257.0	2.50
1650	—	—
1663	7,371.1	1.55
1672	17,559.0	1.00
1682	21,399.0	0.80
1688	28,385.5	0.75
1700	37,166.0	1.00
1710	23,351.0	0.85
1720	34,138.0	1.19
1730	34,860.0	0.67
1740	35,372.0	0.80
1750	50,785.0	1.16
1760	51,283.0	1.60
1770	38,986.0	2.06

◆ CHAPTER 3

Colonies,
Commerce, and
Empire: The
British Plantation
System in the
Chesapeake and
Caribbean

Source 6: From *Sugar and Slaves: the Rise of the Planter Class in the English West Indies, 1624–1713* by Richard S. Dunn. Published for the Omohundro Institute of Early American History and Culture. Copyright © 1972 by the University of North Carolina Press. Used by permission of the publisher. www.uncpress.unc.edu

6. Indentured Servants Shipped from Bristol to Virginia and Maryland, 1654–1686.

Destination	1654–1659	1660–1669	1670–1679	1680–1686	Total
Virginia	796	2,484	1,477	117	4,874
Maryland	1	20	81	35	137
Totals	797	2,504	1,558	152	5,011

Source 7 from Richard S. Dunn, "Servants and Slaves: The Recruitment and Employment of Labor," in Greene and Pole, *Colonial British America*, p. 165, Table 6.1. © 1991 The Johns Hopkins University Press. Reprinted with permission of The Johns Hopkins University Press.

7. English Slave Imports to America, 1600–1780 (in thousands).

Years	West Indies	Southern[19] Mainland	Mid-Atlantic	New England	Total
1601–1625	—	—	—	—	—
1626–1650	21	—	—	—	21
1651–1675	69	—	—	—	69
1676–1700	174	10	—	—	184
1701–1720	160	28	2	—	190
1721–1740	199	64	4	2	269
1741–1760	267	63	1	1	332
1761–1780	335	80	2	—	417
Total	1,225	245	9	3	1,482
Black population in 1780	346	519	42	14	921

Source 8: From *Slave Counterpoint: Black Culture in the Eighteenth-Century Chesapeake and Low Country* by Philip D. Morgan. Published for the Omohundro Institute of Early American History and Culture. Copyright © 1988 by the University of North Carolina Press. Used by permission of the publisher. www.uncpress.unc.edu

19. The Southern Mainland included Maryland, Virginia, North Carolina, South Carolina, and Georgia.

8. Plantation Size in Virginia by Number of Slaves, 1700–1779.

	Number of Slaves on Plantations			
Decade	1–5	6–10	11–20	21+
1700–1709	39%	19%	32%	10%
1710–1719	30	20	27	23
1720–1729	30	29	27	13
1730–1739	28	27	20	25
1740–1749	25	25	32	17
1750–1759	18	22	29	31
1760–1769	15	22	29	33
1770–1779	13	22	35	29

Source 9: From *Adapting to a New World: English Society in the Seventeenth-Century Chesapeake* by James Horn. Published for the Omohundro Institute of Early American History and Culture. Copyright © 1994 by the University of North Carolina Press. Used by permission of the publisher. www.uncpress.unc.edu

9. Number of Servants and Slaves per Household, Lower Western Shore of Maryland, 1658–1700.

No. of Servants and Slaves per Household	No. of Households Owning	Proportion of All Households Owning	Proportion of All Households in Class Owning Mostly Slaves
1658–1674			
1–3	2	10.5%	0%
4–6	8	42.1	37.5
7–9	5	26.3	20.0
10+	4	21.1	25.0
Overall	19	100.0	26.3
1675–1684			
1–3	8	17.8%	12.5%
4–6	18	40.0	5.6
7–9	8	17.8	25.0
10+	11	24.4	36.4
Overall	45	100.0	17.8
1685–1700			
1–3	24	28.2%	33.3%
4–6	25	29.4	48.0
7–9	12	14.1	58.3
10+	24	28.2	66.7
Overall	85	99.9	50.6

Source 12 from Robert D. Mitchell, *Commercialism and Frontier: Perspectives on the Early Shenandoah Valley* (Charlottesville, Va.: University Press of Virginia, 1977), pp. 95–100.

12. Virginia Population West of Blue Ridge Mountains, 1745–1790.

Date	Total Population	Slave Population
1745	c. 10,200	—
1750	c. 17,000	—
1755	c. 20,800	760
1782	—	6,744
1790	74,767	10,715

BARBADOS

Source 13 from Dunn, *Sugar and Slaves*, p. 87; and Beckles, *History of Barbados*, p. 53.

13. Population Estimates, Barbados, 1655–1770.

Year	Whites	Slaves	Slaves as % of Total Population
1655	23,000	20,000	46.5%
1673	21,309	33,184	60.9
1684	19,568	46,602	70.4
1700	15,400	50,100	76.5
1720	17,700	58,800	76.9
1740	17,800	72,100	80.2
1760	17,800	86,600	83.0
1770	17,200	92,000	84.2

Source 14 from Russell R. Menard, *Sweet Negotiations: Sugar, Slavery, and Plantation Agriculture in Early Barbados* (Charlottesville: University of Virginia Press, 2006), p. 27.

14. Land Prices (per acre in Barbadian currency), 1638–1650.

1638	£1.20
1640	1.30
1645	4.70
1650	5.50

◆ CHAPTER 3

Colonies,
Commerce, and
Empire: The
British Plantation
System in the
Chesapeake and
Caribbean

Source 15: Hilary McD. Beckles, *A History of Barbados: From Amerindian Settlement to Caribbean Single Market.* Copyright © 2006 by Cambridge University Press. Reprinted with the permission of Cambridge University Press.

15. Landed Proprietors, Barbados, 1645–1680.

Year	Number of Landed Proprietors
1645	11,200
1667	745
1680	1,406

Source 16: Hilary McD. Beckles, *A History of Barbados: From Amerindian Settlement to Caribbean Single Market.* Copyright © 2006 by Cambridge University Press. Reprinted with the permission of Cambridge University Press.

16. Wealth Distribution, Wealthy Planters, 1673 and 1680.

1673—74 "most eminent" planters (those who owned 200–1,000 acres) owned 31.6% of all arable land.

1680—175 wealthiest planters (those who owned 60+ slaves) owned approx. 60% of all landed property and 60% of all enslaved Africans.

Source 17: From *Sugar and Slaves: the Rise of the Planter Class in the English West Indies, 1624–1713* by Richard S. Dunn. Published for the Omohundro Institute of Early American History and Culture. Copyright © 1972 by the University of North Carolina Press. Used by permission of the publisher. www.uncpress.unc.edu

17. Wealth Distribution, Jamaica, 1674–1701 (percentages).[20]

Appraised Value	% of Estates
£1–99	34.4%
100–499	37.9
500–999	12.8
1,000–1,990	9.4
2,000+	5.5

20. Unfortunately, no such figures are available for Barbados. Jamaica, however, was similar to Barbados and even exceeded Barbados in sugar production in the mid-eighteenth century. At the same time that 14.9% of Jamaican planters owned estates valued at £1,000 or more, that figure in Maryland in 1690–1699 was 1.5%.

Sources 18–20 from Menard, *Sweet Negotiations*, p. 18.

18. Commodities Transactions in Barbados, 1639–1652 (percentages).

Year	% Tobacco	% Cotton	% Sugar
1639	57%	43%	0%
1640	21	79	0
1644	43	26	8
1647	12	47	41
1648	8	32	60
1649	0	0	100

19. Estimated Sugar Exports from Barbados to London, 1651–1706 (tons).

Year	Sugar Exported (in tons)
1651	3,750
1655	7,787
1669	9,525
1683	10,000
1691	9,191
1696	7,613
1698	15,587
1700	12,170
1706	10,236

20. Prices of Cotton, Indigo, and Sugar in Amsterdam, 1624–1650 (in guilders per Dutch pound).

Year	Cotton	Indigo	Sugar
1624	0.81	4.13	0.30
1630	0.53	3.72	0.57
1634	0.48	3.75	0.50
1640	0.34	8.10	0.49
1645	0.61	2.78	0.57
1650	0.28	2.79	0.49

◆ CHAPTER 3

Colonies,
Commerce, and
Empire: The
British Plantation
System in the
Chesapeake and
Caribbean

Source 21: From *Sugar and Slaves: the Rise of the Planter Class in the English West Indies, 1624-1713* by Richard S. Dunn. Published for the Omohundro Institute of Early American History and Culture. Copyright © 1972 by the University of North Carolina Press. Used by permission of the publisher. www.uncpress.unc.edu

21. Indentured Servants Shipped from Bristol to Barbados, 1654–1686.

1654–1659	1660–1669	1670–1679	1680–1686	Total
1,405	948	252	73	2,678

Source 22 from Menard, *Sweet Negotiations*, p. 47; and Philip D. Curtin, *The Atlantic Slave Trade, A Census* (Madison: University of Wisconsin Press, 1969), p. 55.

22. Estimated Slave Imports into Barbados, 1630s–1766.

Years	Est. Number Imports
1630s	1,000
1640s	18,000
1650s	31,364
1660s	28,650
1670s	22,219
1680s	21,885
1690s	35,027
1698–1701	36,400
1708–1729	71,700
1730–1752	56,500
1753–1766	46,900

Source 23 from Menard, *Sweet Negotiations*, p. 32.

23. Sample of Servants and Slaves per Estate, Barbados, 1635–1670.

Years	# Estates	Servants per Estate	Slaves per Estate
1635–1640	8	15.4	0.1
1641–1643	9	12.0	3.4
1646–1649	6	9.5	11.1
1650–1657	7	18.4	24.0
1658–1670	10	3.1	111.1

24. Average Prices for Slaves, Barbados, 1638–1710 (in pounds sterling).

Year	Average Price
1638	£40.88
1639	44.15
1640	30.03
1643	20.54
1645	20.98
1681	13.21
1686	13.28
1694	16.94
1705	26.22
1710	20.97

25. Estimated Deaths of Slaves, British West Indies, 1640–1762.

1640–1700 Approx. 264,000 slaves were brought to the British West Indies. In 1700, the total black population was approx. 100,000.

1712–1762 Approx. 150,000 slaves were brought to the British West Indies. In 1762, the total black population was approx. 128,000.

26. Whites Who Left Barbados, 1645–1700.

1645–1700 Approx. 30,000 whites left Barbados, most without any land or capital.

1679—593 persons left Barbados (35% to England, 38% to British mainland colonies, 26% to other British Caribbean colonies).

◆ CHAPTER 3

Colonies,
Commerce, and
Empire: The
British Plantation
System in the
Chesapeake and
Caribbean

◆

Questions to Consider

When analyzing statistics, look at each set individually and ask the following questions:

1. What does this set of statistics measure?
2. How did what is being measured change over time?
3. Why does that change take place? As noted earlier, the answer to this question often can be found in another statistical set or sets. When you are able to connect one set to another in this way, statisticians say that you have made a *linkage*.

Begin by examining all the Chesapeake statistics. Sources 1 and 2 show that the white population generally increased in both Virginia and Maryland throughout most of the colonial period. However, did the *rate* of that growth change over time? How might you explain this phenomenon (see Source 6)? What does the increase of the black population suggest (see Sources 6, 7, and 10)?

From the late seventeenth century to the mid-eighteenth century, a socioeconomic revolution took place in the Chesapeake. What were the principal features of that revolution (see Sources 4, 8, 9, and 10)? Clearly the adoption of tobacco was a key factor. How did the tobacco culture cause other important changes (Sources 4, 6, 7, 8, 9, 12)?

Tobacco is an extremely labor intensive crop, requiring continuous hoeing and worming as well as topping the plants (to prevent flowering and stimulate existing leaves), suckering (removal of new growth to force the plant's energy into existing leaves), cutting, hanging, curing, stripping, bundling, and packing into hogsheads (large barrels holding over 300 pounds of tobacco leaves). Therefore, a great deal of labor was needed to grow a good crop of tobacco. What were the traditional sources of agricultural labor in the Chesapeake? How did those sources change over time? Can you account for this change?

In addition to labor, those who would raise tobacco needed land, preferably a large amount of it because continuous cultivation of tobacco resulted in serious soil exhaustion. How did patterns of landholding change over time (see Sources 3, 4, 8, and 10)? Combined with changing labor patterns, what kind of economy and society was emerging in the Chesapeake by the mid-18th century?

At this point, allow us to remind you that statistical analysis requires extreme care. For example, as you examine wealth distribution in Middlesex County, Virginia (Source 3), be very careful to note that the "wealth clusters" in the three time periods are different. For example, in the wealth distribution through 1699, the poorest group represents 31.2 percent of the male population, whereas in 1700 to 1719 the poorest group is 42.5 percent and in 1720 to 1750 it is 35.3 percent. In spite of the apparent inconsistency of this pattern, you nevertheless will be able to see general trends of wealth distribution. What are those trends?

There is little question that by the eighteenth century the evolving Chesapeake society was beginning to face increasingly severe demographic and economic troubles. What was the nature of those difficulties? Your chain of evidence should be able to give you insight into the Chesapeake residents' approaching demographic and economic crisis. Was there such a thing as raising *too much* tobacco (see Source 5)? What growing problem does Source 11 reveal? How would you link that to Source 5? Finally, the consolidation of land into larger and larger plantations clearly affected small farmers, to say nothing of those who had lost their holdings to their wealthier neighbors. How did some of them respond to this (Source 12), a trend that continued in the Chesapeake until Civil War times?

To summarize, what factors were responsible for the evolution of a mature society in the Chesapeake region by the mid-1700s? What part did the Chesapeake region play in England's emergence as a major economic power? Were there any negative aspects to that region's growth and change?

Now repeat the process for Barbados. Looking at Source 13, how did the rate of white population growth change over time (see Sources 14 through 17, and Sources 21 and 22)? How did landholding patterns change (Sources 14–17)? How can you explain these changes?

Obviously the shift to sugar production was a crucial factor in the growth and change of Barbadian society. Why was there a shift to sugar and away from tobacco, cotton, and indigo (Sources 18–20)? How did *that* change prompt a change in the source of labor (Sources 21–25)? Why did Barbados continue to import slaves from Africa when the Chesapeake was able to fill its labor needs through slaves' natural increase? What happened to whites who were negatively affected by these changes? Finally, what role did Barbados play in England's emergence as a major power? How did Barbadian society change in this period? Were there any negative aspects to those changes?

Finally you are ready to put the Chesapeake and Barbadian statistics together. While there are significant similarities in those societies' demographics, there are some striking and crucial differences as well. As you look at the major factors (population, landholding, adoption of a one-crop agricultural system, changes in labor system, and so forth), what are the similarities? The major differences?

◆

Epilogue

To a person traveling through the Chesapeake Bay region in the mid-eighteenth century, all appeared well. The plantation system—complete with great planters' houses, private tutors, imported furniture, clothes, and wines, and even seasons of parties and balls—seemed to be a grander reproduction of the lives of England's country squires—except that a large percentage of the wealthiest planters had come from the "middling sort," small land-owners

◆ CHAPTER 3

Colonies,
Commerce, and
Empire: The
British Plantation
System in the
Chesapeake and
Caribbean

whose hard work and good fortune had brought them to the apex of one of British North America's grandest elites.[21]

And yet, beneath the gilded surface not all was well. As the statistics clearly show, the lion's share of the Chesapeake society's benefits went to the wealthiest 10 percent of the landholders (Source 4), whereas free white smallholders' positions were eroding. Too, the shift to slave labor required an increasingly rigid and harsh system to prevent insurrections. As Thomas Jefferson later put it, such a system of bondage restricted the liberties of free and slave alike.[22]

Although only a few sensed it, the zenith of Virginia already had passed by the outbreak of the American Revolution. Overproduction of tobacco and the resulting soil exhaustion,[23] continued reliance on imported manufactured goods, the opening of new plantation lands to the south and west, the emigration of whites from eastern Virginia, and the overpopulation of slaves acted together to increase Virginia's economic troubles. By the time of Thomas Jefferson's death in 1826, the leadership of the southern states had passed from the Chesapeake to a more strident South Carolina.

Finally, one is tempted to wonder if there was any relationship between the Chesapeake's demographic and economic concerns and the region's ultimate revolution against Great Britain. Did planters' growing debts to British merchants (see Source 11) play any role in the Chesapeake's uprising against the mother country? To be sure, Patriot leaders from the Chesapeake doubtless were sincere when they avowed that they took up arms in defense of their liberties. Is it possible, however, that other, unacknowledged reasons also were pushing the colonists of the Chesapeake toward rebellion? Over a century and a half, they had laboriously constructed the Chesapeake society; but even as the revolution approached, that society was under increasing strain and tension. How to maintain the plantation system and slavery while simultaneously advocating equality and freedom became the Chesapeake—and the American—dilemma.

At first glance Barbados remained "that fair jewel of your Majesty's Crown" into the nineteenth century. To begin with, England's demand for sugar was nearly insatiable. Originally affordable only by England's wealthiest elite, by the mid-18th century virtually all of England could partake of sugar, "even the poor wretches living in slumhouses will not be without it." Largely responsible was England's infatuation with tea. In 1770, England imported only 91,260 pounds of tea, whereas by 1770 an astounding 11 *million* pounds was being imported. As tea consumption rose, so also did the consumption of sugar in Britain, from

21. See Lois Green Carr, Russell R. Menard, and Lorena S. Walsh, *Robert Cole's World: Agriculture and Society in Early Maryland* (Chapel Hill: University of North Carolina Press, 1991), p. 15.
22. For examples of the increasing repressiveness of the Chesapeake's slave system, see Warren M. Billings, ed., *The Old Dominion in the Seventeenth Century: A Documentary History of Virginia, 1606–1689* (Chapel Hill: University of North Carolina Press, 1975), pp. 172–174.
23. See Avery Odelle Craven, *Soil Exhaustion as a Factor in the Agricultural History of Virginia and Maryland, 1606–1860* (Champaign: University of Illinois Press, 1926), esp. pp. 32–35.

roughly 4 pounds annually per capita to 18 pounds in 1800. By 1750, "the poorest English farm laborer's wife took sugar in her tea."[24] When the mainland colonies invited Barbados to join in their "revolution" in 1775, the Barbadians firmly refused. They should, they reasoned, remain in the British Empire where their sugar would be bought . . . and sold.

And still, like the Chesapeake, Barbados encountered severe difficulties. Soil exhaustion led to falling crop yields, and Barbados's eminent position was taken over by Jamaica. The share of Barbados's sugar imports to England fell from 47% in 1705–1709 to a bare 5.5% in 1775–1779. Most of this can be explained by the phenomenal rise of Jamaica, whose sugar production leaped from 19.4% of all sugar imports into England and Wales in 1700 to 39.5% in 1770. Clearly Barbados was facing difficulty. The slave rebellion in what ultimately became Haiti (the largest producer of sugar in the Caribbean) artificially raised prices, but only temporarily.[25]

Efforts by England and the new nation of the United States to end the slave trade in 1807–1808 did not excessively alarm the planters of Barbados, since by that time natural increase caused no need for further imports.

Barbadian planters actually offered incentives to slave women to have numerous children (one overseer reported that "I encourage the slaves to breed as much as I can"). Indeed, Barbadian planters even sold their excess slaves.

As a member of the British Empire, the end of the international slave trade in 1807–1808 and the emancipation of slaves in 1834 clearly affected the colony. Yet freedom came gradually, with compensation to the former owners. And most former slaves found themselves continuing to work on their former plantations or scraping out a meager existence as tenants on subpar land. Food rebellions and laborers' riots occurred regularly (the 1876 revolt resulted in 700 to 800 blacks killed). Self-rule came gradually. Finally, in 1966, Barbados achieved full independence. Comparatively speaking, Barbados has achieved a better living standard than have most of Europe's former Caribbean colonies, in terms of literacy, life expectancy, birth rate, and so forth.

The planters of Barbados refused to join their mainland brethren in their revolution against their mother country. Similar in many ways to the planters of the Chesapeake, their differences were significant enough to cause them to choose a different path. Their own revolution would come later.

24. For tea imports see Schumpeter, *English Overseas Trade*, pp. 48–55. For English usage see Edward Long (1774), Quoted in Richard B. Sheridan, *Sugar and Slaves: An Economic History of the British West Indies, 1623–1775* (Barbados: Caribbean Universities Press, 1974), p. 26; Davis, *The Rise of the Atlantic Economies,* p. 251.

25. By 1770 Britain was making enormous profits by re-exporting sugar. See Sheridan, *Sugar and Slaves*, pp. 493–495, 500–501.

4

What Really Happened in the Boston Massacre? The Trial of Captain Thomas Preston

◆

The Problem

On the chilly evening of March 5, 1770, a small group of boys began taunting a British sentry (called a *centinel or sentinel*) in front of the Boston Custom House. Pushed to the breaking point by this goading, the soldier struck one of his tormentors with his musket. Soon a crowd of fifty or sixty gathered around the frightened soldier, prompting him to call for help. The officer of the day, Captain Thomas Preston, and seven British soldiers hurried to the Custom House to protect the sentry.

Upon arriving at the Custom House, Captain Preston must have sensed how precarious his position was. The crowd had swelled to more than one hundred, some anxious for a fight, others simply curiosity seekers, and still others called from their homes by the town's church bells, a traditional signal that a fire had broken out. Efforts by Preston and others to calm the crowd proved useless. And because the crowd had

enveloped Preston and his men as it had the lone sentry, retreat was nearly impossible.

What happened next is a subject of considerable controversy. One of the soldiers fired his musket into the crowd, and the others followed suit, one by one. The colonists scattered, leaving five dead[1] and six wounded, some of whom were probably innocent bystanders. Preston and his men quickly returned to their barracks, where they were placed under house arrest. They were later taken to jail and charged with murder.

---

1. Those killed were Crispus Attucks (a part African, part Native American seaman in his forties, who also went by the name of Michael Johnson), James Caldwell (a sailor), Patrick Carr (an immigrant from Ireland who worked as a leather-breeches maker), Samuel Gray (a ropemaker), and Samuel Maverick (a seventeen-year-old apprentice).

Preston's trial began on October 24, 1770, delayed by the authorities in an attempt to cool the emotions of the townspeople. The anger of most Bostonians, however, did not abate. The day after what some people already were beginning to call "the massacre," an enormous town meeting demanded that the British troops be removed, a demand that Lieutenant Governor Thomas Hutchinson rejected. That same day, witnesses began to appear before the town's justices of the peace to give sworn depositions of their versions of what had taken place, depositions that leaked out in a pamphlet undoubtedly published by anti-British extremists.[2] Then, on March 8, a massive funeral procession of 10,000 to 12,000 mourners accompanied the four caskets to the burial ground.[3] Four days later, Paul Revere's engraving (Source 4 in the Evidence section of this chapter) appeared in *Boston Gazette*. Therefore, when Preston's trial finally began seven months after the event, emotions still were running high.

John Adams, Josiah Quincy, and Robert Auchmuty had agreed to defend Preston,[4] even though the first two were staunch Patriots. They believed that the captain was entitled to a fair trial and did their best to defend him. After a difficult jury selection, the trial began, witnesses for the prosecution and the defense being called mostly from those who had given depositions to the grand jury. The trial lasted for four days, an unusually long trial for the times. The case went to the jury at 5:00 P.M. on October 29. Although it took the jury only three hours to reach a verdict, the decision was not announced until the following day.

In this chapter, you will be using portions of the evidence given at the murder trial of Captain Thomas Preston to reconstruct what actually happened on that March evening in Boston, Massachusetts. Was Preston guilty as charged? Or was he innocent? Only by reconstructing the event that we call the Boston Massacre will you be able to answer these questions.

2. For the ninety six depositions, see *A Short Narrative of the Horrid Massacre in Boston* (Boston: Edes and Gill, 1770). Thirty-one depositions were taken by those favorable to Preston, delivered to London, and published as *A Fair Account of the Late Unhappy Disturbance at Boston* (London: B. White, 1770).
3. Patrick Carr lived until March 14.

4. Adams, Quincy, and Auchmuty (pronounced Auk'muty) also were engaged to defend the soldiers, a practice that would not be allowed today because of the conflict of interest (defending more than one person charged with the same crime).

♦ CHAPTER 4

What Really
Happened in the
Boston Massacre?
The Trial of
Captain Thomas
Preston

♦
Background

The town of Boston[5] had been uneasy throughout the first weeks of 1770. Tension had been building since the early 1760s because the town was increasingly affected by the forces of migration, change, and maturation. The protests against the Stamp Act had been particularly bitter there, and in the wake of a new slate of taxes known as the Townshend Duties (1767), men such as Samuel Adams were encouraging their fellow Bostonians to be even bolder in their remonstrances. In response, in 1768, the British government ordered two regiments of soldiers to Boston to restore order and enforce the laws of Parliament. Knowing the colonists better than did the British government, three years earlier Benjamin Franklin had quipped, "They will not *find* a rebellion; they may indeed *make* one."[6]

Instead of bringing calm to Boston, the presence of soldiers, as Franklin had predicted, only increased tensions. Clashes between Bostonians and redcoats were common on the streets, in taverns, and at the places of employment of British soldiers who sought part-time jobs to supplement their meager salaries. Known British sympathizers and informers were harassed, and Crown officials were openly insulted. Indeed, the town of Boston seemed to be a power keg just waiting for a spark to set off an explosion.

On February 22, 1770, British sympathizer and informer Ebenezer Richardson tried to tear down an anti-British sign. He was followed to his house by an angry crowd that proceeded to taunt him and break his windows with stones. One of the stones struck Richardson's wife. Enraged, he grabbed a musket and fired almost blindly into the crowd. Eleven-year-old Christopher Seider[7] fell to the ground with eleven pellets of shot in his chest. The boy died eight hours later. The crowd, by now numbering about one thousand, dragged Richardson from his house and through the streets, finally delivering him to the Boston jail. Four days later, the town conducted a huge funeral for Christopher Seider, probably arranged and organized by Samuel Adams. Seider's casket was carried through the streets by children, and approximately two thousand mourners (one-seventh of Boston's total population) took part. All through the next week Boston was an angry town. Gangs of men and boys roamed the streets at night looking for British soldiers foolish enough to venture out alone. Similarly, off-duty soldiers prowled the same streets looking for someone to challenge them. A fight broke out at a ropewalk

5. Although Boston was one of the largest urban centers in the colonies, the town was not incorporated as a city. Several attempts were made, but residents opposed them, fearing they would lose the institution of the town meeting.
6. For Franklin's statement, see "Testimony to the House of Commons, February 13, 1755," quoted in Walter Isaacson, *Benjamin Franklin, An American Life* (New York: Simon and Schuster, 2003), p. 230.

7. Christopher Seider is sometimes referred to as Christopher Snider.

between some soldiers who worked there part time and some unemployed colonists. Tempers grew even uglier, and only two days before the "massacre" British Lieutenant Colonel Maurice Carr complained to the Lieutenant Governor "of the frequent abuses offered to his men, and of very insolent, provoking language given to some of them. . . ."[8]

Crowd disturbances had been an almost regular feature of life in both England and America. Historian John Bohstedt has estimated that England was the scene of at least one thousand crowd disturbances and riots between 1790 and 1810.[9] Colonial American towns were no more placid; demonstrations and riots were almost regular features of the colonists' lives. Destruction of property and burning of effigies were common in these disturbances. In August 1765, in Boston, for example, crowds protesting against the Stamp Act burned effigies and destroyed the homes of stamp distributor Andrew Oliver and Massachusetts Lieutenant Governor Thomas Hutchinson.[10] Indeed, it was almost as if the entire community was willing to countenance demonstrations and riots as long as they were confined to parades, loud gatherings, and limited destruction of property. In almost no cases were there any deaths and authorities almost never fired into the crowds, no matter how loud and demonstrative they became. Yet on March 5, 1770, both the crowd and the soldiers acted uncharacteristically. The result was the tragedy that colonists dubbed the "Boston Massacre." Why did the crowd and the soldiers behave as they did?

To repeat, your task is to reconstruct the so-called Boston Massacre so as to understand what really happened on that fateful evening. Spelling and punctuation in the evidence have been modernized only to clarify the meaning.

◆

The Method

Many students (and some historians) like to think that facts speak for themselves. This is especially tempting when analyzing a single incident like the Boston Massacre, many eyewitnesses of which testified at the trial. However, discovering what really happened, even when there are eyewitnesses, is never quite that easy. Witnesses may be confused at the time; they may see

8. Thomas Hutchinson, *The History of the Colony and Province of Massachusetts-Bay*, ed. Lawrence Shaw Mayo (Cambridge: Harvard University Press, 1936). vol. 3, p. 195. For some accounts of the fight at the ropewalk, see *A Short Narrative*, pp. 17–20.

9. John Bohstedt, *Riots and Community Politics in England and Wales*, 1790–1810 (Cambridge, Mass.: Harvard University Press, 1983), p. 5.

10. Thomas Hutchinson, *The History of the Colony and Province of Massachusetts-Bay*, ed. Lawrence Shaw Mayo (Cambridge: Haward University Press, 1936), vol. 3, pp. 88–91. See also Edmund S. Morgan and Helen M. Morgan, *The Stamp Act Crisis: Prologue to Revolution* (Chapel Hill: University of North Carolina Press, 1953), pp. 123–127.

✦ CHAPTER 4

What Really
Happened in the
Boston Massacre?
The Trial of
Captain Thomas
Preston

only part of the incident; or they may unconsciously "see" only what they expect to see. Obviously, witnesses also may have reasons to lie. Thus the testimony of witnesses must be carefully scrutinized, for both what the witnesses *mean* to tell us and other relevant information as well. Therefore, historians approach such testimony with considerable skepticism and are concerned not only with the testimony itself but also with the possible motives of the witnesses.

Of the 81 people who gave depositions to the justices of the peace, only 15 were called by the crown as witnesses. Many of those that were discarded maintained that the soldiers had planned the March 5 incident and, after the shootings, "seemed bent on a further massacre of the inhabitants." On the other side several pro-Preston depositions asserted that the colonists had planned the incident and were preparing to attack the main barracks. None of these depositions could be admitted as evidence in the trial, although their publication in pamphlets meant that the jurors almost surely knew about them.[11]

As for Preston himself, neither he nor the soldiers were allowed to testify at the captain's trial. English legal custom prohibited defendants in criminal cases from testifying on their own behalf, the expectation being that they would perjure themselves. One week after the "massacre," however, in a sworn statement or deposition, Captain Thomas Preston gave his account

of the incident. Although the deposition could not be introduced at the trial, it too had been published in one of the local newspapers, and therefore the jury very likely also was aware of what Preston had said. For this reason, we have reproduced a portion of Preston's statement. How does it agree or disagree with other eyewitness accounts?[12]

Three months before his trial was scheduled to begin, Preston complained to his commanding general that witnesses favorable to him "are being spirited away or intimidated into silence." While intimidation of potential witnesses would not have been unlikely, especially since their depositions had been published, there is no corroborating evidence to support Preston's charge.[13]

No transcript of Preston's trial survives, if indeed one was ever made. Trial testimony comes from an anonymous person's summary of what each person said, the notes of Robert Treat Paine (one of the lawyers for the prosecution), and one witness's (Richard Palmes's) reconstruction of his testimony and cross-examination. Although historians would prefer to use the original trial transcript and would do so if one were available, the anonymous summary, Paine's notes, and one witness's recollections are acceptable substitutes because probably all three people were present in the courtroom (Paine and Palmes certainly were) and

11. For examples of unreliable depositions, see *A Short Narrative*, pp. 14–29: *A Fair Account*, pp. 14–20; and Frederic Kidder, *History of the Boston Massacre* (Albany: Joel Munsell, 1870), pp. 10–12.

12. Preston's statement appeared in the *Boston Gazette*, March 12, 1770. *See Publications of the Colonial Society of Massachusetts* (Boston: The Colonial Society, 1905). p. 6.
13. For Preston's charge see Preston to Gen. Thomas Gage, August 6, 1770, in Randolph G. Adams, "New Light on the Boston Massacre," in American Antiquarian Society *Proceedings*, New Series, vol. 47 (Oct. 1937), pp. 321–322.

the accounts tend to corroborate one another.

Almost all the witnesses were at the scene, yet not all their testimony is of equal merit. First, try to reconstruct the scene itself: the actual order in which the events occurred and where the various participants were standing. Whenever possible, look for corroborating testimony—that of two or more reliable witnesses who heard or saw the same things.

Be careful to use all the evidence. You should be able to develop some reasonable explanation for the conflicting testimony and those things that do not fit into your reconstruction very well.

Almost immediately you will discover that some important pieces of evidence are missing. For example, it would be useful to know the individual backgrounds and political views of the witnesses. Unfortunately, we know very little about the witnesses themselves, and we can reconstruct the political ideas of only about one-third of them. Therefore, you will have to rely on the testimonies given, deducing which witnesses were telling the truth, which were lying, and which were simply mistaken.

The fact that significant portions of the evidence are missing is not disastrous. Historians seldom have all the evidence they need when they attempt to tackle a historical problem. Instead, they must be able to do as much as they can with the evidence that is available, using it as completely and imaginatively as they can. They do so by asking questions of the available evidence.

Where were the witnesses standing? Which one seems more likely to be telling the truth? Which witnesses were probably lying? When dealing with the testimony of the witnesses, be sure to determine what is factual and what is a witness's opinion. A rough sketch of the scene has been provided. How can it help you?

Also included in the evidence is Paul Revere's famous engraving of the incident, probably plagiarized from a drawing by artist Henry Pelham. It is unlikely that either Pelham or Revere was an eyewitness to the Boston Massacre, yet Revere's engraving gained widespread distribution, and most people—in 1770 and today—tend to recall that engraving when they think of the Boston Massacre. Do not examine the engraving until you have read the trial account closely. Can Revere's engraving help you find out what really happened that night? How does the engraving fit the eyewitnesses' accounts? How do the engraving and the accounts differ? Why?

Keep the central question in mind: What really happened in the Boston Massacre? Throughout this exercise, you will be trying to determine whether an order to fire was actually given. If so, by whom? If not, how can you explain why shots were fired? As commanding officer, Thomas Preston was held responsible and charged with murder. You might want to consider the evidence available to you from the point of view of either a prosecution or defense attorney. Which side had the stronger case?

◆ CHAPTER 4

What Really
Happened in the
Boston Massacre?
The Trial of
Captain Thomas
Preston

◆

The Evidence

Source 1 from Paul Revere, *Plan of the Boston Massacre of 1770* (Boston: The Boston
Public Library).

1. Paul Revere's Sketch of the Boston Massacre Scene, in Boston Public Library.[14]

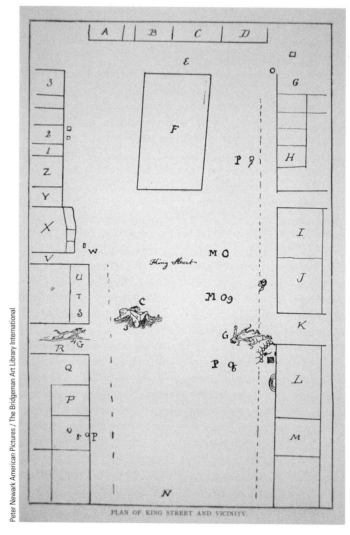

PLAN OF KING STREET AND VICINITY.

14. Note that Revere's sketch contained only four dead, proof that the sketch was done prior to
March 14, when the fifth person, Patrick Carr, died.

Source 2 from *Publications of The Colonial Society of Massachusetts* (Boston: The Colonial Society of Massachusetts, 1905), Vol. VII, pp. 8–9.

2. Deposition of Captain Thomas Preston, March 12, 1770 (excerpt).

The mob still increased and were outrageous, striking their clubs or bludgeons one against another, and calling out, come on you rascals, you bloody backs, you lobster scoundrels, fire if you dare, G-d damn you, fire and be damned, we know you dare not, and much more such language was used. At this time I was between the soldiers and the mob, parleying with, and endeavoring all in my power to persuade them to retire peaceably, but to no purpose. They advanced to the points of the bayonets, struck some of them and even the muzzles of the pieces, and seemed to be endeavoring to close with the soldiers. On which some well behaved persons asked me if the guns were charged. I replied yes. They then asked me if I intended to order the men to fire. I answered no, by no means, observing to them that I was advanced before the muzzles of the men's pieces, and must fall a sacrifice if they fired; that the soldiers were upon the half cock[15] and charged bayonets, and my giving the word fire under those circumstances would prove me to be no officer. While I was thus speaking, one of the soldiers, having received a severe blow with a stick, stepped a little to one side and instantly fired. . . . On this a general attack was made on the men by a great number of heavy clubs and snowballs being thrown at them, by which all our lives were in imminent danger, some persons at the same time from behind calling out, damn your bloods—why don't you fire. Instantly three or four of the soldiers fired. . . . On my asking the soldiers why they fired without orders, they said they heard the word fire and supposed it came from me. This might be the case as many of the mob called out fire, fire, but I assured the men that I gave no such order; that my words were, don't fire, stop your firing.[16]

15. The cock of a musket had to be fully drawn back (cocked) for the musket to fire. In half cock, the cock was drawn only halfway back so that priming powder could be placed in the pan. The musket, however, would not fire at half cock. This is the origin of "Don't go off half cocked."
16. Depositions also were taken from the soldiers, three of whom claimed, "We did our Captain's orders and if we don't obey his commands should have been confined and shot."

◆ CHAPTER 4

What Really
Happened in the
Boston Massacre?
The Trial of
Captain Thomas
Preston

Source 3: Reprinted by permission of the publisher from The Adams Papers: *The Legal Papers of John Adams* – Volume III, Cases 63 & 64, edited by L. Kinvin Wroth and Hiller B. Zobel, pp. 50, 53, 54, 56, 57, 58, 59, 61, 63, 65–66, 67, 68, 69, 72, 74, 76, 77, 79, 80–81, 92–93, Cambridge, Mass.: The Belknap Press of Harvard University Press, Copyright © 1965 by the Massachusetts Historical Society.

3. The Trial of Captain Thomas Preston (*Rex* v. *Preston*), October 24–29 (excerpt).

Witnesses for the King (Prosecution)

Edward Gerrish (or Garrick)

I heard a noise about 8 o'clock and went down to Royal Exchange Lane. Saw some Persons with Sticks coming up Quaker Lane. I said [to the sentry] Capt. Goldsmith owed my fellow Apprentice. He said he was a Gentleman and would pay every body. I said there was none in the Regiment.[17] He asked for me. I went to him, was not ashamed of my face. . . . The Sentinel left his Post and Struck me. I cried. My fellow Apprentice and a young man came up to the Sentinel and called him Bloody back.[18] He called to the Main Guard. . . . There was not a dozen people when the Sentinel called the Guard.

William Wyat

I went to Town House. Some hallowing, and crying where are they. 8 or 10 Soldiers came out[.] Prisoner walk'd at the left with a Stick. Somebody took him by [the] arm and said for G[od]'s Sake Captain . . . mind what you are about and keep the Soldiers in Order. They drew up. He bid 'em face about and then load.[19] The Officer in Rear . . . 100 people, shouting, they called fire, I then heard some Body say fire and took it to be the prisoner. Somebody called him Capt. Preston . . . Prisoner stood behind soldiers[;] I think he had a Cloath Coloured Surtot[20] on. Stampt and said damn your blood fire[,] let the consequence be what it will. They fired and people scattered. . . . After firing Capt. Preston knocked up Guns and reprimanded 'em for firing. It was the same Person who gave Orders to fire.

17. To say that there was no gentleman in the regiment was an insult to the sentry's superior officer, Captain Goldsmith.
18. British soldiers' coats were red.
19. Muskets were loaded from the muzzle with powder, wadding, a ball, and more wadding. The hammer was drawn back halfway, and powder was poured into the small pan under the hammer. There was a small piece of flint attached to the cock so that when the trigger was pulled, the cock would come down and the flint would spark and ignite the gunpowder in the pan. The fire would then ignite the gunpowder in the breech and fire the gun. If the powder in the pan exploded but did not ignite the powder in the breech, the result was a "flash in the pan" and a musket that did not fire.
20. Surtout: a type of overcoat.

John Cox

I saw the officer after the firing and spoke to the Soldiers and told 'em it was a Cowardly action to kill men at the end of their Bayonets. They were pushing at the People who seemed to be trying to come into the Street. The Captain came up and stamped and said Damn their bloods fire again and let 'em take the consequence. I was within four feet of him. He had no surtout but a red Coat with a Rose on his shoulder. . . . I said don't kill us who are carrying of[f] the Dead. I were within 4 or 5 feet of the Soldiers. . . . I heard no Threats.

Benjamin Burdick

When I came into King Street about 9 o'Clock I saw the Soldiers round the Centinel. I asked one if he was loaded and he said yes. I asked him if he would fire, he said yes by the Eternal God and pushd his Bayonet at me. After the firing the Captain came before the soldiers and put up their Guns with his arm and said stop firing, dont fire no more or don't fire again. I heard the word fire and took it and am certain that it came from behind the Soldiers. I saw a man passing busily behind who I took to be an Officer. The firing was a little time after. I saw some persons fall. Before the firing I saw a stick thrown at the Soldiers. The word fire I took to be a word of Command. I had in my hand a highland broad Sword which I brought from home. Upon my coming out I was told it was a wrangle[21] between the Soldiers and people, upon that I went back and got my Sword. I never used to go out with a weapon. I had not my Sword drawn till after the Soldier pushed his Bayonet at me. I should have cut his head off if he had stepd out of his Rank to attack me again. At the first firing the People were chiefly in Royal Exchange lane, there being about 50 in the Street. After the firing I went up to the Soldiers and told them I wanted to see some faces that I might swear to them another day. The Centinel in a melancholy tone said perhaps Sir you may.

Daniel Calef

I was present at the firing. I heard one of the Guns rattle. I turned about and lookd and heard the officer who stood on the right in a line with the Soldiers give the word fire twice. I lookd the Officer in the face when he gave the word and saw his mouth. He had on a red Coat, yellow Jacket and Silver laced hat, no trimming on his Coat.[22] The Prisoner is the Officer I mean. I saw his face plain, the moon shone on it. I am sure of the man though I have not seen

21. A quarrel.
22. The 29th Regiment, to which Preston belonged, wore uniforms that exactly matched Calef's description.

✦ CHAPTER 4

What Really
Happened in the
Boston Massacre?
The Trial of
Captain Thomas
Preston

him since before yesterday when he came into Court with others. I knew him instantly. I ran upon the word fire being given about 30 feet off. The officer had no Surtout on.

Robert Goddard

The Soldiers came up to the Centinel and the Officer told them to place themselves and they formd a half moon. The Captain told the Boys to go home least[23] there should be murder done. They were throwing Snow balls. Did not go off but threw more Snow balls. The Capt. was behind the Soldiers. The Captain told them to fire. One Gun went off. A Sailor or Townsman struck the Captain. He thereupon said damn your bloods fire think I'll be treated in this manner. This Man that struck the Captain came from among the People who were seven feet off and were round on one wing. I saw no person speak to him. I was so near I should have seen it. After the Capt. said Damn your bloods fire they all fired one after another about 7 or 8 in all, and then the officer bid Prime and load again. He stood behind all the time. Mr. Lee went up to the officer and called the officer by name Capt. Preston. I saw him coming down from the Guard behind the Party. I went to Gaol[24] the next day being sworn for the Grand Jury to see the Captain. Then said pointing to him that's the person who gave the word to fire. He said if you swear that you will ruin me everlastingly. I was so near the officer when he gave the word fire that I could touch him. His face was towards me. He stood in the middle behind the Men. I looked him in the face. He then stood within the circle. When he told 'em to fire he turned about to me. I lookd him in the face.

Diman Morton

Between 9 and 10 I heard in my house the cry of fire but soon understood there was no fire but the Soldiers were fighting with the Inhabitants. I went to King Street. Saw the Centinel over the Gutter, his Bayonet breast high. He retired to the steps—loaded. The Boys dared him to fire. Soon after a Party came down, drew up. The Captain ordered them to load. I went across the Street. Heard one Gun and soon after the other Guns. The Captain when he ordered them to load stood in the front before the Soldiers so that the Guns reached beyond him. The Captain had a Surtout on. I knew him well. The Surtout was not red. I think cloth colour. I stood on the opposite corner of Exchange lane when I heard the Captain order the Men to load. I came by my knowledge of the Captain partly by seeing him lead the Fortification Guard.

23. Lest: for fear that.
24. Gaol: jail.

◆ CHAPTER 3

Colonies,
Commerce, and
Empire: The
British Plantation
System in the
Chesapeake and
Caribbean

Source 10: Gloria L. *Main, Tobacco Colony: Life in Early Maryland, 1650-1720.*
Copyright © 1982 Princeton University Press. Reprinted by permission of Princeton
University Press; data from probate records of six counties, Maryland, in Hall of
Records, Annapolis.

10. Percentage of Slaves in Small and Large Bound Labor Groups, 1656–1719.

Years	Number of Laborers in Group	
	2–5	6+
1656–1683	9% slave	40% slave
1684–1696	18	57
1697–1704	32	70
1705–1712	66	89½
1713–1719	68	94

Source 11 data from Census Bureau, *Historical Statistics of the United States*, pt. 2,
pp. 1176–1177.

11. Value of Exports to and Imports from England by Virginia and Maryland, 1700–1770 (in pounds sterling).

Year	Exports (£)	Imports (£)
1700	317,302	173,481
1705	116,768	174,322
1710	188,429	127,639
1715	174,756	199,274
1720	331,482	110,717
1725	214,730	195,884
1730	346,823	150,931
1735	394,995	220,381
1740	341,997	281,428
1745	399,423	197,799
1750	508,939	349,419
1755	489,668	285,157
1760	504,451	605,882
1765	505,671	383,224
1770	435,094	717,782

Nathaniel Fosdick

Hearing the Bells ring, for fire I supposed I went out and came down by the Main Guard. Saw some Soldiers fixing their Bayonets on. Passed on. Went down to the Centinel. Perceived something pass me behind. Turned round and saw the Soldiers coming down. They bid me stand out of the way and damnd my blood. I told them I should not for any man. The party drew up round the Centinel, faced about and charged their Bayonets. I saw an Officer and said if there was any disturbance between the Soldiers and the People there was the Officer present who could settle it soon. I heard no Orders given to load, but in about two minutes after the Captain step'd across the Gutter. Spoke to two Men—I don't know who— then went back behind his men. Between the 4th and 5th men on the right. I then heard the word fire and the first Gun went off. In about 2 minutes the second and then several others. The Captain had a Sword in his hand. Was dressd in his Regimentals. Had no Surtout on. I saw nothing thrown nor any blows given at all. The first man on the right who fired after attempting to push the People slipped down and drop'd his Gun out of his hand. The Person who stepd in between the 4th and 5th Men I look upon it gave the orders to fire. His back was to me. I shall always think it was him. The Officer had a Wig on. I was in such a situation that I am as well satisfied there were no blows given as that the word fire was spoken.

Isaac Pierce

The Lieut. Governor asked Capt. Preston didn't you know you had no power to fire upon the Inhabitants or any number of People collected together unless you had a Civil Officer to give order. The Captain replied I was obliged to, to save my Sentry.

Joseph Belknap

The Lieut. Governor said to Preston Don't you know you can do nothing without a Magistrate. He answered I did it to save my Men.

Witnesses for the Prisoner (Preston)

Edward Hill

After all the firing Captain Preston put up the Gun of a Soldier who was going to fire and said fire no more you have done mischief enough.

Richard Palmes

Somebody there said there was a Rumpus in King Street. I went down. When I had got there I saw Capt. Preston at the head of 7 or 8 Soldiers at the Custom

✦ CHAPTER 4

What Really
Happened in the
Boston Massacre?
The Trial of
Captain Thomas
Preston

house drawn up, their Guns breast high and Bayonets fixed. Found Theodore Bliss talking with the Captain. I heard him say why don't you fire or words to that effect. The Captain answered I know not what and Bliss said God damn you why don't you fire. I was close behind Bliss. They were both in front. Then I step'd immediately between them and put my left hand in a familiar manner on the Captains right shoulder to speak to him. Mr. John Hickling then looking over my shoulder I said to Preston are your Soldiers Guns loaded. He answered with powder and ball. Sir I hope you dont intend the Soldiers shall fire on the Inhabitants. He said by no means. The instant he spoke I saw something resembling Snow or Ice strike the Grenadier[25] on the Captains right hand being the only one then at his right. He instantly stepd one foot back and fired the first Gun. I had then my hand on the Captains shoulder. After the Gun went off I heard the word fire. The Captain and I stood in front about half between the breech and muzzle of the Guns. I dont know who gave the word fire. I was then looking on the Soldier who fired. The word was given loud. The Captain might have given the word and I not distinguish it. After the word fire in about 6 or 7 seconds the Grenadier on the Captains left fired and then the others one after another. . . .

Q. Did you situate yourself before Capt. Preston, in order that you might be out of danger, in case they fired?
A. I did not apprehend myself in any danger.
Q. Did you hear Captain Preston give the word *Fire*?
A. I have told your Honors, that after the first gun was fired, I heard the word, *fire*! but who gave it, I know not.

Matthew Murray

I heard no order given. I stood within two yards of the Captain. He was in Front talking with a Person, I don't know who. I was looking at the Captain when the Gun was fired.

Andrew, a Negro servant to Oliver Wendell[26]

I jump'd back and heard a voice cry fire and immediately the first Gun fired. It seemed to come from the left wing from the second or third man on the left. The Officer was standing before me with his face towards the People. I am certain the voice came from beyond him. The Officer stood before the Soldiers at a sort of a corner. I turned round and saw a Grenadier who stood on the Captain's right swing his Gun and fire. . . .

25. A soldier in the British Grenadier Guards.
26. Andrew was Oliver Wendell's slave. Wendell appeared in court to testify as to Andrew's veracity.

Daniel Cornwall

Capt. Preston was within 2 yards of me—before the Men—nearest to the right—facing the Street. I was looking at him. Did not hear any order. He faced me. I think I should have heard him. I directly heard a voice say Damn you why do you fire. Don't fire. I thought it was the Captain's then. I now believe it. . . .

Jane Whitehouse

A Man came behind the Soldiers walked backwards and forward, encouraging them to fire. The Captain stood on the left about three yards. The man touched one of the Soldiers upon the back and said fire, by God I'll stand by you. He was dressed in dark colored clothes. . . . He did not look like an Officer. The man fired directly on the word and clap on the Shoulder. I am positive the man was not the Captain. . . . I am sure he gave no orders. . . . I saw one man take a chunk of wood from under his Coat throw it at a Soldier and knocked him. He fell on his face. His firelock[27] was out of his hand. . . . This was before any firing.

Newton Prince, a Negro, a member of the South Church

Heard the Bell ring. Ran out. Came to the Chapel. Was told there was no fire but something better, there was going to be a fight. Some had buckets and bags and some Clubs. I went to the west end of the Town House where [there] were a number of people. I saw some Soldiers coming out of the Guard house with their Guns and running down one after another to the Custom house. Some of the people said let's attack the Main Guard, or the Centinel who is gone to King street. Some said for Gods sake don't lets touch the main Guard. I went down. Saw the Soldiers planted by the Custom house two deep. The People were calling them Lobsters, daring 'em to fire saying damn you why don't you fire. I saw Capt. Preston out from behind Soldiers. In the front at the right. He spoke to some people. The Capt. stood between the Soldiers and the Gutter about two yards from the Gutter. I saw two or three strike with sticks on the Guns. I was going off to the west of the Soldiers and heard the Guns and saw the dead carried off. Soon after the Guard Drums beat to arms.[28] People whilst striking on the Guns cried fire, damn you fire. I have heard no Orders given to fire, only the people in general cried fire.

27. Musket.
28. A special drumbeat used as a signal to soldiers to arm themselves.

✦ CHAPTER 4

What Really
Happened in the
Boston Massacre?
The Trial of
Captain Thomas
Preston

James Woodall

I saw one Soldier knocked down. His Gun fell from him. I saw a great many sticks and pieces of sticks and Ice thrown at the Soldiers. The Soldier who was knocked down took up his Gun and fired directly. Soon after the first Gun I saw a Gentleman behind the Soldiers in velvet of blue or black plush[29] trimmed with gold. He put his hand toward their backs. Whether he touched them I know not and said by God I'll stand by you whilst I have a drop of blood and then said fire and two went off and the rest to 7 or 8. . . . The Captain, after, seemed shocked and looked upon the Soldiers. I am very certain he did not give the word fire.

Cross-Examination of Captain James Gifford

Q. Did you ever know an officer order men to fire with their bayonets charged?
A. No, Officers never give order to fire from charged bayonet. They would all have fired together, or most of them.

Thomas Handaside Peck

I was at home when the Guns were fired. I heard 'em distinct. I went up to the main guard and addressed myself to the Captain and said to him What have you done? He said, Sir it was none of my doings, the Soldiers fired of their own accord, I was in the Street and might have been shot. His character is good as a Gentleman and Soldier. I think it exceeds any of the Corps.

Lieutenant Governor Thomas Hutchinson

I was pressed by the people almost upon the Bayonets. The People cried the Governor. I called for the Officer. He came from between the Ranks. I did not know him by Moon light. I had heard no circumstances. I inquired with some emotion, How came you to fire without Orders from a Civil Magistrate? I am not certain of every word. I cannot recollect his answers. It now appears to me that it was imperfect. As if he had more to say. I remember by what he said or his actions I thought he was offended at being questioned. Before I could have his full answer the people cried to the Town house, to the Town house. A Gentleman by me (Mr. Belknap) was extremely civil. I thought he press'd my going into the Town house from a concern for my safety. I was carried by the crowd into the Council Chamber. After some hours Capt. Preston was brought there to be examined. I heard him deny giving Orders. I am very sure it did not occur to me that he had said anything in answer to my question in the Street which would not consist with this denial. My intention in going up was to enquire into the

29. A fabric with a thick, deep pile.

affair. I have no particular intimacy with Capt. Preston. His general character is extremely good. Had I wanted an Officer to guard against a precipitate action I should have pitched upon him as soon as any in the Regiment.

The Evidence was ended.

Closing Arguments

For the Defense

[No transcript of John Adams's closing arguments exists. From his notes, however, we can reconstruct his principal arguments. Adams began by citing cases that ruled that "it is always safer to err in acquitting rather than punishing" when there was doubt as to the defendant's guilt. He also argued that there was ample provocation and that Preston was merely defending himself and his men and was, in all, a victim of self-defense. Adams then reviewed the evidence, stating that there was no real proof that Preston had ordered his men to fire into the crowd. Adams also called into question the testimony of the prosecution witnesses, saying that Robert Goddard "is not capable of making observations" and that other witnesses were in error (he made much of the surtout). He called William Wyatt "diabolically malicious."]

Conclusion of Prosecution's Summary to the Jury

Now Gentlemen the fact being once proved, it is the prisoner's part to justify or excuse it, for all killing is, *prima facie*,[30] Murder. They have attempted to prove, that the People were not only the aggressors, but attacked the Soldiers with so much Violence, that an immediate Danger of their own Lives, obliged them to fire upon the *Assailants*, as they are pleased to call them. Now this *violent Attack* turns out to be nothing more, than a few Snow-balls, thrown by a parcel of Boys; the most of them at a considerable distance, and as likely to hit the Inhabitants as the Soldiers (*all this is but* which is a common Case in the Streets of Boston at that Season of the Year, when a Number of People are collected in a Body), and one Stick, that struck Grenadier, but was not thrown with sufficient force to wound, or even sally him, whence then this Outrage, fury and abuse so much talk'd of? The Inhabitants collected, Many of them from the best of Motives, to make peace; and some out of mere Curiosity, and what was the Situation of Affairs when the Soldiers begun the fire? In addition to the Testimony of many others, you may collect it from the Conduct of Mr. Palmes, a Witness on whom they principally build their Defence. Wou'd he place himself before a party of Soldiers, and risque his Life at the Muzzels of their Guns, when he thought them under a Necessity of firing to defend their

30. At first sight; on first appearance.

◆ CHAPTER 4

What Really
Happened in the
Boston Massacre?
The Trial of
Captain Thomas
Preston

Life? 'Tis absurd to suppose it; and it is impossible you should ever seriously believe, that their Situation could either justify or excuse their . . . Conduct I would contend, as much as any Man, for the tenderness and Benignity[31] of the Law; but, if upon such trifling and imaginary provocation. Men may o'er leap the Barriers of Society, and carry havock and Desolation among their defenceless Fellow Subjects; we had better resign an unmeaning title to protection in Society and range the Mountains uncontrol'd. Upon the whole Gentlemen the facts are with you, and I doubt not, you will find such a Verdict as the Laws of God, of Nature and your own Conscience will ever approve.

Source 4 from Library of Congress.

4. Paul Revere's Engraving of the Boston Massacre.

[Notice how he dubbed the Custom House "Butcher's Hall."]

Library of Congress

31. A kindly act.

Questions to Consider

In reconstructing the event, begin by imagining the positions of the various soldiers and witnesses. Where were the soldiers standing? Where was Captain Preston standing? Which witnesses were closest to Preston (that is, in the best positions to see and hear what happened)? Where were the other witnesses? Remember that the event took place around 9:00 P.M., when Boston was totally dark.

Next, read closely Preston's deposition and the trial testimony. What major points did Preston make in his own defense? Do you find those points plausible? More important, do the witnesses who were closest to Preston agree or disagree with his recounting, or with each other's? On what points? Be as specific as possible.

Now consider the other witnesses, those who were not so near. What did they hear? What did they see? To what degree do their testimonies agree or disagree, both with each other and with Preston and those closest to him?

Lawyers for both sides spent considerable time trying to ascertain what Captain Preston was wearing on that evening. Why did they consider this important? Based on the evidence, what do you think Preston was wearing on the evening of March 5, 1770? What conclusions could you draw from that?

The attorneys also were particularly interested in the crowd's behavior *prior to* the firing of the first musket. Why did they consider that important? How would you characterize the crowd's behavior? Are you suspicious of testimony that is at direct odds with your conclusion about this point?

Several witnesses (especially Jane Whitehouse) tell a quite different story. To what extent is her recounting of the event plausible? Is it corroborated by other witnesses?

We included Paul Revere's engraving, even though he probably was not an eyewitness, because by the time of Preston's trial, surely all the witnesses would have seen it and, more important, because later Americans have obtained their most lasting visual image of the event from that work. How does the engraving conform to what actually happened? How does it conflict with your determination of what actually took place? If there are major discrepancies, why do you think this is so? (Revere certainly knew a number of the eyewitnesses and could have ascertained the truth from them.)

After you have answered these questions and carefully weighed the eyewitnesses' evidence, answer the central question: What really happened in the Boston Massacre?

✦ CHAPTER 4

What Really
Happened in the
Boston Massacre?
The Trial of
Captain Thomas
Preston

✦

Epilogue

In his closing arguments in defense of Captain Preston, John Adams noted that the crowd not only had been harassing the soldiers but also had actually threatened to attack them. Yet there was no reliable evidence to prove that Preston had ordered his men to fire into the crowd, Adams insisted. In such doubtful cases, he concluded, the jury must vote for an acquittal. The prosecution's closing summary portrayed Preston as a murderer. The crowd's actions, the prosecution maintained, were "a few Snow-balls, thrown by a parcel of *Boys*." According to the prosecution, the rest of the people who gathered in the square were peaceful and simply curious about what was happening.

In the trial of Thomas Preston, the jury took only three hours to reach its decision, although the verdict of "not guilty" was not announced until the next morning. Some of the jurors were sympathetic to the British, and thus were determined to find Preston innocent no matter what evidence was presented. Also, the leaking of the depositions ultimately helped the captain's defense because his attorneys knew in advance what the potentially most damaging witnesses would say in court. Once the trial began, defense attorney John Adams's tactics (to create so much confusion in the minds of the jurors that they could not be certain what actually had taken place) were extremely effective. Finally, it was generally believed that, even if he were found guilty, Preston would be pardoned.

As it turned out, the captain had the advantage from the very beginning.[32]

As for Thomas Preston himself, the British officer was quickly packed off to England, arriving in London in February 1771. He retired from military service and received a pension £200 per year from the king "to compensate him for his suffering." For years afterwards he continued to maintain his innocence and insisted that he never gave the orders to fire. Years later John Adams and Thomas Preston saw one another in London and passed without speaking.[33] Of the eight soldiers, six were acquitted and two were convicted of manslaughter and punished by being branded on the thumb. From there they disappeared into the mists and crevices of history.

Although they loudly asserted that the verdicts were gross miscarriages of justice, Patriot leaders Sam Adams, Joseph Warren, Josiah Quincy, and others probably were secretly delighted by Preston's and the majority of the redcoats' acquittals. Those verdicts outraged many colonists and allowed Patriot propagandists to whip up even more sentiment against British "tyranny." Speaking of Samuel Adams, one

32. Of the 12 jurors, 5 of them left Massachusetts in 1775 and became loyalist exiles. Of the rumors that Preston would be pardoned if convicted, see Zobel, *Legal Papers of John Adams*, vol. 3, p. 13.
33. On Preston's maintaining his innocence see Kidder, *Boston Massacre*, p. 288. On the meeting of Adams see Zobel, *Legal Papers of John Adams*, vol. 3, p. 34.

historian has claimed that "[n]o one in the colonies realized more fully than he the primary necessity of arousing public opinion, [and] no one set about it more assiduously."[34]

The so-called Boston Massacre not only was an important event that led to the American Revolution, but it also helped shape Americans' attitudes as to what their revolution was all about. Samuel Adams and others organized annual remembrances of the event. At the 1775 ceremony, held only a month before the battles of Lexington and Concord Bridge, Joseph Warren brought his audience to a near frenzy when he thundered, "[T]ake heed, ye infant babes, lest, whilst your streaming eyes are fixed on the ghastly corpse, your feet slide on the stones bespattered with your father's brains."[35]

More than one hundred years after the event, the Massachusetts legislature authorized a memorial honoring the martyrs to be placed on the site of the so-called massacre. The Bostonians' convictions were bolstered by Irish immigrants whose ancestors had known British "tyranny" firsthand, and the Bostonians remained convinced that the American Revolution had been caused by Britain's selfishness and oppression. But at the annual meeting of the members of the Massachusetts Historical Society that elite group opposed the monument, one of them describing the five who were killed as "vulgar ruffians" and another member asserting that "those who died . . . were victims

of their own folly!" The General Court ignored the society and the monument was erected in 1889.[36]

Then, in 1917, the year that the United States entered the Great War against Germany as an ally of Britain, distinguished American historian Albert Bushnell Hart's textbook *New American History* was published. In his book, Hart devoted only 33 words to the events of March 5, 1770, and avowed that the "unsuitable name of 'Boston Massacre' was applied to the unfortunate affair." As American alliances changed, so also did its history.[37]

Today the site of the Boston Massacre is on a traffic island beside the Old State House (formerly called the Town House and seen in the background of Paul Revere's famous engraving) in the midst of Boston's financial district. With the exception of the State House (now a tasteful museum), the site is ringed by skyscrapers that house, among other institutions, the Bank of America. Thousands of Bostonians and tourists stand on the Boston Massacre site every day, waiting for the traffic to abate.

For his part, John Adams believed that the Boston Massacre was an event "which had been intentionally wrought up by designing men, who knew what

---

34. Philip Davidson, *Propaganda and the American Revolution* (Chapel Hill: University of North Carolina Press, 1941), p. 7.
35. *Ibid.*, p. 9.
36. Adams, "New Light on the Boston Massacre." pp. 261–262.
37. Albert Bushnell Hart, *New American History* (New York: American Book Co., 1917), p. 131. For a fine example of American efforts to "sanitize" their own revolution, see Alfred F. Young, *The Shoemaker and the Tea Party: Memory and the American Revolution* (Boston: Beacon Press, 1999). The subject of the first part of Young's book, George Robert Twelves Hewes, was a participant in the Boston Massacre.

◆ CHAPTER 4

What Really
Happened in the
Boston Massacre?
The Trial of
Captain Thomas
Preston

they were aiming at. . . ."[38] Even so, the Patriot leader claimed that "the foundation of American independence was laid" on the evening of March 5, 1770. Although he may have overstated the case, clearly many Americans living *today* have come to see the event as a crucial one in the buildup to the revolution against Great Britain.

Now that you have examined the evidence, do you think the Boston Massacre of March 5, 1770, was a justifiable reason for rebellion against the mother country? Could the crowd action on that evening secretly have been directed by the Patriot elite, or was it a spontaneous demonstration of anti-British fury? Why was Paul Revere's engraving at such variance with what actually took place?

Few Americans have stopped to ponder what actually happened on that fateful evening. Like the American Revolution itself, the answer to that question may well be more complex than we think.

38. Quoted in John C. Miller, *Sam Adams, Pioneer in Propaganda* (Stanford, Cal.: Stanford University Press, 1936), p. 187.

The Evolution of American Citizenship: The Louisiana Purchase, 1803–1812

◆

The Problem

In 1782, J. Hector St. John,[1] naturalized citizen living in New York, wrote a series of letters about his adopted country that were published in London but soon reached the United States, where they were read with enormous interest.

In Letter III, St. John posed his central question: "What then is the American, this new man?" As a small part of the answer to his question, he explained

> He is an American, who, leaving behind him all his ancient prejudices and manners, receives new ones from the new mode of life he has embraced, the new government he obeys, and the new rank he holds. . . . Here individuals of all nations are melted into a new race of men, whose labours and posterity

will one day cause great changes in the world. . . .[2]

One reason so many Americans pored over St. John's letters is that they were asking that same question themselves: What, indeed, was an American? Those who lived in one of the former thirteen colonies and who supported the Patriot cause automatically became citizens of their respective states, and former Loyalists who took an oath of allegiance also were granted citizenship. Immigrants who arrived in the United States after the war went through a citizenship process in the states where they settled. Then, after the ratification of the Constitution in 1788 and the beginning of the new government in 1789, Congress passed a

1. Born Michael Gullaume Jean de Crevecoeur in France in 1735, he served in the French army in Canada during the French and Indian War, resigned his commission at war's end, and ultimately settled in New York where he became a citizen and changed his name to John Hector St. John. He died in France in 1813.

2. J. Hector St. John, *Letters from an American Farmer*, originally published in London in 1783 (New York: Oxford University Press ed., 1997). Letter III, pp. 43–44.

✦ CHAPTER 5

The Evolution
of American
Citizenship:
The Louisiana
Purchase,
1803–1812

series of acts to establish a process of conferring American citizenship on individuals. The first such act was passed in 1790, setting out the requirements for free white people of a two-year residency period in the United States, proof of "good character," and the taking of an oath "to support the constitution of the United States." Subsequent laws were passed in 1795, 1798, and 1802, the major difference being the residency requirement.[3]

Although citizenship had been granted to free white individuals of all ethnic groups who resided either in the thirteen original states or in states created from lands ceded by the British in the 1783 treaty that ended the War for Independence, citizenship had never been awarded to any group of people *en masse* who were living in lands acquired by the United States *after* the Revolution. In 1803, however, the United States purchased from France an immense territory of 828,000 square miles, roughly equal to the size of the nation. Moreover, the majority of those living in the Louisiana Territory were of French background, with significant Spanish and German minorities. Finally, in 1803, there were approximately 3,200 *gens de couleur libre* or free people of color (approximately 11.26% of the total population) who enjoyed most of the rights of free people.[4] Here was

a population that for the most part did not speak English, was unfamiliar with Anglo-American political and judicial institutions, and had enjoyed the easygoing colonial administrations of France and Spain.

The Louisiana Purchase forced Americans to come to grips with the issue of citizenship. Article III of the 1803 treaty ceding Louisiana to the United States stated clearly that

> The inhabitants of the ceded territory shall be incorporated in the union of the United States, and admitted as soon as possible, according to the principles of the Federal Constitution, to the enjoyment of all the rights, advantages, and immunities of citizens of the United States. . . .

The residents of Louisiana interpreted Article III to mean that they would be admitted to statehood immediately or, at the very least, they would be allowed the same rights and privileges as were granted to residents of the territories under the 1787 Northwest Ordinance.[5] But most United States leaders thought this would not be feasible. Why not? What alternative did they propose? How did Louisianans react? What alterations to the original plan were made? Finally, why was statehood ultimately granted to the Territory of Orleans (the present state of Louisiana) in 1812? By answering these

3. See United States Constitution, Article One, Section 8. For an excellent work on the subject, see James H. Kettner, *The Development of American Citizenship, 1608–1870* (Chapel Hill: Univ. of North Carolina Press, 1978), especially pp. 225–247.
4. For Louisiana's 1803 population, see Peter J. Kastor, ed., *The Louisiana Purchase: Emergence of an American Nation* (Washington, D.C.: CQ Press, 2002), pp. 261–262.

5. The Northwest Ordinance mandated that when a territory's population reached 5,000 free adult males a bicameral legislature would be established. When the population reached 60,000 it would be permitted to draw up a state constitution and, when approved, would be admitted as a state. The Ordinance originally applied to the states of Ohio, Indiana, Illinois, Michigan, and Wisconsin, but later was applied to the Mississippi Territory.

questions, you will ultimately be able to answer this chapter's central question: How did the Louisiana Purchase influence the United States' ideas and policies of citizenship?

Just about every schoolboy and schoolgirl knows how the United States was able to purchase Louisiana from France in 1803. And yet, as we shall see, an equally important aspect of that purchase took place *after* 1803, as Americans struggled with the concept of and criteria for citizenship, since the process of admitting large populations of non-Anglo-Americans to citizenship was repeated numerous times after 1803.

Background

The history of Louisiana can best be understood within the larger fabric of European and world history. As Europe's population began to recover from the devastating plagues of the 1300s,[6] economic recovery spurred a revival of trade that reached as far as Asia and the Middle East, the growth of towns and cities, and the beginnings of national consolidation into early forms of nation-states. As evolving monarchical dynasties supported merchants, bankers, and manufacturers as a way of increasing royal treasuries and as a check against the declining but still powerful feudal lords, these new monarchs attempted to consolidate their reigns through warfare against other monarchs, control of the church, and amassing huge treasuries through new taxes, fees, and conquests.

The capture of Constantinople by the Ottoman Turks in 1453 gave them control of the eastern Mediterranean

Sea, allowing them to block European trade routes into China. Beginning with the emerging nation of Portugal, European monarchs began to encourage and often support explorers searching for alternative trade routes to the East, acting in roughly the same chronological order as their emergence as nation-states. For its part, Portugal charted new routes and established fortified trading stations along the African coast, rounding the tip of Africa in 1498. The consolidation of Spain resulting from the marriage of the two feudal houses of Aragon and Castille (Ferdinand and Isabella) financed explorers such as Columbus and conquerors such as Cortes and Pizarro who enriched Spain (and, in fact, much of Europe) with the gold and silver taken from the "New World" which they encountered while searching for another passage to the Far East.

France was late in exploring, colonizing, and exploiting the Americas, due in large part to a bloody civil war that wracked the area from 1562 to 1598. French explorers and would-be colonizers such as Jacques Cartier and Jean Ribault made attempts at

6. Due to the plagues, it took approximately 200 years for Europe to reach the same population that it had in 1300.

✦ CHAPTER 5

The Evolution
of American
Citizenship:
The Louisiana
Purchase,
1803–1812

founding French settlements, which came to naught. The consolidation of the French nation under Louis XIV (king from 1643 to 1715, nicknamed the "Sun King") gave France the internal order and economic power it needed both to engage in a series of wars and to support American colonization. In 1604, Samuel de Champlain took two ships filled with convicts, adventurers, Protestant exiles, and Roman Catholic priests southward on the St. Lawrence River (that Cartier earlier had found ran into the Great Lakes) and founded Quebec in 1608. From there the French built a series of forts at Montreal, Frontenac, St. Joseph, St. Louis, Detroit, and others. Settlements grew slowly.

A Spanish expedition already had discovered the mouth of the Mississippi River in 1519. Yet it was the French who first settled the region. In 1673, Father Jacques Marquette and Louis Joliet traveled the entire Mississippi River and claimed all of its valley for France. Thus France laid claim to all of North America from Canada to the mouth of the Mississippi, an enormous expanse of territory.

In 1684, Louis XIV named Robert Cavelier, Sieur de La Salle, the first governor of the territory. In return, La Salle named the area "Louisiana" in honor of Louis XIV. As in Canada, initial settlement was slow until, in 1718, the French crown granted John Law a contract to send 6,000 white settlers and 3,000 slaves to Louisiana. That same year Jean Baptiste Lemoyne, Sieur de Bienville, the new governor, built a new settlement and named it New Orleans, in honor of France's

Prince Regent.[7] In the meantime, English settlements along the coast of North America were burgeoning in population, largely because these colonies for the most part contained more permanent settlers and fewer soldiers, traders, and missionaries. For example, by 1720, the population of the English North American colonies was over 450,000, whereas the white population of Louisiana was only around 8,000.

A series of wars with England chipped away at French territory in North America. In 1717, the British acquired Acadia (later Nova Scotia) and, in 1763, gained all of New France (later Canada). Meanwhile, in 1761, France had secretly ceded all of Louisiana to Spain in return for a declaration of war against England. Therefore, by the end of the French and Indian War (1754–1763), France had lost her entire empire in North America, retaining only some valuable sugar islands in the Caribbean. At the end of the war, England expelled a large number of Acadians and turned their homes over to Protestant Scots immigrants (hence the new name Nova Scotia, or New Scotland). Many Acadians migrated to Louisiana, "only to find they were almost as unwelcome there as they were in the English colonies."[8] Moving into the swamps

---

7. At Louis XIV's death in 1715, the heir to the French throne, Louis's great-grandson, was only five years old. Therefore the duc d' Orleans, an elder cousin of the child king, became Prince Regent. The child, eventually Louis XV, later took the throne and lived until 1774. His grandson was the unfortunate Louis XVI.

8. John Keats, *Eminent Domain: The Louisiana Purchase and the Making of America* (New York: Charterhouse, 1973), p. 171.

and bayous of the backcountry, they became known as "Cajuns," a corruption of "Acadians." Elsewhere in Louisiana, when French settlers learned of the secret cession to Spain in 1764, they protested and undertook an ill-fated revolt that was brutally crushed by Spanish General Alejandro O'Reilly and 3,600 soldiers.

It was no secret that the new nation of the United States strongly coveted Louisiana. By the American Revolution, merchants from Philadelphia, Boston, and New York virtually dominated commerce in New Orleans. Agricultural goods coming down the Mississippi and its tributaries were almost exclusively from American farmers and traders. Even before the War for Independence was over, the London *Morning Post* claimed that the United States is "not content with independence, it aims at conquest." A short time later, in 1797, one worried French official warned foreign minister Charles Maurice de Talleyrand, "The Americans are gathering in crowds upon the banks of the Mississippi. If Spain delays in fortifying Louisiana . . . she will unquestionably be dispossessed. The Americans . . . are spreading out like oil upon cloth. . . . In a few years there will be no halt to their expansion." For his part, Talleyrand himself was deeply concerned: "Americans . . . meant at any cost to rule alone in America." And as for Americans, Massachusetts clergyman and geographer Jedediah Morse (the father of F.S.B. Morse, of the telegraph and Morse code) opined, "We cannot but anticipate the period, as not far distant, when the AMERICAN EMPIRE will comprehend millions of souls, west of the Mississippi."[9]

Thus Americans in general and President Jefferson in particular were extremely disturbed when they learned, in May 1801, that France had forced Spain to return Louisiana, which it had ceded to Spain in 1761. By 1801, Spain was very nearly impotent, whereas France was the strongest nation in Europe, perhaps in the entire world. As U.S. Secretary of State Timothy Pickering explained to American minister to Britain, Rufus King, "The Spaniards will actually be more safe, quiet and useful neighbors." For his part, Jefferson actually contemplated seizing Louisiana as soon as France and England resumed warfare: "The day that France takes possession of New Orleans . . . we must marry ourselves to the British fleet and nation." Since Jefferson instructed his friend and personal messenger to pass along that threat to French foreign minister Talleyrand and, if it could be done, to Napoleon himself, it is possible that the American president was bluffing. If so, however, that would have been a very dangerous ploy.

9. The London *Morning Post* (August 21, 1782) and Jedediah Morse are quoted in Alexander DeConde, *This Affair of Louisiana*, pp. 38, 41. Letombe to Talleyrand, November 25, 1797, quoted in Lewis William Newton, "The Americanization of French Louisiana: A Study of the Process of Adjustment between the French and the Anglo-American Populations of Louisiana, 1803–1860" (Ph.D. dissertation, University of Chicago, 1929), p. 30. For Talleyrand, see Henry Adams, *History of the United States of America during the First Administration of Thomas Jefferson* (New York: Charles Scribner's Sons, 1891), vol. I, p. 356.

◆ CHAPTER 5
The Evolution
of American
Citizenship:
The Louisiana
Purchase,
1803–1812

And yet, the stakes could not have been higher."[10]

Since coming to power as First Consul in 1799, army officer Napoleon Bonaparte had envisioned a resurrection of the French Empire in America. Many Frenchmen referred to the cession of Louisiana to Spain as "a crime," and any efforts to rebuild that empire would have been exceedingly popular. The nuclei of that empire would be the Caribbean sugar islands of Saint Domingue, Martinique, Guadeloupe, and St. Barthelemey, which would provide the funds necessary for Napoleon's hopeful future conquests in Europe, the Mediterranean, and North Africa. Louisiana would provide foodstuffs for the Caribbean islands, could be used as a base for an attack to regain Canada from the British, and even block American and British expansionist ambitions in North America.

Napoleon had no trouble getting the Spanish to return Louisiana (one Spanish official wrote, "Louisiana cost us more than it is worth"), but a slave rebellion that had broken out in Saint Domingue was another matter altogether. Napoleon's order to re-enslave former slaves in the French colonies (the revolutionary National Council had abolished slavery in 1794), and his ruse to get rebellion leader Tous-saint Louverture to turn himself in to French authorities (he was hustled off to France, where he died in prison in 1803), intensified the rebellion rather than ended it. A massive French army sent to Saint Domingue was decimated by disease (by March 1803, roughly 50,000 soldiers had perished), and Napoleon's dream of a new North American empire simply collapsed.

Meanwhile, even as Jefferson was giving the French the impression that he was considering seizing Louisiana, he was urging Livingston to begin negotiations to purchase New Orleans and West Florida. Because Livingston was very hard of hearing and did not seem to be making much progress, Jefferson sent James Monroe as minister plenipotentiary to try to speed things along.

Before negotiations even had begun, however, Napoleon was considering selling all of Louisiana to the United States. Not only was he in need of money, but there was a growing fear in France that the British would attack Louisiana by sending a force from Canada down the Mississippi River before the Americans could stop them. "They shall not have Mississippi, which they covet," Napoleon told his ministers. "The conquest of Louisiana would be easy if they only took the trouble to make a descent there. I have not a moment to lose in putting it out of their reach. . . . I think of ceding it to the United States."[11] The treaty of cession

10. Pickering to King, February 15, 1797, quoted in DeConde, *This Affair of Louisiana*, p. 84. Jefferson to American minister to France Robert L. Livingston, April 18, 1802, in Paul Leicester Ford, ed., *The Writings of Thomas Jefferson* (New York: G. P. Putnam's Sons, 1897), Vol. IX, pp. 363–368. Although the United States did not learn of the retrocession until May 1801, the treaty actually was signed the previous October.

11. Napoleon Bonaparte to his ministers, in Frangois de Barbe-Marbois, *History of Louisiana* (Philadelphia: Carey and Lee, 1830), quoted in Keats, *Eminent Domain*, p. 323. Barbe-Marbois was French Minister of the Treasury and the chief French negotiator of the Louisiana Purchase treaty.

was finalized on April 30, 1803, and formally signed on May 2.

News of the Louisiana Purchase swept through the United States like wildfire. Writing to Livingston, President Jefferson stated, "Perhaps nothing since the revolutionary war had produced more uneasy sensations through the body of the nation."[12] Some Americans doubted whether the Constitution gave the president the authority to add territory to the United States, while others worried that the cession itself was invalid since France had promised Spain that it "would not sell, give or otherwise dispose of Louisiana to any third party."[13] For their part, northeasterners feared that adding this immense territory would decrease the power of their section. And many Americans wondered what the status of the territory would be: permanent colony, immediate statehood, or a gradual process that eventually ended in statehood? In all, the purchase of Louisiana left Americans with more questions than the purchase itself actually answered.

Ratification of the Louisiana Purchase treaty on October 20, 1803, brought many of those issues to the surface. Almost immediately the critical issue arose of how Louisiana would be governed and, related to that, the status of the people of Louisiana and the role they would play in the establishment and leadership of their government. Would Louisiana be granted immediate statehood and self-government, as implied by Article III of the cession treaty? Or would President Jefferson and Congress create conditions that Louisianans would have to meet before being granted citizenship? As Postmaster General Gideon Granger informed Governor William Claiborne, "There appears to be about as many opinions as to the mode of governing Louisiana as there are members of the National Legislature."[14]

As you examine and analyze the evidence in this chapter, you will see that the debate over the citizenship of the people of Louisiana continued until the eventual granting of statehood in 1812, and perhaps even longer. How did the American concept of citizenship evolve during this crucial period? What parts did Congress, the territorial government, and Louisianans themselves play in this evolution? In sum, how did the Louisiana Purchase help the United States to develop its concept and policies of citizenship?

12. Jefferson to Livingston, April 18, 1802, in Merrill Peterson, ed., *Thomas Jefferson Writings* (New York: Library of America, 1984), p. 1107.
13. For France's promise to Spain in the October 1800 treaty, see DeConde, *The Affair of Louisiana*, p. 95.

14. Quoted in Merrill D. Peterson, *Thomas Jefferson and the New Nation: A Biography* (New York: Oxford University Press, 1970). p. 777.

✦ CHAPTER 5

The Evolution
of American
Citizenship:
The Louisiana
Purchase,
1803–1812

The Method

The evidence you will be using to answer this chapter's central question begins with an excerpt from the 1803 cession treaty (Source 1) and concludes with the 1811 Enabling Act granting Louisianans the power to draw up a state constitution for their admission to statehood (Source 8). As you will see, the central issue in the dialogue between United States leaders and Louisianans was the criteria Louisianans would have to meet before being granted citizenship. Also, you will quickly recognize that the criteria were not static but instead changed over time. How did they change? Why did they change? What role, if any, did Louisianans play in effecting those changes? What other factors influenced American leaders?

The debate proved to be exceedingly confusing. For one thing, the author of the Declaration of Independence who wrote that "governments are instituted among men, deriving their just powers from the consent of the governed" as president was willing to ignore both his own words and the 1803 Louisiana Purchase treaty. Too, Federalist leaders who in the 1790s had embraced a broad interpretation of the Constitution in 1803–1804 attacked Jefferson for his excessive use of executive authority. Finally, in 1787, the Articles of Confederation government had approved the Northwest Ordinance that established a clear process of a region moving from territorial status to statehood. Yet at first few even considered using that standard in Louisiana. Why not? Why did American leaders change their minds? As you examine and analyze each piece of evidence, consider the above questions. They will help you answer the central question.

Take notes as you go along, remembering that the debate over the nature of American citizenship was not static but instead changed over the years.

The Evidence

Source 1 from Perley Poore, comp., *The Federal and State Constitutions, Colonial Charters, and Other Organic Laws of the United States* (Washington: Government Printing Office, second edition, 1878), part I, pp. 687–689.

1. Article 3 of Treaty ceding Louisiana, October 30, 1803.

ART. 3. The inhabitants of the ceded territory shall be incorporated in the Union of the United States, and admitted as soon as possible, according to the principles of the Federal Constitution, to the enjoyment of all the rights, advantages, and immunities, of citizens of the United States; and, in the mean time, they shall be maintained and protected in the free enjoyment of their liberty, property, and the religion which they profess.[15]

Source 2 from Jefferson to DeWitt Clinton, December 2, 1803, in Ford, *Writings of Thomas Jefferson*, vol. VIII, p. 283.

2. Jefferson letter to Clinton, December 2, 1803.

More difference of opinion seems to exist as to the manner of disposing of Louisiana, than I had imagined possible: and our leading friends are not yet sufficiently aware of the necessity of accommodation and mutual sacrifice of opinion for conducting a numerous assembly, where the opposition too is drilled to act in phalanx on every question. Altho' it is acknowledged that our new fellow citizens are as yet as incapable of self government as children, yet some cannot bring themselves to suspend its principles for a single moment. The temporary or territorial government of that country therefore will encounter great difficulty.

Source 3 is excerpts from letters of Louisiana Governor W. C. C. Claiborne to Secretary of State James Madison, January 2, 10, 1804, in Dunbar Rowland, ed., *Official Letter Books of W. C. C. Claiborne*, 1801–1816 (Jackson, MS: Dept. of Archives and History, 1917), vol. I, pp. 322, 327–330.

3. Claiborne to Madison, January 2, 1804.

The tranquility in which I found this Province is uninterrupted, and every appearance promises a continuation of it. This is the Season of Festivity here, and I am pleased to find that the change of Government [from French to United States] has given additional Spirit to the Public amusements. . . .

15. Foreseeing difficulties that might arise from granting Louisianans immediate citizenship, in an earlier letter to the American negotiators Secretary of State James Madison proposed the following article be included in the treaty: "To incorporate the inhabitants of the hereby ceded territory with the citizens of the United States on an equal footing, being a provision, which cannot now be made, it is to be expected . . . that such footing will take place without unnecessary delay. In the mean time, they shall be secure in their persons and property, and in the free enjoyment of their religion." Madison to Livingston and Monroe, March 2, 1802, quoted in Peter J. Kastor, *The Nation's Crucible: The Louisiana Purchase and the Creation of America* (New Haven: Yale University Press, 2004), p. 43. Note the difference between Madison's suggestion and the final Article.

✦ CHAPTER 5

The Evolution
of American
Citizenship:
The Louisiana
Purchase,
1803–1812

[B]y far the greater part of the people are deplorably uninformed. The wretched Policy of the late Government having discouraged the Education of youth. . . . Frivolous diversions seem to be among their primary pleasures. . . .

Republicanism has many profound admirers here. There is something in the plain principle of equal rights which comes within the Scope of the meanest Capacity, and is sure to be agreeable because it is flattering to. . . every individual. But I fear that Republicanism among all her Friends here will find but a few who have cultivated an acquaintance with her principles. . . .

Permit me before I conclude to repeat my Solicitude for the early establishment of some permanent Government for this province . . . for the sake of the country. When the charms of novelty have faded, and the people have leisure to reflect, they will I fear become very impatient in their present situation. I could wish that the Constitution to be given to this District may be as republican as the people can be safely intrusted with. But the principles of a popular Government are utterly beyond their comprehension. The Representative System is an enigma that at present bewilders them. . . . Not one in fifty of the old inhabitants appear to me to understand the English Language. Trials by Jury at first will only embarrass the administration of Justice. . . .

Claiborne to Madison, January 10, 1804.

The more I become acquainted with the inhabitants of this Province, the more I am convinced of their unfitness for a representative Government. The Credulity of the People is indeed great, and a virtuous Magistrate resting entirely for Support on the Suffrages and good will of his fellow Citizens in this quarter, would often be exposed to immediate ruin by the Machinations of a few base individuals who with some exertion and address, might make many of the people think against their will, and act against their Interests. . . .

Until therefore the progress of information shall in some degree remove that mental darkness which at present so unhappily prevails, and a general knowledge of the American Language, laws and customs be understood, I do fear that a representative Government in Louisiana, would be a dangerous experiment.

God forbid that I should recommend for this people Political provisions under which oppression of any kind could be practised with impunity, by persons in power, but I do think that their own happiness renders it advisable that they remain for some years under the immediate Guardianship of Congress, and that for the present a local and temporary Government for Louisiana upon principles somewhat Similar to our Territorial Government in their first grade, be established.

I have discovered with regret that a strong partiality for the French Government still exists among many of the inhabitants of this City, and it appears to me, that Mr. Laussat[16] is greatly Solicitous to encrease that partiality. With what views I know not, but I have learned in some circles a Sentiment is cherished, that at the close of the War between England and France, the great Buonaparte will again raise his standard in this country. For my part, I attach no importance to this little Political Speculation;—It is directed more by the wishes of those who busy themselves on the subject, than by any reasonable ground of expectation. . . .

Source 4 from *Debates and Proceedings in the Congress of the United States*. 8th Congress, 1st Session (Washington: Gales and Seaton, 1852), pp. 461–462, 479–481.

4. Excerpt from Speech by Congressman Roger Griswold (Conn.), October 25, 1803.

The third article of the treaty is thus expressed.

"The inhabitants of the ceded territory shall be incorporated in the union of the United States, and admitted as soon as possible, according to the principles of the Federal Constitution, to the enjoyment of all the rights, advantages and immunities of citizens of the United States; and in the mean time they shall be maintained and protected in the free enjoyment of their liberty, property, and the religion which they profess."

By this article it is declared: "That the inhabitants of the ceded territory shall be incorporated in the union of the United States, and admitted as soon as possible, according to the principles of the Constitution, to the enjoyment of all the rights, advantages, and immunities of citizens." It is, perhaps, somewhat difficult to ascertain the precise effect which it was intended to give the words which have been used in this stipulation. It is, however, clear, that it was intended to incorporate the inhabitants of the ceded territory into the Union, by the treaty itself, or to pledge the faith of the nation that such an incorporation should take place within a reasonable time. It is proper, therefore, to consider the question with a reference to both constructions.

16. Pierre Clement de Laussat (1765–1835) was appointed by Napoleon as the prefect for Louisiana, the highest civilian office in the colony. Because the formal ceremony of transferring Louisiana from France to the United States did not take place until December 20, 1803, Laussat remained in New Orleans, where he was a constant thorn in Claiborne's side. See Laussat's *Memoirs of My Life* trans. Sister Agnes-Josephine Pastwa (Baton Rouge: Louisiana State University Press, 1978), esp., p. 88–91.

✦ CHAPTER 5

The Evolution
of American
Citizenship:
The Louisiana
Purchase,
1803–1812

It is, in my opinion, scarcely possible for any gentlemen on this floor to advance an opinion that the President and Senate may add to the members of the Union by treaty whenever they please, or, in the words of this treaty, may "incorporate in the union of the United States" a foreign nation who, from interest or ambition, may wish to become a member of our Government. Such a power would be directly repugnant to the original compact between the States, and a violation of the principles on which that compact was formed. It has been already well observed that the union of the States was formed on the principle of a copartnership, and it would be absurd to suppose that the agents of the parties who have been appointed to execute the business of the compact, in behalf of the principals, could admit a new partner, without the consent of the parties themselves. And yet, if the first construction is assumed, such must be the case under this Constitution, and the President and Senate may admit at will any foreign nation into this copartnership without the consent of the States.

The Government of this country is formed by a union of States, and the people have declared, that the Constitution was established "to form a more perfect union of the United States." The United States here mentioned cannot be mistaken. They were the States then in existence, and such other new States as should be formed, within the then limits of the Union, conformably to the provisions of the Constitution. Every measure, therefore, which tends to infringe the perfect union of the States herein described, is a violation of the first sentiment expressed in the Constitution. The incorporation of a foreign nation into the Union, so far from tending to preserve the Union, is a direct inroad upon it; it destroys the perfect union contemplated between the original parties by interposing an alien and a stranger to share the powers of Government with them.

The Government of the United States was not formed for the purpose of distributing its principles and advantages to foreign nations. It was formed with the sole view of securing those blessings to ourselves and our posterity. It follows from these principles that no power can reside in any public functionary to contract any engagement, or to pursue any measure which shall change the Union of the States. Nor was it necessary that any restrictive clause should have been inserted in the Constitution to restrain the public agents from exercising these extraordinary powers, because the restriction grows out of the nature of the Government. The President, with the advice of the Senate, has undoubtedly the right to form treaties, but in exercising these powers, he cannot barter away the Constitution, or the rights of particular States. It is easy to conceive that it must have been considered very important, by the original parties to the Constitution, that the limits of the United States should not be extended. The

Government having been formed by a union of States, it is supposable that the fear of an undue or preponderating influence, in certain parts of this Union, must have great weight in the minds of those who might apprehend that such an influence might ultimately injure the interests of the States to which they belonged; and although they might consent to become parties to the Union, as it was then formed, it is highly probable they would never have consented to such a connexion, if a new world was to be thrown into the scale, to weigh down the influence which they might otherwise possess in the national councils. . . .

Excerpt from Speech by Congressman Samuel Latham Mitchill (NY), October 25, 1803.

But the gentleman from Connecticut, Mr. Chairman, (Mr. GRISWOLD) contends that even if we had a right to purchase soil, we have no business with the inhabitants. His words, however, are very select; for he said and often repeated it that the treaty-making power did not extend to the admission of foreign nations into this confederacy. To this it may be replied that the President and Senate have not attempted to admit foreign nations into our confederacy. They have bought a tract of land, out of their regard to the good of our people and their welfare. And this land, Congress are called upon to pay for. Unfortunately for the bargain, this region contains civilized and Christian inhabitants; and their existence there, it is alleged, nullifies the treaty. The gentleman construed the Constitution of the United States very differently from the manner in which Mr. M. himself did. By the third section of the third article of that instrument, it is declared, that Congress shall have power to dispose of and make all needful rules and regulations respecting the territory and other property of the United States, and nothing therein contained shall be construed so as to prejudice any claim of the United States or of any particular State.

In the case of Louisiana no injury is done either to the nation or to any State belonging to that great body politic. There was nothing compulsory upon the inhabitants of Louisiana to make them stay and submit to our Government. But if they chose to remain, it had been most kindly and wisely provided, that until they should be admitted to the rights, advantages, and immunities of citizens of the United States, they shall be maintained and protected in the enjoyment of their liberty, property, and the religion which they profess. What would the gentleman propose that we shall do with them? Send them away to the Spanish provinces, or turn them loose in the wilderness? No, sir, it is our purpose to pursue a much more dignified system of measures. It is intended, first, to extend to this newly acquired people the blessings of law and social order. To protect them from rapacity, violence, and anarchy. To make them

◆ CHAPTER 5

The Evolution
of American
Citizenship:
The Louisiana
Purchase,
1803–1812

secure in their lives, limbs, and property, reputation, and civil privileges. To make them safe in the rights of conscience. In this way they are to be trained up in a knowledge of our own laws and institutions. They are thus to serve an apprenticeship to liberty; they are to be taught the lessons of freedom; and by degrees they are to be raised to the enjoyment and practice of independence. All this is to be done as soon as possible; that is, as soon as the nature of the case will permit; and according to the principles of the Federal Constitution. Strange! that proceedings declared on the face of them to be Constitutional, should be inveighed against as violations of the Constitution! Secondly, after they shall have been a sufficient length of time in this probationary condition, they shall, as soon as the principles of the Constitution permit, and conformably thereto, be declared citizens of the United States. Congress will judge of the time, manner, and expediency of this. The act we are now about to perform will not confer on them this elevated character. They will thereby gain no admission into this House, nor into the other House of Congress. There will be no alien influence thereby introduced into our councils. By degrees, however, they will pass on from the childhood of republicanism, through the improving period of youth and arrive at the mature experience of manhood. And then, they may be admitted to the full privileges which their merit and station will entitle them to. At that time a general law of naturalization may be passed. For I do not venture to affirm that, by the mere act of cession, the inhabitants of a ceded country become, of course, citizens of the country to which they are annexed. It seems not to be the case, unless specially provided for. By the third article it is stipulated, that the inhabitants of Louisiana shall hereafter be made citizens; *ergo* they are not made citizens of the United States by mere operation of treaty.

Source 5 from Ford, ed., *The Writings of Thomas Jefferson*, Vol. VIII, pp. 279–280.

5. Jefferson to John Breckinridge.[17]

DEAR SIR,—I thought I perceived in you the other day a dread of the job of preparing a constitution for the new acquisition. With more boldness than wisdom I therefore determined to prepare a canvass, give it a few daubs of outline, and send it to you to fill up. I yesterday morning took up the subject

17. John Breckinridge (1760–1806) was a Senator from Kentucky and a political ally and confidante of Jefferson. In 1798 he introduced the Kentucky Resolutions (secretly authored by Jefferson) in the Kentucky legislature and in 1804 did the same with the Louisiana Governance bill. He was grandfather of John C. Breckinridge, who ran for president in 1860 as the candidate of the southern wing of the fractured Democratic Party.

and scribbled off the inclosed. In communicating it to you I must do it in confidence that you will never let any person know that I have put pen to paper on the subject and that if you think the inclosed can be of any aid to you you will take the trouble to copy it & return me the original. I am this particular, because you know with what bloody teeth & fangs the federalists will attack any sentiment or principle known to come from me, & what blackguardisms & personalities they make it the occasion of vomiting forth.

Source 6 from Everett Somerville Brown, ed., *William Plumer's*[18] *Memorandum of Proceedings in the United States Senate, 1803–1807* (New York: Macmillan, 1923), pp. 110–144.

6. Excerpts from the U.S. Senate Debate of the Louisiana Governance Bill, January 24–February 18, 1804.

Mr. Jackson, The inhabitants of Louisiana are not citizens of the United States—they are now in a state of probation—they are too ignorant to elect a legislature—they would consider jurors as a curse to them.

Mr. Maclay, Those people are men and capable of happiness—they ought to elect a legislature & have jurors.

Mr. Saml. Smith, Those people are absolutely incapable of governing themselves, of electing their rulers or appointing jurors. As soon as they are capable & fit to enjoy liberty & a free government I shall be for giving it to them.

Mr. Cocke, The people of that country are free—let them have liberty & a free government—This bill I hope will not pass—it is tyrannical.

Mr. Nicholas, I approve of the bill as it is—I am opposed to giving them the rights of election, or the power of having jurors. We ought not *yet* to give that people *self-government*. As soon as it is necessary I will give my assent to that Country's being admitted as a state into the Union.

Mr. Anderson, Several gentlemen of the Senate, I am sorry to say it, appear to have no regard for the third article of the treaty—they seem opposed to freedom. This bill has not a single feature of our government in it—it is a system of tyranny, destructive of elective rights—We are bound by treaty, & must give that people, a free elective government.

Mr. Pickering, That people are incapable of performing the duties or enjoying the blessings of a free government—They are too ignorant to elect suitable men.

18. William Plumer (1759–1850) was a U.S. Senator from New Hampshire from 1802 to 1807, keeping careful notes on the Senate debates during some of that period. Originally a Federalist, he became a Democratic Republican in 1808.

◆ CHAPTER 5

The Evolution
of American
Citizenship:
The Louisiana
Purchase,
1803–1812

MR. JACKSON, Slaves must be admitted into that territory, it cannot be cultivated without them.

MR. BRACKENRIDGE, I am against slavery—I hope the time is not far distant when not a slave will exist in this Union. I fear our slaves in the south will produce another St. Domingo.

MR. FRANKLIN, I am wholly opposed to slavery.

MR. DAYTON, Slavery must be tolerated, it must be established in that country, or it can never be inhabited. White people cannot cultivate it—your men cannot bear the burning sun & the damp dews of that country—I have traversed a large portion of it. If you permit slaves to go there only from your States, you will soon find there the very worst species of slaves— The slave holders in the United States will collect and send into that country their slaves of the worst description.

MR. JOHN SMITH, I know that country—I have spent considerable time there—white men can cultivate it. And if you introduce slaves from foreign Countries into that territory, they will soon become so numerous as to endanger the government & ruin that country. I wish slaves may be admitted there from the United States—I wish our negroes were scattered more equally, not only through the United States, but through our territories—that their power might be lost. I can never too much admire the deep policy of New England in excluding slavery—I thank God we have no slaves in Ohio. —

MR. FRANKLIN, Slavery is in every respect an evil to the States in the south & in the west, it will, I fear, soon become a dreadful one—Negro insurrections have already been frequent—they are alarming—Look in the laws of Virginia & North Carolina made for the purpose of guarding against & suppressing these rebellions, & you will learn our dangers. . . .

MR. HILLHOUSE, Negroes are rapidly encreasing in this country—there encrease for the ten years ending with the last census was near two hundred thousand. I consider slavery as a serious evil, & wish to check it wherever I have authority. Will not your slaves, even in the southern states, in case of a war, endanger the peace & security of those states? Encrease the number of slaves in Louisiana, they will in due time rebel— their numbers in the district of Orleans, are now equal to the whites— Why add fuel to this tinder box, which when it takes fire will assuredly extend to some of your states—Why encrease the evil at a distant part of your territory—which must necessarily require a standing army to protect it? If that country cannot be cultivated without slaves, it will instead of being a paradise prove a curse to this country, particularly to some of the states in its vicinity. . . .

Mr. John Smith, I have traversed many of the settlements in that country—I know that white men labour there—they are capable of cultivating it—Slaves ought not to be permitted to set their feet there. Introduce slaves there, & they will rebel—That country is full of swamps—negroes can retire to them after they have slain their masters. This was in fact the case not eighteen years since—they rose, slew many, & fled to the morasses. Will you encrease their number, & lay the necessary foundation for the horrors of another St. Domingo? If slaves are admitted there, I fear, we shall have cause to lament the acquisition of that country—it will prove a curse—

Mr. Jackson, The treaty forbids this regulation. It will depreciate your lands there fifty per cent. I am a Rice-planter—my negroes tend three acres each per man—I never work them hard, they finish their stint by one or two oClock, & then make three shillings pr diem to themselves. I know that a white man cannot cultivate three acres of rice, & yet Georgia is not so warm as Louisiana. You cannot prevent slavery—neither laws moral or human can do it—Men will be governed by their interest, not the law—We must keep the third article of the treaty always in view. . . .

Mr. Adams, This bill is to establish a form of government for the extensive country of Louisiana. I have from the beginning been opposed to it—& I still am. It is forming a government for that people without their consent & against their will.

All power in a republican government is derived from the *people*—We sit here under their authority.

The people of that country have given no power or authority to us to legislate for them—The people of the United States could give us none, because they had none themselves. The treaty has given us none, for they were not parties to it—it was made without their knowledge. To pass this bill is an encroachment on their rights—it's a commencement of assumed power—it's establishing a precedent for after Congress's destructive of the essential principles of genuine liberty.

The first territorial Ordinance under the Confederation was made by the then Congress without any legal authority—but the Constitution afterwards sanctioned it.

This bill contains arbitrary principles—principles repugnant to our Constitution—The legislative Council are to be appointed by the Governor, who is a creature of the President's—not elected by the people.

The judges are to legislate—make laws & expound them—this is of the essence of tyranny.

✦ CHAPTER 5

The Evolution
of American
Citizenship:
The Louisiana
Purchase,
1803–1812

In the other territorial governments, even in the departure from liberty, there is a reverence for it—for it provides that when its inhabitants are encreased to a certain number they shall elect a representative. This bill provides that the officers shall be appointed by the President *alone* in the recess of the Senate—why this departure from the Constitution. . . .

Source 7 from the *Pubic Statutes at Large of the United States of America* (Boston: Little & Brown, 1845), Vol. II, pp. 283–289.

7. Excerpts from the Louisiana Governance Bill,[19] introduced into the Senate on December 30, 1803, and supposedly authored by Sen. John Breckinridge.

SEC. 2. The executive power shall be vested in a governor, who shall reside in the said Territory, and hold his office during the term of three years, unless sooner removed by the President of the United States. He shall be commander-in-chief of the militia of the said Territory, shall have power to grant pardons for offences against the said Territory, and reprieves for those against the United States, until the decision of the President of the United States thereon shall be made known; and to appoint and commission all officers, civil and of the militia, whose appointments are not herein otherwise provided for, and which shall be established by law. He shall take care that the laws be faithfully executed. . . .

SEC. 4. The legislative powers shall be vested in the governor, and in thirteen of the most fit and discreet persons of the Territory, to be called the legislative council, who shall be appointed annually by the President of the United States from among those holding real estate therein, and who shall have resided one year at least in the said Territory, and hold no office of profit under the Territory or the United States. The governor, by and with advice and consent of the said legislative council, or of a majority of them, shall have power to alter, modify, or repeal the laws which may be in force at the commencement of this act. Their legislative powers shall also extend to all the rightful subjects of legislation; but no law shall be valid which is inconsistent with the Constitution and laws of the United States, or which shall lay any person under restraint, burden, or disability, on account of his religious opinions, professions, or worship; in all which he shall be free to maintain his own, and not burdened for those of another. The governor shall publish throughout the said Territory all the laws which shall be made, and shall from time to time report the same to the President of the United States to be laid before Congress; which, if

19. Congress approved the Louisiana Governance Act on March 26, 1804.

disapproved of by Congress, shall thenceforth be of no force. The governor or legislative council shall have no power over the primary disposal of the soil, nor to tax the lands of the United States, nor to interfere with the claims to land within the said Territory. The governor shall convene and prorogue the legislative council whenever he may deem it expedient. It shall be his duty to obtain all the information in his power in relation to the customs, habits, and dispositions of the inhabitants of the said Territory, and communicate the same from time to time to the President of the United States.

SEC. 5. The judicial power shall be vested in a superior court, and in such inferior courts, and justices of the peace, as the legislature of the Territory may from time to time establish. The judges of the superior court and the justices of the peace shall hold their offices for the term of four years. . . .

SEC. 6. The governor, secretary, judges, district attorney, marshal, and all general officers of the militia, shall be appointed by the President of the United States in the recess of the Senate; but shall be nominated at their next meeting for their advice and consent. The governor, secretary, judges, members of the legislative council, justices of the peace, and all other officers, civil and of the militia, before they enter upon the duties of their respective offices, shall take an oath or affirmation to support the Constitution of the United States, and for the faithful discharge of the duties of their office. . . .

SEC. 10. It shall not be lawful for any person or persons to import or bring into the said Territory, from any port or place without the limits of the United States, or cause or procure to be so imported or brought, or knowingly to aid or assist in importing or bringing any slave or slaves. . . .

[It would also be illegal to import any slaves from elsewhere in the United States who had been brought to the United States since May 1, 1798.]

Source 8 from Rowland, ed., *Claiborne Letter Book*, vol. II, pp. 124–125, 175–176, 372, 390–392.

8. Excerpts of Letters from Gov. Claiborne to Secretary of State Madison, May 3, 29, October 22, November 5, 1804.

May 3, 1804

The Law for the Government of Louisiana will not be Satisfactory to all the Citizens. Many of the old inhabitants had expected immediate admission into the Union, and the Law does not hold out the means of gratifying the Ambition of Some of the late adventurers from the United States. Complaints therefore upon this subject will be made. For myself however I do firmly believe that the constitution temporarily prescribed is well adapted to the present Situation of Louisiana.

✦ CHAPTER 5

The Evolution
of American
Citizenship:
The Louisiana
Purchase,
1803–1812

May 29, 1804

I am Sorry to inform you that the Citizens here continue dissatisfied on the Subject of the Slave trade, and I find that many natives of the United States who have emigrated hither and some of the old Settlers are by no means pleased with the Government which Congress has prescribed for them. The Governing of Distant Territories has heretofore been an arduous Task, and I fear Louisiana will not form an exception. A state of dependence naturally leads to discontent, and some will be manifested here: as soon therefore, as the State of Society would permit the change, I should like to see the Representative System in its fullest latitude, extended to this Territory: but I shall always think that Congress acted wisely in not immediately confering on these people, the privilege of Self Government. A privilege which in a few years would most probably be used with propriety; but at this time I doubt much whether it would not prove a misfortune to Louisiana. Some few Months ago I have heard certain Politicians contend that so far from a Representative System, nothing but a Military Government would do for the Louisianians. To this Doctrine I never could consent, nor did I ever hear a good reason in support of such opinions, but these same Politicians believing now that the people would be better pleased with the power of electing their council, join in censuring the act of Congress. . . .

The Louisianians or rather the Natives of Louisiana are a pacific amiable people much attached to this Country, and to peace and good order: but many adventurers who are daily coming into the Territory from every quarter, possess revolutionary principles and restless, turbulent dispositions:—these Men will for some years give trouble more or less to the local Government, and will unquestionably excite some partial discontents, for although the Louisianians are by nature as amiable a people as I ever lived among, yet for the want of general information they are uncommonly credulous, and a few designing intrigueing men may easily excite some inquietude in the public mind. . . .

October 22, 1804

I have the Honor to enclose you a List of the Christian names of the Gentlemen commissioned by the President members of the Legisative Council,[20] as also the Christian name of the Gentleman appointed Marshal.

---

20. The Louisiana Governance Act established a council of thirteen men appointed by Jefferson to serve as a territorial legislature. But a majority of his nominees refused to serve, led by Evan Jones, a merchant who opposed Claiborne, and Etienne Bore, the mayor of New Orleans.

Three of the Councillors, to wit Messrs. Dowe, Boré and Jones, have declined serving: Messrs. Watkins, Morgan & Debuys have accepted.—I have taken measures, to inform the others of their appointments, but have not yet receiv'd their answers.—I have issued a proclamation convening the Council on the 12th of next month; but I very much fear I shall not be enabled to form a Quorum.—The opinion of Mr. Jones, in relation to his political consistency, seems to have been adopted by Mr. Boré, and I fear may also be embrac'd by other Gentlemen nam'd.—You will see, therefore, the necessity of the Vacancies being early fill'd.

November 5, 1804.

Since my last letter Mr. Canterelle and Mr. Clarke have also declined accepting their commissions as Members of the Legislative Council.—There is no doubt that some of the promoters of the Memorial[21] have taken these means to embarrass the local Government, and to force Congress to accede to their wishes;—but such Imprudencies seem to me illy calculated to benefit their cause. . . .

If a Council is not formed on the 12th inst.—I fear the People will experience much inconvenience, and of which when fully apprised, they will confide less in the Discretion, Patriotism and Wisdom of their present influential Characters.—

I had no Idea that any Citizen here named a Councillor would decline, from party motives, until after I had received the nominations of the President, and I early communicated to you, my fears, that the Sentiments conveyed by Mr. Jones in his letter to me would be embraced by others, and that it was doubtful, whether a Council would be formed.—. . .

Source 9 from Jared William Bradley, ed., *Interim Appointment: W. C. C. Claiborne Letter Book, 1804–1805* (Baton Rouge: Louisiana State University Press, 2002), pp. 110–115.

9. Gov. Claiborne's Speech to the First Legislative Council of the Territory of Orleans, December 5, 1804.

To you Gentlemen is first committed the important trust of giving Such Laws to this flourishing District, as local wants Shall Suggest, and the Interest of the Citizens may require. I trust important and arduous, but one of which Patriotism and Talents will insure a faithful and able discharge. I confidently

21. For the Memorial, see Source 12.

◆ CHAPTER 5

The Evolution
of American
Citizenship:
The Louisiana
Purchase,
1803–1812

look to you Gentlemen for these qualifications, and I doubt not but your Labors will be brought to a fortunate close. The obstacles however we have to Surmount, ought not to be concealed. To miscalculate them in any way might prove injurious. To esteem our duties too light to require extraordinary execution, would be err in one extreme, to be dismayed by an apprehension of their gigantic weight would be equally unfortunate on the other. To know that they are within the compass of our powers and not much below them, is the happy mean which encourages exertion and insures Success. For my part I am deeply Sensible of the delicacy and importance of the Situation in which my present office places me. I enter upon it with a degree of Diffidence produced by existing circumstances, and the expectations of the Districts— My only Sources of confidence are in your wisdom and experience, and in an honest intention on my part to assist your Councils in every measure that may tend to promote the public good. . . .

The first object of your attention, I trust will be, to provide a system of Jurisprudence suited to the Interest, and as much as possible adapted to the habits of the Citizens. This Subject Should indeed, receive the earliest attention, for until Some Judicial organization is directed by the Legislature, the Territory will remain exposed to great inconvenience. . . .

A System of Criminal Jurisprudence is also matter for your consideration;—I think it probable, that on examination you will find the existing Code of Criminal Law imperfect, and not adapted to the present constitution of The [sic] Territory. On this Subject I cannot forebear recommending an energetic System. But by the Term energetic, I do not mean a Sanguinary or cruel System. Laws are not the weaker by being merciful; it is not the Severity but the celerity and certainty of punishment that repress crimes. While there is a hope of impunity Sons of rapine would brave even the axe or the wheel, who would tremble at detection, when followed by a prompt and certain, tho a light Suffering. . . .

In adverting to your primary duties, I have yet to Suggest one, than which none can be more important or interesting; I mean Some general provision for the education of youth. If we revere Science for her own Sake, or for the innumberable benefits She confers on Society;—if we love our children and cherish the laudable ambition of being respected by our posterity, let not this great duty be overlooked. Permit me to hope then that under your Patronage, Seminaries of Learning will prosper, and the means of acquiring infomation, be placed within the reach of each growing family. Under a free Government, every Citizen has a Country, because he partakes of the Sovereignty and may fill the highest offices. Free America will always present flattering prospects for talents and merit. Let exertions then be made to rear up our Children in the Paths of Science and virtue, and to impress upon their tender hearts a love of civil and religious liberty. Among the Several States of the union an ingenuous emulation happily prevails, in encouraging Literature, and literary institutions, and Some of these are making rapid Strides towards rivaling the proudest establishments of Europe. In this Sentiment So favorable to the general good, you Gentlemen, I am certain will not hesitate to Join. I deem it unnecessary to trouble you with any detail of arrangements—I am however persuaded that parsimonious plans will Seldom Succeed. My advice therefore is that your System be extensive and liberally Supported. . . .

Before I conclude Gentlemen I should be wanting in duty did I not Solicit your attention to the Militia of the Territory—In the age in which we live, as well as in almost every one that has preceded it, we find that neither moderation nor wisdom nor Justice can protect a people against the encroachments of Tyrannical power. The abundance of agriculture, the advantages of Legislation, the usefulness of the arts, in a word any thing dear to a *free people* may be considered as insecure unless they are prepared to resist aggression—Hence we find that the Congress of the United States, and the Legislatures of the Several States, are particularly Solicitous to keep the Citizens armed and disciplined, and I persuade myself that a Policy So favorable to the general Safety will be pursued by this assembly. . . .

Source 10 from Brown, ed., *William Plumer's Memorandum*, p. 223.

10. Recollections of a Dinner Held on December 15, 1804, with Plumer, Massachusetts Senator Timothy Pickering, and Three Louisianans.

They complain in decent but firm language of the government that Congress established over them at the last session. They say nothing will satisfy that people but an elective government.

That Claiborne, their present governor, is unable to speak a word of French, the language that is most generally used in that country. That the proceedings in the courts of law are in a language that most of the people do not understand—That they have in many instances been convicted of breaches of laws the existence of which they were ignorant. That Claiborne is incompetent to discharge the duties of Governor.

That the President had selected some very respectable men whom he has appointed members of the legislative Council. That out of these all except three have positively declined the appointment. That no man who wishes to enjoy the friendship and esteem of the people of that country can accept of an office under the existing system of government.

◆ CHAPTER 5

The Evolution
of American
Citizenship:
The Louisiana
Purchase,
1803–1812

They say that they have visited Mr. Jefferson—that he has not made my enquires of them relative either to their government, or the civil or natural history of their country—That he studiously avoided conversing with them upon every subject that had relation to their mission here. . . [22]

Source 11 from Rowland, ed., *Claiborne Letter Book*, vol. III, p. 35.

11. Claiborne to Madison, December 31, 1804.

A great anxiety exists here to learn the fate of the Memorial to Congress.[23] The importation of Negroes continues to be a favorite object with the Louisianans, and I believe the privilege of Electing one Branch of the Legislature would give very general satisfaction. Immediate admission into the Union is not expected by the reflecting part of society, nor do I think there are many who would wish it. I find in some anonymous publications to the Northward, I have been represented as opposing the assemblage of the people to sign in Memorial, and that on one occasion the Troops were called out in order to intimidate the Citizens.

These statements are incorrect. I never did oppose the meeting of the People; but it is true, that in the then unsettled State of the Government, I saw with regret any manifestation of public discontent, and the more so, since I suspected there were many designing men among us, whose attachments were foreign, that might labour to give an improper direction to the public deliberations.

I remember to have been strongly urged, to suppress by force the first meeting which took place in March last, and by some of those who are now great advocates of the Memorial. But I answered that "the people had a right peaceably to assemble together to remonstrate against grievances" and would not be prevented by me. In consequence several subsequent public meetings took place in this City, without experiencing interruption by me. . . .

The Troops were under Arms on the first day of July, and on that day there was a meeting of a part of the Memorialists;—But the Parade was altogether accidental. . . .

22. The mission of Sauve, Destrehan, and Derbigny was to present a memorial to Congress. See Source 12.
23. See Source 12.

Source 12 from *American State Papers. Documents, Legislative and Executive, of the Congress of the United States, Miscellaneous* (Washington, DC: Gales and Seaton, 1834), vol. I, pp. 400–405.

12. Remonstrance and Petition the House of Representatives by the Freemen of Louisiana, January 4, 1805.[24]

[The Memorial began by stating how happy the petitioners were to learn that Louisiana had been ceded to the United States. That delight, however, turned to disappointment when they read the Louisiana Governance Act that Congress had approved on March 26, 1804.]

May we not be long doomed, like the prisoners of Venice, to read the word LIBERTY on the walls of prisons! We trust to your wisdom and goodness; you are the guardians of our constitutional rights, and we repose our hopes in you as in the sanctuary of honor.

The right of the people peaceably to assemble and petition the Government for a redress of grievances is declared and warranted by the first amendment to the constitution. To this constitution we appeal; we learned from you to resist, by lawful means, every attempt to encroach on our *rights and liberties*; the day we became Americans we were told that we were associated to a free people. We cannot suppose that the language of men jealous of their freedom can possibly be unwelcome to your ears.

By the third article of the treaty between the United States and the French republic, it is agreed "that the inhabitants of the ceded territory shall be incorporated in the Union of the United States, and admitted as soon as possible, according to the principles of the federal constitution, to the enjoyment of all the rights, advantages, and immunities of citizens of the United States, and in the mean time they shall be maintained and protected in the free enjoyment of their liberty, property, and the religion they profess."

Your petitioners beg leave to represent to your honorable Houses, that according to the principles contained in the third article of the treaty above quoted, they conceive that had not Congress thought proper to divide Louisiana into two Territories, they should now be entitled by their population to be incorporated in the Union as an independent State. . . .

[The Louisiana Governance Act divided Louisiana into two territories: the Territory of Orleans (approximately modern-day Louisiana) and the District of Louisiana, to

---

24. Although his name appears nowhere in the Memorial, its author undoubtedly was Edward Livingston (1764–1836), younger brother of minister to France R. R. Livingston and former New York congressman and mayor of the city of New York. The unfortunate victim of a financial scandal in city government, Livingston moved to New Orleans where he hoped to rebuild his financial and political fortunes. He cast his lot with the political opposition to Gov. Claiborne.

♦ CHAPTER 5

The Evolution
of American
Citizenship:
The Louisiana
Purchase,
1803–1812

be governed by the government of the Territory of Indiana. The petitioners referred to the statehood process stated in the 1787 Northwest Ordinance and then compared the governments of the Territory of Indiana and the Territory of Mississippi to their own.]

Your petitioners have thus gone through the painful, yet they conceive indispensable task of remonstrating against grievances, in compliance with the duty they owed to their country, to themselves, and to posterity. Your petitioners are sensible that in the discussion of interests of such magnitude, involving their dearest rights, they may perhaps appear to have deviated a little, either in some of their conclusions or expressions, from the respect they never intended to refuse to the highest authority of their country: but let your honorable Houses remember that your petitioners feel themselves injured, deeply injured. Could they tamely submit, could they even represent with more moderation in such a case, you yourselves would not consider them worthy to be admitted into a portion of the inheritance of the heroes who fought and bled for the independence of America.

Your petitioners ask, 1st, For the repeal of the act erecting Louisiana into two Territories, and providing for the temporary government thereof.

2dly. That legal steps should be immediately taken for the permanent division of Louisiana.

3dly. That a Governor, secretary, and judges, should be appointed by the President, who shall reside in the district Louisiana, and hold property therein to the same amount as is prescribed by the ordinance respecting the Territory northwest of the river Ohio.

4thly. That the Governor, secretary, and judges, to be thus appointed, for the district of Louisiana, should, in preference, be chosen from among those who speak both the English and the French languages.

5thly. That the records of each county, and the proceedings of the courts of justice in the district of Louisiana should be kept, and had in both the English and French languages, as it is the case in a neighboring country, under a monarchical Government, and acquired by conquest.

6thly. That supposing the district of Louisiana to be divided into five counties, ten members, two from each county, shall be elected by the people having a right to vote in each county, according to the rules prescribed by the ordinance respecting the Northwestern Territory every two years, or such another number as Congress may appoint, which said members shall, jointly with the Governor, form the legislative council of said district of Louisiana.

7thly. That Congress would acknowledge the principle of our being entitled, in virtue of the treaty, to the free possession of our slaves, and to the right of importing slaves into the district of Louisiana, under such restrictions as to Congress in their wisdom will appear necessary. . . .

And now your petitioners trust their remonstrances and petition to the justice of your honorable Houses, and they do not entertain the least doubt but that a nation, who, in their declaration of independence, has proclaimed that the governors were intended for the governed, and not the governed for the governors; a nation who complained so loudly of their right of representation, a right inestimable to them, and formidable to tyrants, only being violated; a nation who presented it to the world, as one of their reasons of separation from England, that the King of England had endeavored to prevent the population of their States; a nation who waged war against her mother country for imposing taxes on them without their consent; a nation who styles the Indians "the merciless Indian savages, whose known rule of warfare is an undistinguished destruction of all ages, sexes, and conditions," will not be deaf to their just complaints; and, by redressing their grievances, will deserve forever the must unbounded affection of the inhabitants of this district of Louisiana . . . .

Source 13 from *Public Statutes at Large of the United States of America*, 8th congress, 2nd session, (Boston: Little & Brown, 1845).

13. Second Louisiana Governance Act, March 2, 1805.

Be it enacted by the Senate and House of Representatives of the United States of America in Congress assembled, That the President of the United States be, and he is hereby, authorized to establish within the Territory of Orleans a government in all respects similar (except as is herein otherwise provided) to that now exercised in the Mississippi Territory; and shall, in the recess of the Senate, but to be nominated at their next meeting, for their advice and consent, appoint all the officers necessary therein, in conformity with the ordinance of Congress, made on the thirteenth day of July, one thousand seven hundred and eighty-seven; and that from and after the establishment of the said government, the inhabitants of the Territory of Orleans shall be entitled to and enjoy all the rights, privileges, and advantages secured by the said ordinance, and now enjoyed by the people of the Mississippi Territory.

SEC. 2. *And be it further enacted*, That so much of the said ordinance of Congress as relates to the organization of a general assembly, and prescribes the powers thereof, shall, from and after the fourth day of July next, be in force in the said Territory of Orleans; and in order to carry the same into operation, the governor of the said Territory shall cause to be elected twenty-five representatives, for which purpose he shall lay off the said Territory into

◆ CHAPTER 5

The Evolution
of American
Citizenship:
The Louisiana
Purchase,
1803–1812

convenient election-districts, on or before the first Monday of October next, and give due notice thereof throughout the same; and shall appoint the most convenient time place within each of the said districts, for holding the elections; and shall nominate a proper officer or officers to preside at and conduct the same, and to return him the names of the persons who may have been duly elected. All subsequent elections shall be regulated by the legislature; and the number of representatives shall be determined, and the apportionment made, in the manner prescribed by the said ordinance.

Sec. 3. *And be it further enacted*, That the representatives to be chosen as aforesaid shall be convened by the governor, in the city of Orleans, on the first Monday in November next; and the first general assembly shall be convened by the governor as soon as may be convenient, at the city of Orleans, after the members of the legislative council shall be appointed and commissioned; and the general assembly shall meet, at least once in every year, and such meeting shall be on the first Monday in December, annually, unless they shall, by law, appoint a different day. Neither house, during the session, shall, without the consent of the other, adjourn for more than three days, nor to any other place than that in which the two branches are sitting. . . .

Sec. 7. *And be it further enacted*, That whenever it shall be ascertained by an actual census or enumeration of the inhabitants of the Territory of Orleans, taken by proper authority, that the number of free inhabitants included therein shall amount to sixty thousand, they shall thereupon be authorized to form for themselves a constitution and State government, and be admitted into the Union upon the footing of the original States, in all respects whatever, conformably to the provisions of the third article of the treaty concluded at Paris on the thirteenth of April, one thousand eight hundred and three, between the United States and the French Republic: *Provided*, That the constitution so to be established shall be republican, and not inconsistent with the Constitution of the United States, nor inconsistent with the ordinance of the late Congress, passed the thirteenth day of July, one thousand seven hundred and eighty-seven, so far as the same is made applicable to the territorial government hereby authorized to be established: *Provided, however*, That Congress shall be at liberty, at any time prior to the admission of the inhabitants of the said Territory to the right of a separate State, to alter the boundaries thereof as they may judge proper: *Except only*, That no alteration shall be made which shall procrastinate the period for the admission of the inhabitants thereof to the rights of a State government according to the provision of this act.

Sec. 8. *And be it further enacted*, That so much of an act entitled "An act erecting Louisiana into two Territories, and providing for the temporary government thereof," as is repugnant with this act, shall, from and after the first Monday of November next, be repealed.

Sources 14–17 from Dunbar Rowland, ed., *Official Letter Books of W. C. C. Claiborne,* 1801–1816 (Jackson, MS: State Department of Archives and History, 1917).

14. Claiborne to Judge J. White, October 11, 1808.

The Code[25] will probably be greatly censured by many native Citizens of the United States who reside in the Territory. From principle and habit, they are attached to that system of Jurisprudence, prevailing in the several States under which themselves and their Fathers were reared: For myself I am free to declare the pleasure it would give me to see the Laws of Orleans assimilated to those of the states generally, not only from a conviction, that such Laws are for the most part wise and just, but the opinion I entertain, that in a Country, where a unity of Government and Interests exists, it is highly desirable to introduce thro'out the same Laws and Customs. We ought to recollect however, the peculiar circumstances in which Louisiana is placed, nor ought we to be unmindful of the respect due the sentiments and wishes of the Ancient Louisianians who compose so great a proportion of the population. Educated in a belief of the excellencies of the Civil Law, the Louisianians have hitherto been unwilling to part with them. . . .

15. Claiborne's address to both Houses of the Territorial Legislature, January 14, 1809.

I do not learn Gentlemen that the "act to provide for the means of establishing public schools in the Parishes of the Territory" is likely to produce the desired effect. . . .

The instruction of our children in the various branches of science, should be accompanied with every effort to instil into their minds principles of morality; to cherish their virtuous propensities; to inspire them with an ardent patriotism, & with that spirit of laudable emulation, which "seeks the esteem of posterity for good and virtuous actions". Youths thus reared into life, become the pride of their parents, the ornaments of society & the

25. "The Code" was the new code of civil laws adopted by the territorial legislature. Although Jefferson, Claiborne, and Congress had strongly urged the discarding of the French legal system, over the years it became clear that the vast majority of native Louisianans preferred keeping it. The 1808 code, therefore, was an amalgam of the two systems.

◆ CHAPTER 5

The Evolution
of American
Citizenship:
The Louisiana
Purchase,
1803–1812

pillars of their country's glory. You cannot Gentlemen, but be sensible of the importance of this subject; it embraces the best interest of the community & mingles with the warmest affections of the heart. . . .

16. Claiborne to Robert Smith, November 18, 1809.

[Claiborne reported to Smith that there were seven newspapers published in the city of New Orleans—four in French and English, two in French only, and one in English only.]

The *Moniteur* has a limited circulation, and being published only in French is not taken by the Citizens whose native language is English; so also the *Louisiana Gazette* being published only in English does not circulate among Citizens whose native Language is French.—*The Louisiana Courrier—Orleans Gazette*—and *Telegraph* are subscribed for by both descriptions of citizens.—The *first* is understood to have the most extensive circulation.

As regards European politicks the *Louisiana Courrier* and *Telegraph* appear to take great Interest in the successes of Bonaparte, the *Orleans Gazette*, and the *Louisiana Gazette*, manifest a Bias in favour of England and her allies.

17. Claiborne's address to Both Houses of the Territorial Legislature, January 29, 1811.

I could not avail myself of an occasion as favorable as the present, to renew my entreaties for a more energetic Militia System. The best interest of the Territory; the safety of our families and of our property, united in recommending this subject to your early and most serious consideration. The present lax and disorganised state of the Militia is not attributable to a want of exertion on the part of the Officers. The fault attaches to the Law; that is defective. I do not object to the leading principles of the System; they are believed to be correct, and a radical change would only tend to embarrass and retard the introduction of order and discipline. A few Amendments only to the existing Law are necessary, to effect the purposes for which it is designed. Prescribe the time for Regimental, Batallion and Company Musters, and direct the latter to be more frequent than heretofore: augment considerably the fines for not-attendance (so much so as to make the wealthiest of our Citizens unwilling to incur them) and provide means for their sure and speedy collection; vest the officers with power to enforce their orders; punish the disobedient and disorderly with fines and if necessary with imprisonment; and let the exemptions from duty be as circumscribed as possible. In a word let your Law be as rigid as the Principles of a free Government, can be brought to sanction. The faithful Citizens cannot but approve such a course. They are aware of the many *casualities, internal* and *external* to which the Territory is exposed, and must be sensible of the importance of a well regulated Militia. . . .

Source 18 from *Public Statutes at Large of the United States of America.* Eleventh Congress, Third Session, February 20, 1811, (Boston: Little & Brown, 1845).

18. An Act to Enable the People of the Territory of Louisiana to Form a Constitution and a State Government, and For the Admission of Such State into the Union, on an Equal Footing with the Original States, February 20, 1811.

Be it enacted by the Senate and House of Representatives of the United States of America in Congress assembled, That the inhabitants of all that part of the territory or country ceded under the name of Louisiana, by the treaty made at Paris on the thirtieth of April, one thousand eight hundred and three, between the United States and France. . . . are hereby, authorized to form for themselves a constitution and State government, and to assume such name as they may deem proper, under the provisions and upon the conditions hereinafter mentioned.

SEC. 2. *And be it further enacted*, That all free white male citizens of the United States, who shall have arrived at the age of twenty-one years, and resided within the said Territory at least one year previous to the day of election, and shall have paid a territorial, county, or district, or parish tax, and all persons having in other respects the legal qualifications to vote for representatives in the general assembly of the said Territory, be, and they are hereby, authorized to choose representatives to form a convention, who shall be apportioned amongst the several counties, districts, and parishes in the said Territory of Orleans in such manner as the legislature of the said Territory shall by law direct. The number of representatives shall not exceed sixty, and the elections for the representatives aforesaid shall take place on the third Monday in September next, and shall be conducted in the same manner as is now provided by the laws of the said Territory for electing members for the house of representatives.

SEC. 3. *And be it further enacted*, That the members of the convention, when duly elected, be, and they are hereby, authorized to meet at the city of New Orleans, on the first Monday of November next, which convention, when met, shall first determine, by a majority of the whole number elected, whether it be expected or not, at that time, to form a constitution and State government for

◆ CHAPTER 5

The Evolution
of American
Citizenship:
The Louisiana
Purchase,
1803–1812

the people within the said Territory, and if it be determined to be expedient, then the convention shall in like manner declare, in behalf of the people of the said Territory, that it adopts the Constitution of the United States; whereupon the said convention shall be, and hereby is, authorized to form a constitution and State government for the people of the said Territory : *Provided*, The constitution to be formed, in virtue of the authority herein given, shall be republican, and consistent with the Constitution of the United States; that it shall contain the fundamental principles of civil and religious liberty; that it shall secure to the citizen the trial by jury in all criminal cases, and the privilege of the writ of *habeas corpus*, conformable to the provisions of the Constitution of the United States.

◆

Questions to Consider

The evolution of the concept of American citizenship was a process that was sometimes cooperative and often contentious.[26] As you already have seen, United States leaders were by no means in agreement regarding either the definition or the process of citizenship. Nor were the Louisianans themselves of one mind.

To begin with, Louisianans who insisted that Article 3 of the treaty of cession (Source 1) granted them full citizenship and immediate statehood obviously were naïve. And yet, the Northwest Ordinance of 1787 clearly set forth a process whereby the nation's western lands would become states, and three territories (Ohio, Indiana, and Mississippi) already were at some point in that process.[27] Why didn't President Jefferson or Congress choose to apply that process to Louisiana?

Both Jefferson and Congressman Samuel L. Mitchill referred to Louisianans as "children" (Sources 2 and 4). What did they mean by that? Louisianans doubtless were different in several ways from people living in Ohio, Indiana, Mississippi, and other western lands. But *precisely what was different about them* that caused American leaders to deny them the process laid out in the Northwest Ordinance? See Governor Claiborne's opinions in his letters in Source 3.

Federalists in Congress were genuinely concerned about the constitutionality of what was taking place, the erosion of the political power of New England, and the expansion of slavery. But many of them also used the issue as a way to embarrass President Jefferson. How do the remarks of Roger Griswold (Source 4) and Federalists in Source 6, reveal these points?

26. Contentious: quarrelsome, belligerent.
27. For the process set out by the Northwest Ordinance, consult your text or your instructor. Ohio became a state in 1803, Indiana in 1816, and Mississippi in 1817.

The Louisiana Governance Bill (secretly authored by Jefferson and introduced by Sen. Breckinridge)[28] touched off a fiery debate in the Senate. What were the principal provisions of the bill (Source 7)? What were the major points of contention (Source 6)? Did the bill contain any provisions for eventual statehood?

Claiborne reported the general dissatisfaction with the Louisiana Governance Act among Louisianans (Sources 8 and 11). What were the objections? Note especially Claiborne's inability to put together a Legislative Council (letters of October 22 and November 5, 1804).

A key piece of evidence is Source 9, Governor Claiborne's first address to the Legislative Council. What did Claiborne tell Louisianans they must do in order to impress Congress and achieve statehood? See also his earlier letters to Secretary of State Madison in Source 3.

In Source 10, Senator William Plumer recalled objections that certain Louisianans had regarding the Louisiana Governance Act and Governor Claiborne. What do those points tell you? Add to those the objections you find in the formal Remonstrance and Petition (that had been approved by 150 New Orleans residents and then distributed to adjoining parishes for an additional 2,000 signatures). To what group did the Louisanans compare themselves?

The Second Louisiana Governance Act (Source 13) established a process for being granted statehood and made basic changes in the Louisianan government. Based on the Evidence in this chapter, how had Louisianans conformed to the wishes of Congress and Claiborne *before the Second Governance Act*? In your view, why did Congress make those critical alterations? How do you think the concept of citizenship was changing . . . if indeed it was?

Sources 14–17 demonstrate clearly how, in Claiborne's opinion, the majority of Louisianans had *not* changed. Even so, in 1811, Congress authorized Louisiana to begin the process of moving toward statehood, a process that was finally approved by Congress on April 8, 1812. According to the 1787 Northwest Ordinance, a territory had to reach a white population of 60,000 before being admitted to statehood. Yet the 1810 census reported that the Territory of Orleans had only 34,311 free whites, and all of Louisiana contained only 51,538 whites. In your view, why was the state of Louisiana (the former Territory of Orleans) admitted to the Union with less than the mandated population?[29]

Finally, return to the central question. After examining and analyzing all the evidence and reading between the lines when necessary, determine how the debate following the Louisiana Purchase helped the United States develop its concept and policies of citizenship. Was the new concept more restrictive? More liberal? Support your hypothesis with evidence from the Evidence section of the chapter.

28. See Source 5. Why did Jefferson not want his authorship known?

29. For 1810 census returns, see Kastor, ed., *The Louisiana Purchase*, p. 273. On December 17, 1810, Julien Poydras (1746–1824), the non-voting delegate from the territory to the House of Representatives, reported that the 60,000 population had been reached, although it may not have been. *Debates and Proceedings of Congress*. 11th Congress, 3rd. Session, p. 481.

✦ CHAPTER 5
The Evolution
of American
Citizenship:
The Louisiana
Purchase,
1803–1812

✦

Epilogue

It is virtually impossible to overestimate the significance of the Louisiana Purchase to the United States. Not only was the size of the young nation virtually doubled (all or part of fourteen states were carved from it), but a literal treasure of natural resources was found within it. As Napoleon Bonaparte himself put it, "This accession of territory strengthens for ever the power of the United States; and I have just given to England a maritime rival, that will sooner or later humble her pride."[30]

Nor were Americans themselves unaware of the purchase's importance. Perhaps it was an overstatement uttered by historian Thomas McIntre Cooley, who said in 1887 that "nearly all leading events of later American history were either traceable to or in some measure shaped or determined by it." Uncharacteristically more restrained was Theodore Roosevelt, who wrote, in 1900, "The Purchase therefore provided the impetus for Americans to fulfill their national destiny."[31]

Virtually ignored, however, is the effect the debates after the Louisiana Purchase had on reshaping the concept of American citizenship. For the first time, a sizable body of non-British people with a different language, legal and political systems, customs, and religion had become a part of the United States. Due to these differences, they were not included in the citizenship and statehood process enacted by the Northwest Ordinance. Rather than alter their ways, most Louisianans defied efforts to change them. Without making any attempts to become absorbed into the larger American culture, native Louisianans for the most part stubbornly but peacefully resisted. Thus, even though some congressmen were not convinced that Louisianans had undergone the proper "Americanization" process, they ultimately gave in, hoping that citizenship and statehood would *make* them Americans.[32]

If Louisianans had not been fully accepted as American citizens, the Battle of New Orleans (January 8, 1815) convinced many Americans of the Louisianans' loyalty, if not their desire for cultural homogeneity. Kentucky congressman Solomon Sharp asked whether "there be an American, whose bosom does not beat high with joy to call Louisiana a legitimate daughter of the Union, and hail her citizens as brothers."[33]

If Americans had been willing to accept Louisianans of a different culture than their own to citizenship, this did not set a permanent precedent for later

30. Quoted in DeConde, *This Affair of Louisiana*, p. 173.

31. Thomas McIntre Cooley, "The Acquisition of Louisiana," in *Indiana Historical Society Publications*, vol. 2 (1887), p. 65; Theodore Roosevelt, *The Winning of the West* (New York: P. F. Collier and Sons, 1896), vol. 4, p. 297.

32. *Debates and Proceedings in Congress.* 11th Congress, 3rd. Session, pp. 321, 494–505, 542, 574–576.

33. *Ibid.*, p. 1116.

generations. During the late nineteenth and all of the twentieth century, furious debates took place over groups of immigrants who chose to retain their own languages, customs, religions, and the like, and whether they should be granted full citizenship. Ironically, some Americans who insisted the loudest that these groups should adopt the core American culture were the same who had to struggle the hardest for citizenship and acceptance themselves. Thus the definition of American citizenship remains ever-changing, as is the nation itself.[34]

34. The authors are particularly indebted to Professor Cinnamon Brown of Westminster College for her work on Louisiana and especially the Battle of New Orleans. See her "The Youngest of the Great American Family." The Creation of a Franco-American Culture in Early Louisiana (Ph. D. dissertation, University of Tennessee, 2009).

Church, State, and Democracy: The Sunday Mail Controversy, 1827–1831

⬥

The Problem

On July 4, 1827, most of those who attended the Independence Day service at Philadelphia's Seventh Presbyterian Church probably expected to enjoy a traditional patriotic homily honoring Revolutionary War veterans (some of whom were still alive), General Washington, and the other Founders. Little did they suspect that the religious message they were about to hear would become one of the most important sermons delivered in the still-young republic, one that was widely published and distributed throughout much of the United States.

Instead of paying tribute to heroes of the past, guest pastor Ezra Stiles Ely (1786–1861) issued a ringing call for all Christians of all denominations to unite to elect fellow Christians to office who would enact laws reflecting their own beliefs and social principles:

I propose, fellow-citizens, a new sort of union, or, if you please, a *Christian party*

in politics, which I am exceedingly desirous all good men in our country should join: not by . . . the formation of a new society, . . . but by adopting, avowing, and determining to act upon truly religious principles in all civil matters.[1]

Although Ely denied that he was advocating a political party similar to the emerging coalitions of the early nineteenth century, his call for organization, platforms, and voter drives certainly bore striking similarities to the political parties that were forming in the United States in the 1820s and 1830s.

In one sense Ely's stirring remarks marked the climax of the religious excitement known collectively as the Second Great Awakening. During the

1. Ezra Stiles Ely, *The Duty of Christian Freemen to Elect Christian Rulers: A Discourse Delivered on the Fourth of July, 1827, In the Seventh Presbyterian Church, in Philadelphia* (Philadelphia: William F. Geddes, 1828), p. 8.

period from the late 1790s to the mid-1830s, thousands of Americans attended religious revivals and camp meetings, joined existing denominations or formed new ones, and founded or supported ecumenical "improvement associations" such as the American Bible Society, the American Tract Society, the American Sunday School Union, and countless others. Why, Ely and others reasoned, couldn't this increased interest in religion be channeled in part toward drafting and enacting legislation that would bring secular society more in conformity with Christian moral beliefs and commandments? As Baptist leader John Mason Peck prophesied, "Jesus Christ is about to possess the whole land."[2]

The first test of whether Christians would be able to act together to change federal laws was the effort to pressure Congress to close all post offices on Sundays and prohibit the carrying of mail on the Christian Sabbath. An earlier attempt to do so in the 1810s had collapsed, but supporters reasoned that better organization and leadership would succeed this time where earlier efforts had failed. Such a success, many believed, would be but the first step in an ambitious campaign to legislate Christian principles. In its first annual report, the recently established General Union for Promoting the Observance of the Christian Sabbath explained that the success or failure of the Sunday mail campaign would "in the main determine all the rest [of the Society's efforts]."[3]

Although the men who drafted and ratified the federal Constitution had given a great deal of thought to the proper relationship between the federal government and religious institutions, the vast majority of Americans had paid almost no attention to church-state relations and had never debated the issues arising from them. The efforts to close the post offices on the Christian Sabbath gave them the first opportunity to do so.

Your task in this chapter is to examine arguments for and against the closing of post offices on Sunday. What arguments did those in favor of closings use to lobby Congress as well as their fellow countrymen? What arguments did the opposition use to counter their ideological foes? What tactics did both sides adopt? In your view, what is the historical significance of the conflict?

A historian who is analyzing a particular debate attempts to be fair to all sides. In this chapter, you should do likewise. Remember that those who considered themselves devout Christians were on both sides of the issue, as were those who could not be described as religious. What were the *principal issues* that the Sunday mail controversy revealed?

2. For a partial list of associations, see John R. Bodo, *The Protestant Clergy and Public Issues, 1812–1848* (Princeton: Princeton University Press, 1954), p. 20. For Peck's remark, see *ibid*, p. 22.

3. *First Annual Report of the General Union for Promoting the Observance of the Christian Sabbath: Adopted May 12, 1829* (New York: J. Collard, 1829), p. 13.

♦ CHAPTER 6
Church, State,
and Democracy:
The Sunday Mail
Controversy,
1827–1831

♦

Background

One of the most perceptive visitors to the United States during the nation's first century was the Frenchman Alexis de Tocqueville (1805–1859), who spent nine months in 1831–1832 traveling and observing the government, people, and institutions of the young republic. In his book *Democracy in America*, published in French in 1835 and in English in 1836, Tocqueville offered many comparisons between the United States and his native land, one of the most startling to him being the widespread popularity of religious beliefs and institutions. "In France," Tocqueville claimed, " . . . the spirit of religion and the spirit of liberty almost always pulled in opposite directions. In the United States I found them intimately intertwined: together they ruled the same territory."[4]

And yet, if Tocqueville had come to America with his fellow countryman the Marquis de Lafayette a half century earlier, he would have found a very different environment. In spite of the fact that almost every one of the thirteen original states had a government-supported established church as well as a multitude of state and local ordinances having to do with the Sabbath and many aspects of moral—or immoral—behavior, most Americans were not church members (only about 17 percent in 1789) and regularly ignored laws governing behavior on the Sabbath. Even so, the vast majority of free Americans would have identified themselves as Christians (overwhelmingly Protestant) and do not seem to have wanted to strike down these state and local ordinances so long as they were able to ignore them.[5]

When those who were later called the Founders met in 1787 to draft a new federal constitution, however, they were extremely aware of the dangers inherent in an alliance of the national government and any religion. Indeed, since most of the Founders had come from an English background, their own history made them all too aware that any unification of church and state was potentially disastrous. Even since English King Henry VIII had broken with the Roman Catholic Church in 1534, England had witnessed wholesale religious persecutions and executions, two civil wars, the beheading of one king (Charles I, in 1647), and the overthrow of another (James II, in 1688). To most of the Founders, therefore, any artificial or forced religious conformity could lead, as it had in England, to tyranny and enormous bloodshed. Therefore, they wrote a constitution that purposely made almost no mention of religion. The document was to be, as they saw it, a

---

4. Alexis de Tocqueville, *Democracy in America*, trans. Arthur Goldhammer (New York: Library of America, 2004 ed.), p. 341. Tocqueville and his traveling companion Gustave de Beaumont (1802–1865) carried letters of introduction from Lafayette.

5. For colonial and early state Sabbath ordinances, see William Addison Blakely, comp., *American State Papers Bearing on Sunday Legislation* (Washington, DC: Religious Liberty Association, 1911), pp. 34–57.

framework on how the new central government would be organized and would operate. As such, they believed, perhaps naively, that there was no real need for any statement on religion, since that was in a totally different sphere.

Not unexpectedly, there were complaints. In a June 15, 1789, letter to John Adams, Dr. Benjamin Rush spoke for many when he wrote, "Many pious people wish the name of the Supreme Being had been introduced somewhere in the new Constitution. Perhaps an acknowledgement may be made of his goodness or of his providence in the proposed amendments." As a suggestion to the new Vice President, Rush added, "In all enterprises and parties I believe the *praying* are better allies than the *fighting* part of communities."[6] Ignoring Rush's suggestion, the Constitution's first amendment contained only sixteen words concerning religion:

> Congress shall make no law respecting an establishment of religion, or prohibiting the free exercise thereof.

Clearly the intention of that part of the First Amendment was to protect the state from a religious denomination *and* all religious denominations from the state, creating what President Thomas Jefferson in 1802 described as a "wall of separation." In spite of considerable grumbling, the "wall of separation" held fast.[7]

This did not mean, however, that the Founders intended that there should be an absence of religion in Americans' private and public lives. Indeed, they *hoped* for it. An overwhelming majority of Americans would have agreed with John Adams when he opined, "Religion I hold to be essential to morals. I have never read of an irreligious character in Greek or Roman history, or in any other history, nor have I known one in life who was not a rascal. Name one if you can, living or dead." Even Benjamin Franklin, whose ideas about religion were, to say the least, unconventional, wrote

> I have lived, sir, a long time; and the longer I live, the more convincing proofs I see of this truth: that God governs the affairs of men! And if a sparrow cannot fall to the ground without his notice, is it probable that an empire can rise without his aid?[8]

Thus almost no one objected when President Washington took the presidential oath of office with his hand on a Bible, a practice that has been repeated by every subsequent president except one (Franklin Pierce, in 1853). And while more than a few chafed at state or local ordinances having to do with religion, there appears to have been no general movement to have them repealed. As they joined the Union, most of the new states followed suit. To the Founders and most of their contemporaries, the goal was *not to separate religion from politics*, as Americans hoped that their religious-based

6. Rush to Adams, June 15, 1789, in L. H. Butterfield, ed., *Letters of Benjamin Rush* (Princeton: Princeton University Press, for the American Philosophical Society, 1951), vol. I, p. 517.

7. See Jefferson to the Danbury (CT) Baptist Association, January 1, 1802, cited in Dumas Malone, *Jefferson the President: First Term, 1801–1805* (Boston: Little, Brown, 1970), pp. 108–109.

8. Jon Meacham, *American Gospel: God, the Founding Fathers, and the Making of a Nation* (New York: Random House, 2006), pp. 28, 89.

✦ CHAPTER 6

Church, State,
and Democracy:
The Sunday Mail
Controversy,
1827–1831

moral senses would inform their political decisions. Rather, the goal was to *separate the church from the state*, so that neither institution could infect or dominate the other. To many twenty-first century Americans, these two goals appear to be the same, but to the generation of the Founders they were distinctly different. To that generation, most very likely would have agreed with James Madison when he wrote, "If men were angels, no government would be necessary."[9]

Beginning in the early 1800s, however, a major shift began to take place in American religion. In the new western states, evangelical preachers (mostly Methodist circuit riders, independent Baptist clergymen, and Presbyterian missionaries) began to reach the new communities that were sprouting up west of the original thirteen states. Many of these men and women had never attended a religious service and were initially drawn to the excitement of the huge revivals and camp meetings (week-long revivals in which people came and "camped" on the ground). In August 1801, for example, in Cane Ridge, Kentucky, Presbyterian, Methodist, and Baptist evangelists preached for nearly a week to approximately 20,000 people. According to one of the clergymen, many exhibited their religious spirit by shouting, rolling on the ground, and other physical manifestations of their "salvation." At the same time, in northeastern cities, many people who had grown fearful of rapid changes caused by waves of immigrants, urban growth, technology,

and the market economy, embraced religious institutions as rocks in the swiftly flowing stream. Church membership, once an anemic 17 percent in 1789, had burgeoned to 34 percent by 1850. According to Presbyterian cleric Lyman Beecher (1775–1863), around 100,000 Americans joined churches in 1831 alone. Many were attracted to new religious denominations that had grown up or had broken off from older churches. Cumberland Presbyterians, United Brethren, Republican Methodists, Disciples of Christ, New School Presbyterians, Latter-Day Saints (Mormons), Millerites (Seventh Day Adventists), Unitarians, and several varieties of Baptists all spring from this Second Great Awakening.[10]

At the same time that thousands of American men and women were swept up in this religious excitement, a series of national organizations emerged to marshal these new converts to spread the Gospel even further and demonstrate their own personal salvations through good works. Indeed, many evangelical preachers predicted that good works to improve society would hasten the second coming of Jesus Christ. Often financed by wealthy businessmen such as silk merchant Lewis Tappan and flour merchant Josiah Bissell, these national organizations established state and local chapters to distribute tracts and Bibles, fund missionaries at home and abroad, organize Sunday

9. James Madison, "Federalist #51," in Clinton Rossiter, ed., *The Federalist Papers* (New York: New American Library, 1961), p. 290.

10. For two descriptions of revival meetings, see Frances Trollope, *Domestic Manners of the Americans*, ed. Donald Smalley (New York: Alfred A. Knopf, 1949), pp. 167–175; Anne Royal, "A Tennessee Revival" [1830] in *The Annals of America* (Chicago: Encyclopedia Britannica, 1968), vol. 5, pp. 383–385.

Schools, and support reform movements such as temperance which, in terms of numbers, was the largest reform movement in the United States prior to the Civil War. Leadership of these organizations often overlapped. For example, New Jersey U.S. Senator Theodore Frelinghuysen (1787–1862) was at approximately the same time president of the American Tract Society and the American Bible Society, vice president of the Sunday School Union, the American Education Society, and the Home Mission Society, and an active officer of the Temperance Union and Peace Society. Several other leading clerics were either officers of or participants in numerous "improvement" societies. Not only did all these organizations publish and mass distribute reports and pamphlets (the General Union for Promoting the Observance of the Christian Sabbath, for example, distributed 100,000 copies of its constitution), but each denomination established numerous sectarian newspapers in order to reach their new members.[11]

The first major effort to bring all these people, denominations, and national societies together was the Sunday mail issue. Since most businesses were closed on Sundays, the post office was a "conspicuous exception" to the general Sabbath observance in small-town America, and as such was a good test of the potential power of American Protestants in the political arena.[12]

From independence to around 1830, a United States Postal System employee was often the only federal officer that a vast majority of Americans ever met. With only sixty-nine employees in 1788, the postal system had grown to 8,450 officers by 1830 and was delivering 13.8 million letters and 16.0 million newspapers per year. The mileage of post roads by 1828 had increased approximately 452 percent and, by 1831, 76.3 percent of the federal government's civilian work force were postmasters. To religious leaders, therefore, the postal service was the most visible and, they reasoned, the most vulnerable. Stagecoaches carrying the mail on the Sabbath were noisy reminders that the federal government was not observing the Sabbath. Moreover, most postmasters also were storekeepers who sold alcoholic beverages on Sundays while the post offices were open.[13]

In 1810, Congress passed a law requiring post offices to be open on Sundays for a minimum of one hour. Religious leaders responded with a poorly organized petition effort and from 1814 to 1817 no less than seven bills to overturn the 1810 statute were introduced in Congress, with none ever getting to a vote. But when an 1825 law strengthened the

11. For Frelinghuysen, see Clifford S. Griffin, *Their Brothers' Keepers: Moral Stewardship in the United States, 1800–1865* (New Brunswick: Rutgers University Press, 1960), p. 56. For other leaders, see Bodo, *Protestant Clergy*, pp. 20–22.

12. Daniel Walker Howe, *What Hath God Wrought: The Transformation of America,* *1815–1848* (New York: Oxford University Press, 2007), p. 229.

13. Richard R. John, *Spreading the News: The American Postal System from Franklin to Morse* (Cambridge: Harvard University Press, 1995), pp. 3, 4, 25, 51; Wayne E. Fuller, *Morality and the Mail in Nineteenth Century America* (Urbana: University of Illinois Press, 2003), pp. 2, 22. For Sunday liquor sales see Howe, *What Hath God Wrought*, p. 229.

✦ CHAPTER 6
Church, State,
and Democracy:
The Sunday Mail
Controversy,
1827–1831

1810 statute, leaders of an invigorated religious movement prepared to test their organization and their strength. If even the most excited Christians were becoming lethargic, surely, they believed, this issue would rouse them to do battle.[14]

Your task in this chapter is to examine and analyze the arguments for and against the closing of post offices on Sunday. What arguments did each side employ? What tactics did the two sides use? Finally, what do you think was the historical significance of the conflict?

✦

The Method

Once having gathered all the available evidence, the first thing historians must do is to arrange the evidence. In this chapter, we have arranged the ten pieces of evidence in roughly chronological order, based on when each piece was written, published, or spoken. To answer the central questions, however, you will want to rearrange the evidence by dividing it into two general groups: those pieces of evidence that support the effort to close post offices on Sundays, and those that oppose that effort. When you do that, you will see that there are four pieces of evidence supporting closings, five that oppose it, and one (Source 8) that appears to be on the fence.

Before examining and analyzing the evidence in further detail, however, it would be enormously helpful to know something about the authors of the evidence. Learning about the authors will help you to understand not only their general opinions but also will make your reading of their pieces easier. All but one of the pieces of evidence (Source 3) had individuals who revealed their authorship, and almost all of them can be found

in the multivolume *Dictionary of American Biography* (in print or online), on Google.com, or in other sources.

Now that you have rearranged the evidence and learned something about the authors, you are ready to examine and analyze the evidence in detail. Here it would be very helpful to make a chart, listing on one side all the arguments in favor of closing post offices on Sundays and on the other side all the points against it. As you write down each point, make sure to use numbers to help you remember which piece (or pieces) of evidence made that point. Also be aware that almost all the pieces of evidence contain more than one point. Finally, some pieces of evidence (especially Sources 7 and 10) do not address the issue directly. You will have to infer how the authors stood on the issue.

The last two questions call for "opinion" answers. As to tactics, you will have to infer them from the writings and from the Background section of this chapter. The last question, as to the historical significance of the conflict, will take a good deal of thought and historical imagination. The Epilogue section may be of some help.

14. Blakely, *American State Papers*, pp. 176–185.

◆

The Evidence

Source 1 from Ezra Stiles Ely, *The Duty of Christian Freemen to Elect Christian Rulers: A Discourse Delivered on the Fourth of July, 1827* (Philadelphia: William F. Geddes, 1828), pp. 4–8, 10, 12, 14.

1. Ely, Duty of Christian Freemen, 1827.

We have assembled, fellow citizens, on the anniversary of our Nation's birth day, in a rational and religious manner, to celebrate our independence of all foreign domination, and the goodness of God in making us a free and happy people. On what subject can I, on the present occasion, insist with more propriety, than on the duty of all the rulers and citizens of these United States in the exercise and enjoyment of all their political rights, to honour the Lord Jesus Christ.

Let it then be distinctly stated and fearlessly maintained IN THE FIRST PLACE, that every member of this christian nation, from the highest to the lowest, ought to serve the Lord with fear, and yield his sincere homage to the Son of God. Every ruler *should be* an avowed and a sincere friend of Christianity. He should know and believe the doctrines of our holy religion, and act in conformity with its precepts. This *he ought* to do; because as a man he is required to serve the Lord. . . .

I would guard, however, against misunderstanding and misrepresentation, when I state, that all our rulers ought in their official stations to serve the Lord Jesus Christ. I do not wish any religious test to be prescribed by constitution, and proposed to a man on his acceptance of any public trust. Neither can any intelligent friend of his country and of true religion desire the establishment of any one religious sect by civil law. Let the religion of the Bible rest on that everlasting rock, and on those spiritual laws, on which Jehovah has founded his kingdom: let Christianity by the spirit of Christ in her members support herself: let Church and State be for ever distinct: but, still, let the doctrines and precepts of Christ govern all men, in all their relations and employments. If a ruler is not a Christian he ought to be one, in this land of evangelical light, without delay; and he ought, being a follower of Jesus, to honour him even as he honours the Father. . . .

SECONDLY, Since it is the duty of all our rulers to serve the Lord and kiss the Son of God, it must be most manifestly the duty of all our Christian fellow-citizens to honour the Lord Jesus Christ and promote christianity by electing and supporting as public officers the friends of our blessed Saviour. . . .

◆ CHAPTER 6

Church, State,
and Democracy:
The Sunday Mail
Controversy,
1827–1831

If the wise, the prudent, the temperate, the friends of God and of their country do not endeavour to control our elections, they will be controlled by others: and if *one* good man may, without any reasonable excuse, absent himself, then *all*, may. Fellow Christians, the love of Christ and of our fellow-men should forbid us to yield the choice of our civil rulers into the hands of selfish office hunters, and the miserable tools of their party politics. If all the truly religious men of our nation would be punctual and persevering in their endeavours to have good men chosen to fill all our national and state offices of honour, power and trust, THEIR WEIGHT would soon be felt by politicians; and those who care little for the religion of the Bible, would, for their own interest, consult the reasonable wishes of the great mass of Christians throughout our land. . . .

I propose, fellow-citizens, a new sort of union, or, if you please, a *Christian party in politics*, which I am exceedingly desirous all good men in our country should join: not by *subscribing a constitution* and the formation of a new society, to be added to the scores which now exist; but by adopting, avowing, and determining to act upon, truly religious principles in all civil matters. I am aware, that the true Christians of our country are divided into many different denominations; who have, alas! too many points of jealousy and collision; still, a union to a very great extent, and for the most valuable purposes is not impracticable. . . .

[Here Ely maintained that members of all Christian denominations could agree on what was bad moral character. In addition, he argued that good men "who profess no experimental acquaintance with Christianity, might unite and co-operate with our Christian party."]

All who profess to be Christians of any denomination ought to agree that they will support no man as a candidate for any office, who is not professedly friendly to Christianity, and a believer in divine Revelation. We do not say that true or even pretended Christianity shall be made a constitutional test of admission to office; but we do affirm that Christians may in their elections lawfully prefer the avowed friends of the Christian religion to Turks, Jews, and Infidels.

[Ely then explained that a new Christian party would be able to draw Presbyterians, Baptists, Methodists, Congregationalists, German Christians, Reformed Dutch churchmen, and even "members of the Protestant Episcopal church in our country."]

It deprives no man of his right for me to prefer a Christian to an Infidel. If Infidels were the most numerous electors, they would doubtless elect men of their own sentiments; and unhappily such men not unfrequently get into power in this country, in which ninety-nine hundredths of the people are believers in the divine origin and authority of the Christian religion. If hundreds of thousands of our fellow citizens should agree with us in an effort to elect men to public office who read the Bible, profess to believe it, reverence the Sabbath, attend public worship, and sustain a good moral character, who could complain? Have we not as much liberty to be the supporters of the Christian cause by our votes, as others have to support anti-christian men and measures?

Let us awake, then, fellow Christians, to our sacred duty to our Divine Master; and let us have no rulers, with our consent and co-operation, who are not known to be avowedly Christians. . . .

If they are of no religious denomination, they belong to the party of infidels. . . .

We are a Christian nation: we have a right to demand that all our rulers in their conduct shall conform to Christian morality; and if they do not, it is the duty and privilege of Christian freemen to make a new and a better election.

May the Lord Jesus Christ for ever reign in and over these United States, and call them peculiarly his own.

Amen.

Source 2 from *Report of Senate Committee on Post Offices and Postal Roads, January 19, 1829*. 20th Congress 2nd session, Senate Report #74.

2. Report of Senate Committee on Post Offices and Postal Roads, January 19, 1829. Sen. Richard M. Johnson, Chairman.[15]

We are aware, that a variety of sentiment exists among the good citizens of this nation, on the subject of the Sabbath day; and our government is designed for the protection of one, as much as for another. The Jews, who, in this country are as free as Christians, and entitled to the same protection from the laws, derive their obligation to keep the Sabbath day from the fourth commandment of their decalogue, and in conformity with that injunction, pay religious homage to the seventh day of the week, which we call Saturday. One denomination of Christians among us, justly celebrated for their piety, and certainly as good citizens as any other class, agree with the Jews in the moral obligation of the Sabbath, and observe the same day. There are also many Christians among us, who derive not their obligation to observe the

15. There was considerable doubt at the time, and later, over whether Johnson actually wrote the report. Some attribute the authorship to O. B. Brown, a Baptist minister and federal employee who shared a boardinghouse with Johnson. Others claim that the true author was Alexander Campbell (see Source 9), a Kentucky clergyman who was a friend of Johnson.

Sabbath from the decalogues, but regard the Jewish Sabbath as abrogated. From the example of the Apostles of Christ, they have chosen the first day of the week, instead of that day set apart in the decalogue, for their religious devotions. These have generally regarded the observance of the day as a devotional exercise, and would not more readily enforce it upon others, than they would enforce secret prayer or devout meditations. Urging the fact, that neither their Lord nor his disciples, though often censured by their accusers for a violation of the Sabbath, ever enjoined its observance, they regard it as a subject on which every person should be fully persuaded in his own mind, and not coerce others to act upon his persuasion. Many Christians again differ from these, professing to derive their obligation to observe the Sabbath from the fourth commandment of the Jewish decalogue, and bring the example of the Apostles, who appear to have held their public meetings for worship on the first day of the week, as authority for so far changing the decalogue, as to substitute that day for the seventh. The Jewish government was a theocracy, which enforced religious observances; and though the committee would hope that no portion of the citizens of our country could willingly introduce a system of religious coercion in our civil institutions, the example of other nations should admonish us to watch carefully against its earliest indication.

With these different religious views, the committee are of opinion that Congress cannot interfere. It is not the legitimate province of the legislature to determine what religion is true, or what false. Our government is a civil, and not a religious institution. Our Constitution recognises in every person, the right to choose his own religion, and to enjoy it freely, without molestation. Whatever may be the religious sentiments of citizens, and however variant, they are alike entitled to protection from the government, so long as they do not invade the rights of others.

The transportation of the mail on the first day of the week, it is believed, does not interfere with the rights of conscience. The petitioners for its discontinuance appear to be actuated from a religious zeal, which may be commendable if confined to its proper sphere; but they assume a position better suited to an ecclesiastical than to a civil institution. They appear, in many instances, to lay it down as an axiom, that the practice is a violation of the law of God. Should Congress, in their legislative capacity, adopt the sentiment, it would establish the principle, that the Legislature is a proper tribunal to determine what are the laws of God. It would involve a legislative decision in a religious controversy; and on a point in which good citizens may honestly differ in opinion, without disturbing the peace of society, or endangering its liberties. If this principle is once introduced, it will be impossible to define its bounds. Among all the religious persecutions with which almost every page of modern history is stained, no victim ever suffered, but for the violation of what government denominated the law of God. To prevent a similar train of evils in this country, the Constitution has wisely withheld from our government the power of defining the Divine Law. It is a right reserved to each citizen; and while he respects the equal rights of others, he cannot be held amenable to any human tribunal for his conclusions.

Extensive religious combinations, to effect a political object, are, in the opinion of the committee, always dangerous. This first effort of the kind, calls for the establishment of a principle, which, in the opinion of the committee, would lay the foundation for dangerous innovations upon the spirit of the Constitution, and upon the religious rights of the citizens. If admitted, it may be justly apprehended, that the future measures of government will be strongly marked, if not eventually controlled, by the same influence. All religious despotism commences by combination and influence; and when that influence begins to operate upon the political institutions of a country, the civil power soon bends under it; and the catastrophe of other nations furnishes an awful warning of the consequence. . . .

[Here the report explained that postal employees were fully aware of their workloads when they took employment and were not required to work any hours if that conflicted with their own consciences. In addition, delay of the mails would be inefficient and a burden to private businesses and other government agencies].

Nor can the committee discover where the system could consistently end. If the observance of a holyday becomes incorporated in our institutions, shall we not forbid the movement of an army; prohibit an assault in time of war; and lay an injunction upon our naval officers to lie in the wind while upon the ocean on that day? Consistency would seem to require it. Nor is it certain that we should stop here. If the principle is once established, that religion, or religious observances, shall be interwoven with our legislative acts, we must pursue it to its ultimatum. We shall, if consistent, provide for the erection of edifices for the worship of the Creator, and for the support of Christian ministers, if we believe such measures will promote the interests of Christianity. It is the settled conviction of the committee, that the only method of avoiding these consequences, with their attendant train of evils, is to adhere strictly to the spirit of the Constitution, which regards the general government in no other light than that of a civil institution, wholly destitute of religious authority.

What other nations call religious toleration, we call religious rights. They are not exercised in virtue of governmental indulgence, but as rights, of which government cannot deprive any portion of citizens, however small. Despotic

◆ CHAPTER 6
Church, State,
and Democracy:
The Sunday Mail
Controversy,
1827–1831

power may invade those rights, but justice still confirms them. Let the national legislature once perform an act which involves the decision of a religious controversy, and it will have passed its legitimate bounds. The precedent will then be established, and the foundation laid for that usurpation of the Divine prerogative in this country, which has been the desolating scourge to the fairest portions of the old world. Our constitution recognizes no other power than that of persuasion, for enforcing religious observances. Let the professors of Christianity recommend their religion by deeds of benevolence—by Christian meekness—by lives of temperance and holiness. Let them combine their efforts to instruct the ignorant—to relieve the widow and the orphan—to promulgate to the world the gospel of their Saviour, recommending its precepts by their habitual example: government will find its legitimate object in protecting them. It cannot oppose them, and they will not need its aid. Their moral influence will then do infinitely more to advance the true interests of religion, than any measures which they may call on Congress to enact.

The petitioners do not complain of any infringement upon their own rights. They enjoy all that Christians ought to ask at at the hand of any government— protection from all molestation in the exercise of their religious sentiments.

Resolved, That the Committee be discharged from the further consideration of the subject.

Source 3 from *An Account of Memorials Presented to Congress During the Last session . . . Praying that the Mails May not Be Transported, Nor Post-Offices kept Open, on the Sabbath* (New York: T.R. Marvin, May 1829), pp. 3–4, 30–32.

3. Account of Memorials, May 1829.

Ever since the mail was first transported in the United States on the Sabbath, this violation of the day of rest has been a source of grief and pain to many individuals, who are justly ranked among the most intelligent, useful, and virtuous of our citizens. To the certain knowledge of the compiler of these pages, much regret has been expressed, by persons residing in many parts of the Union, that a practice so pernicious in its tendency and consequences, should have been sanctioned by any department of our national government.

Post-offices, in our large towns, were gradually opened, one after another, for a *part of the Sabbath*; and in 1810, a section was inserted, in the law regulating the post-office, by which post-masters were obliged to deliver letters at all reasonable hours, *on every day of the week*. This law attracted very little attention at the time; and it is supposed, that the section alluded to was scarcely considered at all, except by the Committee that introduced it. A member of congress recently declared it to be very strange, that such a provision should have crept into the law; for it was clearly a repeal of the *Fourth Commandment.* . . .

The keeping open of post-offices, on the day of sacred rest, has been to many hearts a still greater grief and burden, than the transportation of the mail on that day. In many towns, both large and small, the post office is so located, as to attract crowds of idlers, who do not pretend to any plea of necessity. The young, if they have not pious parents or guardians, are led, by this public and authorized show of business to disregard the Sabbath, and to withdraw themselves from public worship. All these consequences were foreseen at once, by those who are accustomed to regard moral causes and their effects. . . .

From that time to the present, the multiplied evils of Sabbath-breaking have become more and more apparent; and the apprehension has been extensively felt, that an irresistible flood of business and pleasure will roll over the sacred institutions of religion, and leave our beloved land a moral desolation. Hence it has been a subject of conversation for years, in many a circle of reflecting and patriotic men, and in many states of the Union, if not in every state, that the friends of the Sabbath should come forward, and plead its claims before the national legislature. . . .

It was with the highest gratification, therefore, that the friends of religion, in different parts of the land, were informed, that a most respectable committee, composed of gentlemen of different religious denominations, had been constituted in the largest of our commercial cities, and sent forth an invitation to their countrymen to join in the petition, which was soon to be presented. This was early in December last; and, before the close of that month, many petitions had been forwarded, and some were before the post-office committee of each house of congress. Others continued to arrive till the last weeks of the session; and, in the whole, *four hundred and forty one* distinct petitions were presented to the House of Representatives, and *twenty six* to the Senate. These were severally referred to the post-office committees. . . .

[The document then listed all the towns in the nineteen states, the District of Columbia, and the territory of Michigan from which the 467 petitions came from, a long list of names of people who had either drafted or signed petitions, and a few excerpts from some of the petitions.]

CONCLUDING OBSERVATIONS

From what has appeared in the preceding pages, it must be manifest to every candid mind, that the petitions to congress, in relation to the transportation and opening of the mail on the Sabbath, did not originate in any transient

◆ CHAPTER 6
Church, State,
and Democracy:
The Sunday Mail
Controversy,
1827–1831

feeling, nor in any narrow, or local, or personal views; but that they were the result of much reflection, and a solemn conviction of duty, in regard to a subject, which is deemed by the petitioners to be vitally important to their country and to individuals—to the present generation and to posterity. It is plain, therefore, that the purpose of the petitioners cannot be relinquished, and that no suitable means of attaining it should be neglected.

The reasons, which they assign, are of the gravest character, resting on a sense of obligation to obey an express command of God,—a full persuasion that a disregard of this command will bring down upon our land the displeasure of Heaven,—a deliberate opinion, that the Sabbath is one of the most glorious proofs of the divine beneficence;—that it is eminently calculated to make communities, wherever it is properly observed, virtuous, prosperous and happy; that the loss of this institution would be a calamity so awful, as that any well-grounded apprehension of it might reasonably excite the most gloomy forebodings; that the present regulations of the post-office tend strongly toward the abolition of the Sabbath; that they are, therefore, in the highest sense, adverse to the public good; that, as the preservation of moral integrity; or a sense of responsibility of God, extensively among the people, is confessedly essential to the continuance of a republican government,—every enlightened patriot, as well as every true Christian, must cherish the institutions of religion, as the great means of perpetuating our free government; that the laws of the several States are disregarded, and the religious privileges of the people invaded, by the present regulations of the post-office; and that the inconvenience of having the mails at rest and the post-offices closed on the Sabbath, is very small, compared with the great and alarming evils of a contrary course.

[The account then addressed the question of whether the nondelivery of mail on Sundays would be damaging to commerce. The account said that this would be an extremely rare occurrence that easily could be dealt with.]

In conclusion, the people of the United States have it in their power to secure their religious freedom, their civil institutions and their national prosperity, to themselves and to future ages, if they will satisfy the Sabbath, and thus enjoy all its benign, restraining, and enlightening influences; but if they unwisely disregard the voice of experience and the voice of God, it may be said of them, by the SUPREME LAWGIVER, as it was said of the Jewish commonwealth: *But if ye will not hearken unto me to hallow* THE SABBATH DAY, *and not to bear a burden, even entering in at the gates of Jerusalem on the Sabbath day; then I will kindle a fire in the gates thereof, and it shall devour the palaces of Jerusalem, and it shall not be quenched.*

Source 4 from [Ezra Stiles Ely], *The Logic and Law of Col. Johnson's Report to the Senate, on Sabbath Mails* (Utica, NY: G. S. Wilson, 1829, pp. 3–10, 21.

4. Logic and Law of Col. Johnson's Report, 1829.

This report appears to have been drawn up by Col. Johnson, and is of course a draught of opinions for which he has committed himself to the public; and in speaking of the Report we shall briefly refer to the author. We greatly respect Col. J. as a man—have the greatest confidence in his patriotism—believe him possessed naturally of a strong mind—but knowing as we do his history, he will not, we presume, set up for his opinions, however honest, the claim of infallibility. The whole Report, is courteous, plausible,—but as we deem, fundamentally erroneous in its principles, and singularly illogical in its deductions. It deserves respectful treatment from the character of the author, but every citizen owes it a thorough examination, since it avowedly intends to "settle a principle;"—a principle too, fundamental to the character of the Government and nation, and designed to be a pole star in all its future policy. The patriot ought to search it well, as it involves one of the most momentous points in the whole affair of government. Col. J. indeed, claims that the point is already settled by the "Constitution," and that his Report is only a necessary application of this decision; neither of which, we trust, will be found correct. The Constitution is from the people; let the people judge of the interpretation. . . .

[The author asserts that similar petitions had failed before, but the question has reappeared "more formidable than ever" due to the "growth of moral principle and intelligence in our country." The pamphlet then asserts the people's constitutional right to petition, especially when they see actions and opinions (Johnson's) "endangering directly or indirectly the moral character of the community." Any notions contrary to that would be opined by "an irreligious DESPOTISM."

Then, countering Sen. Johnson's description of religious combinations as "dangerous," the author states that no denomination ever has advocated a measure in conflict with the Constitution. "Till Col. J. can prove the contrary, we cannot but view his insinuations as unkind and libelous."]

We come now to a review of the fundamental principle of Col. Johnson's Report, that *for Congress* to grant the plea of the petitioners against the transportation of the mails and the obligation to open the Post Offices on Sunday, would be a *violation of the Constitution*. In the language of the Colonel, the petitioners "call for the establishment of a principle which would lay the foundation for dangerous innovations upon the spirit of the Constitution;" and, therefore, "the observance of a holy day cannot be incorporated in our institution." "The spirit of the Constitution regards the General Government in no other light than that of a civil institution."

[153]

◆ CHAPTER 6
Church, State,
and Democracy:
The Sunday Mail
Controversy,
1827–1831

The inference from all this is manifest, though not drawn out. It was enough for the present, to settle the principle, that the good citizens of the States might henceforth abstain from "religious combinations." Colonel J. will please to enlighten us, if this be not the idea he intended the petitioners should receive—that the General Government is ATHEISTICAL: That when government binds a citizen to official duties in the Post Office or any other department, on Sunday, this is not a fit subject for complaint, petition, "religious combination,"—is a political object—the general Government knows no religion. . . .

We knew, that at the formation of the Constitution, some, because it contained neither creed, nor religious establishment, nor religious test, espoused the idea that the Constitution was *atheistical*. We also knew, that the policy of some of our statesmen was *atheistical*, and their measures tending to introduce the principle. But we confess our skill in "discerning spirits" is not great; and we cannot to this day, see any thing in the "spirit of the Constitution," atheistical, or that constitutionally binds the General Government to run over the religious feelings of the nation, or forbids Congress to authorize the Postmaster General to delay a little on any day of the week, till the moral feelings of the nation are removed out of his way. Every citizen of the United States, at the formation of the Constitution, was a subject of an *independent* state or nation, where he enjoyed his rights and his religion, and was satisfied. The delegates to the Convention met to agree on *terms of union between the states*; not to interfere with state laws or annihilate sovereignty. Col. J. well knows the jealousy of the states at that time; that it was difficult enough to agree on general and political terms of union without assuming the delicate and difficult subject of religious creeds and forms:—that did not belong to the Convention, and was never delegated. The independent Sovereignties took care of that, and their citizens were satisfied. The states then had feelings of attachment to the religion of their fathers and laws in relation to the Sabbath. And we pledge ourselves, that at least the sons of the Pilgrims would never have consented to union in any government which claimed the prerogatives of Atheism, and without the pressure of necessity annihilated their Sabbaths. The Convention were too wise to suppose this, and, therefore, like the proceeding Congress, *showed respect* to the religious sentiments and usages of the states. And it well knew, that a regard to the Sabbath had characterized us as a nation from the beginning. The matter stands thus: Independent states sent their delegates to agree on terms of confederation, and delineate a plan which, without impairing the several sovereignties, should unite them for the *general safety*. These terms they settle, and say nothing, if you please, about religion; only they are careful to do no act and pass no article that shall disturb a single religious feeling, or violate a single religious institution. Now, what is the "spirit" of the Constitution? "A social and political instrument," not an ecclesiastical. True enough; but a truism. Are we to infer, as the spirit of the Constitution, because it says *nothing* on the subject of religion, it says something against it? that what is not mentioned in the Constitution is *constitutionally prohibited*. This argument from silence, applied universally, would legitimate conclusions which we are persuaded Col. J. would be among the first to denounce. . . .

Follow Citizens, we are old fashioned republicans. It is a favorite maxim of ours, "that every citizen is free and equal." We wish some committee to settle the question, whether it be not the spirit of the Constitution, to relieve from an obligation to official labor on the Sabbath, equally and impartially, the conscience of a post-master, a stage-driver, an inn-keeper, or an hostler, with the President of the United States? If they report that in the opinion of said committee such relief is a dangerous innovation on the spirit of the Constitution, in the name of republicanism, we second the motion for their "discharge."

So much for the silence of the Constitution, and so much for the voice of the Convention. What indication of the "spirit of the Constitution" is to be obtained from the sentiments and acts of the proper interpreters of olden time or of the nation? This inquiry is superfluous, after what has been said: for after all, the proper place to find the spirit of the Constitution, is where we have found it—in the *body* of the Constitution, approving of a Sabbath and providing for its conscientious enjoyment. But as we love the spirit of the Constitution, we'll seek it any where. Shall we look to the old Continental Congress, who conducted the nation through the perils of the Revolution, and secured the Independence which they first declared; who settled those principles on which the States could harmonize and unite, and laid the foundation of national character and government? They observed a Sabbath! True, on the Sabbath (April 8th, 1781) when the movements of the British troops were jeopardizing all the stores and provisions on the southern peninsula, they met—who blames them? But when the danger was over, they met no more. Shall we inquire of the Convention that formed the Constitution? They recognized a Sabbath. Shall we inquire after the opinions of subsequent meetings of Congress? They always provided a Sabbath occasion for the conscientious—(till recently)—and *now* we are solemnly assured, after the laborious consultations of a Committee of the Senate of the United States, that to *grant a Sabbath cessation from official* business to the Post office department, "would be establishing a principle which would lay the foundation for dangerous *innovations*, (I think I am right, Fellow Citizens,) "*innovations* on the spirit of the Constitution."—Verily, if the constitutional

◆ CHAPTER 6
Church, State,
and Democracy:
The Sunday Mail
Controversy,
1827–1831

accomodation of a Sabbath for the President and the *restoration* of the constitutional accommodation of a Sabbath for Commoners, has now gotten to be adverse to the "spirit of the Constitution," it is high time that a Special Committee be appointed to define the difference between the old and the new "spirit of the Constitution," and by what means the soul of the Constitution has undergone this wondrous change! . . .

Another principle on which Col. J. proceeds, in reasoning down the petitioners, is, that restoring the Sabbath to its ancient quiet, does not comport with the spirit of the government, since *the Government knows no religion.* This too is "news" to the good citizens of the States, which no doubt will make 3,000 copies of the Report exceedingly appropriate. Having lived so long under the Government, and loved it too as we imagined, and carefully noticed its character, we had very charitably, but it seems erroneously, taken up a different fancy. Henceforth we must away with all such vain imaginations. Know all men by these presents, (3,000 copies) that this Government is no longer to be baptized "*christian*"—"The Government knows no religion." Quere; are the oaths and treaties of our Government good in law? What guarantee of their veracity have "we the people?" . . .

[Having claimed that the notion of the federal government "knowing no religion" is a novel idea, the tract then goes into an extended (10 pages) treatise showing the numerous times that colonial and state governments and the federal government referred to God, Nature's God, Divine Providence, and so forth. Especially noted were the openings of legislatures with prayers, special days of fasting and prayer, Benjamin Franklin's (the first Postmaster General) belief "in the Providence of God as governing the world; that the Constitution was influenced, guided, and governed by that omnipotent, omnipresent, and beneficent Ruler," President Washington's remark that "Of all the dispositions and habits which lead to political prosperity, religion and morality are indispensable supports," and the countless use of chaplains, religious-based oaths, and prayers before battles, conventions, legislative sessions, and the like. Especially interesting was Franklin's writing to those who were contemplating immigrating to America.]

Contemplating the preceding facts, we put the question to Col. J. as an honorable man:—Supposing the petitioners to possess the spirit of '76—the standard of pure and enlightened patriotism, might they not, as *patriots*, feel concerned at the introduction of a mercantile or a political system, which "woke up" the very day so generally devoted to cherishing the principles and sentiments of religion, which our Government has assured us was the "*only solid foundation of public liberty?*" Would it have been *charitable* in the petitioners, to have supposed that the religious and moral sentiments of '76 were no longer possessed by the Government? that, enjoying the fruits of former patriotism and piety, "Jeshurun waxed fat and kicked?" Was it rational to suppose that the

Government and nation, in '76, were *not Christian*, and knew no religion?—when "the United States, in Congress assembled," (though there were *then* Jews and possibly a few Deists,) yet officially promoted the circulation of the Old and New Testaments; bound themselves by the sanctity of an oath on that Holy Volume; rejoiced "above all," in the possession of the gospel of peace; attributed all national blessings to Almighty God; and implored, and recommended the people to implore, his directions in their councils and his forgiveness of their sins, through the merits of the Divine Redeemer; and measured our national existence by "the year of our Lord:" when they urged the States to cherish "pure and undefiled religion," which the states never understood other than the Christian; when they carefully provided and paid Christian chaplains of various denominations, that their armies and hospitals might be supplied with Christian instruction and consolation; when they reverently waived national business on the Sabbath, when a Christian nation is engaged in worshipping the Father of Mercies—and even tenderly accommodated those denominations that would celebrate the crucifixion of the Redeemer. We have seen that the spirit of '76 on these subjects was still possessed in the administration of Washington. If, therefore, our Government is no longer Christian, but Jewish, Mahomedan, Pagan, or Atheistical, it is incumbent on Col. J. to point out *when* and *how* the change was introduced! The 3,000 do not suffice. Till then, please to allow the petitioners to abide by the spirit of '76. It is, and they glory in it, their only spirit, as it was once the spirit of Congress and the nation; though now to be baptized "religious combination!"

Source 5 from *First Annual Report of the General Union for Promoting the Observance of the Christian Sabbath: adopted May 12, 1829* (New York: J. Collard, 1829), pp. 8–14.

5. Address by the Rev. Matthias Bruen, Corresponding Secretary of the General Union.

This General Union grew out of the conscious want, on the part of the Christian community, of that equal respect unto all God's commandments which is essential to temporal and spiritual prosperity. It was believed that the public conscience in every branch of Christ's nation might appear, as the Scriptures present it, exceeding sinful. On solemn consideration it was believed that the safety and honor of the Church loudly called for some plan, in which Christians of every name might co-operate to excite a livelier sense of the divine authority and paramount importance of the Christian Sabbath.

It was further considered, that the exact observance of the Lord's day, according to the commandment, is not only the chief support and defense of

✦ CHAPTER 6

Church, State,
and Democracy:
The Sunday Mail
Controversy,
1827–1831

the church of Christ on earth, but is also a wall of safety to the civil community. It was believed that if new energy could be given to the public conscience on this vital subject, that the sum of national happiness would be proportionately increased. The concurrence of all was therefore earnestly asked, and your executive committee were made the organ of expressing this desire.

In conformity with the purpose for which they were appointed, they published, soon after the convention which formed the constitution of this Union, an address to the people of the United States, of which upwards of one hundred thousand copies in pamphlet or newspaper form were circulated. In this age of philanthropy perhaps no single document bearing upon the morals of the land has been more timely and effective.

Communications from different quarters of the United States were received by your temporary Corresponding Secretary, and many auxiliary Unions spontaneously formed. The pulpit and the press, the two great organs for influencing public sentiment, took a new impulse: the fourth commandment, in its length and breadth, began to take hold of the public mind;—and this Union will be remembered with fervent gratitude, should nothing farther result, since it has already elevated by many degrees the moral sense of our republic.

The spirit of the age, which is another name for the all-presiding providence of God, distinguishing different eras of the world by varieties of temper, admits an appeal upon every important subject to its free examination. Opinion has always ruled the world;—as men think, so are they; in former centuries public sentiment was subjugated by monarchy or aristocracy;—in this republican age and country, Providence has led us into the open field of individual opinions, and requires every man submit his conscience only to the Word of his Creator. This Union has entered the field of free inquiry, and has presented to our observant fellow citizens the motives which should secure due reverence for the fourth commandment; being well assured that the voice of reason and the sentiment of religion will prevail where there is sabbath rest;—but that the din of sabbath profanation can drown the loudest argument, and that the very existence of the Christian religion is annulled just so far as this commandment is despised.

Convinced that a more important subject never arrested the eye of a free people, from our post of review we have been rejoiced to observe to what extent it has agitated the land, and that while there has been difference of opinion enough to elicit a full pleading on each side, from every quarter, whether friendly or opposed to our organization, praise of our object has issued. Thousands of unexpected witnesses have appeared upon this great trial of God's holy day, to approve its worth. In this country, where public opinion is the freest and the mightiest upon earth, no line of difference has appeared as to the utility of the sabbath, however the means chosen by this Union may not have escaped censure. The obloquy[16] has been very little, and we bear it cheerfully, as the unavoidable expense of an experiment to gain an end which all consent to, that it is good. We would gladly be shown a better way, if one exists, than that which we have taken. We believe self submission to God's law to be the good old gospel way, and that in this land of freedom, no just offense can be taken with any measures, associated or individual, based upon a conscientious regard to every one of the ten commandments. We have had the pleasure of seeing many, doubtful at first of the utility of this Union, become its warm advocates; and feel assured that nothing but misapprehension or bigotry, the spirit that would lord it over our free institutions, and over liberty of conscience, can object to any association of individuals refusing to trample upon what they believe to be a law of the Highest. Here all profess to respect the rights of conscience. For conscience' sake, more than for this world's wealth, our ancestors converted the forest waste into our fruitful fields; and your committee congratulate this Union upon its operations, because it has drawn forth this voice of conscience from our countrymen, and confirmed that moral sense which alone elevates the character and secures the prosperity of our beloved republic. Republican institutions can never be dissevered from virtue: virtue is but another name for the sense of moral responsibility to God; and this moral sense never lived but in sabbath time.

The churches in this land, however divided on some other subjects, for the most part feel alike in this sabbath question; and with the churches are connected large congregations, embodying the moral strength of our nation. . . .

The mighty march of the Temperance Society over our land, fills your committee with the belief that our Union, based upon the same principle of entire abstinence, will have the same power in reforming public opinion, and can never appeal in vain to the intelligence, the conscience, the desire of self preservation, yet prevalent in our country.

We hope that this Anniversary will fill all our members with the same conviction, and that all will feel that they are pledged for life to entire abstinence, and the effort of complete and universal reform. . . . and when the steam boat or the stage, which systematically runs over the divine law, by night or by day, for one hour, or for four and twenty, is compelled to take the stamp before our public, which God's prohibition of the sin fixes on it, a complete reformation will ensue, and our land will keep her sabbaths. The

16. Obloquy: false, malicious statements.

✦ CHAPTER 6

Church, State,
and Democracy:
The Sunday Mail
Controversy,
1827–1831

whole moral law must be lifted up together, upon one table—each command of equal authority—for the veneration of America and of all the earth;—it must be received altogether, as God gave it together his everlasting commandment. It is only strange that among those who profess to revere the Scriptures, this special effort should be needed. . . .

Yet this comparatively happy republic is overflooded with sabbath profanation. Every canal carries it, every river wafts it down, every bay embosoms it; our great cities are the emporiums of the crime, at once the volcanoes which receive the fuel and disperse the flame;—here the public gardens, the common tippling shops, the capacious steam boats, are filled with those deeply tainted with this sin; and while there is not a command in the decalogue more precise in its prohibitory clause, there is no rest upon God's holy day. The animals subjected to our dominion for six days, and relieved by the divine law from the rigour of unintermitted toil, share the burden;—the whole creation groaneth and travaileth together. In many parts, the stalls of the butchers, the baskets of the bakers, the fruits of the market, the pages of the newspaper, the documents of the lawyer, the accounts of the merchant, have more or less of the odour of this sin. The poor are under slavery to the rich; their children, and orphans hindered from the sabbath school, and the community at large subjected to a training most expensive in its results in pauperism and prisons, ignorance and unhappiness, coupled with the loss of all the benefits of Christianity for the life that is to come. . . .

While renewing their invitation to all to aid in this work, your committee are encouraged by the effects of the question brought before the congress of the United States at its late session, of discontinuing the public mails upon the sabbath. As the object of this Union is not to affect the government directly, but the government through the people; as we appeal from the few to the many, and would make radical reform among those who have the keys of power, that is, the great body of our fellow citizens, and who, if they will reform themselves, will find the work completed, your committee have not regarded in their duty to act in their associate capacity in that important matter. But we have watched its whole movement with great interest, sensible that the result must in the main determine all the rest; and that so long as one steam boat, or one stage, can plead an United States' contract and legislative injunction for sabbath breaking, and thus run over State rights, the rights of conscience, and the rights of God, we are parties to a flagrant violation of the divine law, and to a wide source of temporal and spiritual calamity. . . .

Christianity can only exist where the sabbath is reverenced, and Christianity has here introduced free government and general happiness. Its heavenly spirit alone ever civilized and beautified any region of the globe, and it has done its wonders in soils most uncongenial. It has given the sceptre of this world's opinions to the descendant of the Goth, and of the dwellers in northern wilds, and seems to have entrusted itself for safety, and for universal propagation, to our native language. No state of this Union has grown out of heathenism. Christianity founded all our glorious institutions; and with no other compulsory sway than that of light and love, as the sun reigns over the world, will pour its temporal and eternal riches upon our canals and our rivers, our plains and our mountains. . . .

Source 6 from *Report of the House Committee on Post Offices and Postal Roads, March 4–5, 1830.* 21st Congress 1st Session, House Report #271, pp. 3–5, 7.

6. Report of House Committee on Post Offices and Postal Roads, March 4, 1830. Rep. Richard M. Johnson, Chairman, and Minority Report by Rep. William McCreery.

[The 1830 report was somewhat different from and considerably longer than the Senate Committee's 1829 report. This report began by stating that the committee could find no constitutional power permitting Congress to determine whether any time "has been set apart by the Almighty for religious exercises," and that Congress was not empowered to pass any law respecting the establishment of religion. Moreover, elected officials are chosen to represent voters' political and not their religious views. The committee went on to suggest that the closing of post offices on Sunday would open the door to a plethora of religious laws that eventually would impinge the rights of all.]

With the exception of the United States, the whole human race, consisting, it is supposed, of eight hundred millions of rational beings, is in religious bondage; and, in reviewing the scenes of persecution which history every where presents, unless the committee could believe that the cries of the burning victim, and the flames by which he is consumed, bear to Heaven grateful incense, the conclusion is inevitable, that the line cannot be too strongly drawn between Church and State. If a solemn act of legislation shall, in *one* point, define the law of God, or point out to the citizen one religious duty, it may, with equal propriety, proceed to define every part of divine revelation; and enforce *every* religious obligation, even to the forms and ceremonies of worship; the endowment of the church, and the support of the clergy.

◆ CHAPTER 6
Church, State,
and Democracy:
The Sunday Mail
Controversy,
1827–1831

It was with a kiss that Judas betrayed his Divine Master, and we should all be admonished,—no matter what our faith may be—that the rights of conscience cannot be so successfully assailed as under the pretext of holiness. The Christian religion made its way into the world in opposition to all human Governments. Banishment, tortures, and death, were inflicted in vain to stop its progress. But many of its professors, as soon as clothed with political power, lost the meek spirit which their creed inculcated, and began to inflict on other religions, and on dissenting sects of their own religion, persecutions more aggravated than those which their own apostles had endured. The ten persecutions of Pagan Emperors, were exceeded in atrocity by the massacres and murders perpetrated by Christian hands; and in vain shall we examine the records of Imperial tyranny for an engine of cruelty equal to the *Holy Inquisition*. Every religious sect, however meek in its origin, commenced the work of persecution as soon as it acquired political power. The framers of the constitution recognised the eternal principle, that man's relation with his God is above human legislation, and his rights of conscience inalienable. Reasoning was not necessary to establish this truth: we are conscious of it in our bosoms. It is this consciousness which, in defiance of human laws, has sustained so many martyrs is tortures and in flames. They *fell* that their duty to God was superior to human enactments, and that man could exercise no authority over their consciences: it is an inborn principle which nothing can eradicate.

The bigot, in the pride of his authority, may lose light of it—but strip him of his power; prescribe a faith to him which his conscience rejects; threaten him in turn with the dungeon and the faggot; and the spirit which God has implanted in him, rises up in rebellion and defies you. Did the primitive Christians ask that Government should recognize and observe their religious institutions? All they asked was *toleration*; all they complained of, was persecution. What did the Protestants of Germany, or the Hugenots of France, ask of their Catholic superiors? *Toleration*. What do the persecuted Catholics of Ireland ask of their oppressors? *Toleration*.

Do not all men in this country enjoy every religious right which martyrs and saints ever asked? Whence, then the voice of complaint? Who is it, that, in the full enjoyment of every principle which human laws can secure, wishes to arrest a portion of these principles from his neighbor? Do the petitioners allege that they cannot conscientiously participate in the profits of the mail contracts and post offices, because the mail is carried on Sunday? If this be their motive, then it is worldly gain which stimulates to action, and not virtue or religion. Do they complain that men, less conscientious in relation to the Sabbath, obtain advantages over them, by receiving their letters and attending to their contents?

Still their motive is worldly and selfish. But if their motive be to induce Congress to sanction, by law, their *religious opinions* and *observances*, then their efforts are to be resisted, as in their tendency fatal, both to religious and political freedom. Why have the petitioners confined their prayer to the mails? Why have they not requested that the Government be required to suspend *all* its executive functions on that day? Why do they not require us to enact that our ships shall not sail? that our armies shall not march? that officers of justice shall not seize the suspected, or guard the convicted? They seem to forget that government is as necessary on Sunday as on any other day of the week. The spirit of evil does not rest on that day. It is the Government, ever active in its functions, which enables us all, even the petitioners, to worship in our churches in peace. Our Government furnishes very few blessings like our mails. They bear from the centre of our Republic to its distant extremes, the acts of our legislative bodies, the decisions of the judiciary, and the orders of the Executive. Their speed is often essential to the defence of the country, the suppression of crime, and the dearest interest of the people. Were they suppressed one day of the week, their absence must be often supplied by public expresses; and, besides, while the mail bags might rest, the mail coaches would pursue their journey with the passengers. The mail bears, from one extreme of the Union to the other, letters of relatives and friends, preserving a communion of heart between those far separated, and increasing the most pure and refined pleasures of our existence: also, the letters of commercial men convey the state of the markets, prevent ruinous speculations, and promote general, as well as individual interest: they bear innumerable religious letters, newspapers, magazines and tracts, which reach almost every house throughout this wide Republic. Is the conveyance of these a violation of the Sabbath? The advance of the human race in intelligence, in virtue, and religion itself, depends in part upon the speed with which a knowledge of the past is discriminated. Without an interchange between one country and another, and between different sections of the same country, every improvement in moral or political science, and the arts of life, would be confined to the neighborhood where it originated. The more rapid and the more frequent this interchange, the more rapid will be the march of intellect, and the progress of improvement. The mail is the chief means by which intellectual light irradiates to the extremes of the Republic. Stop it one day in seven, and you retard one seventh the advancement of our country. So far from stopping the mail on Sunday, the committee would recommend the use of all reasonable means to give it a greater expedition and a greater extension. What would be the elevation of our country, if every new conception could be made to strike every mind in the Union at the same time? It is not the distance of a Province or State from the seat of Government, which endangers its separation; but it is

◆ CHAPTER 6

Church, State,
and Democracy:
The Sunday Mail
Controversy,
1827–1831

the difficulty and unfrequency of intercourse between them. Our mails reach Missouri and Arkansas in less time than they reached Kentucky and Ohio in the infancy of their settlement; and now, when there are three millions of people extending a thousand miles West of the Alleghany, we hear less of discontent, than when there were a few thousands scattered along their Western base. . . .

Our fathers did not wait to be oppressed, when the mother country asserted and exercised an unconstitutional power over them. To have acquiesced in the tax of three pence upon a pound of tea, would have led the way to the most cruel exactions; they took a bold stand against the principle, and liberty and independence was the result. The petitioners have not requested Congress to suppress Sunday mails upon the ground of political expediency, but because they violate the sanctity of the first day of the week.

This being the fact, and the petitioners having indignantly disclaimed even the wish to unite politics and religion, may not the committee reasonably cherish the hope, that they will feel reconciled to its decision, in the case; especially, as it is also a fact, that the counter memorials, equally respectable, oppose the interference of Congress, upon the ground that it would be legislating upon a religious subject, and therefore unconstitutional.

Resolved, That the committee be discharged from the further consideration of the subject.

Minority Report by Rep. McCreery, March 5, 1830.

All Christian nations acknowledge the first day of the week, to be the Sabbath. Almost every State in this Union have, by positive legislation, not only recognized this day as sacred, but has forbidden its profanation under penalties imposed by law.

It was never considered, by any of those States, as an encroachment upon the rights of conscience, or as an improper interference with the opinions of the few, to guard the sacredness of that portion of time acknowledged to be holy by the many.

The petitioners ask not Congress to expound the moral law; they ask not Congress to meddle with theological controversies, much less to interfere with the rights of the Jew or the Sabbatarian, or to treat with the least disrespect the religious feelings of any portion of the inhabitants of the Union; they ask the introduction of no religious coercion into our civil institutions; no blending of religion and civil affairs; but they do ask, that the agents of Government, employed in the Post Office Department, may be permitted to enjoy the same opportunities of attending to moral and religious instruction, or intellectual improvement, on that day, which is enjoyed by the rest of their fellow citizens. They approach the Government, not for personal emolument, but as patriots and Christians, to express their high sense of the moral energy and necessity of the Sabbath for the perpetuity of our republican institutions; and respectfully request that Congress will not, by legislative enactments, impair those energies. . . .

The wise and good Ruler of the universe made the appointment, not by a mere arbitrary exercise of authority, but for our good; and whatever difference of opinion may exist in respect to the proper day to be observed, almost all agree, that one day in seven should be devoted to religious exercises. That being admitted, can any thing be more reasonable than the request of the petitioners, that, at least, so much of the law should be repealed, as requires the post offices to be kept open every day of the week. Does not the enactment of that law plainly imply, that mankind is under no moral obligation to refrain from secular labor on any day of the week? Is it not in direct opposition to the received opinion of almost all professing Christians? It is to that part of the law, more particularly, which requires, in terms, all the postmasters throughout the United States to deliver letters, packets, and papers, on every day of the week, to which the minority of your committee object, and which is most offensive to the petitioners. In this statute is at once seen, a palpable encroachment on the rights of conscience. It either drives every man, who feels himself morally bound to observe the Sabbath in a religious manner, from the service of his country, and equal participation in her favors, or subjects him to the hard terms of remaining in office, at the expense of his principles. It is freely acknowledged, that the works of necessity and mercy are not forbidden; and, if the transportation of the mail on Sunday, could be justified on that ground, (which is not admitted) it cannot be contended, that the keeping open offices, where no mail arrives on that day, is the work of necessity.

The arguments which have been urged for the transportation of the mail, &c. on the Sabbath, are mainly derived from commercial convenience, and from alleged derangement of business and intercourse. This doctrine militates against the first principles of good morals. If these are important at all, they are paramount to the claims of expediency; but this plea makes them subservient to the pressure of worldly business, and converts them into mere questions of profit and loss.

Granting the prayer of the petitioners cannot interfere with the religious feelings or consciences of any portion of the citizens; because, they ask no service to be performed; no principle to be professed. It is only asked that certain duties be not required on a certain day. Were it imposing any service, or requiring the profession of any opinions, those whose religious sentiments were different, might justly complain. But he who conscientiously believes that he is bound to observe the seventh day of the week, in a religious manner, can have no just reason to complain; because, Government takes

◆ CHAPTER 6

Church, State,
and Democracy:
The Sunday Mail
Controversy,
1827–1831

nothing from him, in permitting all classes of citizens to observe the first day of the week, as a day of religious rest. The case would be quite different, did the privilege of resting on that day, impose anything on any class of citizens, contrary to their conscience.

Source 7 from Zelotes Fuller, *The Tree of Liberty. An Address in Celebration of the Birth of Washington, Delivered at the Second Universalist Church in Philadelphia, Sunday Morning, February 28, 1830, in The Annals of America* (Chicago: Encyclopedia Britannica, 1968) vol. 5, pp. 358–360.

7. Zelotes Fuller, The Tree of Liberty.[17]

Fifty-three years have we been in possession of national independence and political freedom. Our fathers willed themselves free and independent, and behold, liberty followed the sun in his path! *To continue free, we have but to will it*! And will you not do it, O people of America—ye who know the sweets of liberty? To support the liberties of our country, as did your fathers, so have ye pledged your lives, your fortunes, and your sacred honor. And are ye not ready to make good the pledge? Ye who are the friends of American freedom, and of humankind, have but one answer to give, and that answer is yea! Ye will duly honor the cause, that is committed to your keeping. Ye will never prove false to the liberties of your country—nor violate the pledge of your fathers—the pledge of yourselves as Americans.

Remember that the civil and religious liberty which ye enjoy, and which ye hold to be the birth-right of every man, was purchased with toil, and blood, and suffering. Dear was the price which it cost—precious the lives that were sacrificed. Never, O never suffer yourselves to be robbed of such an invaluable heritage, nor quietly submit to any infringement of the rights and privileges which it confers.

I have said, we fear not that the civil and religious rights and privileges, which our excellent constitution guarantees, will be infringed by those abroad, but they may be by a certain class at home, if no precaution be taken to prevent it. Yea, we deem it a truth, too evident to admit of doubt, and too generally conceded to require proof on the present occasion, that it is the intention of a certain religious sect in our country, to bring about, if possible, a union of church and state. To effect this purpose, a deep and artful scheme has been laid, and which may ultimately be consummated, unless it is speedily and

17. Zelotes Fuller (1773–1857) was a Universalist minister and editor of the newspaper *Philadelphia Liberalist*, which began publication in 1832.

vigorously opposed. Yea, the declaration has gone forth, that in ten years, or certainly in twenty, the political power of our country, will be in the hands of those who shall have been educated to believe in and probably *pledged* to support, a certain creed. Merciful God! forbid the fulfillment of the prophecy! Forbid it all ye, who have at heart, the prosperity and happiness of our nation!

People of this free and happy land! we ask, will you give your consent to the political dominancy of any one religious sect, and the establishment of their religious creed by law? Will you in any way encourage certain popular religious measures, got up by a certain popular religious sect, in our humble opinion, for a very *unpopular* object, but which in the view of many, is very popular to approve? Be assured, whatever may be the *ostensive* objects of these measures, if they should be generally adopted, they will tend to infuse the spirit of religious intolerance and persecution into the political institutions of our country, and in the end, completely to annihilate the political and religious liberty of the people. Are you willing that a connection should be formed between politics and religion, or that the equal rights of conscience, should in any degree be mutilated? Are ye prepared to bow your necks to an intolerant and persecuting system of religion; for instance, like that of England? Are ye prepared to submit to such an unrighteous system of tithes, taxations and exactions, for the support of a *national religion*, as the great mass of her people are compelled to submit to? Are ye prepared to debase yourselves, like so many beasts of burden, before a dissipated nobility and an intolerant corrupted priesthood? It cannot be. I feel certain, that I am addressing those of my countrymen, who are too enlightened and intelligent, too patriotic and independent in their principles, whose feelings are too lofty and whose souls are too noble, who love liberty too well and prize it too highly, ever to submit to such degradation and wretchedness. No! sooner may we perish—sooner let yonder fields be strewed with our bones— sooner shall the tented battle ground, be stained with our blood, as with the blood of our fathers! for what is life without liberty to him, whose bosom glows with the patriotic fire of '76, and who scorns to be a slave? Ye who imbibe the principles and feelings of Washington and his associates, in the days that tried men's souls; ye who are genuine republicans at heart, cannot we think, long debate, which of the two choose, slavery or death. . . .

Never I beseech of you, encourage a certain *"Christian party in politics,"* which under moral and religious pretences, is officiously and continually interfering with the religious opinions of others, and endeavoring to effect by law and other means, equally exceptionable, a systematic course of measures, evidently calculated, to lead to a union of Church and State. If a union of church and state should be effected, which may God avert, then will

◆ CHAPTER 6

Church, State,
and Democracy:
The Sunday Mail
Controversy,
1827–1831

the doctrines of the prevailing sect, become the creed of the country, to be enforced by fines, imprisonment, and doubtless death! Then will superstition and bigotry frown into silence, everything which bears the appearance of liberality; the hand of genius will be palsied, and a check to all further improvements in our country, will be the inevitable consequence. If we now permit the glorious light of liberty to be extinguished, it may never more shine to cheer a benighted world with the splendour of its rays. Was it, may we ask, for a few years only, of freedom and independence, that our fathers raised the standard of rebellion? Was it for no more than this, they braved an empire's power, endured the toil, hardships and suffering, of an unequal and bloody warfare—that they closed their unarmed ports against the navies of Britain, and bid defiance to the authorities of ancient days and the threats of parliaments and thrones? It is for you to say, O people of America. The destinies of your country, are in your own hands. They are committed to your own keeping. It is for you to say, which ye will have, liberty or slavery, knowledge or ignorance, happiness or misery. I have said, *to continue free you have but to will it.*

If we do not choose the wiser and the better part—if by our negligence or want of zeal, we suffer the liberties of our country to be subverted—if we permit a corrupted priesthood to gain ascendancy in the civil government, then shall the like direful fate of other countries, where this has been, and is still the case, be the fate of ours. The abuses which have been practiced, the hellish cruelties which have been perpetrated, and the immense amount of suffering which has been inflicted, under governments where the clergy have borne rule, cannot easily be described. Youth and beauty, age and virtue, genius and rank, were equally unable to relax the iron grasp of clerical tyranny. Even now there are regions where the infuriated demon of persecution unfurles her bloodstained banner, and demands that unnumbered victims should bleed at the foot of her unrighteous throne! The past history of the Christian Church, should be a solemn warning to us, never to permit an alliance to be formed, between the priesthood and the civil magistracy— *between Church and State powers.* . . .

Source 8 from *Christian Messenger*, vol. 4 (1830), pp. 140–141.

8. The Rev. Barton W. Stone on the Sabbath Mail Controversy, May 1830.

We are grieved to see . . . a disposition to destroy the idea of a Sabbath under any name. I should rejoice to see that day more religiously observed by all. I have disapproved the attempt to urge Congress to legislate on the subject, and have been disgusted at the zeal of the clergy in their bold attempts to have it effected; yet I have seen the opposite party run into a criminal extreme . . . . These last by their untempered zeal against stopping the mail on the sabbath, have . . . done real injury to their cause. . . . While the clergy are suspected of having designs to establish their religion by law; these are suspected as having designs to overthrow Christianity *in toto*.

Source 9 from *Christian Baptist*, June 7, 1830.

9. The Rev. Alexander Campell on the Sabbath Mail Controversy, June 1830.

HEAR THE PRIESTLY HIERARCHS!

The intolerant zeal with which some of the most aspiring sectaries urge governmental interference in behalf of the cessation of Sunday mails, has convinced me that political designs are at the bottom of the prayers of many of the petitioners. The leaders evince a spirit of resentment against those who do not coincide with their schemes . . . which illly comports with that zeal for holiness which they profess in favor of the Sabbath.

Source10: William Ellery Channing, "Remarks on Associations" from *Church and State in American History: Key Documents, Decisions, and Commentary from the Past Three Centuries*, 3rd edition. Edited by John F. Wilson and Donald Drakeman. Copyright © 2003 John F. Wilson, Donald Drakeman. Reprinted by permission of Westview Press, a member of the Perseus Books Group.

10. William Ellery Channing, "Remarks on Associations."

In truth, one of the most remarkable circumstances or features of our age is the energy with which the principle of combination, or of action by joint forces, by associated numbers, is manifesting itself. It may be said, without much exaggeration, that every thing is done now by societies. Men have learned what wonders can be accomplished in certain cases by union, and seem to think that union is competent to every thing, you can scarcely name an object for which some institution has not been formed. Would men spread one set of opinions or crush another? They make a society. Would they improve the penal code, or relieve poor debtors? They make societies. Would they encourage agriculture, or manufactures or science? They make societies.

◆ CHAPTER 6

Church, State,
and Democracy:
The Sunday Mail
Controversy,
1827–1831

Would one class encourage horse-racing, and another discourage travelling on Sunday? They form societies. We have immense institutions spreading over the country, combining hosts for particular objects. We have minute ramifications of these societies, penetrating everywhere except through the poor-house, and conveying resources from the domestic, the laborer, and even the child, to the central treasury. This principle of association is worthy the attention of the philosopher, who simply aims to understand society and its most powerful springs. To the philanthropist and the Christian it is exceedingly interesting, for it is a mighty engine, and must act either for good or for evil, to an extent which no man can foresee or comprehend.

That this mode of action has advantages and recommendations is very obvious. The principal arguments in its favor may be stated in a few words. Men, it is justly said, can do jointly what they cannot do singly. The union of minds and hands works wonders. Men grow efficient by concentrating their powers. Joint effort conquers nature, hews through mountains, rears pyramids, dikes out the ocean. Man, left to himself, living without a fellow,—if he could indeed so live,—would be one of the weakest of creatures. Associated with his kind, he gains dominion over the strongest animals, over the earth and the sea, and, by his growing knowledge, may be said to obtain a kind of property in the universe. . . .

The truth is, and we need to feel it most deeply, that our connection with society, as it is our greatest aid, so it is our greatest peril. We are in constant danger of being spoiled of our moral judgment, and of our power over ourselves; and in losing these, we lose the chief prerogatives of spiritual beings. We sink, as far as mind can sink, into the world of matter, the chief distinction of which is, that it wants self-motion, or moves only from foreign impulse. The propensity in our fellow-creatures which we have most to dread is that which, though most severely condemned by Jesus, is yet the most frequent infirmity of his followers,—we mean the propensity to rule, to tyrannize, to war with the freedom of their equals, to make themselves standards for other minds, to be lawgivers, instead of brethren and friends, to their race. Our great and most difficult duty, as social beings, is, to derive constant aid from society without taking its yoke; to open our minds to the thoughts, reasonings, and persuasions of others, and yet to hold fast the sacred right of private judgment; to receive impulses from our fellow-beings, and yet to act from our own souls; to sympathize with others, and yet to determine our own feelings; to act with others, and yet to follow our own consciences; to unite social deference and self-dominion; to join moral self-subsistence with social dependence; to respect others without losing self-respect; to love our friends and to reverence our superiors, whilst our supreme homage is given to that moral perfection which no friend and no superior has realized, and which, if faithfully pursued, will often demand separation from all around us. Such is our great work as social beings, and to perform it we should look habitually to Jesus Christ, who was distinguished by nothing more than by moral independence,—than by revisiting and overcoming the world. . . .

Associations often injure free action by a very plain and obvious operation. They accumulate power in a few hands, and this takes place just in proportion to the surface over which they spread. In a large institution, a few men rule, a few do every thing; and, if the institution happens to be directed to objects about which conflict and controversy exist, a few are able to excite in the mass strong and bitter passions, and by these to obtain an immense ascendancy. Through such an association, widely spread, yet closely connected by party feeling, a few leaders can send their voices and spirit far and wide, and, where great funds are accumulated, can league a host of instruments, and by menace and appeals to interest can silence opposition. Accordingly, we fear that in this country an influence is growing up, through widely spread societies, altogether at war with the spirit of our institutions, and which, unless jealously watched, will gradually but surely encroach on freedom of thought, of speech, an of the press. It is very striking to observe how, by such combinations, the very means of encouraging a free action of men's minds may be turned against it. We all esteem the press as the safeguard of our liberties, as the power which is to quicken intellect by giving to all minds an opportunity to act on all. Now, by means of tract societies spread over a whole community, and acting under a central body, a few individuals, perhaps not more than twenty, may determine the chief reading for a great part of the children of the community, and for a majority of the adults, and may deluge our country with worthless sectarian writings, fitted only to pervert its taste, degrade its intellect, and madden it with intolerance. Let associations devoted to any objects which excite the passions be everywhere spread and leagued together for mutual support, and nothing is easier than to establish a control over newspapers. We are persuaded that, by an artful multiplication of societies, devoted apparently to different objects, but all swayed by the same leaders, and all intended to beat against a hated party, as cruel a persecution may be carried on in a free country as in a despotism. Public opinion may be so combined, and inflamed, and brought to bear on odious individuals or opinions, that it will be as perilous to think and speak with manly freedom as if an inquisition were open before us. It is now discovered that the way to rule in this country is by an array of numbers which a prudent man will not like to face. Of consequence, all

♦ CHAPTER 6

Church, State,
and Democracy:
The Sunday Mail
Controversy,
1827–1831

associations aiming or tending to establish sway by numbers ought to be opposed. They create tyrants as effectually as standing armies. Let them be withstood from the beginning. No matter whether the opinions which they intend to put down be true or false.

We feel, however, that the danger of great associations is increased by the very fact that they are sometimes useful. They are perilous instruments. They ought to be suspected. They are a kind of irregular government created within our constitutional government. Let them be watched closely. As soon as we find them resolved or disposed to bear down a respectable man or set of men, or to force on the community measures about which wise and good men differ, let us feel that a dangerous engine is at work among us, and oppose to it our steady and stern disapprobation.

♦

Questions to Consider

Begin by looking at the evidence in favor of closing the post offices on Sundays. The Rev. Ezra Stiles Ely (Source 1) advocated "a Christian Party in Politics," but denied it would be a political party like the Democrats, National Republicans, or any other organization. What, then, did he mean by a "Christian party"? Does the fact that he tried to recruit Andrew Jackson to seek the presidency as a member of that party clarify Ely's position in your mind? What points do you think Jackson would have made on closing the post offices on Sundays? On Ely, see also Source 4, written anonymously by him. How do the two sources "fit" together?

Joseph L. Blau (1909–1986), a professor of religious studies whose specialties were Jewish history, philosophy, and the history of American liberalism and religious freedom, praised Richard M. Johnson's report as "one of the finest defenses of the principle of religious freedom in the United States."[18] Johnson began the report by stating that there was no general agreement among Americans regarding on what day the Sabbath actually fell, even noting that one denomination of Christians (the Seventh Day Adventists) actually celebrated the Sabbath on Saturday, as did Jews. Why was this point the central core of Johnson's argument? Why did Johnson maintain that he could not honor the many petitions (considerably more than the 467 claimed in Source 3) in favor of closing the post offices on Sundays?

Johnson claimed that "extensive religious combinations to effect a political object are . . . always dangerous." In his opinion, why was this so? What else did Johnson suggest would happen if Congress did act to close post offices on Sunday?

18. Joseph L. Blau, *Cornerstones of Religious Freedom in America* (Boston: Beacon Press, 1950), p. 108.

Source 3 is a summary of all the petitions sent to Congress in favor of closing post offices on Sundays. According to historian Bertram Wyatt-Brown, this was the first time that the tactic of flooding Congress with petitions had been attempted on a national scale.[19] Why did the *Account* (Source 3) claim that allowing the post offices to remain open was bad? What would be the inevitable results?

The exhaustive pamphlet *The Logic and Law of Col. Johnson's Report to the Senate* (Source 4) basically maintained that the Johnson report discriminated against Christians. How did the anonymous author (almost surely the Rev. Ezra Stiles Ely) support that claim? Ely also argued that, even though many American leaders at the time of the drafting and ratification of the Constitution were "atheistical," the Constitution itself contained no such spirit and, indeed, no power "to run over the religious feelings and usages of the nation." Why did the author consider that point important? According to the Tenth Amendment (1791), what governmental body, if any, could legitimately legislate on religion? Was, therefore, Johnson's position grounded in the 1787 Constitution or some "new" notions? How could that accusation be proven?

The excerpt of the *First Annual Report of the General Union for Promoting the Observance of the Christian Sabbath* (Source 5) was an address by the Union's corresponding secretary,

the Rev. Matthias Bruen (1793–1829), a Presbyterian clergyman who had been in poor health for years and would die within months of the meeting. In the opinion of Bruen, why was such a national association necessary? At one point in his address, Bruen stated that the goal of the Union "is not to affect the government directly, but the government through the people." What do you think he meant by that?

By 1830, Johnson was no longer in the Senate but was a member of the House of Representatives. In this position he also wrote the report of the House Committee on Post Offices and Postal Roads. How did the House report differ from the earlier Senate report of 1829? What additional points did he make? How did Rep. William McCreery counter Johnson's assertions?

Sources 7 through 10 all are writings that opposed the closing of the post offices on Sundays, and yet they all were written by Protestant clergymen. Why did these four clerics take that stand? What was Fuller's main concern? Fuller's *Tree of Liberty* (Source 7) was specifically written to counteract Ely's *Duty of Christian Freemen* (Source 1). Review Ely's sermon, comparing it to Fuller's remarks.

Stone and Campbell both were independent clergymen who, in 1832, merged their followers into a movement called the Restoration. Both opposed the efforts to close the post offices on Sunday, principally because they believed that the commandments contained in the Old Testament (including the Ten Commandments) applied only to the Jewish people and to no one else. But in Sources 8 and 9 the two preachers offered another reason for opposing

19. Bertram Wyatt-Brown, "Prelude to Abolitionism: Sabbatarian Politics and the Rise of the Second Party System," *Journal of American History*, vol. 58 (Sept. 1971), p. 329.

◆ CHAPTER 6
Church, State,
and Democracy:
The Sunday Mail
Controversy,
1827–1831

the petitions. What was it? Compare that point to Sources 1 and 7.

William Ellery Channing was one of the founders of the Unitarian movement. In the excerpt you have read, Channing never really mentioned the post office controversy. Where do you think he stood on that issue? What were the main points of his essay?

How did they relate to the post office debate?

Now you should be able to answer the central questions of this chapter: What arguments did each side use in the post office debate? What tactics did both sides employ? In your opinion, what is the historical significance of the conflict over the post office?

◆

Epilogue

In her travel account, *Domestic Manners of the Americans* (1832), British author Frances Trollope commented on the American religious climate: "My residence in the country has shewn me that a religious tyranny may be exerted very effectually without the aid of the government . . . persecution exists to a degree unknown, I believe, in our well-ordered land since the days of Cromwell."[20] Trollope had arrived in the United States in the midst of the great debate over Sabbath mails and post offices (1827–1831). What Trollope clearly failed to see, however, was that the majority of Americans thought more of their individual rights and freedoms than they did of their churches' doctrines. In spite of numerous petitions to Congress that the post offices be closed on Sundays, the signatories were but a fraction of the adult population. Johnson's reports were allowed to stand. When it came to a choice between their individual rights

and their religions' commandments, most Americans chose the former.

Petition leaders tried to get President Andrew Jackson, nominally a Presbyterian, to take up their cause, but he wisely refused. The president had been in office less than a year, and was almost overwhelmed with the Eaton Affair and Cherokee removal. He allowed his allies, principally Johnson, to speak for him. For his part, the politically ambitious Johnson was rewarded by being nominated for vice president as Martin Van Buren's running mate in 1836. But his common-law relationship with one of his slaves and, at her death, two others in succession, along with his 1829 and 1830 reports, probably ended his political career. He failed to receive his party's renomination in 1840 and after that made several unsuccessful attempts to return to national office. Johnson died in 1850.[21]

And yet, the voluntary associations had pioneered tactics that became

20. Trollope, *Domestic Manners of Americans*, pp. 107, 115. She was referring to the English civil war of the 1640s.

21. Johnson was the only vice president chosen by the U. S. Senate, because he had not received enough electoral votes.

influential and important later. National organizations (with state, county, and local chapters) and mass petition drives were adopted by many of these same organizations to advocate temperance, defend Cherokees against removal, and ultimately call for the abolition of slavery. Indeed, many of the leaders of these reform movements had learned these tactics from the Sunday mail controversy.

Nor did the effort to legislate Christian beliefs and morality die with the post office debates. In 1864, a petition was presented to President Abraham Lincoln to alter the Preamble to the Constitution to read:

> We, the people of the United States, humbly acknowledging Almighty God as the source of all authority and power in civil government, The Lord Jesus Christ as the Governor among the Nations, and His revealed will as of supreme authority, in order to constitute a Christian government . . . do ordain and establish this Constitution for the United States of America.[22]

Delegates from the National Reform Association were received cordially and tactfully, but the petition went nowhere. In that same year, however, Lincoln did not oppose putting the phrase "In God We Trust" on United States coins.

In 1885, the Sabbath Question resurfaced, with similar results. In 1892, however, in his opinion in *Church of the Holy Trinity v. United States* (143 U.S. 457), Supreme Court Justice David J. Brewer wrote that "America is a Christian nation" and spent almost half of his text demonstrating the United States' Christian identity. Then, in 1954, Congress changed the Pledge of Allegiance by adding the two words "under God."

In the meantime, states had been pretty much free to do as they wished about religion. The Congregational Church was the established denomination in Massachusetts and Connecticut until the 1830s; five states maintained taxes supporting the clergy; twelve continued religious tests for holding office; prayer was sanctioned in public schools; sales of contraceptives were outlawed in a few states; and "blue laws" remained in force.

In 1940, however, in the Supreme Court case *Cantwell v. Connecticut* (310 U. S. 296), the Court ruled that the First and Fourteenth Amendments applied to the states as well as to the federal government. Almost immediately a veritable flood of cases began to come forward, often striking down many of these state laws. At this point, as in 1829–1830, many concerned Christians arose, believing that the federal government was discriminating against them. The debate continues.

Meanwhile, in 1912, Congress finally repealed regulations requiring post offices to be open on Sundays. Instead of religious petitioners (although there were, again, many of them), however, the victory should be credited to the postal workers' union.

22. From *American Gospel* by Jon Meacham, Copyright © 2006 by Jon Meacham.

Land, Growth, and Justice: The Removal of the Cherokees

◆

The Problem

In the spring of 1838, General Winfield Scott and several units of the U.S. Army (including artillery regiments) were deployed to the Southeast to collect Native Americans known as Cherokees[1] and remove them to lands west of the Mississippi River. Employing bilingual Cherokees to serve as interpreters at $2.50 per day, Scott constructed eleven makeshift stockades and on May 23 began rounding up Native Americans and herding them into these temporary prisons. According to John G. Burnett, a soldier who participated in the removal,

> Men working in the fields were arrested and driven to the stockades. Women were dragged from their homes by soldiers whose language they could not understand. Children were often separated from their parents and driven into the stockades with the sky for a blanket

and the earth for a pillow. And often the old and infirm were prodded with bayonets to hasten them to the stockades.[2]

Just behind the soldiers came whites, eager to claim homesteads, search for gold, or pick over the belongings that the Cherokees did not have time to carry away.

On August 23, 1838, the first of thirteen parties of Cherokees began their forced march to the West, arriving in what had been designated as Indian Territory (later Oklahoma) on January 17, 1839. With some traveling by boat while others journeyed overland, a total of approximately thirteen thousand Cherokees participated in what became known as the Trail of Tears. (See Map 1.) It has been estimated that over four thousand died in the squalid stockades or along the way.[3] But recent

1. The Cherokees referred to themselves as Ani'Yun'wiya ("principal people"). The origin of the term *Cherokee* is unknown, but the name almost certainly was given to them by Native American neighbors. See Russell Thornton, *The Cherokees: A Population History* (Lincoln: University of Nebraska Press, 1990), pp. 7–8.

2. See John G. Burnett, "The Cherokee Removal Through the Eyes of a Private Soldier," *Journal of Cherokee Studies* 3 (1978): 180–185.
3. The official U.S. Army count of those removed to Indian Territory totaled 13,149, of whom 11,504 actually arrived in the West. Based on the tribal census of 1835, at least 2,000 died in the stockades.

research has determined that the figure may have been higher than that, in part because of shoddy record keeping and in part because numerous Cherokees died in an epidemic almost immediately on reaching their destination. In addition, conflict broke out between new arrivals and those Cherokees (around six thousand) who had earlier moved. And, once in the West, those who opposed removal took out their vengeance on the leaders of the Cherokee removal faction. Cherokee advocates of removal (including leaders Major Ridge, John Ridge, Elias Boudinot, and Thomas Watie) were murdered.[4]

The forced removal of the Cherokees marked the end of a debate that was older than the United States itself. As white populations mushroomed and settlements moved ever westward, the question of how to deal with Native Americans came up again and again, especially when Native American peoples refused to sell or give their lands to whites by treaty.

In 1829, Andrew Jackson became president. For at least ten years it was well known that he believed that Native Americans had no legitimate titles to their lands and should be removed from all of their lands east of the Mississippi River in order to make way for

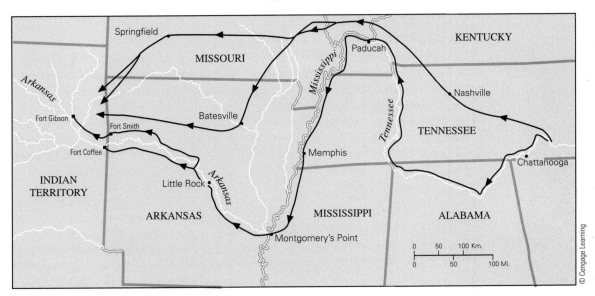

Map 1. The Trail of Tears, 1838–1839.
Adapted from Grace Steele Woodward, *The Cherokees* (Norman: University of Oklahoma Press, 1963), pp. 206–207. Copyright © 1963 by the University of Oklahoma Press, Norman, Publishing Division of the University of Oklahoma. Reprinted by permission.

4. See Russell Thornton, "The Demography of the Trail of Tears Period: A New Estimate of Cherokee Population Losses," in William L. Anderson, ed., *Cherokee Removal: Before and After* (Athens, Ga.: University of Georgia Press, 1991), pp. 75–95.

white settlement. And although he was not known as an accomplished speaker or writer (his spelling was nearly as poor as that of George Washington), in his First Annual Message to Congress (Source 1 in the Evidence section), Jackson almost surely was one of the most articulate voices in favor of removal.[5]

The major difficulty, however, involved the Cherokee lands in the state of Georgia, roughly five million acres. In 1802, the United States government and the state of Georgia had reached an agreement whereby the federal government had promised to "extinguish, for the use of Georgia, as early as the same can be peaceably obtained upon reasonable terms . . . the Indian titles to all lands lying within the limits of the state". The state of Georgia was becoming more insistent that the federal government honor its 1802 promise. At the same time, having already ceded portions of their lands in Georgia in treaties of 1785, 1791, 1794, 1798, 1817, and 1819, the Cherokee National Council reached "a decisive and unalterable conclusion not to cede away any more lands."[6]

5. For Jackson's early opinions, see Joseph McMinn to Secretary of War William Crawford, October 25, 1816, in *American State Papers: Indian Affairs* (Washington, DC: Gales and Seaton, 1834), vol. 2, p. 115.
6. For the 1802 agreement, see *American State Papers: Public Lands* (Washington: Gales and Seaton, 1834), vol. 1, p. 114. For the Cherokee decision, see Joseph McMinn to Secretary of War John C. Calhoun, June 24, 1823, in W. Edwin Hemphill, ed., *The Papers of John C. Calhoun* (Columbia, SC: Univ. of South Carolina Press, 1975), vol. 8, pp. 129–130; Cherokee National Council to Cherokee National Committee, October 25, 1823, in *American State Papers: Indian Affairs*, vol. 2, pp. 470–471; and Cherokee Delegation to the President of the United States, January 19, 1824, in *ibid.*, vol. 2, p. 473.

The hardening of attitudes of both white Georgians and Cherokees presented the federal government with a serious dilemma. Although President Jackson was not the only white person to argue in favor of removal, whites both in and out of the government advocated several alternatives to removal, and these alternatives were debated—sometimes fiercely—both in Congress and among the white population at large.

Of course, the Cherokees themselves were deeply divided as to what response they should make if the federal government ultimately decided to remove them. Here again several possible alternatives were offered and, as with whites, they were debated with considerable ferocity.

In this chapter, you will be analyzing the two debates, the first among whites, who in the end would determine the fate of the Cherokees, and the second, among the Cherokees as to how they would respond to the whites' final decision. What alternatives did whites consider? What were the strengths and weaknesses of each alternative? Then, what alternatives did the Cherokees consider? What were the strengths and weaknesses of each position?

For both whites and Cherokees, significant segments of both populations did not view removal as inevitable. Many years later, people look back on a particular decision (to fire on Fort Sumter, for instance, or to support the Civil Rights Movement of the twentieth century) as inevitable. Most contemporaries, however, did not see it that way. As a historian, you should avoid the concept of "inevitability" as well.

Background

The origins of the Cherokees are clouded in mystery. Linguistically related to the Iroquois of New England and northern New York, it is thought that the Cherokees migrated south into present-day Georgia, Tennessee (itself a derivation of the name of a Cherokee town, Tanasi), South Carolina, and North Carolina and settled the area somewhere between the years 600 and 1000, centuries before the first regular contact with white people in the late 1600s. Spread across much of the Southeast, the Cherokees were divided into three main groups: the Lower Towns, along the upper Savannah River in South Carolina; the Middle Towns, along the Little Tennessee River and its tributaries in western North Carolina; and the Overhill Towns, in eastern Tennessee and extreme western North Carolina. (See Map 2.)

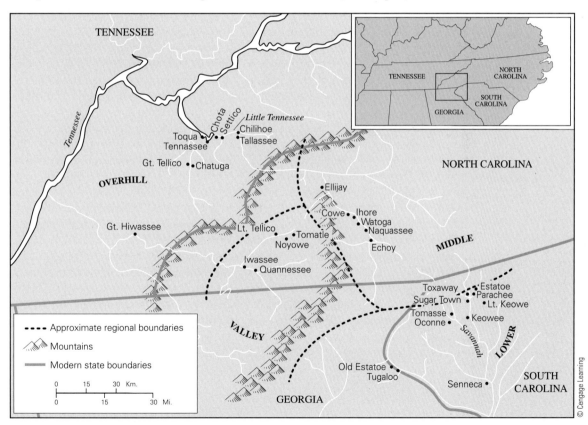

Map 2. Cherokee Settlements, 1775.
From Duane H. King, ed., *The Cherokee Nation: A Troubled History* (Knoxville: University of Tennessee Press, 1979), p. 50. Reprinted by permission.

Sometime before their regular contact with Europeans, the Cherokees became sedentary. Women performed most of the farm duties, raising corn and beans, whereas men hunted deer and turkey and caught fish to complete their diet. The Cherokees built towns organized around extended families. Society was *matrilineal*, meaning that property and position passed from generation to generation through the mother's side of the family. Each town theoretically was autonomous, and there were no leaders (or chiefs, in European parlance) who ruled over all the towns. Local leaders led by persuasion and example, and all adults, including women, could speak in town councils. Indeed, Cherokee governing practices were considerably more democratic and consensual than the Europeans' hierarchical ways.

Initial contacts with Europeans were devastating. Europeans brought with them measles and smallpox, against which Native Americans were not immune. Also, Cherokees were attracted to European goods such as fabrics, metal hoes and hatchets, firearms, and (tragically) alcohol. In order to acquire these goods, Cherokees traded deerskins for them. By the early 1700s, Cherokees were killing an average of fifty thousand deer each year to secure their hides for barter, and estimates are that by 1735 over one million deer had been killed, almost certainly depleting the herds. Gradually, the Cherokees were losing their self-sufficiency and becoming increasingly dependent on European goods.

With European colonization and expansion in North America, the Cherokees inevitably became swept up into European peoples' wars. Initially siding with the British against the French, the Cherokees turned against the British when the colonial governor of South Carolina called thirty-two chieftains to a conference and then killed twenty-nine of them. The British retaliated against a Cherokee outburst by destroying the Lower Towns, killing over one hundred Cherokee warriors, and driving the survivors into the mountains. In the American Revolution, the Cherokees, hoping to stem white western expansion, again sided with the British. American Patriots destroyed over fifty Cherokee towns, scalping men and women indiscriminately.

After the American Revolution, the new U.S. government pursued a policy of attempting to "civilize" the Cherokees. For their part, some Cherokee leaders recognized that less land and fewer deer demanded major changes in their way of life, and they accepted "civilization." As Chief Eskaqua explained to President Washington, "Game is going fast away from us. We must plant corn and raise cattle."[7] Aided by government Indian agent Return J. Meigs (who lived with the Cherokees from 1801 to 1823) and a number of missionaries (sent by the American Board of Commissioners for Foreign Missions), several Cherokees were able to embrace many of the "white man's ways." Many men gave up hunting and took over agriculture from women. Plows, spinning wheels, and looms were introduced, and many

7. Chief Eskaqua to Washington, 1792, quoted in William G. McLoughlin, *Cherokee Renascence in the New Republic* (Princeton: Princeton Univ. Press, 1986), p. 3.

Cherokee women took up the making of cloth and clothing. As it did with white settlers, land ownership and agriculture produced a class system. By 1824, the most affluent Cherokees lived in stately homes and owned 1,277 African American slaves. For some, therefore, the "civilization" process led to a vastly improved standard of living.

Mission boarding schools, supported by white contributions, dotted the landscape. For some of the most promising young boys, the American Board of Commissioners for Foreign Missions founded a school in Cornwall, Connecticut, where two of the Cherokee Nation's most prominent future leaders, John Ridge and Elias Boudinot, were educated.[8] At the same time, a Native American man, Sequoyah, began devising a Cherokee alphabet (he called it a syllabary) of eighty-five phonetic symbols that allowed Cherokees to write what previously had been their oral language. In 1828, the first edition of the bilingual newspaper the *Cherokee Phoenix and Indians' Advocate* appeared, edited by Elias Boudinot.

Governmental and political forms also were modeled after Anglo-European institutions. A Native American police force was instituted in 1808, and in the following year a detailed census was taken. In 1827, a formal constitution was adopted, modeled on the United States Constitution, setting up a representative government and courts for the Cherokee Nation. Women, who were more nearly equal to men in traditional Cherokee society, saw their position deteriorate, as they were prohibited from voting or serving as representatives by the new constitution. In many ways, then, Cherokees remade their economy, society, culture, and government.

Yet, in the eyes of some whites, the Cherokees' progress toward "civilization" was frustratingly slow. Several Cherokees, perhaps a majority, resisted the new ways, refused to adopt Anglo-European gender roles, ignored the mission schools, and opposed efforts to teach them the English language or convert them to Christianity. Moreover, those who interacted with whites realized that no matter how "civilized" they had become, they were still looked down upon, often abused, and generally referred to as "savages." Indeed, the school in Connecticut was forced to close its doors when two of its students (John Ridge and Elias Boudinot) planned to marry two local white girls, as this news very nearly caused a riot. Angered, John Ridge wrote:

> If an Indian is educated in the sciences, has a good knowledge of the classics, astronomy, mathematics, moral and natural philosophy, and his conduct [is] equally modest and polite, yet he is an Indian, and the most stupid and

8. The American Board of Commissioners for Foreign Missions was chartered in 1812. The purpose of the school was to train Native Americans to become Christian missionaries. Elias Boudinot's Cherokee name was (anglicized) Buck Watie. When traveling to the school in Cornwall, he stayed with Elias Boudinot (1740–1821), a former member of the Continental Congress, Director of the United States Mint (1795–1805), and a sponsor of the Board School for Indians in Cornwall. The young student then took Boudinot's name.

illiterate white man will disdain and triumph over this worthy individual.[9]

For those who had lost confidence in the Cherokees' abilities to embrace "white men's civilization," a powerful alternative was removal. Even Indian agent Return J. Meigs had given up hope and advocated it, even though he remained with the Cherokees for the rest of his life.[10]

The Louisiana Purchase (1803) acquired roughly 500 million acres, some of which theoretically could be used for the relocation of the eastern Native Americans. The emergence of harsher white attitudes about Native Americans undoubtedly increased public opinion in favor of removal. The major question, therefore, was how to induce Cherokees and other Native American peoples to cede their lands and accept relocation. Since the founding of the nation, it was generally agreed that no Native American lands could be acquired except by treaty. General Andrew Jackson, however, believed that no such land agreements were necessary and therefore the United States could take these lands by eminent domain, a notion that in 1818 was rejected by the House Committee on Public Lands. But when President James Monroe stated that "there is no obligation on the United States to remove the Indians by force," a showdown had become very nearly unavoidable. In an effort to avoid violence, in 1818, a trickle of Cherokees began to migrate to lands west of the Mississippi River.[11]

The vast majority of Cherokees, however, refused to move. They had built farms, sawmills, tanneries, ferries, stores, and towns. The Treaty of Hopewell (1785) had promised that they would be able to hold onto their lands "forever." In addition, Christian missionaries who lived among the Cherokees strengthened their resolve to resist removal, believing that the Cherokees were making great strides at becoming "civilized" right where they were. Yet one Cherokee chieftain's 1775 statement turned out to be prophetic: "Indian Nations before the Whites are like balls of snow before the sun."[12]

The conclusion of the War of 1812 touched off a tremendous white population boom in the West, thereby increasing the difficulty of Native Americans holding onto their lands. From 1810 to 1830, the white population of the area that comprised the states of Georgia, Tennessee, Mississippi, and Alabama more than tripled, and the white population of Georgia alone more than doubled. Ignoring treaty lines, whites

---

9. *Christian Herald*, December 20, 1823, quoted in Thurman Wilkins, *Cherokee Tragedy: The Story of the Ridge Family and of the Decimation of a People* (New York: Macmillan, 1970), p. 145.
10. Meigs to Secretary of War Henry Dearborn, June 11, 1808, quoted in Theda Perdue and Michael D. Green, *The Cherokee Nation and the Trail of Tears* (New York: Viking Books, 2007), p. 38.
11. *Ibid.*, p. 92. For Jackson's opinion, see Jackson to Monroe, March 4, 1817, in *ibid.*, p. 50. For Monroe's view, see Wilkins, *Cherokee Tragedy*, p. 155. The early migrants initially moved to the Arkansas Territory but were forced to relocate to the Indian Territory (Oklahoma) in 1836 when Arkansas became a state. Those who migrated prior to the Trail of Tears became known as the Old Settlers.
12. J. G. M. Ramsey, *Annals of Tennessee* (Charleston, S.C.: Walker and James, 1853), pp. 117–118.

began drifting into Cherokee country. Cherokees retaliated by attacking and burning the buildings and crops of the white settlers; federal troops had to be dispatched to restore order. In the past, the federal government had been able to restore order by negotiating treaties to obtain lands that whites had overrun. But the decision by Cherokee leaders not to give up any more lands heightened an already tense situation. For its part, Georgia increased its demands that the federal government honor its 1802 agreement and remove the Cherokees immediately.

The election of Andrew Jackson in 1828 was a signal to Georgians that they now could move with impunity. In December 1828, over three months before Jackson's inauguration, the Georgia legislature passed an act declaring that as of June 1, 1830, all Cherokee territory would be subject to Georgia laws, and Cherokee laws (including their constitution) would be null and void. At roughly the same time, the Georgia legislature also made provisions for a lottery to be used to distribute Cherokee lands to whites. The discovery of gold in Cherokee territory touched off another land rush of around four thousand whites, accompanied by predictable violence.[13]

Against almost insurmountable odds, the Cherokees continued to resist, supported by a number of white missionaries

who had built churches and schools throughout the territory. Here again the American Board of Commissioners for Foreign Missions was at the center of missionary activity as well as efforts to strengthen Cherokee resolve to stand firm against the Georgia state government and white encroachment. As a result, Georgia passed an act requiring all whites living in Cherokee territory to secure licenses, an obvious attempt to expel the missionaries. When the missionaries refused to apply for the required licenses, eleven of them were arrested and sentenced to terms of four years in the Milledgeville state penitentiary. When the Georgia governor offered executive clemency to all those who would leave voluntarily, only two (Samuel Worcester and Elizur Butler) refused. Worcester appealed to the United State Supreme Court, and in *Worcester v. Georgia* Chief Justice John Marshall declared that the Cherokee territory was a distinct, independent political community in which Georgia laws did not apply. President Jackson ignored Marshall's decision, and Worcester served out his term of four years, then moved to the West to establish a mission among the Cherokees. Before his death in 1859, he had translated the Bible into the Cherokee language.[14]

13. Some of those who made a great deal of money from the Georgia gold rush included the South Carolina political leader John C. Calhoun, his son-in-law Thomas G. Clemson (who used some of the profits to found Clemson College in South Carolina), and future governor of New York and Democratic presidential candidate Samuel J. Tilden.

14. Both Worcester and Butler were American Board missionaries. For their difficulties, see Jack Frederick Kilpatrick and Anna Gritts Kilpatrick, *New Echota Letters: Contributions of Samuel A. Worcester to the Cherokee Phoenix* (Dallas: Southern Methodist University Press, 1968), p. 113. Worcester, one of the American Board's original commissioners, corresponded with the Rev. Ezra Stiles Ely, another officer of the American Board. Worcester to Ely, March 10, 1830, in *ibid.*, pp. 74–77. For Ely, see Chapter 6.

By the time Worcester was released from prison, however, the conflict was almost over. In his First Annual Message to Congress of December 8, 1829 (see Source 1), President Jackson made his case for the "voluntary" removal of all Native Americans east of the Mississippi River. Responding to the president's message in February 1830, the House of Representatives took up the Indian Removal Bill. The bill, however, reignited a furious debate both in Congress and among the general public. Hundreds of petitions were sent to Congress, the majority from religious groups and benevolent societies opposed to removal. Many congressional opponents of the bill were genuinely concerned about the welfare of Native Americans, but at least an equal number were Jackson's political opponents, seeking to embarrass the president. On April 23, 1830, the Senate approved the Indian Removal Bill by a vote of 28–19, the House following suit on May 24 by the close margin of 102–97. Jackson signed the bill on May 28, 1830.[15] The act empowered the president to trade land in the West for lands on which Native Americans east of the Mississippi then resided, to pay Native Americans for improvements they had made to lands they were giving up, to assist and protect Native Americans during their migration, and to superintend and care for them once they had reached their destinations.

The Removal Act, however, only *authorized* removal, and longstanding United States policy still required that all land cessions or sales of Native American lands must be completed by treaty. Therefore, while Cherokees debated over how to respond to the Removal Act, the federal government began to search for pliable Cherokee leaders who would approve a removal treaty.

By 1835, the Ridge-Watie-Boudinot extended family provided the core of a small minority of Cherokees that originally had vehemently opposed relocation but had come to see it as the only realistic alternative. President Jackson then named John F. Schermerhorn, a retired Dutch Reformed minister, to negotiate a treaty. The Treaty of New Echota finally was approved, in late 1835, by a "council" of twenty and a committee of eighty-six Cherokees. Neither group, however, had the authority to negotiate such an agreement and had no legal standing with the Cherokees' National Council.[16]

Meanwhile, the state of Georgia instituted its lottery. In late 1832, surveying had begun and some lottery winners began to move into Cherokee territory

---

15. For the text of the Removal Act, see Wilcomb E. Washburn, ed. *The American Indian and the United States: A Documentary History* (New York: Random House, 1973), Vol. III, pp. 2169–2171.

16. For biographies of the principal "Treaty Party" leaders, see Edward Everett Dale and Gaston Litton, eds., *Cherokee Cavaliers: Forty Years of Cherokee History As Told in the Correspondence of the Ridge-Watie-Boudinot Family* (Norman: Univ. of Oklahoma Press, 1939). Most of the Treaty Party leaders were well-educated Cherokees, had numerous white ancestors, and in some cases had married white women. For his part, Schermerhorn was nicknamed the "Devil's Horn" by Cherokees because of his reputation as a "notorious womanizer." Perdue and Green, *Cherokee Nation*, p. 111.

to claim their prizes, resulting in more violence. In the same month that the Treaty of New Echota was approved by the "Treaty Party," the Georgia legislature authorized all lottery winners to take possession of their lands by November 1836, an obvious ploy to induce Cherokees to leave the state.

Outraged by the actions of both the "Treaty Party" (as they had been derisively labeled) and the state of Georgia, Principal Chief John Ross and the National Council circulated a petition to the United States Congress that was purportedly signed by 15,665 Cherokees. The petition maintained that the Treaty of New Echota was invalid because it never had been approved by the National Council, and begged that Congress would reverse its position on removal and protect the Cherokees from the incursions of white Georgians. At last, on April 9, 1838, the United States Senate, which earlier had ratified the Treaty of New Echota by a single vote, voted to table the petition, and General Winfield Scott was given his orders.

About eleven hundred Cherokees remained in North Carolina, principally because these Cherokees convinced a white merchant named William Holland Thomas to use money from the Treaty of New Echota to purchase thousands of acres in western North Carolina on which these Cherokees settled (he kept the land title in his own name). In 1837, the North Carolina General Assembly acknowledged the Cherokees' right to remain in North Carolina. The fact that the land Thomas purchased for the Cherokees was land that virtually no one else wanted probably was a factor in the legislature's decision. In addition to the eleven hundred Cherokees who were allowed to stay in North Carolina, an additional three hundred remained scattered throughout Georgia, Alabama, and Tennessee. Some had hidden themselves from Scott's soldiers; others were related by blood and marriage to their white neighbors.

Eyewitness accounts of the Trail of Tears, by both Native Americans and U.S. Army escorts, make for grim reading. As many as twenty-five hundred or more died in the makeshift stockades prior to the journey. And of the 13,149 (cited by army records) who began the trip, only 11,504 arrived in Indian Territory. In addition, several hundred died soon after their arrival, by either disease or violence between the new arrivals and earlier migrants or between the "accommodationists" and the last-ditch resisters.[17]

What alternatives did whites consider? What were the strengths and weaknesses of each alternative? For the Cherokees, answer the same two questions. Note that some Cherokees actually favored relocation. What were their reasons for doing so?

17. Burnett, "The Cherokee Removal Through the Eyes of a Private Soldier," pp. 180–185; Vicki Rozema, ed., *Voices from the Trail of Tears* (Winston-Salem, N. C.: John F. Blair, 2003); and Theda Perdue and Michael D. Green, eds., *The Cherokee Removal: A Brief History with Documents* (Boston: Bedford St. Martin's, 2005).

✦

The Method

As you examine and analyze the principal arguments both in favor of and opposed to Cherokee removal, almost immediately you will see that some of the speakers and writers chose to *rephrase* the question. For example, instead of listing the reasons the Cherokees should be removed, President Jackson preferred to discuss *why the Cherokees could not remain where they were* (Source 1). By carefully reading his answers (there were several) to that question, you will be able to infer what his answers would have been to the question of *why the Cherokees ought to be removed*.

The same holds true for speakers and writers opposed to Cherokee removal. In some cases, they offered what they thought were alternatives that would have been superior to that of removal. As with Jackson's message, you will have to infer from what opponents said or wrote what they *would have* said or written regarding why the Cherokees ought *not to have been removed*.

Similarly to Jackson, many other speakers and writers offered more than one answer to the question. Therefore, as you examine and analyze the evidence, be sure to take notes carefully.

The second central question in this chapter regards the strengths and weaknesses of the principal points both in favor of and opposed to Cherokee removal. This is not nearly so easy as it may first appear. For one thing, you may not be able to uncover the real reasons a speaker or writer took a particular position. For example, almost no one in favor of removal said that Cherokees should be removed because whites wanted their lands. Even Georgia Governor Wilson Lumpkin (Source 5), who allowed whites to begin settling on Cherokee lands before any treaty was negotiated and who wanted to speed up the process so that he would still be in office when the issue was finally settled, was not willing to be so obvious. Similarly, no opponent of removal would have been crass enough to say that the opponent's true motive was to embarrass President Jackson politically. Without considerably more information than is available here, you will have to take the speaker's or writer's comments at face value. Jackson, for example, always claimed that removal was the most humane policy for the Cherokees themselves. Is there any evidence to the contrary?

Moreover, as you assess the strengths and weaknesses of each speaker's or writer's position, you will almost inevitably be drawn into the interesting but highly dangerous process of evaluating the alternatives to removal. Typically, historians concern themselves with what *actually did* happen rather than what *might have* happened. To be sure, some of the opponents of removal did advocate alternatives to removal, and in some cases you may have to deal with such alternatives as you determine the strengths and weaknesses of a particular position. If you plan to do this, however, use the actual facts at your disposal to assess a particular alternative. Do not *create* facts to fit your hypothesis—perhaps the worst charge that can be made against a historian. Also remember that you are dealing with people from the early 1800s, *not* the twenty-first century. Avoid putting ideas and thought processes contemporary to you into their minds.

The process of removing Cherokees from the East took decades. During that period, several principal figures in this drama actually changed their minds regarding removal. For example, several members of the Treaty party at first had vehemently opposed relocation, but in the end came to embrace it. Is there any clue in the evidence as to why they might have done so? What arguments did they use?

Let us offer a final note of caution. As you examine each piece of evidence, avoid the temptation to "take sides" in the debate or to make the historical individuals into one-dimensional heroes or villains. Analyze the logic of each of the arguments, even when you find the conclusions of a speaker or writer to be reprehensible.

Beneath the surface of all the arguments is the *image* of Native Americans, both in the eyes of European Americans and in those of Native Americans. What underlying assumptions regarding Cherokees can you detect in both the white and Cherokee evidence?

Now proceed to the Evidence section of the chapter. Take notes as you read each selection. Once again, a chart may prove helpful.

◆

The Evidence

WHITE SOURCES

Source 1 from James D. Richardson, *A Compilation of the Messages and Papers of the Presidents* (New York: Bureau of National Literature, 1897), vol. III, pp. 1019–1022.

1. Excerpt from President Andrew Jackson's First Annual Message to Congress, December 8, 1829.[18]

The condition and ulterior destiny of the Indian Tribes within the limits of some of our States, have become objects of much interest and importance. It has long been the policy of Government to introduce among them the arts of civilization, in the hope of gradually reclaiming them from a wandering life.

---

18. From George Washington to Woodrow Wilson, no president of the United States appeared in person before Congress. All communications between the president and Congress were conducted in writing.

[187]

This policy has, however, been coupled with another, wholly incompatible with its success. Professing a desire to civilize and settle them, we have, at the same time, lost no opportunity to purchase their lands, and thrust them further into the wilderness. By this means they have not only been kept in a wandering state, but been led to look upon us as unjust and indifferent to their fate. Thus, though lavish in its expenditures upon the subject, Government has constantly defeated its own policy; and the Indians, in general, receding further and further to the West, have retained their savage habits. A portion, however, of the Southern tribes, having mingled much with the whites, and made some progress in the arts of civilized life, have lately attempted to erect an independent government, within the limits of Georgia and Alabama. These States, claiming to be the only Sovereigns within their territories, extended their laws over the Indians; which induced the latter to call upon the United States for protection. . . .

Actuated by this view of the subject, I informed the Indians inhabiting parts of Georgia and Alabama, that their attempt to establish an independent government would not be countenanced by the Executive of the United States; and advised them to emigrate beyond the Mississippi, or submit to the laws of those States.

Our conduct towards these people is deeply interesting to our national character. Their present condition, contrasted with what they once were, makes a most powerful appeal to our sympathies. Our ancestors found them the uncontrolled possessors of these vast regions. By persuasion and force, they have been made to retire from river to river, and from mountain to mountain; until some of the tribes have become extinct, and others have left but remnants, to preserve, for a while, their once terrible names. Surrounded by the whites, with their arts of civilization, which, by destroying the resources of the savage, doom him to weakness and decay; the fate of the Mohegan, the Narragansett, and the Delaware, is fast overtaking the Choctaw, the Cherokee, and the Creek. That this fate surely awaits them, if they remain within the limits of the States, does not admit of a doubt. Humanity and national honor demand that every effort should be made to avert so great a calamity. It is too late to inquire whether it was just in the United States to include them and their territory within the bounds of new States whose limits they could control. That step cannot be retraced. A State cannot be dismembered by Congress, or restricted in the exercise of her constitutional power. But the people of those States, and of every State, actuated by feelings of justice and a regard for our national honor, submit to you the interesting question, whether something cannot be done, consistently with the rights of the States, to preserve this much injured race?

As a means of effecting this end, I suggest, for your consideration, the propriety of setting apart an ample district West of the Mississippi, and without the limits of any State or Territory, now formed, to be guarantied to the Indian tribes, as long as they shall occupy it: each tribe having a distinct control over the portion designated for its use. There they may be secured in the enjoyment of governments of their own choice, subject to no other control from the United States than such as may be necessary to preserve peace on the frontier, and between the several tribes. There the benevolent may endeavor to teach them the arts of civilization; and, by promoting union and harmony among them, to raise up an interesting commonwealth, destined to perpetuate the race, and to attest the humanity and justice of this Government.

This emigration should be voluntary: for it would be as cruel as unjust to compel the aborigines to abandon the graves of their fathers, and seek a home in a distant land.[19] But they should be distinctly informed that, if they remain within the limits of the States, they must be subject to their laws. In return for their obedience, as individuals, they will, without doubt, be protected in the enjoyment of those possessions which they have improved by their industry. But it seems to me visionary to suppose, that, in this state of things, claims can be allowed on tracts of country on which they have neither dwelt nor made improvements, merely because they have seen them from the mountain, or passed them in the chace [sic]. Submitting to the laws of the States, and receiving, like other citizens, protection in their persons and property, they will, ere long, become merged in the mass of our population.

Source 2 from Andrew A. Lipscomb and Albert Ellergy Bergh, eds., *The Writings of Thomas Jefferson* (Washington, D.C.: Thomas Jefferson Memorial Association, 1903), vol. XVI, pp. 450–454.

2. President Thomas Jefferson to Captain Hendrick, the Delawares, Mohicans, and Munries, December 21, 1808.

The picture which you have drawn, my son, of the increase of our numbers and the decrease of yours is just, the causes are very plain, and the remedy depends on yourselves alone. You have lived by hunting the deer and buffalo— all these have been driven westward; you have sold out on the seaboard and moved westwardly in pursuit of them. As they became scarce there, your

19. Jackson believed, perhaps naively, that a majority of Cherokees would move to the West voluntarily. See his Third Annual Message to Congress, December 6, 1831, in Richardson, *Messages and Papers of the Presidents*, vol. III, p. 1117.

food has failed you; you have been a part of every year without food, except the roots and other unwholesome things you could find in the forest. Scanty and unwholesome food produce diseases and death among your children, and hence you have raised few and your numbers have decreased. Frequent wars, too, and the abuse of spirituous liquors, have assisted in lessening your numbers. The whites, on the other hand, are in the habit of cultivating the earth, of raising stocks of cattle, hogs, and other domestic animals, in much greater numbers than they could kill of deer and buffalo. Having always a plenty of food and clothing they raise [an] abundance of children, they double their numbers every twenty years, the new swarms are continually advancing upon the country like flocks of pigeons, and so they will continue to do. Now, my children, if we wanted to diminish our numbers, we would give up the culture of the earth, pursue the deer and buffalo, and be always at war; this would soon reduce us to be as few as you are, and if you wish to increase your numbers you must give up the deer and buffalo, live in peace and cultivate the earth. You see then, my children, that it depends on yourselves alone to become a numerous and great people. Let me entreat you, therefore, on the lands now given you to begin to give every man a farm; let him enclose it, cultivate it, build a warm house on it, and when he dies, let it belong to his wife and children after him. Nothing is so easy as to learn to cultivate the earth; all your women understand it, and to make it easier, we are always ready to teach you how to make ploughs, hoes, and necessary utensils. If the men will take the labor of the earth from the women they will learn to spin and weave and to clothe their families. In this way you will also raise many children, you will double your numbers every twenty years, and soon fill the land your friends have given you, and your children will never be tempted to sell the spot on which they have been born, raised, have labored and called their own. When once you have property, you will want laws and magistrates to protect your property and persons, and to punish those among you who commit crimes. You will find that our laws are good for this purpose; you will wish to live under them, you will unite yourselves with us, join in our Great Councils and form one people with us, and we shall all be Americans; you will mix with us by marriage, your blood will run in our veins, and will spread with us over this great island. Instead, then, my children, of the gloomy prospect you have drawn of your total disappearance from the face of the earth, which is true, if you continue to hunt the deer and buffalo and go to war, you see what a brilliant aspect is offered to your future history, if you give up war and hunting. Adopt the culture of the earth and raise domestic animals; you see how from a small family you may become a great nation by adopting the course which from the small beginning you describe has made us a great nation.

Source 3 from Theda Perdue and Michael D. Green, eds., *The Cherokee Removal: A Brief History with Documents* (Boston: Bedford Books, 1995), pp. 98–102.

3. Excerpt from William Penn (pseudonym for Jeremiah Evarts of the American Board of Commissioners for Foreign Missions), "A Brief View of the Present Relations Between the Government and People of the United States and the Indians Within Our National Limits," November 1829.

The positions here recited are deemed to be incontrovertible. It follows, therefore,

That the removal of any nation of Indians from their country by force would be an instance of gross and cruel oppression:

That all attempts to accomplish this removal of the Indians by bribery or fraud, by intimidation and threats, by withholding from them a knowledge of the strength of their cause, by practising upon their ignorance, and their fears, or by vexatious opportunities, interpreted by them to mean nearly the same thing as a command;—all such attempts are acts of oppression, and therefore entirely unjustifiable:

That the United States are firmly bound by treaty to protect the Indians from force and encroachments on the part of a State; and a refusal thus to protect them would be equally an act of bad faith as a refusal to protect them against individuals: and

That the Cherokees have therefore the guaranty of the United States, solemnly and repeatedly given, as a security against encroachments from Georgia and the neighboring States. By virtue of this guaranty the Cherokees may rightfully demand, that the United States shall keep all intruders at a distance, from whatever quarter, or in whatever character, they may come. Thus secured and defended in the possession of their country, the Cherokees have a perfect right to retain that possession as long as they please. Such a retention of their country is no just cause of complaint or offence to any State, or to any individual. It is merely an exercise of natural rights, which rights have been not only acknowledged but repeatedly and solemnly confirmed by the United States.

Although these principles are clear and incontrovertible, yet many persons feel an embarrassment from considering the Cherokees as *living in the State of Georgia.* All this embarrassment may be removed at once by bearing in mind, that the Cherokee country is not in Georgia. . . .

[Here Penn argued that the Cherokees owned their land by treaty with the U.S. government, that in 1825 the state of Georgia made a treaty with the Creek Nation to acquire their land, and hence would have to do so with the Cherokees as well.]

If the separate existence of the Indian tribes *were* an inconvenience to their neighbours, this would be but a slender reason for breaking down all the barriers of justice and good faith. Many a rich man has thought it very inconvenient, that he could not add the farm of a poor neighbour to his possessions. Many a powerful nation has felt it to be inconvenient to have a weak and dependent state in its neighbourhood, and has therefore forcibly joined the territory of such state to its own extensive domains. But this is done at the expense of honour and character, and is visited by the historian with his severest reprobation.

In the case before us the inconvenience is altogether imaginary. If the United States were examined, with a view to find a place where Indians could have a residence assigned them, so that they might be as little as possible in the way of the whites, not a single tract, capable of sustaining inhabitants, could be found more secluded than the present country of the Cherokees. It is in the mountains, among the head waters of rivers diverging in all directions; and some parts of it are almost inaccessible. The Cherokees have ceded to the United States all their best land. Not a twentieth part of what remains is of a very good quality. More than half is utterly worthless. Perhaps three tenths may produce moderate crops. The people of the United States have a free passage through the country, secured by treaty. What do they want more? If the Cherokee country were added to Georgia, the accession would be but a fraction joined to the remotest corner of that great State;—a State now scarcely inferior in size to any State in the Union except Virginia; a State having but six or seven souls to a square mile, counting whites and blacks, and with a soil and climate capable of sustaining a hundred to the square mile with the greatest of ease. There is no mighty inconvenience, therefore, in the arrangement of Providence, by which the Cherokee claim a resting place on the land which God gave to their fathers. . . .

There is one remaining topic, on which the minds of many benevolent men are hesitating; and that is, *whether the welfare of the Indians would not be promoted by a removal.* Though they have a right to remain where they are; though the whole power of the United States is pledged to defend them in their possessions; yet it is supposed by some, that they would act wisely, if they would yield to the pressure, quietly surrender their territory to the United States, and accept a new country beyond the Mississippi, with a new guaranty.

In support of this supposition, it is argued, that they can never remain quiet where they are; that they will always be infested by troublesome whites; and that the states, which lay claim to their territory, will persevere in measures to vex and annoy them.

Let us look a moment at this statement. Is it indeed true, that, in the very prime and vigour of our republican government, and with all our boasted reliance upon constitutions and laws, we cannot enforce as plain an act of Congress as is to be found in our national statute-book? Is it true, that while treaties are declared in the constitution to be the supreme law of the land, a whole volume of these supreme laws is to be at once avowedly and utterly disregarded? Is the Senate of the United States, that august body, as our newspapers have called it a thousand times, to march in solemn procession, and burn a volume of treaties? Are the archives of state to be searched, and a hundred and fifty rolls, containing treaties with the Indians, to be brought forth and consigned to the flames on Capitol Hill, in the presence of the representatives of the people, and all the dignitaries of our national government? When ambassadors from foreign nations inquire, *What is the cause of all this burning?* are we to say, "Forty years ago President Washington and the Senate made treaties with the Indians, which have been repeated and confirmed by successive administrations. The treaties are plain, and the terms reasonable. But the Indians are weak, and their white neighbors will be lawless. The way to please these white neighbours is, therefore, to burn the treaties, and then call the Indians our dear children, and deal with them precisely as if no treaties had ever been made." Is this answer to be given to the honest inquires of intelligent foreigners? Are we to declare to mankind, that in our country law is totally inadequate to answer the great end for which human laws are made, that is, the protection of the weak against the strong? And is this confession to be made without feeling and without shame? It cannot be. The people of the United States will never subject themselves to so foul a reproach.

Source 4 from *Speeches on the Passage of the Bill for the Removal of the Indians, Delivered in the Congress of the United States, April and May, 1830* (Boston: Perkins and Marvin, 1830), pp. 25–28.

4. Excerpt from Speech of Senator Theodore Frelinghuysen[20] of New Jersey.

It is alleged, that the Indians cannot flourish in the neighborhood of a white population—that whole tribes have disappeared under the influence of this propinquity. As an abstract proposition, it implies reproach somewhere. Our virtues certainly have not such deadly and depopulating power. It must, then, be our vices that possess these destructive energies—and shall we commit injustice, and put in, as our plea for it, that our intercourse with the Indians has been so demoralizing that we must drive them from it, to save them? True, Sir, many tribes have melted away—they have sunk lower and lower—and

20. Theodore Frelinghuysen (1787–1862) was president of the American Board of Commissioners for Foreign Missions from 1841 to 1857. For more on Frelinghuysen, see Chapter 6.

what people could rise from a condition to which policy, selfishness, and cupidity, conspired to depress them?

Sir, had we devoted the same care to elevate their moral condition, that we have to degrade them, the removal of the Indians would not now seek for an apology in the suggestions of humanity. But I ask, as to the matter of fact, how stands the account? Wherever a fair experiment has been made, the Indians have readily yielded to the influences of moral cultivation. Yes, Sir, they flourish under this culture, and rise in the scale of being. They have shown themselves to be highly susceptible of improvement, and the ferocious feelings and habits of the savage are soothed and reformed by the mild charities of religion. They can very soon be taught to understand and appreciate the blessings of civilization and regular government. . . .

Prompted and encouraged by our counsels, they have in good earnest resolved to become men, rational, educated, Christian men; and they have succeeded beyond our most sanguine hopes. They have established a regular constitution of civil government, republican in its principles. Wise and beneficent laws are enacted. The people acknowledge their authority, and feel their obligation. A printing press, conducted by one of the nation, circulates a weekly newspaper, printed partly in English, and partly in the Cherokee language. Schools flourish in many of their settlements. Christian temples, to the God of the Bible, are frequented by respectful, devout, and many sincere worshippers. God, as we believe, has many people among them, whom he regards as the "apple of his eye." They have become better neighbors to Georgia. . . .

Let the general government come out, as it should, with decided and temperate firmness, and officially announce to Georgia, and the other States, that if the Indian tribes choose to remain, they will be protected against all interference and encroachment; and such is my confidence in the sense of justice, in the respect for law, prevailing in the great body of this portion of our fellow-citizens, that I believe they would submit to the authority of the nation. I can expect no other issue.

Source 5 from Wilson Lumpkin, *The Removal of the Cherokee Indians from Georgia* (New York: Dodd, Mead & Co., 1907), vol. 1, pp. 95–102.

5. Georgia Governor Wilson Lumpkin to the Georgia Assembly, December 2, 1831.

Executive Department, Georgia, Milledgeville, December 2nd, 1831.

It is believed that a crisis has arrived, in which we cannot permit the course of our policy in relation to the Cherokee part of Georgia to remain in its present perplexed and extraordinary condition without jeopardizing the interest and prosperity, if not the peace and safety, of the State.

Circumstances within the recollection of our whole people emperiously demanded the extension of the laws and jurisdiction of our State over our entire population and territory.

This step has been taken, and cannot be retraced. The State cannot consent to be restricted in the exercise of her constitutional rights.[21] It is now too late for us to theorize on this subject; we are called upon to act; the public functionaries of the State stand pledged to their constituents, and the world, to sustain the ground which they have taken. It is our constitutional right, and moral duty, fortwith [sic] to interpose and save that part of our State from confusion, anarchy, and perhaps from bloodshed . . .

A few thousand half civilized men, both indisposed and incompetent to the faithful discharge of the duties of citizenship, and scattered over a territory so extensive, can never enjoy the inestimable blessing of civil government.

Whatever may be the nominal character of our legislation, we cannot govern the country under consideration with honor to our character, and benefit and humanity to the Indians, until we have a settled, freehold, white population, planted on the unoccupied portion of that territory, under the influence of all the ordinary inducements of society, to maintain a good system of civil government. Our government over that territory in its present condition, in order to be efficient, must partake largely of a military character, and consequently must be more or less arbitrary and oppressive in its operations. If the present system be continued, it is important that ample powers should be afforded to the Executive, to regulate the conduct, and control the operations, of the agents employed to administer the Government in that part of the State; but it is doubtful, even with this power, whether any vigilance and energy on the part of the Executive can wholly prevent injustice and oppression being committed on the Indians, and at the same time maintain the laws inviolate.

If Georgia were at this day to relinquish all right, title and claim to the Cherokee country, what would be its situation? The impotency and incompetency of the Cherokees to maintain a regular government, even for a few months, perhaps for a few weeks, would at once be demonstrated. The country would be speedily overrun, chiefly by the most abandoned portions of society from all quarters.

The gold mines would hold out an irresistible temptation to all such characters. The existence alone of the rich gold mines utterly forbids the idea of a state of quiescence on this all engrossing subject.

---

21. In his memoirs, Governor Lumpkin stated that "at the very threshold of my Executive administration it became my duty to resist Federal usurpation [and] . . . Federal encroachments." Lumpkin, *Removal of the Cherokee*, vol. 1, p. 94. What was Lumpkin referring to here?

Our true situation and motives on this question are still misunderstood, and often misrepresented, by those at a distance. In order to appreciate our policy, our true situation must be understood. I will not attempt to enumerate the wrongs, embarrassments, and perplexities, which this State has encountered, by what I am constrained to deem the impertinent intermeddling of "busy-bodies." Officious persons of various descriptions have unfortunately succeeded in inducing our Indian people to believe that we are their enemies and oppressors, and in alienating their affections from us. These various intermeddlings hastened the crisis which compelled the State to the course which she has taken; and the day must speedily arrive when all the heart-burnings on this subject must be put to final rest. The combined and combining influences now in operation against the character, interest, peace, and prosperity of the State, cannot be much longer deplored in silent inaction; nor ought we to place any reliance on inefficient measures. Unfounded calumny and prejudice, kept at a distance, may be endured; but domestic and household enemies produce unceasing disquietude and danger.

The unfortunate remnant of Cherokee Indians remaining in Georgia ought now to consider themselves the admitted charge of our peculiar care; and if possible we ought, as their friends and benefactors, to preserve and cherish them. They ought not forcibly to be dispossessed of their homes, or driven from the land of their fathers; they ought to be guarded and protected in the peaceable enjoyment of a sufficient portion of land to sustain them, with their families, in their present abodes, so long as they may choose to remain; and their rights and property should be as well secured from all lawless depredation as those of the white man. It would be as cruel as unjust, to compel the aborigines to abandon the graves of their fathers; but in the present extraordinary state of things it would be visionary to suppose, that the Indian claim can be allowed to this extensive tract of country—to lands on which they have neither dwelt, nor made improvements.[22]

Principles of natural law and abstract justice have often been appealed to, to show that the Indian tribes within the territorial limits of the States ought to be regarded as the absolute owners and proprietors of the soil they occupy.

All civilized nations have acknowledged the validity of the principles appealed to, with such modifications and interpretations of these principles as the truth of history has verified, especially in the settlement of this country.

The foundations of the States which form this confederacy were laid by civilized and Christian nations who considered themselves instructed in the nature of their duties by the precepts and examples contained in the Sacred Volume which they acknowledged as the basis of their religious creed and

22. See similarity to Jackson's phrase in Source 1, pg. 189.

obligations. To go forth, subdue, and replenish the earth, were considered Divine commands. . . .

The present state of things in the Cherokee country, it is believed, is strengthening the adversaries of Georgia, at home and abroad.

In order to secure and protect the Indians in their abodes, and their property of every kind under our laws, their individual and separate possessions ought to be defined by actual survey; in accomplishing which it will be least expensive and most compatible with the views of the State (as provided by the act of the Legislature at its last session), to survey the entire country.

Until we have a population planted upon the unoccupied portion of this territory, possessed of all the ordinary inducements of other communities to sustain our laws and government, our present laws providing for the government of this part of the State should not only be continued, but ample power should be afforded to enforce obedience to their requirements. To effect this object, the Executive should be vested with full power promptly to control the agents who have been, or may be, selected to maintain the authority of the laws in that portion of the State. . . .

CHEROKEE SOURCES

Sources 6 and 7 from Perdue and Green, *The Cherokee Removal: A Brief History with Documents*, pp. 43–44, 131–132.

6. Petition of Cherokee Women, May 2, 1817.

The Cherokee ladys now being present at the meeting of the chiefs and warriors in council have thought it their duty as mothers to address their beloved chiefs and warriors now assembled.

Our beloved children and head men of the Cherokee Nation, we address you warriors in council. We have raised all of you on the land which we now have, which God gave us to inhabit and raise provisions. We know that our country has once been extensive, but by repeated sales has become circumscribed to a small track [sic], and [we] never have thought it our duty to interfere in the disposition of it till now. If a father or mother was to sell all their lands which they had to depend on, which their children had to raise their living on, which would be indeed bad & to be removed to another country. We do not wish to go to an unknown country [to] which we have understood some of our children wish to go over the Mississippi, but this act of our children would be like destroying your mothers.

Your mothers, your sisters ask and beg of you not to part with any more of our land. We say ours. You are our descendants; take pity on our request. But keep it for our growing children, for it was the good will of our creator to place us here, and you know our father, the great president,[23] will not allow his white children to take our country away. Only keep your hands off of paper talks for its our own country. For [if] it was not, they would not ask you to put your hands to paper, for it would be impossible to remove us all. For as soon as one child is raised, we have others in our arms, for such is our situation & will consider our circumstance.

Therefore, children, don't part with any more of our lands but continue on it & enlarge your farms. Cultivate and raise corn & cotton and your mothers and sisters will make clothing for you which our father the president has recommended to us all. We don't charge any body for selling any lands, but we have heard such intentions of our children. But your talks become true at last; it was our desire to forwarn you all not to part with our lands.[24]

7. John Ridge (a Cherokee leader) to Albert Gallatin,[25] February 27, 1826.

[In this long letter, Ridge began by giving a geographic location of the Cherokee Nation, its population, its successful adoption of agriculture, its government, the status of women, its religious beliefs, and its educational institutions.]

Col. Silas Dinsmore was appointed by Genl. Washington as Agent of the Nation, who from the Indian Testimony itself labored indefatigably in Teaching the Cherokees the art of agriculture by distributing hoes & ploughs & giving to the women Spinning wheels, cards & Looms. It appears when this change of Hunter life to a civilized one was proposed by the Agent to the Chiefs in Council, that he was unanimously laughed at by the Council for attempting [to] introduce white peoples' habits among the Indians, who were created to pursue the chase. Not discouraged here, the Agent turned to Individuals & succeeded to gain some to pay their attention to his plan by way of experiment, which succeeded. An anecdote is related of a Chief who was heartily opposed to the Agent's view. He came to Col. Dinsmore & said, "I don't want you to recommend these things to my people. They may suit white people, but will do [nothing] for the Indians. I am now going to hunt &

---

23. President James Monroe.

24. Despite the women's petition, Cherokees signed two more treaties, in 1817 and 1819, before deciding to cede no more land. See Cherokee Delegation to the U.S. Senate, April 16, 1824, "Views of the Cherokees in Relation to Further Cessions of Their lands," *American State Papers: Indian Affairs*, vol. 2, p. 502.

25. Albert Gallatin (1761–1849) was a congressman, secretary of the treasury, and diplomat. When Ridge wrote to Gallatin, Gallatin had just been nominated as U.S. minister to Great Britain.

shall be gone six moons & when I return, I shall expect to hear nothing of your talks made in [my] absence to induce my people to take hold of your plan." But in his absence the Agent induced his wife & daughters to Spin & weave with so much assiduity as to make more cloth in value, than the Chief's Hunt of six months amounted to. He was astonished & came to the Agent with a smile, accusing him for making his wife & daughters better hunters than he & requested to be furnished a plough & went to work on his farm. In the meantime, the Moravians opened their School for the Indians, cleared a farm, cultivated a garden & planted an orchard. The Venerable Rev. John Gambold & his amiable Lady were a standing monument of Industry, Goodness & friendship. As far as they had means, they converted the "Wilderness to blossom as the Rose." There the boys & girls were taught to read & write, & occasionally labor in the Garden & in the field. There they were first taught to sing & pray to their Creator, & here Gospel Worship was first Established. Never shall I forget father Gambold & mother Mrs. Gambold. By them the clouds of ignorance which surrounded me on all sides were dispersed. My heart received the rays of civilization & my intellect expanded & took a wider range. My superstition vanished & I began to reason correctly. . . .

Source 8 from Francis Paul Prucha, ed., *Cherokee Removal: The "William Penn" Essays and Other Writings By Jeremiah Evarts* (Knoxville: Univ. of Tennessee Press, 1981), pp. 259–262.

8. Address of the Committee and Council of the Cherokee Nation . . . to the People of the United States, July 24, 1830.[26]

We are aware that some persons suppose it will be for our advantage to remove beyond the Mississippi. We think otherwise. Our people universally think otherwise. Thinking that it would be fatal to their interests, they have almost to a man sent their memorial to Congress, deprecating the necessity of a removal. This question was distinctly before their minds when they signed their memorial. Not an adult person can be found, who has not an opinion on the subject; and if the people were to understand distinctly, that they could be protected against the laws of the neighboring States, there is probably not an adult person in the nation, who would think it best to remove; though

26. Although the address was issued by the General Council of the Cherokee Nation and published in the *Cherokee Phoenix* on July 24, 1830, it actually was written by Jeremiah Evarts (1781–1831), secretary of the American Board of Commissioners for Foreign Missions. See Source 3. The Council added the last paragraph in this excerpt.

possible a few might emigrate individually. There are doubtless many who would flee to an unknown country, however beset with dangers, privations and sufferings, rather than be sentenced to spend six years in a Georgia prison for advising one of their neighbors not to betray his country. And there are others who could not think of living as outlaws in their native land, exposed to numberless vexations, and excluded from being parties or witnesses in a court of justice. It is incredible that Georgia should ever have enacted the oppressive laws to which reference is here made, unless she had supposed that something extremely terrific in its character was necessary, in order to make the Cherokees willing to remove. We are not willing to remove; and if we could be brought to this extremity, it would be, not by argument; not because our judgment was satisfied; not because our condition will be improved—but only because we cannot endure to be deprived of our national and individual rights, and subjected to a process of intolerable oppression.

We wish to remain on the land of our fathers. We have a perfect and original right to claim this, without interruption or molestation. The treaties with us, and laws of the United States made in pursuance of treaties, guaranty our residence, and our privileges, and secure us against intruders. Our only request is, that these treaties may be fulfilled, and these laws executed. . . .

It is under a sense of the most pungent feelings that we make this, perhaps our last appeal to the good people of the United States. It cannot be that the community we are addressing, remarkable for its intelligence and religious sensibilities, and pre-eminent for its devotion to the rights of man, will lay aside this appeal, without considering that we stand in need of its sympathy and commiseration. We know that to the Christian and the philanthropist, the voice of our multiplied sorrows and fiery trials will not appear as an idle tale. In our own land, our own soil, and in our dwellings, which we reared for our wives and for our little ones, when there was peace on our mountains and in our valleys, we are encountering troubles which cannot but try our very souls. But shall we, on account of these troubles, forsake our beloved country? Shall we be compelled by a civilized and Christian people, with whom we have lived in perfect peace for the last forty years, and for whom we have willingly bled in war, to bid a final adieu to our homes, our farms, our streams, and our beautiful forests? No. We are still firm. We intend still to cling, with our wonted affection, to the land which gave us birth, and which, every day of our lives, brings to us new and stronger ties of attachment. We appeal to the Judge of all the earth, who will finally award us justice, and to the good sense of the American people, whether we are intruders upon the land of others. Our consciences bear us witness that we are the invaders of no man's rights—we have robbed no man of his territory—we have usurped no man's authority, nor have we deprived any one of his unalienable privileges. How then shall we indirectly confess the right of another people to our land by leaving it forever? On the soil which contains the ashes of our beloved men, we wish to live, on this soil we wish to die. . . .

Source 9 from Theda Perdue, ed., *Cherokee Editor: The Writings of Elias Boudinot* (Knoxville: Univ. of Tennessee Press, 1983), pp. 175–179. Copyright © 1983 by The University of Tennessee Press. Reproduced by permission.

9. Elias Boudinot, "Resolutions," October 2, 1832.

Whereas, a crisis of the utmost importance, in the affairs of the Cherokee people has arrived, requiring from every individual the most serious reflection and the expression of views as to the present condition and future prospects of the Nation; and whereas a portion of the Cherokees have entertained opinions which have been represented as hostile to the true interest and happiness of the people, merely because they have not agreed with the Chiefs and leading men; and as these opinions have not heretofore been properly made known, therefore.

Resolved, That it is our decided opinion, founded upon the melancholy experience of the Cherokees within the last two years, and upon facts which history has furnished us in regard to other Indian nations, that our people cannot exist amidst a white population, subject to laws which they have no hand in making, and which they do not understand; that the suppression of the Cherokee Government, which connected this people in a distinct community, will not only check their progress in improvement and advancement in knowledge, but, by means of numerous influences and temptations which this new state of things has created, will completely destroy every thing like civilization among them, and ultimately reduce them to poverty, misery, and wretchedness.

Resolved, That, considering the progress of the States authorities in this country, the distribution and settlement of the lands, the organization of counties, the erection of county seats and Courthouses, and other indications of a determined course on the part of the surrounding States, and considering, on the other hand, the repeated refusal of the President and Congress of the United States to interfere in our behalf, we have come to the conclusion that this nation cannot be reinstated in its present location, and that the question left to us and to every Cherokee, is, whether it is more desirable to remain here, with all the embarrassments with which we must be surrounded, or to seek a country where we *may* enjoy our own laws, and live under our own vine and fig-tree.

Resolved, That in expressing the opinion that this nation cannot be reinstated, we do it from a thorough conviction of its truth—that we never will encourage our confiding people with hopes that can never be realized, and with expectations that will assuredly be disappointed—that however unwelcome and painful the truth may be to them, and however unkindly it may be received from us, we cannot, as *patriots* and well-wishers of the Indian race, shrink from doing our duty in expressing our decided convictions. That we scorn the charge of selfishness and a want of patriotic feelings alleged against us by some of our countrymen, while we can appeal to our consciences and the searcher of all hearts for the rectitude of our motives and intentions.

Resolved, That, although *we love the land* of our fathers, and should leave the place of our nativity with as much regret as any of our citizens, we consider the lot of the *Exile* immeasurably more to be preferred than a submission to the laws of the States, and thus becoming witnesses of the ruin and degradation of the Cherokee people.

Resolved, That we are firmly of the opinion, that a large majority of the Cherokee people would prefer to remove, if the true state of their condition was properly made known to them.[27]—We believe that if they were told that they had nothing to expect from further efforts to regain their rights as a *distinct community*, and that the only alternatives left to them is either to remain amidst a white population, subject to the white man's laws, or to remove to another country, where they may enjoy peace and happiness, they would unhesitatingly prefer the latter. . . .

Resolved, that we consider the policy pursued by the Red Clay Council,[28] in continuing a useless struggle from year to year, as destructive to the present peace and future happiness of the Cherokees, because it is evident to every observer that while this struggle is going on, their difficulties will be accumulating, until they are ruined in their property and character, and the only remedy that will then be proposed in their case will be, *submission to the laws of the States* by taking reservations.

27. Boudinot accused Principal Chief John Ross and the National Council of not telling the Cherokees "how seemingly hopeless their situation was." Perdue, *Cherokee Editor*, p. 228, n. 29.
28. "Red Clay Council": the National Council.

Source 10 from John Ross, et. al., to President Andrew Jackson, January 23, 1835, in Gary F. Moulton, ed., *The Papers of Chief John Ross* (Norman: Univ. of Oklahoma Press, 1985), vol. 1, pp. 317–318.

10. John Ross[29] et al. to President Andrew Jackson, January 23, 1835.

It is known to your Excellency, that the history of the Cherokee Nation since the year 1829 up to the present, has been on its part, one of repeated, continued unavailing struggle against the cruel policy of Georgia; on the part of that State, it has been one, of unparalleled aggravated acts of oppression upon the Nation. Actuated by an unextinguishable love of country, confiding implicitly in the good faith of the American Govt. and believing that the Govt. priding itself, as it does upon its justice and humanity would, not only not, disregard its own plighted faith, but would eventually interpose to prevent it from being disregarded, and trampled into dust by the State of Georgia. Being fully convinced in their own judgement that they could not prosper as well any where else as upon their native land, the Cherokees have successively appealed to the Executive, Legislative and Judiciary Departments of this Govt. for redress of wrongs committed and security against injuries apprehended, but as yet those appeals have been unavailing; In defiance of Acts of Congress, decisions of the Supreme Court, and of solemn treaties, Georgia has gone on first, to despoil them of their laws & Govt. and impose upon them laws the most obnoxious, then to distribute their lands unbought, to her own citizens by lottery, and lastly she has put forth her hand under the last Act of her Legislature to expel them from their homes & firesides, to drive them out to hunger and perish in the wild forests—to accomplish this last cruel purpose, armed bands of her citizens are now parading thro' their Country. The Undersigned deeply affected with this deploreable, condition of their people would ask you, Dear Sir, to pity and save them. For, upon the exercise of your power alone, they are firmly persuaded the salvation of their people depend. Let the comforts and enjoyments of life which have been so profusely scattered around you, by a bountiful providence remind you, that hundreds of their people, many of whom are women and children, may now be homeless wanderers, suffering with cold & hunger, for no crime, but, because they did not love their Country less.

The crisis of the fate of the Cherokee people, seems to be rapidly approaching—and the time has come, when they must be relieved of their sufferings— They having fully determined against a removal to Arkansas. The undersigned

29. John Ross (1790–1866), the Principal Chief from 1828 to 1860, was one-eighth Cherokee, well-educated and became a wealthy landowner and businessman. In 1836, his property was appraised at $23,665 ($446,085 in 2001 dollars).

Delegation would therefore most respectfully and earnestly ask to be informed, upon what terms will the President negotiate for a final termination of those sufferings, that their people may repose in peace and comfort on the land of their nativity, under the enjoyment of such rights and privileges as belongs to freemen. And the Delegation would in conclusion beg leave to assure the President in great sincerity, that after a due deliberation on the terms which he may offer, should they be found to have been dictated in that spirit of liberality and justice, as in their best judgement would afford their people ample relief and sattisfaction by adopting them; it may be done. With sentiments of great respect, they remain, yr. Excellency's most Hble. Servts.

Source 11 from John Ridge to Major Ridge, et al., March 10, 1835, in Dale and Litton, eds., *Cherokee Cavaliers*, pp. 12–13.

11. John Ridge[30] to Major Ridge et al., March 10, 1835.

I have delayed this long in writing to you in the consequence of the hard struggles I had to make against John Ross & his party. At the outset they told Congress that our people had decided that they would choose to be citizens of the U. States [rather] than to remove. We contradicted this & he has failed to get an answer from Congress. From various indications we ascertained that he was going to act falsely to his people & sell the Nation either by getting Reservations of land or taking the whole in money on pretense of going out of the limits of the U. States. We protested against this & we have succeeded to get a treaty made to be sent home for the ratification of the people.[31] It is very liberal in its terms—an equal measure is given to all. The poor Indian enjoys the same rights as the rich—there is no distinction. We are allowed to enjoy our own laws in the west. Subsistence for one year, $25. for each soul for transportation, fair valuation for ferries & Improvements, $150 for each individual, more than forty thousand dollars perpetual annuity in the west, & a large sum of money to pay for the losses of the Cherokees against the white people. In fact—we get four milions & a half in money to meet all expenses & large addition in land to that already possessed by our brethren in the west. John Ross and his party tried hard to treat & get the whole in money & go as they said out of the limits of the U. States, but they have failed.[32] Jackson

30. John Ridge (Cherokee name Yellow Bird) was born in 1792, the son of Major Ridge and cousin of Elias Boudinot. He initially opposed Cherokee relocation but changed his mind after President Jackson's refusal to enforce the Supreme Court decision in *Worchester v. Georgia*.
31. The Treaty of New Echota.
32. Ridge's charge that Ross intended to steal the money appropriated for removal was not true.

said that he would not trust them with the money of the people. The Indians here under his care wish that he would refer the whole to the people. Ross has failed before the Senate, before the Secretary of War, & before the President. He tried hard to cheat you & his people, but he has been prevented. In a day or two he goes home no doubt to tell lies. But we will bring all his papers & the people shall see him as he is. . . .

The Congress has allowed money enough to pay the expenses of our Councils while the people are signing this treaty if they approve it. We are all well. I shall go to the north & see my wife's parents & in great haste will return to you. Stand, stay. All will be right. The U. States will never have any thing more to do with John Ross. Thus it becomes of selfish men. . . .

Source 12 from Protest of the Cherokee Delegation, laid before the Senate and House of Representatives, June 21, 1836, (Washington, DC: s.n., 1836) in Southeastern Native American Documents 1790–1842, accessible through the Georgia Virtual Library, Galileo, www.galileo.usg.edu.

12. "Protest of the Cherokee Delegation," June 21, 1836.

To the honourable Senate and House of Representatives of the United States of North America, in Congress assembled:

The undersigned representatives of the Cherokee nation, east of the river Mississippi, impelled by duty, would respectfully submit, for the consideration of your honourable body, the following statement: An instrument purporting to be a treaty with the Cherokee people, has recently been made public by the President of the United States, that will have such an operation, if carried into effect. This instrument, the delegation aver before the civilized world, and in the presence of Almighty God, is fraudulent, false upon its face, made by unauthorized individuals, without the sanction, and against the wishes, of the great body of the Cherokee people. Upwards of fifteen thousand of those people have protested against it, solemnly declaring they will never acquiesce. The delegation would respectfully call the attention of your honourable body to their memorial and protest, with the accompanying documents, submitted to the Senate of the United States, on the subject of the alleged treaty, which are herewith transmitted. . . .

It is the expressed wish of the Government of the United States to remove the Cherokees to a place west of the Mississippi. That wish is said to be founded in humanity to the Indians. To make their situation more comfortable, and to preserve them as a distinct people. Let facts show how this *benevolent* design has been prosecuted, and how faithfully to the spirit and letter has the promise of the President of the United States to the Cherokees been fulfilled—that *"those who remain may be assured of our patronage; our aid, and good neighbourhood."* The delegation are not deceived by empty professions, and fear their race is to be destroyed by the mercenary policy of the present day, and their lands wrested from them by physical force; as proof, they will refer to the preamble of an act of the General Assembly of Georgia, in reference to the Cherokees, passed the 2d of December, 1835, where it is said, "from a knowledge of the Indian character, and from the present feelings of these Indians, it is confidently believed, that the right of occupancy of the lands in their possession should be withdrawn, *that it would be a strong inducement to them to treat with the General Government, and consent to a removal to the west;* and whereas, the present Legislature openly avow that their primary object in the measures intended to be pursued, *are founded on real humanity to these Indians,* and with a view, in a distant region, to perpetuate them with their old identity of character, *under the paternal care of the Government of the United States;* at the same time frankly disavowing *any selfish or sinister motives towards them in their present legislation."* This is the profession. Let us turn to the practice of *humanity,* to the Cherokees, by the State of Georgia. In violation of the treaties between the United States and the Cherokee nation, that State passed a law requiring all white men, residing in that part of the Cherokee country, in her limits, to take an oath of allegiance to the State of Georgia. For a violation of this law, some of the ministers of Christ, missionaries among the Cherokees, were tried, convicted, and sentenced to hard labor in the penitentiary. Their case may be seen by reference to the records of the Supreme Court of the United States.

Valuable gold mines were discovered upon the Cherokee lands, within the chartered limits of Georgia, and the Cherokees commenced working them, and the Legislature of that State interfered by passing an act, making it penal for an Indian to dig for gold within Georgia, no doubt *"frankly disavowing any selfish or sinister motives towards them."* Under this law many Cherokees were arrested, tried, imprisoned, and otherwise abused. Some were even shot in attempting to avoid an arrest; yet the Cherokee people used no violence, but humbly petitioned the Government of the United States for a fulfilment of treaty engagements, to protect them, which was not done, and the answer given that the United States could not interfere. Georgia discovered she was not to be obstructed in carrying out her measures, *"founded on real humanity to these Indians,"* she passed an act directing the Indian country to be surveyed into districts. This excited some alarm, but the Cherokees were quieted with the assurance it would do no harm to survey the country. Another act was shortly after passed, to lay off the country into lots. As yet there was no authority to take possession, but it was not long before a law was made, authorizing a lottery for the lands laid off into lots. In this act the Indians were secured in possession of all the lots touched by their improvements, and the balance of the country allowed to be occupied by white men. This was a direct violation of the 5th article of the treaty of the 27th of February, 1819. The Cherokees made no resistance, still petitioned the United States for protection, and received the same answer that the President could not interpose. After the country was parcelled out by lottery, a horde of speculators made their appearance, and purchased of the "fortunate drawers," lots touched by Indian improvements, at reduced prices, declaring it was uncertain when the Cherokees would surrender their rights, and that the lots were encumbered by their claims. The consequence of this speculation was that, at the next session of the Legislature, an act was passed limiting the Indian right of occupancy to the lot upon which he resided. . . .

[The memorial gives several examples of Cherokees who were cheated out of their lands or who lost them to white speculators or squatters.]

The delegation must repeat, the instrument entered into at New Echota, purporting to be a treaty, is deceptive to the world, and a fraud upon the Cherokee people. If a doubt exist as to the truth of their statement, a committee of investigation can learn the facts, and it may also learn that if the Cherokees are removed under that instrument, it will be by force.

◆

Questions to Consider

Remember that your task in this chapter is a dual one. First, you must examine and analyze the five sources by white writers concerning how to deal with Native Americans east of the Mississippi River, noting the strengths and weaknesses of each argument. Then you must repeat the process for the seven sources by Cherokee writers[33] on the best course for the Cherokee nation to pursue.

President Andrew Jackson gave four principal reasons why, in his opinion, the Cherokees should not remain where they were as a political entity separate from the state of Georgia (Source 1). What were those four reasons? How important was it, in Jackson's opinion, that the Cherokees become "civilized"? In his view, what would be the results of permitting the Cherokees to remain in the East? Finally, Jackson strongly maintained that any such emigration "should be voluntary," but, in his view, what would happen to the Cherokees

33. See fn. 26.

who refused to leave? Why couldn't the president of the United States intervene to help the Cherokees remain where they were?

President Thomas Jefferson's letter of December 21, 1808 (Source 2), while not specifically referring to the Cherokees, accurately summarized his general policy with regard to Native Americans living within the boundaries of the United States. What did Jefferson believe were the causes of population decline among Native American people (note that Jackson also dealt with this problem, and in a way not terribly different from that of Jefferson)? How, in Jefferson's view, could that situation be reversed? In return for staying on their lands, what would Native Americans have had to give up? What was Jackson's opinion on this topic? In your view, which president was more eager to eliminate Native American cultures: Jackson or Jefferson? Also note that Jefferson realized that Native Americans were not simply wandering hunters, but that they already cultivated the earth ("all your women understand it"). What stereotype did Jefferson seem to believe? What do you make of the phrase, "you will unite yourselves with us, join in our Great Councils and form one people with us"? What was Jefferson proposing? How did Jackson treat the same subject?

Jeremiah Evarts (Source 3) also opposed removal. How did Evarts contest President Jackson's opinion that the Cherokees' position was unconstitutional, according to Article IV, Section 3 of the Constitution? (Remember that even though Evarts wrote months before Jackson's message, the president's position was well known.) What was Evarts's opinion of the much-circulated notion in Georgia that Cherokees were inhabiting some of the best land in the state? What was his position on the inability of the government to protect the Cherokees where they were from intruding whites?

Senator Theodore Frelinghuysen was deeply and genuinely concerned about the fate of Native Americans. The speech excerpted here (Source 4) took approximately six hours to deliver, so it is not possible to include all of the points he made in opposition to removal. Frelinghuysen began his speech by admitting that many Native Americans living in close proximity to whites had experienced great difficulties. Yet why does he say this has happened? Why does he believe that removal will not work and, moreover, is not necessary? What alternative (by inference) might Frelinghuysen have supported? How important was it to Frelinghuysen that the Cherokees become "civilized"? Did he seem less concerned than Andrew Jackson about making the Cherokees more like their white neighbors?

Georgia Governor Wilson Lumpkin (Source 5) maintained that, like Frelinghuyson, he too was genuinely concerned about the fate of the Cherokees but, unlike Frelinghuyson, Lumpkin argued for their removal. In Governor Lumpkin's opinion, why was this the only alternative? What did he believe would happen if the Cherokees were allowed to remain? Lumpkin maintained that the Cherokees were influenced by "busy-bodies." Who were they? How convincing was Lumpkin?[34]

The seven Cherokee sources reveal deep divisions over how—or whether—to oppose their removal. What arguments did the Cherokee women make in opposition to removal (Source 6)? What were the strengths and weaknesses of their position?

John Ridge appears twice in the evidence, once in 1826 (Source 7) and the other in 1835 (Source 11). What was the major difference in Ridge's position in the two sources? What was his major point in Source 7? How would that relate to his opinion in 1826 regarding removal? Source 11?

According to the Cherokee leaders' address in 1830 (Source 8), why were some Cherokees abandoning lands in Georgia and moving west? In their opinion, who were the real "intruders" in Georgia? How would you describe their appeal?

The re-election of President Jackson, and his statement that he would not enforce the Supreme Court's decision in *Worcester v. Georgia* (1832), convinced some Cherokee leaders that the only realistic alternative was to relocate to Indian Territory. In Elias Boudinot's "Resolutions" (Source 9), what arguments did he offer in support of removal? Why did he claim that most Cherokees still opposed relocation? How did Principal Chief John Ross attempt to counter Boudinot's arguments (Source 10)? Which person do you believe had

the stronger argument? How would you describe the Cherokee protest in Source 12? What were the major points?

Having extracted from the evidence the principal arguments for and against removal, now use your text, the Background section of this chapter, and the help of your instructor to explain the strengths and weaknesses of each principal argument. In order to do so, take each argument for or against removal and use historical facts to determine its strengths and weaknesses. In some cases, another piece of evidence will assist you. For example, President Jackson claimed that the Cherokees' position was unconstitutional. Jeremiah Evarts, however, attempted (with some success) to challenge Jackson's position.

One more example will suffice. In his essay opposing removal, Evarts maintained that the Cherokees already had given up their best lands and what remained in their hands were lands that were "utterly worthless." What fact, however, did Evarts omit? In what way might that fact weaken his position?

Always keep in mind that a statement of opinion (a hypothesis) must be proved by using *facts*, and *not* by using other statements of opinion. What is the matter with the following two statements? (1) The Cherokees should be removed because they lack the industry to make their lands produce. (2) The Cherokees ought not to be removed because their lifestyle is superior to that of whites.

---

34. Lumpkin's opinion of Native Americans coincided with Jackson's. In his Fifth Annual Message to Congress (1833), the President stated that the Cherokees "have neither the intelligence, the industry, the moral habits, nor the desire of improvement . . . in their condition." James D. Richardson, *A Compilation of the Messages and Papers of the Presidents* (New York: Bureau of National Literature, 1897), vol. 3, p. 1252.

✦

Epilogue

The war between the older immigrants and the newer arrivals to Indian territory went on for seven years, until peace between the two factions of Cherokees finally was made in 1846. During that period, some Cherokees reversed their trek and returned to North Carolina. When the Civil War broke out in 1861, factionalism once again emerged, with some Cherokees supporting the Confederacy and others backing the Union. Fighting between these factions (a "mini–Civil War") claimed the lives of as much as 25 percent of the Cherokee population.

In 1868, Congress recognized the obvious fact that the Cherokees who remained in the East had become a distinct group, named the Eastern Band of the Cherokees (as opposed to the migrating group, which was called the Cherokee Nation).[35] In 1875, the federal government began to acquire land in North Carolina for a reservation, named the Qualla Boundary, which ultimately contained around 56,000 acres. In 1889, the Eastern Band received a charter from North Carolina granting the Cherokees what amounted to home rule in the Qualla Boundary. Then the federal government began an intensive program to "civilize" the eastern Cherokees, an effort that was ultimately

unsuccessful. Cherokees clung stubbornly to their own language and traditions, and by 1900, less than one-fourth of the population could speak English—approximately half of them young people in white-administered boarding schools. Because they consistently voted Republican, after 1900 the Democratic majority in North Carolina disfranchised both the African Americans and the Cherokees by passing a law requiring literacy tests prior to voting.

Meanwhile the Cherokee Nation (in the West) was experiencing its own difficulties. In spite of the fact that the 1830 Indian Removal Act guaranteed that Native Americans would always hold the land onto which they were placed, land grants to railroad companies and a territorial land rush stripped a good deal of land away from the Cherokees. In 1891, the Cherokee Nation owned 19.5 million acres. By 1971, it owned but 146,598.

In North Carolina, the creation of the Great Smoky Mountains National Park in 1934 offered the Eastern Band a way out of its economic quagmire. In November 1934, the council appropriated $50,000 for tourist facilities, and in 1937, the first Cherokee-owned motel (Newfound Lodge) was opened for business. In 1939, an estimated 169,000 people visited the national park and purchased around $30,000 worth of Cherokee crafts.

The development of tourism undoubtedly helped alleviate a severe economic crisis for the Eastern Band. In 1932, at the low point of the Great Depression,

35. Technically there is a third group of Cherokees, the United Keetoowah Band, composed mostly of "full-blooded" Old Settlers who were strictly traditionalists. They were recognized as a separate group by the Oklahoma Indian Welfare Act of 1936 and by an act of Congress in 1950.

it was estimated that 200 of the 496 Cherokee families in North Carolina needed public assistance. The New Deal did provide some jobs, through the Indian Emergency Conservation Work Program, a separate version of the Civilian Conservation Corps. But tourism also presented the Eastern Band with the problem of whether Cherokees could retain their cultural identity while at the same time catering to the desires of visitors with money.[36] In the 1990s, the Eastern Band turned to casino gambling to increase their revenues, although income from tourism and gambling is not evenly dispersed and many Cherokees still live extremely modestly.

By then, of course, the principal voices on both sides of the issue had long been stilled. In 1837 (one year before the beginning of the Trail of Tears), Andrew Jackson left the presidency to his hand-picked successor, Martin Van Buren, and retired to his plantation, the Hermitage, near Nashville, Tennessee. He died in 1845, still convinced that his advocacy of Cherokee removal was the most humane alternative for the Native Americans themselves.

For his part, however, before his death in 1826, Thomas Jefferson had changed his position to one of supporting removal. Frustrated over what he considered to be the slow progress Native Americans were making in adopting "civilization," the principal author of the Declaration of Independence came to believe that Native American people and white people could not live side by side unless the Native Americans abandoned their own culture in favor of that of the whites.[37]

The removal of most of the Cherokees in 1838–1839 (and in a second forced migration in 1841 to 1844) is an important, if tragic, chapter in the history of the United States that is important to know. It is also important to understand that there were many voices on both sides of the removal issue, thus making the subject of Cherokee removal not only a tragic one but an exceedingly complex one as well.

36. Because tourists expected to see Native Americans with ornate feathered headdresses (typical of Plains Indians but never worn by Cherokees), Cherokees accommodatingly wore them.

37. See Bernard W. Sheehan, *Seeds of Extinction: Jeffersonian Philanthropy and the American Indian* (Chapel Hill: University of North Carolina Press, 1973).

CHAPTER

8

Women's Equality

◆

The Problem

In early February 1906, Susan B. Anthony, though in declining health, made a difficult midwinter journey from Rochester, New York, to Baltimore, Maryland. The National American Woman Suffrage Association (NAWSA) annual convention coincided with her eighty-sixth birthday, and the organization was eager to celebrate with her. By 1906, Anthony had spent literally a lifetime advocating women's citizenship. She and her longtime collaborator, Elizabeth Cady Stanton (1815–1902), fought more than fifty years for basic rights for women: to own property, to divorce abusive husbands, to claim custody of minor children, to collect wages, and to vote.

Stanton, Anthony, and a generation of what are now termed "first-wave" feminists introduced the idea of female civil equality in the 1840s. They pursued their cause through the judicial system, in the court of public opinion, and by lobbying state legislatures and the U.S. government. While the decades of work resulted in some reforms, in divorce law and property rights, for example, in 1906 the cornerstone of citizenship—the right to vote—remained a strictly male privilege. The defeats had, amazingly, not dampened Anthony's zeal for her cause nor her optimism about its eventual success.

Anthony's failing health precluded her giving a full address to the convention. But she would not disappoint the crowd, and so rose to briefly talk. Anthony spoke eloquently of all the women of her generation who had dedicated their lives to the yet-unrealized goal of female equality; she assured the rapt audience, "with such women consecrating their lives . . . failure is impossible!"[1]

These were the last words Susan B. Anthony spoke in public. She died within a month of addressing the NAWSA. Despite sacrificing so much, so long, for her goal, Anthony died having never cast a legitimate ballot. Stanton had passed four years earlier. Not until 1920, seventy-two years after the Seneca Falls Convention, where Stanton drafted a Declaration of Sentiments, modeled after the Declaration of Independence and similarly declaring female independence, did white women in the United States secure suffrage rights.

For 131 years after the ratification of the United States Constitution, females could not vote. In this chapter

1. Susan B. Anthony "Speech to the National American Woman Suffrage Association," February 1906. In Ida Husted Harper, *The Life and Work of Susan B. Anthony*, Vol. 3 (Indianapolis: The Hollenbeck Press, 1908), 1409.

you will be reading evidence from first-wave feminists explaining their justification for women's rights alongside rebuttals from their critics. Why did changing American political traditions matter so much to women like Susan B. Anthony? Why were women's civil rights so controversial?

Background

It is difficult today to imagine the world that Susan B. Anthony lived in and therefore to appreciate why many Americans in that era perceived her message to be so radical. In 2010, women serve as governors, senators in the U.S. Congress, and in every part of state and national government. Women run Fortune 500 corporations, Hollywood studios, network news bureaus, and leading universities, including Harvard. They work as lawyers, physicians, ministers, and soldiers. Both Republican President George W. Bush and Democratic President Barack Obama appointed a woman to head the State Department, to be the global representative of American policy. Women had a higher voting rate (66 percent) than males (62 percent) in the 2008 presidential election, just as they did in 2004.

In the America of Susan B. Anthony's youth, women could not vote. They rarely owned property; wives' assets automatically fell under the control of their husbands. White women were discouraged from pursuing an extensive education, from speaking in public, and from traveling alone. Although the colonial mindset that women were morally inferior to men and more sexually aggressive than them had been replaced by the opposite stereotype—that women were virtuous, passive, and ethereal—belief in female intellectual inferiority remained, commonplace. Some antebellum physicians even told their female patients that too much intellectual activity would draw blood from their uteruses to their brains and, as a result, make them infertile.

In white middle-class and elite families, women were taught that their proper place was within the household, raising patriotic, pious children and making a peaceful refuge for their husbands. Ideally, wives occupied the domestic realm and left politics and finance to their husbands. Cultural conventions called for public and private, male and female, to remain largely separated in middling and elite families. Furthermore, for those families, the domestic world, or "sphere" of middle- and upper-class women was subordinate to the public "sphere" of men. So, for women born into households like Susan B. Anthony's—educated, religious, middling rank New Englanders—the path in life was highly gendered and quite narrow. It was these conventions that they challenged in their fight for women's suffrage.

These societal values generally did not apply to African American, immigrant, or poorer white women. The economic realities of their lives made their adopting these conventions highly unlikely. In the case of black women—the great majority of whom were enslaved—their labor was exploited at the same level as that of slave men.

The advocacy of women such as Anthony was thus limited by race and class, and, to a lesser degree, by region. The majority of women in America did not identify with the concerns of Anthony's cohort. Some faced far more vexing difficulties: impoverishment, labor exploitation, enslavement. Others who did belong to the middle and upper class rejected the critique of the women's sphere, fearing the cost of abandoning gender conventions would vastly outweigh any gains made by attaining equal citizenship with men. Southern whites overwhelmingly privileged preserving their region's racial hierarchy over any other reformist concerns, including women's rights. First-wave feminists persisted, however, believing that expanding citizenship in the American Republic would benefit all women, and that it was a just and proper expression of America's founding principles.

Feminists wanted to claim citizenship in a young nation already undergoing a series of major political and cultural changes in the antebellum era (1820s–1850s). The republican vision of the founding generation, in which learned, civic-minded, elite men reasoned together to determine the best interests of the nation, was giving way to comparatively raucous democratic reforms. Leaders of the Revolution assumed that only men who owned

substantial property held a stake in civic life, and only they could exercise the independent-mindedness required to put the common good above self-interest. As John Jay argued, "those who own the country ought to run it." So, in most states in the 1790s, only property owners could vote. The property qualification for serving in government was even higher.

In the early nineteenth century, these republican values were supplanted by a growing zeal for democracy—open competition over ideas and power. Rather than reasoning together to determine the common good, political leaders increasingly believed that the best ideas should triumph at the polls. The franchise was expanded in most states to include all adult white males. Political parties competed openly for votes; partisan contests determined national policy. But this expansion of the practical implications of the language of the Declaration of Independence—that "all men are created equal"—did not include African American men. And citizenship continued to be strictly gendered.

The rise of evangelical Christianity, shepherded in through a series of religious revivals known as the Second Great Awakening, was also profoundly altering the nation. Unlike political innovations, however, the Awakening did cross racial and gender lines. The Awakening legitimized previously fringe groups such as the Baptists, and embraced a more emotional, individualistic religious experience. Awakening ministers preached the centrality of the conversion experience: God came into the lives of true believers, irrespective of all concerns other than faith. How learned or rich a person was mattered little to salvation; God welcomed all, regardless of race, class, or gender. Conversion typically brought an outpouring of emotions: contrition, lamentation, euphoria, and sometimes physical spasms. Awakening ministers and converts also placed a great deal of emphasis on post-conversion behavior. Transformed men and women should daily bear the mark of their faith, and they should work to perfect society—to ready themselves and their communities for the return of Christ.

More women than men embraced evangelicalism which, along with the emotionalism displayed in the conversion experience, led to what historians have called the "feminization" of American Christianity. In other words, women became increasingly attracted to and engaged in religious life, and the expressions of evangelical piety seemed decidedly feminine. Church attendance, particularly among women, skyrocketed because of evangelical zeal. Thousands flocked to outdoor revivals to hear charismatic preachers and witness dramatic, impromptu conversions. Upstate New York was the scene of so many fiery revivals that it came to be known as the "burned over district."[2]

As the movement spread south, it bore the imprint of the region's increasingly peculiar institution of racial slavery. Early on, Great Awakening ministers who journeyed south preached the equality of all believers. They sought to convert slaves to evangelical Christianity and taught the immorality of slavery. As a result, evangelical Christianity became the dominant faith of the nation's free blacks and slaves. This initial level of egalitarianism was unacceptable to the region's planter elites, so Awakening ministers gradually made concessions to the South's gentry culture and racial hierarchy. As a consequence, many evangelical denominations split along regional lines, with northern Baptists, for example, continuing to embrace egalitarianism and southern Baptists opting to preach the godliness of slavery. The South, which had been the least religious region from the early colonial period through the close of the eighteenth century, became the "Bible Belt," and evangelical Christianity the dominant religion of white southerners.[3]

While evangelical Christianity helped preserve traditionalism in the South, in the North it fueled a progressive set of social reforms. Combined with a series of other changes occurring in the nation, including a rise in immigration and the growth of a market-centered economy, Awakening values, particularly the emphasis on post-conversion behavior, inspired Americans to seek to redress a number of societal problems. Excessive drinking, inadequate educational institutions, prostitution, and, outside the South, slavery were targeted as moral crises imperiling the young nation. Through moral reform the republic could be perfected. Women, who peopled the evangelical churches in disproportionate numbers, championed

---

2. See Paul E. Johnson, *A Shopkeeper's Millennium: Society and Revivals in Rochester, New York, 1815–1937* (New York: Hill and Wang, 1978).

3. For a fuller discussion of the evolution of evangelical Christianity in the early national South, see Christine Leigh Heyrman, *Southern Cross: The Beginnings of the Bible Belt* (New York: Knopf, 1997).

these reform movements. Sometimes in solely female organizations and sometimes partnering with like-minded men, reformist women sought to address the moral failings they saw afflicting America.

The Beecher family of New England reflected the interconnections of reform efforts in their region. Lyman Beecher was a theologian and minister who adopted Awakening ideals and then founded the American Temperance Society in 1826. Temperance quickly became a nationwide movement, with over two thousand local chapters founded within five years. Lyman Beecher's daughter, Catherine, was an educational innovator. She founded the Hartford Female Seminary in Connecticut, one of the nation's first major educational institutions for women. Her brothers, Charles and Henry, followed their father into the ministry. (Charles also composed hymns.) Many of the siblings also committed themselves to abolitionist activism. When Edward Beecher moved to Illinois, he started that state's first antislavery society. Sister Isabella attended Catherine's Hartford Academy and then informally educated herself in the law (women were never lawyers in those days). Harriett, perhaps the most renowned member of the family, was a teacher, abolitionist, and famous writer. *Uncle Tom's Cabin*, published in 1852, was the bestselling novel of the century.

Participation in these interconnected reform associations, particularly the immediatist, abolitionist movement that emerged in the North in the 1830s, taught women the practical skills required for successful political activism.[4] Reformism in general and abolitionism in particular

also instilled in women who joined these organizations a commitment to social justice and human equality. And, for some women, it threw into high relief their disfranchisement and legalized subordination. While clearly not on a par with the cruelty and debasement that slavery inflicted on African Americans, the denial of civil rights to white women distressed some reformers. Of course this was roundly rejected in the gentry-dominated, slaveholding South. It was controversial to some reform-minded women as well— including the Beecher sisters. But to other northern activists, male and female, the subjection of women, like the enslavement of blacks, seemed antithetical to American democracy and patently immoral.

It was an antislavery conference that roused feminists to action. A delegation of American activists had gone to London in 1840 to attend the World Anti-Slavery Convention. Among the group was Lucretia Mott, a veteran of reform organizations, and Elizabeth Cady Stanton, a young bride on her honeymoon. The convention fell into heated debate over the presence of the women, since mixed-gender groups, particularly ones in which women might speak, remained deeply controversial. The organization refused to accept the American women

4. The outset of the abolition movement is usually marked by the publication of William Lloyd Garrison's *Liberator* in 1831. Variously termed "immediatism," "Garrisonianism," or, most often, "abolitionism," this approach to anti-slavery called for the immediate end to racial slavery and the full and equal inclusion of African Americans into American life. Earlier approaches had focused on gradualism— freeing individuals once they reached a certain age or skill level or gradually outlawing slavery in a territory or state over a period of decades.

as participants, and finally compromised by allowing them to sit, silently, behind a curtain in the convention hall. Before they left London, Mott and Stanton determined to launch a women's rights movement in the United States.

Even in their own circle of like-minded reformers, feminists faced major obstacles. Women such as Lucretia Mott, Elizabeth Cady Stanton, Susan B. Anthony, and the Beecher sisters did not necessarily agree on the method, the scope, or even the advisability of challenging social conventions. For a whole host of reasons, the majority of white Americans found the idea of female equality absurd; to others it seemed downright dangerous. Certainly it was a radical break from a very long past. In 1848, when Mott and Stanton's London dream was finally commenced and the Seneca Falls Convention called for women to claim full citizenship, nowhere in the Western World did women vote. What lay behind the intense debates over women's civil rights? What did women's equality mean for the advocates and the critics of "first-wave" feminism?

✦

The Method

While there are biological differences between males and females, what societies read into those differences varies greatly. Manhood and womanhood—the roles and the defining traits ascribed to males and females—are shaped by larger cultural assumptions and societal needs. In short, gender is socially constructed. Certainly not every male or every female upholds his or her community's values. Massachusetts exile Anne Hutchinson offers us one powerful example of a woman rejecting societal expectations—and the high price that can accompany such independent-mindedness. Of course, seventeenth-century Massachusetts residents placed a premium on conformity and order, so their reaction to Anne's violation of established ethics was particularly strident. Other communities at other times have allowed for more latitude. Women and men in modern America enjoy far more flexibility in pursuing individual interests than their seventeenth-century counterparts. But in our own time, cultural assumptions that differentiate between women and men still exist. Can you list jobs, personality traits, or familial and community responsibilities that are gendered? What do those differences tell you about our assumptions about men and women? What are our gendered values?

In this chapter you will apply that skill to the past. You will focus on what the nineteenth-century men and women who argued about women's rights said. You will also engage in cultural analysis—exploring the underlying, sometime unexpressed, assumptions behind their words.

Part of why the first-wave feminists faced such an uphill battle in winning women's civic equality was that their efforts ran counter to a whole set of deeply entrenched beliefs about the proper role of women (at least white middle-class and elite women) in antebellum America. It should be apparent as you read this chapter's documents that opinions on women's proper roles and responsibilities varied enormously. Some authors support an expansion of women's opportunities and rights; others oppose such changes. Still others find themselves in the middle, embracing some changes and rejecting others.

Try not to take sides when you read the sources. It is deceptively easy to criticize our forebears. Remember that your purpose is not to determine who was right or wrong, or even to critique the various opinions. You are trying to use the materials to understand the culture in which these debates took shape. What inspired the feminists to take their stand? Why did this reform emerge in the 1840s? And why did it spark such a diversity of passionate opinions? Always keep in mind the central question posed:

Why was women's rights such a divisive, controversial issue for nineteenth-century Americans?

As you review the documents, make a list of the contested rights. What new opportunities did women seek? A comprehensive list will require you to consider not only the advocacy pieces supporting women's rights, but also the critiques. Reading both sides of the debate will allow you to enumerate all the changes the women's rights movement either intentionally pursued or, by implication, would foster.

Now, look again at the documents. What common patterns do you see? What values, what worldview do these authors—all middle-ranking whites—have in common? One obvious commonality is religion. But press this issue further: What particular religious ethics and beliefs appear to link the authors together? What other general cultural values do you see? Consider the texts as pieces of writing. How did the authors use language and tone and structure to express their opinions?

✦

The Evidence

Source 1 from Thomas R. Drew, "Dissertation on the Characteristic Differences Between the Sexes," *Southern Literary Messenger* 1 (May 1835): 439–512, in Winston E. Langley and Vivian C. Fox. eds., *Women's Rights in the United States: A Documentary History* (Westport, CT: Greenwood Press, 1994), pp. 62–63.

1. Dissertation on the Characteristic Differences Between the Sexes (1835).

The relative position of the sexes in the social and political world, may certainly be looked upon as the result of organization. The greater physical strength of man, enables him to occupy the foreground in the picture. He leaves the domestic scenes; he plunges into the turmoil and bustle of an active, selfish world; in his journey through life, he has to encounter innumerable difficulties, hardships and labors which constantly beset him. His mind must be nerved against them. Hence courage and boldness are his attributes. It is his province, undismayed, to stand against the rude shocks of the world; to meet with a lion's heart, the dangers which threaten him. He is the shield of woman, destined by nature to guard and protect her. Her inferior strength and sedentary habits confine her within the domestic circle; she is kept aloof from the bustle and storm of active life; she is not familiarized to the out of door dangers and hardships of a cold and scuffling world: timidity and modesty are her attributes. In the great strife which is constantly going forward around her, there are powers engaged which her inferior physical strength prevents her from encountering. She must rely upon the strength of others; man must be engaged in her cause. How is he to be drawn over to her side? Not by menace—not by force; for weakness cannot, by such means, be expected to triumph over might. No! It must be by conformity to that character which circumstances demand for the sphere in which she moves; by the exhibition of those qualities which delight and fascinate—which are calculated to win over to her side the proud lord of creation, and to make him an humble suppliant at her shrine. Grace, modesty and loveliness are the charms which constitute her power. By these, she creates the magic spell that subdues to her will the more mighty physical powers by which she is surrounded. Her attributes are rather of a passive than active character. Her power is more emblematical of that of divinity: it subdues without an effort, and almost creates by mere volition; whilst man must wind his way through the difficult and intricate mazes of philosophy; with pain and toil, tracing effects to their causes, and unraveling the deep mysteries of nature—storing his mind with useful knowledge, and exercising, training and perfecting his intellectual powers, whilst he cultivates his strength and hardens and matures his courage; all with a view of enabling him to assert his rights, and exercise a greater sway over those around him.

Source 2 from Angelina Grimké, "Letter XII: Human Rights Not Founded on Sex," in Angelina Emily Grimké, *Letters to Catherine Beecher: In Reply to an Essay on Slavery and Abolitionism, Addressed to A.E. Grimké, Revised by the Author* (Boston: Isaac Knapp, 1838), pp. 114–121.

2. Angelina Grimké letter to Catherine Beecher (1836).

[Angelina Grimké and her sister, Sarah, descended from a wealthy, prominent South Carolina slaveholding family. They rejected their family's long history of racial slavery, however. In 1833, Angelina published a letter in William Lloyd Garrison's

Liberator *calling for the immediate liberation of slaves. In 1837, she and Sarah went on a 67-city tour, speaking out against slavery and breaking new ground as females addressing mixed-gender crowds. Catherine Beecher, though a lifelong advocate for women teachers, was an anti-suffragist. She believed that women should exert influence in the home and in schools—but not through direct action as citizens.]*

. . . . The investigation of the rights of the slave has led me to a better understanding of my own. I have found the Anti-Slavery cause to be the high school of morals in our land—the school in which *human rights* are more fully investigated, and better understood and taught, than in any other. Here a great fundamental principle is uplifted and illuminated, and from this central light, rays innumerable stream all around. Human beings have *rights*, because they are *moral* beings: the rights of *all* men grow out of their moral nature; and as all men have the same moral nature, they have essentially the same rights. These rights may be wrested from the slave, but they cannot be alienated: his title to himself is as perfect *now*, as is that of Lyman Beecher:[5] it is stamped on his moral being, and is, like it, imperishable. Now if rights are founded in the nature of our moral being, then the *mere circumstance of sex* does not give to man higher rights and responsibilities, than to woman. To suppose that it does, would be to deny the self-evident truth, that the 'physical constitution is the mere instrument of the moral nature.' To suppose that it does, would be to break up utterly the relations, of the two natures, and to reverse their functions, exalting the animal nature into a monarch, and humbling the moral into a slave; making the former a proprietor, and the latter its property. When human beings are regarded as *moral* beings, sex, instead of being enthroned upon the summit, administering upon rights and responsibilities, sinks into insignificance and nothingness. . . .

Source 3 from Sarah M. Grimké, "Letters on the Equality of the Sexes and the Condition of Woman, addressed to Mary S. Parker, President of the Boston Female Anti-Slavery Society," in *The Original Equality of Woman* (Boston: Isaac Knapp, 1838), reprinted in Larry Ceplair, ed., *The Public Years of Sarah and Angelina Grimké: Selected Writings 1835–1839* (New York: Columbia University Press, 1989), pp. 204–210.

3. Sarah Grimké letter to Mary S. Parker, *The Original Equality of Woman* (1837).

[Sarah Grimké was raised in a devout Episcopal family. She attended church faithfully as a young woman and led Bible study among her family's slaves—

5. Lyman Beecher was Catherine Beecher's father, and one of the most respected and high profile ministers in the United States.

much to her parents' alarm. As an adult, she converted to the Quaker faith and took an active role in that community, teaching weekly Bible classes. Her confident understanding of scripture and theology is evident in this letter.]

My Dear Friend, —In attempting to comply with thy request to give my views on the Province of Woman, I feel that I am venturing on nearly untrodden ground, and that I shall advance arguments in opposition to a corrupt public opinion, and the perverted interpretation of Holy Writ, which has so universally obtained. But I am in search of truth; and no obstacle shall prevent my prosecuting that search, because I believe the welfare of the world will be materially advanced by every new discovery we make of the designs of Jehovah in the creation of woman. It is impossible that we can answer the purpose of our being, unless we understand that purpose. It is impossible that we should fulfill our duties, unless we comprehend them; or live up to our privileges, unless we know what they are.

In examining this important subject, I shall depend solely on the Bible to designate the sphere of woman, because I believe almost every thing that has been written on this subject, has been the result of a misconception of the simple truths revealed in the Scriptures, in consequence of the false translation of many passages of Holy Writ. My mind is entirely delivered from the superstitious reverence which is attached to the English version of the Bible. King James's translators certainly were not inspired. I therefore claim the original as my standard, *believing that to have been inspired*, and I also claim to judge for myself what is the meaning of the inspired writers, because I believe it to be the solemn duty of every individual to search the Scriptures for themselves, with the aid of the Holy Spirit, and not be governed by the views of any man, or set of men.

We must first view woman at the period of her creation. "And God said, Let us make man in our own image, after our likeness; and let them have dominion over the fish of the sea, and over the fowl of the air, and over the cattle, and over all the earth, and over every creeping thing that creepeth upon the earth. So God created man in his own image, in the image of God created he him, male and female created he them." In all this sublime description of the creation of man, (which is a generic term including man and woman,) there is not one particle of difference intimated as existing between them. They were both made in the image of God; dominion was given to both over every other creature, but not over each other. Created in perfect equality, they were expected to exercise the viceregency intrusted to them by their Maker, in harmony and love.

Let us pass on now to the recapitulation of the creation of man: — "The Lord God formed man of the dust of the ground, and breathed into his nostrils the breath of life; and man became a living soul. And the Lord God said, it is not good that man should be alone, I will make him an help meet for him."[6] All creation swarmed with animated beings capable of natural affection, as we know they still are; it was not, therefore, merely to give man a creature susceptible of loving, obeying, and looking up to him, for all that the animals could do and did do. It was to give him a companion, *in all respects* his equal; one who was like himself a *free agent*, gifted with intellect and endowed with immortality; not a partaker merely of his animal gratifications, but able to enter into all his feelings as a moral and responsible being. If this had not been the case, how could she have been a help meet for him? I understand this as applying not only to the parties entering into the marriage contract, but to all men and women, because I believe God designed woman to be a help meet for man in every good and perfect work. She was a part of himself, as if Jehovah designed to make the oneness and identity of man and woman perfect and complete; and when the glorious work of their creation was finished, "the morning starts sang together, and all the sons of God shouted for joy."

This blissful condition was not long enjoyed by our first parents. Eve, it would seem from the history, was wandering alone amid the bowers of Paradise, when the serpent met with her. From her reply to Satan, it is evident that the command not to eat "of the tree that is in the midst of the garden," was given to both, although the term man was used when the prohibition was issued by God. "And the woman said unto the serpent, WE may eat of the fruit of the trees of the garden, God hath said, YE shall not eat of it, neither shall YE touch it, lest YE die." Here the woman was exposed to temptation from a being with whom she was unacquainted. She had been accustomed to associate with her beloved partner, and to hold communion with God and with angels; but of satanic intelligence, she was in all probability entirely ignorant. Through the subtlety of the serpent, she was beguiled. And "when she saw that the tree was good for food, and that it was pleasant to the eyes, and a tree to be desired to make one wise, she took of the fruit thereof and did eat."

We next find Adam involved in the same sin, not through the instrumentality of a super-natural agent, but through that of his equal, a being whom he must have known was liable to transgress the divine command, because he must have felt that he was himself a free agent, and that he was restrained from disobedience only by the exercise of faith and love towards his Creator. Had Adam tenderly reproved his wife, and endeavored to lead her to repentance instead of sharing in her guilt, I should be much more ready to accord to man that superiority which he claims; but as the facts stand

---

6. Genesis, chapters 1 and 2. The chapters recount two differing narratives of the creation story. Grimké's critics pointed to the second accounting, of Eve being formed from Adam's rib, to counter her analysis.

disclosed by the sacred historian, it appears to me that to say the least, there was as much weakness exhibited by Adam as by Eve. They both fell from innocence, and consequently from happiness, *but not from equality*.

Let us next examine the conduct of this fallen pair, when Jehovah interrogated them respecting their fault. They both frankly confessed their guilt. "The man said, the woman whom thou gavest to be with me, she gave me of the tree and I did eat. And the woman said, the serpent beguiled me and I did eat." And the Lord God said unto the woman, "Thou wilt be subject unto thy husband, and he will rule over thee." That this did not allude to the subjection of woman to man is manifest, because the same mode of expression is used in speaking to Cain of Abel. The truth is that the curse, as it is termed, which was pronounced by Jehovah upon woman, is a simple prophecy. The Hebrew, like the French language, uses the same word to express *shall* and *will*. Our translators having been accustomed to exercise lordship over their wives, and seeing only through the medium of a perverted judgment, very naturally, though I think not very learnedly or very kindly, translated it *shall* instead of *will*, and thus converted a prediction to Eve into a command to Adam; for observe, it is addressed to the woman and not to the man. The consequence of the fall was an immediate struggle for dominion, and Jehovah foretold which would gain the ascendancy; but as he created them in his image, as that image manifestly was not lost by the fall, because it is urged in Gen. 9:6, as an argument why the life of man should not be taken by his fellow man, there is no reason to suppose that sin produced any distinction between them as moral, intellectual and responsible beings. Man might just as well have endeavored by hard labor to fulfil the prophecy, thorns and thistles will the earth bring forth to thee, as to pretend to accomplish the other, "he will rule over thee," by asserting dominion over his wife.

> Authority usurped from God, not given.
> He gave him only over beast, flesh, fowl,
> Dominion absolute: that right he holds
> By God's donation: but man o'er woman
> He made not Lord, such title to himself
> Reserving, human left from human free.

Here then I plant myself. God created us equal; — he created us free agents; — he is our Lawgiver, our King and our Judge, and to him alone is woman bound to be in subjection, and to him alone is she accountable for the use of those talents with which Her Heavenly Father has entrusted her. One is her Master even Christ.

Thine for the oppressed in the bonds of womanhood,

Sarah M. Grimké

[223]

Source 4 from "'Pastoral Letter.' Extract from a Pastoral Letter of 'the General Association of Massachusetts (Orthodox) to the Churches under their care'—1837," in Elizabeth Cady Stanton, Susan B. Anthony, and Matilda Joslyn Gage, eds. *History of Woman Suffrage*, Vol. 1 (1848–1861) (Rochester, NY: Charles Mann, 1887), pp. 81–82.

4. Extract from a Pastoral Letter of the General Association of Massachusetts (Orthodox) to the Churches Under Their Care (1837).

. . . . The appropriate duties and influence of woman are clearly stated in the New Testament. Those duties and that influence are unobtrusive and private, but the source of mighty power. When the mild, dependent, softening influence of woman upon the sternness of man's opinions is fully exercised, society feels the effects of it in a thousand forms. The power of woman is her dependence, flowing from the consciousness of that weakness which God has given her for her protection, (!) and which keeps her in those departments of life that form the character of individuals, and of the nation. There are social influences which females use in promoting piety and the great objects of Christian benevolence which we can not too highly commend.

We appreciate the unostentatious prayers and efforts of woman in advancing the cause of religion at home and abroad; in Sabbath-schools; in leading religious inquirers to the pastors (!) for instruction; and in all such associated effort as becomes the modesty of her sex; and earnestly hope that she may abound more and more in these labors of piety and love. But when she assumes the place and tone of man as a public reformer, our care and protection of her seem unnecessary; we put ourselves in self-defence (!) against her; she yields the power which God has given her for her protection, and her character becomes unnatural. If the vine, whose strength and beauty is to lean upon the trellis-work, and half conceal its clusters, thinks to assume the independence and the overshadowing nature of the elm, it will not only cease to bear fruit, but fall in shame and dishonor into the dust. We can not, therefore, but regret the mistaken conduct of those who encourage females to bear an obtrusive and ostentatious part in measures of reform, and countenance any of that sex who so far forget themselves as to itinerate in the character of public lecturers and teachers. . . .

Source 5 from "Declaration of Sentiments," in Elizabeth Cady Stanton, Susan B. Anthony, and Matilda Joslyn Gage, eds. *History of Woman Suffrage*, Vol. 1 (1848–1861), (Rochester, NY: Charles Mann, 1887), pp. 70–73.

5. Seneca Falls Convention, Declaration of Sentiments (1848).

[The Declaration of Sentiments, modeled after the Declaration of Independence, emerged out of the Women's Rights Convention, held July 19–20, 1848, in Seneca

Falls, New York. With less than a week's notice, the event drew nearly 300 people, including forty men. Elizabeth Cady Stanton was the principal architect of the Declaration. Telling of that age, none of the women present chose to preside; Lucretia Mott's husband, James, led the deliberations.]

When, in the course of human events, it becomes necessary for one portion of the family of man to assume among the people of the earth a position different from that which they have hitherto occupied, but one to which the laws of nature and of nature's God entitle them, a decent respect to the opinions of mankind requires that they should declare the causes that impel them to such a course.

We hold these truths to be self-evident: that all men and women are created equal; that they are endowed by their Creator with certain inalienable rights; that among these are life, liberty, and the pursuit of happiness; that to secure these rights governments are instituted, deriving their just powers from the consent of the governed. Whenever any form of government becomes destructive of these ends, it is the right of those who suffer from it to refuse allegiance to it, and to insist upon the institution of a new government, laying its foundation on such principles, and organizing its powers in such form, as to them shall seem most likely to effect their safety and happiness. Prudence, indeed, will dictate that governments long established should not be changed for light and transient causes; and accordingly all experience hath shown that mankind are more disposed to suffer, while evils are sufferable, than to right themselves by abolishing the forms to which they were accustomed. But when a long train of abuses and usurpations, pursuing invariably the same object evinces a design to reduce them under absolute despotism, it is their duty to throw off such government, and to provide new guards for their future security. Such has been the patient sufferance of the women under this government, and such is now the necessity which constrains them to demand the equal station to which they are entitled.

The history of mankind is a history of repeated injuries and usurpations on the part of man toward woman, having in direct object the establishment of an absolute tyranny over her. To prove this, let facts be submitted to a candid world.

He has never permitted her to exercise her inalienable right to the elective franchise.

He has compelled her to submit to laws, in the formation of which she had no voice.

He has withheld from her rights which are given to the most ignorant and degraded men—both natives and foreigners.

Having deprived her of this first right of a citizen, the elective franchise, thereby leaving her without representation in the halls of legislation, he has oppressed her on all sides.

He has made her, if married, in the eye of the law, civilly dead.

He has taken from her all right in property, even to the wages she earns.

He has made her, morally, an irresponsible being, as she can commit many crimes with impunity, provided they be done in the presence of her husband. In the covenant of marriage, she is compelled to promise obedience to her husband, he becoming, to all intents and purposes, her master—the law giving him power to deprive her of her liberty, and to administer chastisement.

He has so framed the laws of divorce, as to what shall be the proper causes, and in case of separation, to whom the guardianship of the children shall be given, as to be wholly regardless of the happiness of women—the law, in all cases, going upon a false supposition of the supremacy of man, and giving all power into his hands.

After depriving her of all rights as a married woman, if single, and the owner of property, he has taxed her to support a government which recognizes her only when her property can be made profitable to it.

He has monopolized nearly all the profitable employments, and from those she is permitted to follow, she receives but a scanty remuneration. He closes against her all the avenues to wealth and distinction which he considers most honorable to himself. As a teacher of theology, medicine, or law, she is not known.

He has denied her the facilities for obtaining a thorough education, all colleges being closed against her.

He allows her in Church, as well as State, but a subordinate position, claiming Apostolic authority for her exclusion from the ministry, and, with some exceptions, from any public participation in the affairs of the Church.

He has created a false public sentiment by giving to the world a different code of morals for men and women, by which moral delinquencies which exclude women from society, are not only tolerated, but deemed of little account in man.

He has usurped the prerogative of Jehovah himself, claiming it as his right to assign for her a sphere of action, when that belongs to her conscience and to her God.

He has endeavored, in every way that he could, to destroy her confidence in her own powers, to lessen her self-respect, and to make her willing to lead a dependent and abject life.

Now, in view of this entire disfranchisement of one-half the people of this country, their social and religious degradation—in view of the unjust laws above mentioned, and because women do feel themselves aggrieved, oppressed, and fraudulently deprived of their most sacred rights, we insist that they have immediate admission to all the rights and privileges which belong to them as citizens of the United States.

In entering upon the great work before us, we anticipate no small amount of misconception, misrepresentation, and ridicule; but we shall use every instrumentality within our power to effect our object. We shall employ agents, circulate tracts, petition the State and National legislatures, and endeavor to enlist the pulpit and the press in our behalf. We hope this Convention will be followed by a series of Conventions embracing every part of the country. . . .

. . . WHEREAS, The great precept of nature is conceded to be, that "man shall pursue his own true and substantial happiness." Blackstone in his Commentaries remarks, that this law of Nature being coeval with mankind, and dictated by God himself, is of course superior in obligation to any other. It is binding over all the globe, in all countries, and at all times; no human laws are of any validity if contrary to this, and such of them as are valid, derive all their force, and all their validity, and all their authority, mediately and immediately, from this original; therefore,

Resolved, That such laws as conflict, in any way, with the true and substantial happiness of woman, are contrary to the great precept of nature and of no validity, for this is "superior in obligation to any other."

Resolved, That all laws which prevent woman from occupying such a station in society as her conscience shall dictate, or which place her in a position inferior to that of man, are contrary to the great precept of nature, and therefore of no force or authority.

Resolved, That woman is man's equal—was intended to be so by the Creator, and the highest good of the race demands that she should be recognized as such.

Resolved, That the women of this country ought to be enlightened in regards to the laws under which they live, that they may no longer publish their degradation by declaring themselves satisfied with their present position, nor their ignorance, by asserting that they have all the rights they want.

Resolved, That inasmuch as man, while claiming for himself intellectual superiority, does accord to woman moral superiority, it is pre-eminently his duty to encourage her to speak and teach, as she has as opportunity, in all religious assemblies.

Resolved, That the same amount of virtue, delicacy, and refinement of behavior that is required of woman in the social state, should also be required of man, and the same transgressions should be visited with equal severity on both man and woman.

Resolved, That the objection of indelicacy and impropriety, which is so often brought against woman when she addresses a public audience, comes with a very ill-grace from those who encourage, by their attendance, her appearance on the stage, in the concert, or in feats of the circus.

Resolved, That woman has too long rested satisfied in the circumscribed limits which corrupt customs and a perverted application of the Scriptures have marked out for her, and that it is time she should move in the enlarged sphere which her great Creator has assigned her.

Resolved, That it is the duty of the women of this country to secure to themselves their sacred right to the elective franchise.[7]

Resolved, That the equality of human rights results necessarily from the fact of the identity of the race in capabilities and responsibilities.

Resolved, therefore, That, being invested by the Creator with the same capabilities, and the same consciousness of responsibility for their exercise, it is demonstrably the right and duty of woman, equally with man, to promote every righteous cause by every righteous means; and especially in regard to the great subjects of morals and religion, it is self-evidently her right to participate with her brother in teaching them, both in private and in public, by writing and by speaking, by any instrumentalities proper to be used, and in any assemblies proper to be held; and this being a self-evident truth growing out of the divinely implanted principles of human nature, any custom or authority adverse to it, whether modern or wearing the hoary sanction of antiquity, is to be regarded as a self-evident falsehood, and at war with mankind.

Source 6 from "Female Department: Women out of their Latitude," *Mechanic's Advocate* (Albany, NY: 1846–1848), 12 August 1848. Vol. 2, Iss. 34, p. 264. Accessed 31 January 2010. Available online through the American Periodicals Series: < http://proquest.umi.com/pqdw eb?did=1217678512&Fmt=10&clientId=20270&RQT=309&VName=HNP >.

6. "Women out of their Latitude" (1848).

We are sorry to see that the women, in several parts of this State, are holding what they call "Woman's Rights Conventions," and setting forth a formidable list of those Rights, in a parody upon the Declaration of American Independence.

The papers of the day contain extended notices of these Conventions. Some of them fall in with their objects, and praise the meetings highly; but the majority either deprecate or ridicule both.

7. All the other resolutions passed unanimously. But suffrage was so radical that even Lucretia Mott initially balked at the idea. The renowned abolitionist and eloquent former slave, Frederick Douglass, persuaded the crowd to endorse women's voting rights.

The women who attend these meetings, no doubt at the expense of their more appropriate duties, act as committees, write resolutions and addresses, hold much correspondence, make speeches, etc. etc. They affirm, as among their rights, that of unrestricted franchise, and assert that it is wrong to deprive them of the privilege to become legislators, lawyers, doctors, divines, etc. etc.; and they are holding conventions and making an agitatory movement, with the object in view of revolutionising public opinion and the laws of the land, and changing their relative position in society in such a way as to divide with the male sex the labors and responsibilities of active life, in every branch of arts, science, trades and professions!

Now it requires no argument to prove that this is all wrong. Every true-hearted female will instantly feel that it is unwomanly, and that to be practically carried out, the males must change their position in society to the same extent in an opposite direction, in order to enable them to discharge an equal share of the domestic duties which now appertain to females, and which must be neglected, to a great extent, if women are allowed the exercise of all the "rights" that are claimed by these Convention-holders. Society would have to be radically remodelled, in order to accommodate itself to so great a change in the most vital part of the compact of the social relations of life; and the order of things established at the creation of mankind, and continued six *thousand years*, would be completely broken up. The organic laws of our country, and of each State, would have to be licked into new shapes, in order to admit of the introduction of the vast change that is contemplated. In a thousand other ways that might be mentioned, if we had room to make, and our readers had patience to hear them, would this sweeping reform be attended, by fundamental changes in the public and private, civil and religious, moral and social relations of the sexes, of life, and of government.

But this change is impracticable, uncalled for and unnecessary. *If effected*, it would get the world by the ears, make "confusion worse confounded," demoralise, and degrade from their high sphere and noble destiny, women of all respectable and useful classes and prove a monstrous injury to all mankind. It would be productive of no positive good, that would not be outweighed, ten fold, by positive evil. It would alter the relations of females, without bettering their condition.

Besides all, and above all, it presents no remedy for the *real* evils that the millions of the industrious, hardworking and much-suffering women of our country groan under and seek to redress.

Source 7 from Elizabeth Cady Stanton, *National Reformer* (Rochester, NY), 14 September 1848, in Susan Groag Bell and Karen M. Offen, eds., *Women, the Family, and Freedom,* Volume 1, 1750–1880 (Stanford, CA: Stanford University Press, 1983), pp. 259–260. Reprinted from Elizabeth Cady Stanton, Susan B. Anthony, and Matilda Joslyn Gage, eds. *History of Woman Suffrage*, Vol. 1, 1848–1861 (Rochester, NY: Charles Mann, 1887), p. 806.

7. Elizabeth Cady Stanton on Women's Rights (1848).

. . . . There is no danger of this question dying for want of notice. Every paper you take up has something to say about it, and just in proportion to the refinement and intelligence of the editor, has this movement been favorably noticed. But one might suppose from the articles that you find in some papers, that there were editors so ignorant as to believe that the chief object of these recent Conventions was to seat every lord at the head of a cradle, and to clothe every woman in her lord's attire. Now, neither of these points, however important they be considered by humble minds, were touched upon in the Conventions. . . . For those who do not yet understand the real objects of our recent Conventions at Rochester and Seneca Falls, I would state that we did not meet to discuss fashions, customs, or dress, the rights or duties of man, nor the propriety of the sexes changing positions, but simply our own inalienable rights, our duties, our true sphere. If God has assigned a sphere to man and one to woman, we claim the right to judge ourselves of His design in reference to *us*, and we accord to man the same privilege. We think a man has quite enough in this life to find out his own individual calling, without being taxed to decide where every woman belongs; and the fact that so many men fail in the business they undertake, calls loudly for their concentrating more thought on their own faculties, capabilities, and sphere of action. We have all seen a man making a jackass of himself in the pulpit, at the bar, or in our legislative halls, when he might have shone as a general in our Mexican war, captain of a canal boat, or as a tailor on his bench. Now, is it to be wondered at that woman has some doubts about the present position assigned her being the true one, when her every-day experience shows her that man makes such fatal mistakes in regard to himself?

There is no such thing as a sphere for a sex. Every man has a different sphere, and one in which he may shine, and it is the same with every woman; and the same woman may have a different sphere at different times. The distinguished Angelina Grimké was acknowledged by all the anti-slavery host to be in her sphere, when, years ago, she went through the length and breadth of New England, telling the people of her personal experience of the horrors and abominations of the slave system, and by her eloquence and power as a public speaker, producing an effect unsurpassed by any of the highly gifted men of her day. Who dares to say that in thus using her splendid talents in speaking for the dumb, pleading the cause of the poor friendless slave, that she was out of her sphere? Angelina Grimké is now a wife and the mother of several children. We hear of her no more in public. Her sphere and her duties have changed. She deems it her first and her most sacred duty to devote all her time and talents to her household and to the education of her children. We do not say that she is not *now* in her sphere. The highly gifted Quakeress, Lucretia Mott, married early in life, and brought up a large family of children. All who have seen her at home agree that she was a pattern as a wife, mother, and housekeeper. No one ever fulfilled all the duties of that sphere more perfectly than did she. Her children are now settled in their own homes. Her husband and herself, having a comfortable fortune, pass much of their time in going about and doing good. Lucretia Mott has now no domestic cares. She has a talent for public speaking; her mind is of a high order; her moral perceptions remarkably clear; her religious fervor deep and intense; and who shall tell us that this divinely inspired woman is out of her sphere in her public endeavors to rouse this wicked nation to a sense of its awful guilt, to its great sins of war, slavery, injustice to woman and the laboring poor.

Questions to Consider

Obviously the authors of these various texts did not agree about women's rights. They proclaimed their opinions clearly and emphatically. These disputes took place within a particular historical and cultural context. The parameters of the debate—the assumptions that were shared by the authors and the issues they disagreed about—tell us a great deal about antebellum America. In this chapter you should discover not only the sources of the controversy surrounding women's rights, but also develop a deeper understanding of antebellum culture.

Once you have listed the specific points of contention, think about why these issues mattered so much to the authors. What assumptions—about civic life, about the future of the nation, about morality, and about human nature—appear in these texts? Can you see the influences of the American Revolution? Of evangelical Christianity? The documents should also help you see changes that had already taken place—in women's civic engagement, in their formal education, in their religiosity—by the time of the Seneca Falls meeting. While critics of gender equality found the Declaration of Sentiments dangerous, advocates such as Elizabeth Cady Stanton and Lucretia Mott saw women's rights as essential.

These disagreements reflected profound changes that divided antebellum Americans. What were those changes?

Consider the essay by Thomas Drew. How does he understand social order? In his view, what is the basic nature of women and of men? Why and in what specific ways are men and women different? What are their proper roles in society? Compare his perceptions with the letter written by Angelina Grimké. Does she agree with Drew about physical differences determining social roles? How does she understand social order and gender differences? What does she think is the basic nature of women and men? What about the General Association of Massachusetts? The signers of the Declaration of Sentiments?

Compare the letter written by Sarah Grimké to the one sent to Massachusetts churches. What religious values do they have in common? Where do they part ways? What underlying assumptions about religion and gender can you see in these two documents? How does the church leaders' understanding of women's proper place in society differ from that of Sarah and her sister, Angelina?

Review again each document, thinking of each as a piece of writing that reflects the values of the author as well as the culture of that era. Compare and contrast the tone of each piece. The recipients of the texts varied, but all the authors sought to persuade readers to adopt their views. Think about the different tactics—ridicule, logic, hyperbole, emotionalism, persuasion—employed by the writers. How might audiences respond to these differing approaches? What can you glean about the women's rights debate by the tone and the structure of the writing? For example, what does Elizabeth Cady Stanton's authoring of the Declaration of Sentiments tell us about women's education and civic engagement? What does Stanton's 1848 essay tell us about her perception of her critics?

For all the authors you've read, the stakes of the debate appeared extraordinarily high. Each writes as if the fate of American society depends on widespread adoption of their views. Why were they so adamant? What deeper cultural assumptions did their advocacy reflect? Why was "first-wave" feminism so controversial?

According to the advocates of women's rights, what will be the costs to American society if their position is rejected? According to their opponents, what will be the consequences of embracing women's equality? What do these stakes tell us about antebellum America? To answer these questions, begin with the Declaration of Sentiments. According to that document, in what ways have women been exploited? At what cost? What are the consequences of women continuing to accept those prescribed parameters? What specific changes do they seek? What would this require of women? Of men? In the essay, "Women out of their Latitude," the author maintains that embracing women's rights will cause "monstrous injury to all mankind" and result in society being "radically remodelled." First, does the author accurately report on the Seneca Falls objectives? Second, what does the author mean that society would be "radically remodelled" with "monstrous injury"? What sort of changes would embracing women's equality force? In her rebuttal to the critics of women's rights, Elizabeth Cady Stanton roundly rejects the entire idea of women's "sphere." How does she attempt to recast this paradigm? If her argument holds sway, what would this reimagination of women's proper roles mean for antebellum America?

Epilogue

Elizabeth Cady Stanton and like-minded women and men did not secure women's legal equality in the antebellum era. Certainly there were some successes. Several states adopted women's property rights in the 1850s. Changes came in divorce law as well, with more states allowing abused and abandoned wives to end their marriages.[8] But what they defined as the foundation for female equality—the right to vote—eluded nineteenth-century feminists. Stanton and Susan B. Anthony became close friends in the 1850s, and lifelong allies in the fight for women's rights. They made a terrific team: Stanton the compelling, forceful writer, and Anthony the consummate strategist. Over the course of the next half-century, they tried every approach. They waged their fight in newspapers; they founded organizations; they engaged in public displays of civil disobedience and went to jail; they lobbied legislatures; they filed lawsuits. The movement fractured in the wake of the Civil War, with some feminists endorsing the 14th and 15th Amendments (which extended civil equality and voting rights to former enslaved men), while others withheld their support until women, too, could enjoy citizenship. In 1890, the two sides reconciled, creating the National American Woman Suffrage Association. Elizabeth Cady Stanton served as the first president; Susan B. Anthony succeeded her a few years later.

Neither woman lived to see her dream of women's suffrage realized. Stanton died in 1902. Anthony followed four years later. It fell to a new generation of feminists to shepherd their vision. Carrie Chapman Catt was president of the NAWSA, and the face of the women's suffrage movement, when the 19th Amendment passed Congress in the summer of 1919. It was ratified by the requisite number of states and added to the United States Constitution on August 26, 1920.

But the 19th Amendment applied principally to white women. In 1920, the majority of African Americans lived in the South, where Reconstruction had collapsed under the weight of white southern intransigence, northern apathy, and racial violence. Segregation reigned there, and black women, like

8. For divorce law, see Hendrik Hartog, *Man and Wife in America: A History* (Cambridge, MA: Harvard University Press, 2000); and Norma Bosch, *Framing American Divorce: From the Revolutionary Generation to the Victorians* (Berkeley, CA: University of California Press, 1999).

black men, were threatened and intimidated away from the polls. Not until 1965 could the majority of African American women vote in the United States—one hundred years after the defeat of the Confederacy and nearly two hundred years after Thomas Jefferson's eloquent call for equality and self-government launched the American republic. In the twenty-first century, women vote in larger numbers than men. But egalitarianism at the voting booth has not produced a gender-neutral society. In 2009, American women held 49.8 percent of all jobs, but they earned 77 cents to every dollar paid to a man.[9]

9. "The New Gender Gap," *The New York Times*, 30 September 2009.

9

The "Peculiar Institution": Slaves Tell Their Own Story

The Problem

With the establishment of its new government in 1789, the United States became a virtual magnet for foreign travelers, perhaps never more so than during the three decades preceding the Civil War. Middle to upper class, interested in everything from politics to prison reform to the position of women in American society, these curious travelers fanned out across the United States, and almost all of them wrote about their observations in letters, pamphlets, and books widely read on both sides of the Atlantic. Regardless of their particular interests, however, few travelers failed to comment on the "peculiar institution" of African American slavery.

As did many nineteenth-century women writers, English author Harriet Martineau showed keen interest in those aspects of American society that affected women and children. She was appalled by slavery, believing it degraded marriage by allowing southern white men to sexually exploit female slaves, a practice that often produced interracial children born into bondage.

The young Frenchman Alexis de Tocqueville came to study the American penitentiary system and stayed to investigate politics and society. In his book *Democracy in America* (1842), Tocqueville expressed his belief that American slaves had completely lost their African culture—their customs, languages, religions, and even the memories of their countries. The enormously popular English novelist, Charles Dickens, also visited in 1842. He spent very little time in the South but collected and published advertisements for runaway slaves that contained gruesome descriptions of their burns, brandings, scars, and shackles. As Dickens departed for a steamboat trip to the West, he wrote that he left "with a grateful heart that I was not doomed to live where slavery was, and had never had my senses blunted to its wrongs and horrors in a slave-rocked cradle."[1]

---

1. Charles Dickens, *American Notes and Pictures from Italy* (London: Oxford University Press, 1957), p. 137.

In the turbulent 1850s, Fredrika Bremer, a Swedish novelist, traveled throughout the United States for two years and spent considerable time in South Carolina, Georgia, and Louisiana. After her first encounters with African Americans in Charleston, Bremer wrote her sister that they "appear for the most part cheerful and well-fed."[2] Her subsequent trips to the plantations of the backcountry, however, increased her sympathy for slaves and her distrust of white southerners' assertions that "slaves are the happiest people in the world."[3] In fact, by the end of her stay, Bremer was praising the slaves' morality, patience, talents, and religious practices.

These travelers—and many more—added their opinions to the growing literature about the nature of American slavery and its effects. But the overwhelming majority of this literature was written by white people. What did the slaves themselves think? How did they experience the institution of slavery?

✦

Background

By the time of the American Revolution, what had begun in 1619 as a trickle of Africans intended to supplement the farm labor of indentured servants from England had swelled to a slave population of approximately 500,000 people held in bondage in mainland British America.

Slavery existed in every North American colony. Slaves worked in cities and on farms, in homes and businesses, and in the thriving Atlantic maritime trades. For most of the colonial era, few white colonists other than the Quakers ever questioned the efficacy and morality of holding Africans as chattel. Racial slavery, in sum, was central to building stable and profitable American colonies.

While slavery had a long history in colonial America, the nature of the institution changed substantively over time. In the seventeenth century, African men and women often labored alongside white servants, apprentices, and small landowners and craftsmen. Slavery was racially based and brutal, but it was one of several forms of exploitative, unfree labor. Historian Ira Berlin has described this pattern, common throughout North America, as "societies with slaves." By the middle of the eighteenth century, the southern provinces had evolved into "slave societies." Slavery was no longer *a* labor system but had become *the* labor system and a foundational institution in society. By mid-century the economy, culture, and social order of southern colonies, most notably South Carolina and Virginia, depended on racial slavery. The majority of slaves worked on plantations in these two colonies, producing lucrative agricultural commodities such as tobacco and rice. Slavery became more rigid and pervading.

2. Fredrika Bremer, *America of the Fifties: Letters of Fredrika Bremer,* ed. Adolph B. Benson (New York: American Scandinavian Foundation, 1924), p. 96.

3. *Ibid.*, p. 100.

Laws increasingly defined blacks as inferior to whites and attempted to grant owners nearly unchecked power over slaves.

Although it unleashed a flood of debates about slavery, the American Revolution did not reverse those trends in the South. The founding generation clearly understood the contradiction of allowing slavery in a republic. Slaveholders such as Thomas Jefferson, principal author of the Declaration of Independence, and James Madison, architect of the Constitution, engaged in anguished discussions about the problem of perpetuating racial slavery in the new nation they were designing. Jefferson famously confessed, "I tremble for my country when I reflect that God is just; that his justice cannot sleep forever." But he, Madison, and the great majority of their fellow southern planters failed to act on their concerns. (Jefferson freed some of his children with Sally Hemings, but neither he nor Madison undertook any substantive emancipatory plan during their lives or in their wills.)

Meanwhile, northern states, where African American slavery was not so deeply rooted, began instituting gradual emancipation programs after the Revolution. These new laws, which often freed men and women upon their reaching a certain age, sometimes took decades to reach fruition. As late as the 1840 census, slaves still resided in New England states. And, in some cases, freedom came with strings. In 1818 and 1822, Connecticut and Rhode Island, respectively, rescinded the voting rights of free black men. When New York revised its state constitution in 1821, it disfranchised African Americans as well. Some New England towns

even revived the colonial practice of "warning out"—expelling undesirable transients—in decidedly racialized terms. Still, the differences between the increasingly free North and the slave South appeared stark enough to James Madison in 1787 that he declared, "the real difference of interests" at the Constitutional Convention, "lay, not between the large & small but between the N. & Southern States. The institution of slavery & its consequences formed the line of discrimination."[4]

The South's commitment to slavery was spurred on by the invention of the cotton gin in the 1790s. The gin enabled seeds to be removed from the easily grown short staple cotton, which, in turn, allowed southern planters to expand into commercial cotton production. The subsequent cotton boom proved transformative for the American South and for African American men and women held in bondage. Cotton extended plantation culture by fueling the westward movement of commercial agriculture and racial slavery. In the early nineteenth century, southern planters carried slavery into nearly every area of the South, including Tennessee, Kentucky, Alabama, Mississippi, Missouri, and ultimately Texas. Simultaneously, the slave population burgeoned, roughly doubling every thirty years (from approximately 700,000 in 1790 to 1.5 million in 1820 to more than 3.2 million in 1850). Because importation of slaves from Africa was banned in 1808 (although there was some illegal slave smuggling), slave

4. James Madison, *Notes of Debates in the Federal Convention of 1787* (New York: W. W. Norton, 1966), 295.

population growth derived principally from natural increase.

As the institution of slavery changed, so too did the experiences of men and women held in bondage. In colonial America, differences in nationality, language, and customs, owing to the prevalence of slaves imported directly from Africa, had worked against the ability of bondspersons to forge a common, shared culture. Moreover, because slaves engaged in a wide range of occupations in the various colonies, African American cultures tended to be regionally rooted. The lives of slaves in colonial South Carolina differed significantly from those in Virginia; the culture that emerged in urban areas diverged from that forged on plantations. But in the antebellum era, slave cultures converged. Second- and third-generation native-born African Americans dominated the slave populations on cotton plantations in the southern frontier. They spoke the same language as whites, many had converted to Christianity, and some knew how to read and write (since this was illegal, most kept it secret from their white owners).

Antebellum slaveholders, for their part, grew ever more anxious about and defensive of the South's racial order. This derived in part from the clear fact that the American South was increasingly isolated in maintaining slavery in the early nineteenth century. In addition to the gradual emancipation programs of many older northern states, slavery had been forbidden in the Northwest Territory. Britain abolished the slave trade in 1807 and ended slavery in 1833. France outlawed slavery in 1794. (Napoleon reinstated it during his reign; it was abolished a second, final time in 1848.) A number of widely publicized slave uprisings only added to the conviction of southern whites that their way of life was under siege. In 1791, a revolution on the French colony of Saint Domingue resulted in the abolition of slavery on the Caribbean island and the creation of the first free black republic, Haiti. The Haitian Revolution was the most successful slave rebellion in history, and it horrified southern whites. The Nat Turner Rebellion in Virginia in 1831, in which fifty-five whites were killed, many as they slept, deepened slaveholders' insecurities. In response, southern states passed a series of laws that made the system of slavery even more restrictive. Manumission statutes grew far more rigid; in Mississippi every manumission required a special act of the state legislature, and Virginia mandated the outmigration of any freed slave. It became illegal even for owners to teach their slaves to read. Compulsory slave patrols policed the southern countryside, acting as sheriff, judge, and jury if they found a slave separated from his or her owner without written permission. Postmasters searched the mails for banned abolitionist literature.

Slaveholding southerners constructed a remarkably complete and diverse set of arguments to defend their "peculiar institution." By the 1830s, gone was the founding generation's lament about slavery being a necessary evil. Now, southerners promoted slavery as a positive good—for blacks and whites alike—that they intended to preserve at any cost. Law, economics, science, theology, and history were all mustered in defense of slaveholding. Prominent proslavery advocate George Fitzhugh argued that African Americans were so inferior to whites that if freed "gradual but certain extermination would be their fate." "Our negroes," he further insisted, "are confessedly better off than any free laboring population in the world." In an 1837 speech before the United States Senate, the famous South Carolina politician John C. Calhoun pronounced slavery ennobling to the South, and maintained the institution "is indispensible to the peace and happiness of both" blacks and whites. Southerners argued that slavery was a more humane system than northern capitalism. After all, they insisted, slaves were fed, clothed, sheltered, and cared for when they were ill and aged, whereas northern factory workers were paid pitifully low wages and then discarded when they were no longer useful. Furthermore, many white southerners bragged that slavery introduced "barbarous" Africans to "civilized" American ways, including to Christianity.[5]

In such an atmosphere, in which many of the South's intellectual efforts went into defending slavery, dissent and freedom of thought were not welcome. White southerners who disagreed with the proslavery agenda remained silent, were cowed into submission, or decided to leave the region. In some ways, then, the enslavement of African Americans partly rested on the limitation of freedoms for southern whites as well.

On the other hand, racial slavery afforded all whites certain benefits. Even the poorest white person enjoyed a social status superior to all African Americans. Slavery created a racial divide in the South that superseded class divisions and promoted white solidarity. As historian Edmund S. Morgan elegantly argued in his magisterial study of slavery and freedom in early Virginia, all white men could imagine themselves free and equal because they would never be black and enslaved.[6] Fear of black uprisings also prompted many non-slaveholders to fall in line with their planter neighbors. And some whites believed that emancipation would bring them into direct economic competition with blacks, which, they assumed, would drive down wages.

For all these reasons, non-slaveholding whites—who represented the majority of the South's population—propped up the institution. The proportion of white southern families who owned slaves actually declined in the nineteenth century, from one-third in 1830 to roughly one-fourth by 1860. Moreover, nearly three-fourths of these slaveholders owned fewer than ten slaves. Slaveholders, then, were a

5. See George Fitzhugh, *Sociology for the South: Or the Failure of Free Society* (Richmond, VA: A. Morris, 1854), in Paul Finkelman, ed., *Defending Slavery: Proslavery Thought in the Old South, A Brief History with Documents* (Boston: Bedford/St. Martin's, 2003), 190; Fitzhugh, *Cannibals All! Or Slaves without Masters*, in Finkelman, 199; and John C. Calhoun, "Speech on the Reception of Abolition Petitions, Delivered in the Senate, February 6th, 1837," in Richard R. Crallé, ed., *Speeches of John C. Calhoun, Delivered in the House of Representatives and in the Senate of the United States* (New York: D. Appleton, 1853), 625–33, in Finkelman, 58.

6. Edmund S. Morgan, *American Slavery, American Freedom: The Ordeal of Colonial Virginia* (New York: Norton, 1975).

distinct minority of the white southern population, and those men who owned large plantations and hundreds of slaves were an exceedingly small group. But because they maintained the solid support of their non-slaveholding neighbors, elite slaveholders controlled the region.

While white southerners used oceans of ink to insist that their slaves were happy and content, evidence of the perceptions of slaves themselves is woefully limited. Given the restrictive nature of the slave system, the relative paucity of literary sources is hardly surprising. The major exception to this pattern can be found in the writings of slaves who escaped to the North. Harriet Jacobs and Frederick Douglass numbered among the women and men who succeeding in fleeing bondage and in telling their life stories in compelling, widely read narratives. Although the great majority of slaves did not escape and most never learned to read and write, they still left a remarkable amount of evidence that can help us understand their perspectives. We just have to be imaginative in how we approach and use that material.

In an earlier chapter, you discovered that statistical information (about births, deaths, age at marriage, farm size, inheritance, and so forth) can reveal a great deal about ordinary people, such as the colonists on the eve of the American Revolution. Demographic evidence can help historians form a picture of these people and of socioeconomic trends at the time, even if the individuals themselves were not aware of those patterns. In this chapter, you will employ a similar method, although you will be using a different kind of evidence. Your sources come not from white southerners (whose stake in maintaining slavery was enormous), foreign travelers (whose cultural biases often influenced what they reported), or even white abolitionists in the North (whose urgent need to eradicate the "sin" of slavery sometimes led them to exaggerate). You will be using stories and songs from the rich oral tradition of African Americans, supplemented by narratives of runaways, to investigate peoples' experiences inside the institution of racial slavery.

Some oral traditions were collected soon after emancipation. However, much of the evidence did not come to light until many years later, when the former slaves were very old. In fact, not until the 1920s did concerted efforts to preserve the reminiscences of these men and women begin. In the 1920s, Fisk University collected a good deal of evidence. In the 1930s, the government-financed Federal Writers' Project accumulated more than two thousand narratives from ex-slaves in every southern state except Louisiana and deposited them in the Library of Congress in Washington, D.C.

Like the narratives of self-liberating slaves, these sources derived from personal memory must be used with imagination and care. In particular, you will want to think about how the passage of time and changed circumstances—securing personal freedom through flight, the end of slavery after the Civil War—shaped memory.

The central question you are to answer is this: How did African Americans experience the institution of slavery?

The Method

Historians must always try to be aware of the limitations of their evidence. In the Federal Writers' Project, most of the former slaves were in their eighties or nineties (quite a few were older than one hundred) at the time they were interviewed. In other words, most of the interviewees had been children or young people in 1860. It is also important to know that although some of the interviewers were black, the overwhelming majority were white. Last, although many of the former slaves had moved to another location or a different state after the Civil War, many others were still living in the same county.

As historian Ira Berlin pointed out in his edited collection of slave narratives, former slaves were always patronized and sometimes intimidated by local white interviewers.[7] Once in a while, the actual interviews were written up in a stereotypical black dialect form, and occasionally the content itself was edited by the interviewers until the Federal Writers' Project issued directives to stop these practices. But Berlin also notes that many, perhaps most, elderly blacks did not fear retaliation, were eager to tell their stories, and answered obliquely or indirectly when the interviewers' questions touched on sensitive racial issues. For example, former slaves might say that they themselves were treated all right but then tell about "other situations"

elsewhere where slaves were badly mistreated. For an excellent example of an oblique answer, notice how a former slave responds to a question about whether slavery was "good" for the slaves by telling a story about a raccoon and a dog (Source 3).

Like all historical evidence, slave narratives have both strengths and weaknesses. They are firsthand reports that, when carefully evaluated and corroborated by other testimony, can provide insight into the last years of slavery in the United States from the viewpoint of the slaves themselves. These narratives reveal much about these people's thoughts about slavery. Some of the stories or anecdotes may not actually be true, but they still convey a great deal about the perceptions of former slaves. Apocryphal stories can, in fact, reveal larger truths about African American experiences and cultures. Therefore, often you must pull meaning from a narrative, inferring what the interviewee meant and believed as well as what he or she said.

As for their songs, slaves often hid their true meanings through the use of symbols, metaphors, and allegories. Here again, you must be able to read between the lines, extracting thoughts and attitudes that were purposely concealed.

Finally, included in the evidence are three accounts of runaway slaves who escaped to the North before the Civil War. Frederick Bailey (who later changed his name to Douglass) ran away when he was about nineteen years old, but he was captured and returned.

---

7. Ira Berlin et al., eds. *Remembering Slavery* (New York: New Press, 1998).

Two years later, he was able to escape, and he moved to Massachusetts, where he worked as a laborer. After joining an antislavery society and becoming an extraordinarily successful speaker, he published his autobiography (1845) and edited his own abolitionist newspaper, the *North Star*. Harriet Jacobs (who used the pen name Linda Brent) was twenty-seven years old when she ran away in 1845, but her narrative was not published until the beginning of the Civil War. Throughout her story, Jacobs used fictitious names and places to protect those who had helped her and to conceal the escape route she had used. Both Douglass and Jacobs were self-educated people who wrote their own books—both of which were widely read in the nineteenth century and continue to be popular teaching texts today.

John Thompson represents yet another kind of slave narrative. He did not become famous, like Douglass or Jacobs, and little is known about his life aside from the information contained in his narrative. After he escaped to Philadelphia, Thompson feared he might be returned to slavery, so he took to the seas. He worked for several years in the whaling industry, traveling the world before contributing his story to an abolitionist press in Massachusetts. Like the rest of your sources, Thompson's narrative rested on his memories of a life in bondage long since left behind.

As you examine each source, jot down enough notes to allow you to recall that evidence later. But also, perhaps in a separate column, write down the *attitude* that each text communicates. What is the hidden message? After you have examined each piece of evidence, look back over your notes. What attitudes about slavery stand out?

◆

The Evidence

Sources 1 through 14 from B. A. Botkin, Federal Writers' Project, *Lay My Burden Down: A Folk History of Slavery* (Chicago: The University of Chicago Press, 1945), pp. 4–5, 7, 14, 22–23, 25, 26, 27, 34, 55, 91, 106, 121, 124. Copyright 1945. Reprinted by permission.

1. Hog-Killing Time.

I remember Mammy told me about one master who almost starved his slaves. Mighty stingy, I reckon he was.

Some of them slaves was so poorly thin they ribs would kinda rustle against each other like corn stalks a-drying in the hot winds. But they gets even one hog-killing time, and it was funny, too, Mammy said.

They was seven hogs, fat and ready for fall hog-killing time. Just the day before Old Master told off they was to be killed, something happened to all them porkers. One of the field boys found them and come a-telling the master: "The hogs is all died, now they won't be any meats for the winter."

When the master gets to where at the hogs is laying, they's a lot of Negroes standing round looking sorrow-eyed at the wasted meat. The master asks: "What's the illness with 'em?"

"Malitis," they tells him, and they acts like they don't want to touch the hogs. Master says to dress them anyway for they ain't no more meat on the place.

He says to keep all the meat for the slave families, but that's because he's afraid to eat it hisself account of the hogs' got malitis.

"Don't you all know what is malitis?" Mammy would ask the children when she was telling of the seven fat hogs and seventy lean slaves. And she would laugh, remembering how they fooled Old Master so's to get all them good meats.

"One of the strongest Negroes got up early in the morning," Mammy would explain, "long 'fore the rising horn called the slaves from their cabins. He skitted to the hog pen with a heavy mallet in his hand. When he tapped Mister Hog 'tween the eyes with the mallet, 'malitis' set in mighty quick, but it was a uncommon 'disease,' even with hungry Negroes around all the time."

2. The Old Parrot.

The mistress had an old parrot, and one day I was in the kitchen making cookies, and I decided I wanted some of them, so I tooks me out some and put them on a chair; and when I did this the mistress entered the door. I picks up a cushion and throws [it] over the pile of cookies on the chair, and Mistress came near the chair and the old parrot cries out, "Mistress burn, Mistress burn." Then the mistress looks under the cushion, and she had me whupped, but the next day I killed the parrot, and she often wondered who or what killed the bird.

3. The Coon and the Dog.

Every time I think of slavery and if it done the race any good, I think of the story of the coon and dog who met. The coon said to the dog, "Why is it you're so fat and I am so poor, and we is both animals?" The dog said: "I lay round Master's house and let him kick me and he gives me a piece of bread right on." Said the coon to the dog: "Better, then, that I stay poor." Them's my sentiment. I'm like the coon, I don't believe in 'buse.

[243]

4. The Partridge and the Fox.

A partridge and a fox 'greed to kill a beef. They kilt and skinned it. Before they divide it, the fox said, "My wife says send her some beef for soup." So he took a piece of it and carried it down the hill, then come back and said, "My wife wants more beef for soup." He kept this up till all the beef was gone 'cept the liver. The fox come back, and the partridge says, "Now let's cook this liver and both of us eat it." The partridge cooked the liver, et its parts right quick, and then fell over like it was sick. The fox got scared and said that beef is pizen, and he ran down the hill and started bringing the beef back. And when he brought it all back, he left, and the partridge had all the beef.

5. The Rabbit and the Tortoise.

I want to tell you one story 'bout the rabbit. The rabbit and the tortoise had a race. The tortoise git a lot of tortoises and put 'em 'long the way. Ever' now and then a tortoise crawl 'long the way, and the rabbit say, "How you now, Br'er Tortoise?" And he say, "Slow and sure, but my legs very short." When they git tired, the tortoise win 'cause he there, but he never run the race, 'cause he had tortoises strowed out all 'long the way. The tortoise had other tortoises help him.

6. Same Old Thing.

The niggers didn't go to the church building; the preacher came and preached to them in their quarters. He'd just say, "Serve your masters. Don't steal your master's turkey. Don't steal your master's chickens. Don't steal your master's hogs. Don't steal your master's meat. Do whatsomever your master tells you to do." Same old thing all the time.

7. Freedom.

I been preaching the gospel and farming since slavery time. I jined the church 'most 83 years ago when I was Major Gaud's slave, and they baptizes me in the spring branch close to where I finds the Lord. When I starts preaching I couldn't read or write and had to preach what Master told me, and he say tell them niggers iffen they obeys the master they goes to Heaven; but I knowed there's something better for them, but daren't tell them 'cept on the sly. That I done lots. I tells 'em iffen they keeps praying, the Lord will set 'em free.

8. Prayers.

My master used to ask us children, "Do your folks pray at night?" We said "No," 'cause our folks had told us what to say. But the Lord have mercy, there was plenty of that going on. They'd pray, "Lord, deliver us from under bondage."

9. Buck Brasefield.

They was pretty good to us, but old Mr. Buck Brasefield, what had a plantation 'jining us'n, was so mean to his'n that 'twa'n't nothing for 'em to run away. One nigger, Rich Parker, runned off one time, and whilst he gone he seed a hoodoo man, so when he got back Mr. Brasefield took sick and stayed sick two or three weeks. Some of the darkies told him, "Rich been to the hoodoo doctor." So Mr. Brasefield got up outen that bed and come a-yelling in the field, "You thought you had old Buck, but by God he rose again." Them niggers was so scared they squatted in the field just like partridges, and some of 'em whispered, "I wish to God he had-a died."

10. Papa's Death.

My papa was strong. He never had a licking in his life. He helped the master, but one day the master says, "Si, you got to have a whopping," and my poppa says, "I never had a whopping and you can't whop me." And the master says, "But I can kill you," and he shot my papa down. My mama took him in the cabin and put him on a pallet. He died.

11. Forbidden Knowledge.

None of us was 'lowed to see a book or try to learn. They say we git smarter than they was if we learn anything, but we slips around and gits hold of that Webster's old blue-back speller and we hides it till 'way in the night and then we lights a little pine torch, and studies that spelling book. We learn it too. I can read some now and write a little too.

They wasn't no church for the slaves, but we goes to the white folks' arbor on Sunday evening, and a white man he gits up there to preach to the niggers. He say, "Now I takes my text, which is, Nigger obey your master and your mistress, 'cause what you git from them here in this world am all you ever going to git, 'cause you just like the hogs and the other animals—when you dies you ain't no more, after you been throwed in that hole." I guess we believed that for a while 'cause we didn't have no way finding out different. We didn't see no Bibles.

12. Broken Families.

I seen children sold off and the mammy not sold, and sometimes the mammy sold and a little baby kept on the place and give to another woman to raise. Them white folks didn't care nothing 'bout how the slaves grieved when they tore up a family.

13. Burning in Hell.

We was scared of Solomon and his whip, though, and he didn't like frolicking. He didn't like for us niggers to pray, either. We never heard of no church, but us have praying in the cabins. We'd set on the floor and pray with our heads down low and sing low, but if Solomon heared he'd come and beat on the wall with the stock of his whip. He'd say, "I'll come in there and tear the hide off you backs." But some the old niggers tell us we got to pray to God that He don't think different of the blacks and the whites. I know that Solomon is burning in hell today, and it pleasures me to know it.

14. Marriage.

After while I taken a notion to marry and Massa and Missy marries us same as all the niggers. They stands inside the house with a broom held crosswise of the door and we stands outside. Missy puts a little wreath on my head they kept there, and we steps over the broom into the house. Now, that's all they was to the marrying. After freedom I gits married and has it put in the book by a preacher.

15. Pompey.

Pompey, how do I look?
O, massa, mighty.
What do you mean "mighty," Pompey?
Why, massa, you look noble.
What do you mean by "noble"?
Why, sar, you just look like one *lion*.
Why, Pompey, where have you ever seen a lion?
I see one down in yonder field the other day, massa.
Pompey, you foolish fellow, that was a *jackass*.
Was it, massa? Well you look just like him.

16. A Grave for Old Master.

Two slaves were sent out to dig a grave for old master. They dug it very deep. As I passed by I asked Jess and Bob what in the world they dug it so deep for. It was down six or seven feet. I told them there would be a fuss about it, and they had better fill it up some. Jess said it suited him exactly. Bob said he would not fill it up; he wanted to get the old man as near *home* as possible. When we got a stone to put on his grave, we hauled the largest we could find, so as to fasten him down as strong as possible.

17.

We raise de wheat,
Dey gib us de corn;
We bake de bread,
Dey gib us de crust;
We sif de meal,

Dey gib us de huss;
We [peel] de meat,
Dey gib us de skin;
And dat's de way
Dey take us in;
We skim de pot,
Dey gib us de liquor,
And say dat's good enough for nigger.

18.

He delivered Daniel from the lion's den,
Jonah from de belly ob de whale,
And de Hebrew children from de fiery furnace,
And why not every man?

Source 19 from Sterling Stuckey, "Through the Prism of Folklore: The Black Ethos in Slavery," *Massachusetts Review* 9 (1968): 421. Reprinted by permission from *The Massachusetts Review.*

19.

When I get to heaven, gwine be at ease,
Me and my God gonna do as we please.
Gonna chatter with the Father, argue with the Son,
Tell um 'bout the world I just come from.

Source 20 from Frederick Douglass, *Narrative of the Life of Frederick Douglass,* pp. 1–3, 13–15, 36–37, 40–41, 44–46, 74–75. Copyright 1963 by Doubleday. Reprinted by permission of Doubleday, a division of Bantam, Doubleday, Dell Publishing Group, Inc.

20. Excerpts from the Autobiography of Frederick Douglass.

I was born in Tuckahoe, near Hillsborough, and about twelve miles from Easton, in Talbot county, Maryland. I have no accurate knowledge of my age, never having seen any authentic record containing it. By far the larger part of the slaves know as little of their ages as horses know of theirs, and it is the wish of most masters within my knowledge to keep their slaves thus ignorant. I do not remember to have ever met a slave who could tell of his birthday. They seldom come nearer to it than planting-time, harvesting-time, cherry-time, spring-time, or fall-time. . . .The nearest estimate I can give makes me now between twenty-seven and twenty-eight years of age. I come to this, from hearing my master say, some time during 1835, I was about seventeen years old.

My mother was named Harriet Bailey. She was the daughter of Isaac and Betsey Bailey, both colored, and quite dark. My mother was a darker complexion than either my grandmother or grandfather.

My father was a white man. He was admitted to be such by all I ever heard speak of my parentage. The opinion was also whispered that my master was my father; but of the correctness of this opinion, I know nothing; the means of knowing was withheld from me. . . .

[His mother, a field hand, lived twelve miles away and could visit him only at night.]

. . . I do not recollect of ever seeing my mother by the light of day. She was with me in the night. She would lie down with me, and get me to sleep, but long before I waked she was gone. Very little communication ever took place between us. Death soon ended what little we could have while she lived, and with it her hardships and suffering. She died when I was about seven years old, on one of my master's farms, near Lee's Mill. I was not allowed to be present during her illness, at her death, or burial. She was gone long before I knew any thing about it. Never having enjoyed, to any considerable extent, her soothing presence, her tender and watchful care, I received the tidings of her death with much the same emotions I should have probably felt at the death of a stranger. . . .

The slaves selected to go to the Great House Farm,[8] for the monthly allowance for themselves and their fellow-slaves, were peculiarly enthusiastic. While on their way, they would make the dense old woods, for miles around, reverberate with their wild songs, revealing at once the highest joy and the deepest sadness. They would compose and sing as they went along, consulting neither time nor tune. The thought that came up, came out—if not in the word, in the sound;—and as frequently in the one as in the other. . . .

I did not, when a slave, understand the deep meaning of those rude and apparently incoherent songs. I was myself within the circle; so that I neither saw nor heard as those without might see and hear. They told a tale of woe which was then altogether beyond my feeble comprehension; they were tones

---

8. Great House Farm was the huge "home plantation" that belonged to Douglass's owner.

loud, long, and deep; they breathed the prayer and complaint of souls boiling over with the bitterest anguish. Every tone was a testimony against slavery, and a prayer to God for deliverance from chains. . . .

I have often been utterly astonished, since I came to the north, to find persons who could speak of the singing, among slaves, as evidence of their contentment and happiness. It is impossible to conceive of a greater mistake. Slaves sing most when they are most unhappy. The songs of the slave represent the sorrows of his heart; and he is relieved by them, only as an aching heart is relieved by its tears. At least, such is my experience. I have often sung to drown my sorrow, but seldom to express my happiness. Crying for joy, and singing for joy, were alike uncommon to me while in the jaws of slavery. . . .

[Douglass was hired out as a young boy and went to live in Baltimore. His mistress began to teach him the alphabet, but when her husband found out, he forbade her to continue. After Douglass overheard his master's arguments against teaching slaves to read and write, he came to believe that education could help him gain his freedom.]

The plan which I adopted, and the one by which I was most successful, was that of making friends of all the little white boys whom I met in the street. As many of these as I could, I converted into teachers. With their kindly aid, obtained at different times and in different places, I finally succeeded in learning to read. When I was sent on errands, I always took my book with me, and by doing one part of my errand quickly, I found time to get a lesson before my return. I used also to carry bread with me, enough of which was always in the house, and to which I was always welcome; for I was much better off in this regard than many of the poor white children in our neighborhood. This bread I used to bestow upon hungry little urchins, who, in return, would give me that more valuable bread of knowledge. I am strongly tempted to give the names of two or three of those little boys, as a testimonial of the gratitude and affection I bear them; but prudence forbids;—not that it would injure me, but it might embarrass them; for it is almost an unpardonable offence to teach slaves to read in this Christian country. . . .

I was now about twelve years old, and the thought of being a *slave for life* began to bear heavily upon my heart. . . . After a patient waiting, I got one of our city papers, containing an account of the number of petitions from the north, praying for the abolition of slavery in the District of Columbia, and of the slave trade between the States. From this time I understood the words *abolition* and *abolitionist,* and always drew near when that word was spoken, expecting to hear something of importance to myself and fellow-slaves. The light broke in upon me by degrees. . . .

[After talking with two Irish laborers who advised him to run away, Douglass determined to do so.]

. . . I looked forward to a time at which it would be safe for me to escape. I was too young to think of doing so immediately; besides, I wished to learn how to write, as I might have occasion to write my own pass.[9] I consoled myself with the hope that I should one day find a good chance. Meanwhile, I would learn to write. . . .

[Douglass first copied the letters written on the planks of wood used in ship construction. Later, he dared small boys in the neighborhood to prove that they could spell better than he could; in that way, he began to learn how to write.]

. . . During this time, my copy-book was the board fence, brick wall, and pavement; my pen and ink was a lump of chalk. With these, I learned mainly how to write. I then commenced and continued copying the Italics in Webster's Spelling Book, until I could make them all without looking on the book. By this time, my little Master Thomas had gone to school, and learned how to write, and had written over a number of copy-books. These had been brought home, and shown to some of our near neighbors, and then laid aside. My mistress used to go to class meeting at the Wilk Street meetinghouse every Monday afternoon, and leave me to take care of the house. When left thus, I used to spend the time in writing in the spaces left in Master Thomas's copy-book, copying what he had written. I continued to do this until I could write a hand very similar to that of Master Thomas. Thus, after a long, tedious effort for years, I finally succeeded in learning how to write. . . .

[After the death of his owner, Douglass was recalled to the plantation and put to work as a field hand. Because of his rebellious attitude, he was then sent to work for a notorious "slave-breaker" named Covey. When Covey tried to whip Douglass, who was then about sixteen years old, Douglass fought back.]

We were at it for nearly two hours. Covey at length let me go, puffing and blowing at a great rate, saying that if I had not resisted, he would not have whipped me half so much. The truth was, that he had not whipped me at all. I considered him as getting entirely the worst end of the bargain; for he had drawn no blood from me, but I had from him. The whole six months afterwards, that I spent with Mr. Covey, he never laid the weight of his finger upon me in anger. He would occasionally say, he didn't want to get hold of me again. "No," thought I, "you need not; for you will come off worse than you did before." . . .

9. In many areas, slaves were required to carry written passes stating that they had permission from their owners to travel to a certain place.

[This fight was a turning point for Douglass, who felt his self-confidence increase greatly along with his desire to be free. Although he was a slave for four more years, he was never again whipped.]

It was for a long time a matter of surprise to me why Mr. Covey did not immediately have me taken by the constable to the whipping-post, and there regularly whipped for the crime of raising my hand against a white man in defense of myself. And the only explanation I can now think of does not entirely satisfy me; but such as it is, I will give it. Mr. Covey enjoyed the most unbounded reputation for being a first-rate overseer and negro-breaker. It was of considerable importance to him. That reputation was at stake; and had he sent me—a boy about sixteen years old—to the public whipping-post, his reputation would have been lost; so, to save his reputation, he suffered me to go unpunished. . . .

[During the Civil War, Douglass actively recruited African American soldiers for the Union, and he worked steadfastly after the war for African American civil rights. Douglass also held a series of federal jobs that culminated in his appointment as the U.S. minister to Haiti in 1888. He died in 1895 at the age of seventy-eight.]

Source 21 from Linda Brent, *Incidents in the Life of a Slave Girl*, pp. xiii–xiv, 7, 9–10, 26–28, 48–49, 54–55, 179, 201–203, 207. Copyright © 1973 and renewed 2001 by Walter Magnus Teller. Reprinted by permission of Harcourt, Inc.

21. Excerpts from the Autobiography of Linda Brent (Harriet Jacobs).

I wish I were more competent to the task I have undertaken. But I trust my readers will excuse deficiencies in consideration of circumstances. I was born and reared in Slavery; and I remained in a Slave State twenty-seven years. Since I have been at the North, it has been necessary for me to work diligently for my own support, and the education of my children. This has not left me much leisure to make up for the loss of early opportunities to improve myself; and it has compelled me to write these pages at irregular intervals, whenever I could snatch an hour from household duties. . . .

[Brent explains that she hopes her story will help northern women realize the suffering of southern slave women.]

I was born a slave; but I never knew it till six years of happy childhood had passed away. My father was a carpenter, and considered so intelligent and skillful in his trade, that when buildings out of the common line were to be erected, he was sent for from long distances, to be head workman. On condition of paying his mistress two hundred dollars a year, and supporting himself, he was allowed to work at his trade, and manage his own affairs. His strongest wish was to purchase his children; but, though he several times offered his hard earnings for that purpose, he never succeeded. In complexion my parents were a light shade of brownish yellow, and were termed mulattoes. They lived together in a comfortable home; and, though we were all slaves, I was so fondly shielded that I never dreamed I was a piece of merchandise, trusted to them for safe keeping, and liable to be demanded of them at any moment. I had one brother, William, who was two years younger than myself—a bright, affectionate child. I had also a great treasure in my maternal grandmother, who was a remarkable woman in many respects. . . .

[When Linda Brent was six years old, her mother died, and a few years later the kind mistress to whom Brent's family belonged also died. In the will, Brent was bequeathed to the mistress's five-year-old niece, Miss Emily Flint. At the same time, Linda Brent's brother William was purchased by Dr. Flint, Emily's father.]

My grandmother's mistress had always promised her that, at her death, she would be free; and it was said that in her will she made good the promise. But when the estate was settled, Dr. Flint told the faithful old servant that, under existing circumstances, it was necessary she should be sold. . . .

[Brent's grandmother, widely respected in the community, was put up for sale at a local auction.]

. . .Without saying a word, she quietly awaited her fate. No one bid for her. At last, a feeble voice said, "Fifty dollars." It came from a maiden lady, seventy years old, the sister of my grandmother's deceased mistress. She had lived forty years under the same roof with my grandmother; she knew how faithfully she had served her owners, and how cruelly she had been defrauded of her rights; and she resolved to protect her. The auctioneer waited for a higher bid; but her wishes were respected; no one bid above her. She could neither read nor write; and when the bill of sale was made out, she signed it with a cross. But what consequence was that, when she had a big heart overflowing with human kindness? She gave the old servant her freedom. . . .

During the first years of my service in Dr. Flint's family, I was accustomed to share some indulgences with the children of my mistress. Though this seemed to me no more than right, I was grateful for it, and tried to merit the kindness by the faithful discharge of my duties. But I now entered on my fifteenth year—a sad epoch in the life of a slave girl. My master began to whisper foul words in my ear. Young as I was, I could not remain ignorant of their import. I tried to treat them with indifference or contempt. The master's age, my extreme youth, and the fear that his conduct would be reported to my grandmother, made him bear this treatment for many months. He was a crafty man, and resorted to many means to accomplish his purposes. . . .The mistress, who ought to protect the helpless victim, has no other feelings towards her but those of jealousy and rage. . . . Even the little child, who is accustomed to wait on her mistress and her children, will learn, before she is twelve years old, why it is that her mistress hates such and such a one among the slaves. . . . She listens to violent outbreaks of jealous passion, and cannot help understanding what is the cause. She will become prematurely knowing in evil things. Soon she will learn to tremble when she hears her master's footfall. She will be compelled to realize that she is no longer a child. If God has bestowed beauty upon her, it will prove her greatest curse. That which commands admiration in the white woman only hastens the degradation of the female slave. . . .

[*Afraid to tell her grandmother about Dr. Flint's advances, Brent kept silent. But Flint was enraged when he found out that Brent had fallen in love with a young, free, African American carpenter. The doctor redoubled his efforts to seduce Brent and told her terrible stories about what happened to slaves who tried to run away. For a long time, she was afraid to try to escape because of stories such as the one she recounts here.*]

In my childhood I knew a valuable slave, named Charity, and loved her, as all children did. Her young mistress married, and took her to Louisiana. Her little boy, James, was sold to a good sort of master. He became involved in debt, and James was sold again to a wealthy slaveholder, noted for his cruelty. With this man he grew up to manhood, receiving the treatment of a dog. After a severe whipping, to save himself from further infliction of the lash, with which he was threatened, he took to the woods. He was in a most miserable condition—cut by the cowskin, half naked, half starved, and without the means of procuring a crust of bread.

Some weeks after his escape, he was captured, tied, and carried back to his master's plantation. This man considered punishment in his jail, on bread and water, after receiving hundreds of lashes, too mild for the poor slave's offence. Therefore he decided, after the overseer should have whipped him to his satisfaction, to have him placed between the screws of the cotton gin, to stay as long as he had been in the woods. This wretched creature was cut with the whip from his head to his feet, then washed with strong brine, to prevent the flesh from mortifying. . . . He was then put into the cotton gin, which was screwed down, only allowing him room to turn on his side when he could not lie on his back. Every morning a slave was sent with a piece of bread and bowl of water, which were placed within reach of the poor fellow. The slave was charged, under penalty of severe punishment, not to speak to him.

Four days passed, and the slave continued to carry the bread and water. On the second morning, he found the bread gone, but the water untouched. When he had been in the press four days and five nights, the slave informed his master that the water had not been used for four mornings, and that a horrible stench came from the gin house. The overseer was sent to examine into it. When the press was unscrewed, the dead body was found partly eaten by rats and vermin. . . .

[Dr. Flint's jealous wife watched his behavior very closely, so Flint decided to build a small cabin out in the woods for Brent, who was now sixteen years old. Still afraid to run away, she became desperate.]

And now, reader, I come to a period in my unhappy life, which I would gladly forget if I could. The remembrance fills me with sorrow and shame. . . . The influences of slavery had had the same effect on me that they had on other young girls; they had made me prematurely knowing, concerning the evil ways of the world. I knew what I did, and I did it with deliberate calculation. . . .

I have told you that Dr. Flint's persecutions and his wife's jealousy had given rise to some gossip in the neighborhood. Among others, it chanced that a white unmarried gentleman had obtained some knowledge of the circumstances in which I was placed. He knew my grandmother, and often spoke to me in the street. He became interested for me, and asked questions about my master, which I answered in part. He expressed a great deal of sympathy, and a wish to aid me. He constantly sought opportunities to see me, and wrote to me frequently. I was a poor slave girl, only fifteen years old.

So much attention from a superior person was, of course, flattering; for human nature is the same in all. I also felt grateful for his sympathy, and encouraged by his kind words. It seemed to me a great thing to have such a friend. By degrees, a more tender feeling crept into my heart. He was an educated and eloquent gentleman; too eloquent, alas, for the poor slave girl who trusted in him. Of course I saw whither all this was tending. I knew the impassable gulf between us; but to be an object of interest to a man who is not married, and who is not her master, is agreeable to the pride and feelings of a slave, if her miserable situation has left her any pride or sentiment. It seems less degrading to give one's self, than to submit to compulsion. There is something akin to freedom in having a lover who has no control over you, except that which he gains by kindness and attachment. A master may treat you as rudely as he pleases, and you dare not speak; moreover, the wrong does not seem so great with an unmarried man, as with one who has a wife to be made unhappy. There may be sophistry in all this; but the condition of a slave confuses all principles of morality, and, in fact, renders the practice of them impossible.

[Brent had two children, Benjy and Ellen, as a result of her relationship with Mr. Sands, the white "gentleman." Sands and Brent's grandmother tried to buy Brent, but Dr. Flint rejected all their offers. However, Sands was able (through a trick) to buy his two children and Brent's brother, William. After he was elected to Congress, Sands married a white woman. William escaped to the North, and Brent spent seven years hiding in the tiny attic of a shed attached to her grandmother's house. Finally, Brent and a friend escaped via ship to Philadelphia. She then went to New York City, where she found work as a nursemaid for a kind family, the Bruces, and was reunited with her two children. However, as a fugitive slave, she was not really safe, and she used to read the newspapers every day to see whether Dr. Flint or any of his relatives were visiting New York.]

But when summer came, the old feeling of insecurity haunted me. It was necessary for me to take little Mary[10] out daily, for exercise and fresh air, and the city was swarming with Southerners, some of whom might recognize me. Hot weather brings out snakes and slaveholders, and I like one class of the venomous creatures as little as I do the other. What a comfort it is, to be free to *say* so! . . .

I kept close watch of the newspapers for arrivals; but one Saturday night, being much occupied, I forgot to examine the Evening Express as usual. I went down into the parlor for it, early in the morning, and found the boy about to kindle a fire with it. I took it from him and examined the list of arrivals. Reader, if you have never been a slave, you cannot imagine the acute sensation at my heart, when I read the names of Mr. and Mrs. Dodge,[11] at a hotel in Courtland Street. It was a third-rate hotel, and that circumstance convinced me of the truth of what I had heard, that they were short of funds and had need of my value, as *they* valued me; and that was by dollar and cents. I hastened with the paper to Mrs. Bruce. Her heart and hand were always open to every one in distress, and she always warmly sympathized with mine. It was impossible to tell how near the enemy was. He might have passed and repassed the house while we were sleeping. He might at that moment be waiting to pounce upon me if I ventured out of doors. I had never seen the husband of my young mistress, and therefore I could not distinguish him from any other stranger. A carriage was hastily ordered; and, closely veiled, I followed Mrs. Bruce, taking the baby again with me into exile. After various turnings and crossings, and returnings, the carriage stopped at the

10. Mary was the Bruces' baby.
11. Emily Flint and her husband.

house of one of Mrs. Bruce's friends, where I was kindly received. Mrs. Bruce returned immediately, to instruct the domestics what to say if any one came to inquire for me.

It was lucky for me that the evening paper was not burned up before I had a chance to examine the list of arrivals. It was not long after Mrs. Bruce's return to her house, before several people came to inquire for me. One inquired for me, another asked for my daughter Ellen, and another said he had a letter from my grandmother, which he was requested to deliver in person.

They were told, "She *has* lived here, but she has left."

"How long ago?"

"I don't know, sir."

"Do you know where she went?"

"I do not, sir." And the door was closed. . . .

[Mrs. Bruce was finally able to buy Brent from Mr. Dodge, and she immediately gave Brent her freedom.]

Reader, my story ends with freedom; not in the usual way, with marriage. I and my children are now free! We are as free from the power of slaveholders as are the white people of the north; and though that, according to my ideas, is not saying a great deal, it is a vast improvement in *my* condition. The dream of my life is not yet realized. I do not sit with my children in a home of my own. I still long for a hearthstone of my own, however humble. I wish it for my children's sake far more than for my own. But God so orders circumstances as to keep me with my friend Mrs. Bruce. Love, duty, gratitude, also bind me to her side. It is a privilege to serve her who pities my oppressed people, and who has bestowed the inestimable boon of freedom on me and my children. . . .

[Harriet Jacobs's story was published in 1861, and during the Civil War she did relief work with the newly freed slaves behind Union army lines. For several years after the war ended, she worked tirelessly in Georgia to organize orphanages, schools, and nursing homes. Finally, she returned to the North, where she died in 1897 at the age of eighty-four.]

Source 22 from John Thompson, "The Life of John Thompson, a Fugitive Slave; Containing His History of 25 Years in Bondage, and His Providential Escape. Written by Himself" (1856). Documenting the American South Project, 2000. Accessible online November 21, 2009: <http://docsouth.unc.edu/neh/thompson/thompson.html>.

22. Excerpt from "The Life of John Thompson, a Fugitive Slave."

. . .MR. W. was a very cruel slave driver. He would whip unreasonably and without cause. He was often from home, and not unfrequently three or four weeks at a time, leaving the plantation, at such times, in care of the overseer. When he returned, he sometimes ordered all the slaves to assemble at the house, when he would whip them all round; a little whipping being, as he thought, necessary, in order to secure the humble submission of the slaves.

Sometimes he forced one slave to flog another, the husband his wife; the mother her daughter; or the father his son. This practice seemed very amusing to himself and his children, especially to his son, John, who failed not to walk in his father's footsteps, by carrying into effect the same principle, until he became characteristically a tyrant.

When at home from school, he would frequently request his grandmother's permission, to call all the black children from their quarters to the house, to sweep and clear the yard from weeds, &c., in order that he might oversee them. Then, whip in hand, he walked about among them, and sometimes lashed the poor little creatures, who had on nothing but a shirt, and often nothing at all, until the blood streamed down their backs and limbs, apparently for no reason whatever, except to gratify his own cruel fancy.

This was pleasing to his father and grandmother, who, accordingly, considered him a very smart boy indeed! Often, my mother, after being in the field all day, upon returning at night, would find her little children's backs mangled by the lash of John Wagar, or his grandmother; for if any child dared to resist the boy, she would order the cook to lash it with a cowhide kept for that purpose.

I well remember the tears of my poor mother, as they fell upon my back, while she was bathing and dressing my wounds. But there was no redress for her grievance, she had no appeal for justice, save to high heaven; for if she complained, her own back would be cut in a similar manner.

Sometimes she wept and sobbed all night, but her tears must be dried and her sobs hushed, ere the overseer's horn sounded, which it did at early dawn, lest they should betray her. And she, unrefreshed, must shake off her dull slumbers, and repair, at break of day, to the field, leaving her little ones to a similar, or perhaps, worse fate on the coming day, and dreading a renewal of her own sorrows the coming evening. Great God, what a succession of crimes! Is there no balm in Gilead; is there no physician there, that thy people can be healed? . . .

Questions to Consider

The evidence in this chapter falls into three categories: reminiscences from former slaves, culled from interviews conducted in the 1930s (Sources 1 through 16); songs transcribed soon after the Civil War, recalled by runaway slaves, or remembered years after (Sources 17 through 19); and the autobiographies of Frederick Douglass, Harriet Jacobs, and John Thompson, three slaves who escaped to the North (Sources 20 through 22).

Since the evidence contains a number of subtopics, thinking about the documents in the context of these themes should be profitable. For example:

1. How did slaves perceive their owners?
2. What mechanisms of control did slaveholders employ? To what effect?
3. In what ways did African Americans resist enslavement and debasement?
4. What role did religion play in the lives of slaves?
5. How was family defined and experienced by slaves?
6. How did gender shape the perceptions and experiences of slaves?

Within all these themes, keep in mind the importance of historical memory. How did the passage of time and distance from the immediate experience of slavery shape recollections? What can we learn about African Americans' experiences from the long-term view of former slaves regarding their bondage?

Regrouping the evidence into subtopics should help you answer the central question: How did African Americans experience—and remember—the institution of slavery?

As mentioned, some slaves and former slaves chose to be direct in their messages (see, for example, Sources 10 and 17), but many more communicated their thoughts more indirectly or obliquely. Several of the symbols and metaphors used are easy to figure out (see Source 3), but others will take considerably more deliberation. The messages are there; historians must take the time and care to engage them.

Reflect as well on the importance of audience. Frederick Douglass and Harriet Jacobs wrote their autobiographies for northern readers. Furthermore, both worked as abolitionists, and they hoped their writings would contribute to their political cause. (Thompson's memoir was published by an abolitionist press, but he worked as a seaman.) Certainly the abolitionist leanings of these writers do not invalidate their work, but historians should bear in mind those facts when analyzing these sources. Does the other evidence, from songs, interviews, and stories, corroborate what these three authors wrote? How do the writings and memories of individuals who successfully fled slavery in the antebellum era compare with those emancipated after the Civil War?

◆

Epilogue

Even before the Civil War formally ended, thousands of African Americans began casting off the shackles of slavery. Some ran away to meet the advancing Union armies; after 1863, 200,000 black men enlisted in the United States military. African American soldiers represented nearly 10 percent of the nation's fighting forces. Although casualties were high—roughly one-third of the African American soldiers who saw action were wounded or killed—their desertion rate was lower than that of the U.S. Army as a whole. Twenty-one African Americans won the Congressional Medal of Honor for heroic service during the Civil War. As men took to the battlefield, many families migrated into cities, where they hoped to find work and new opportunities. Others stayed on the land, expecting to become free-holding farmers. At the end of the war, African Americans quickly established their own churches, independent of the racist preaching that marked antebellum services. Knowing the power of education in preserving freedom and autonomy, adults joined children in enrolling in schools they established in partnership with the Freedmen's Bureau. And for decades African Americans searched for lost kin, seeking reunions with spouses, children, and siblings long sold away. Generations of white southerners had dreaded the violence they predicted would accompany black liberation. As it turned out, African Americans did not seek revenge; they wanted a new start and an equal stake in their country.

Reconstruction, effected by the military occupation of the rebellious states, temporarily addressed many of the former slaves' ambitions—particularly those of African American men. Ratification of three constitutional amendments guaranteed a permanent end to slavery, equal protection under the law for all citizens, and voting rights. As a result, black men participated in the political process and served in Reconstruction governments. African American delegates to the South Carolina state legislature outnumbered whites, and Blanche Bruce and Hiram Revels, both black men, represented Mississippi in the United States Senate.

In 1865, Massachusetts Senator Charles Sumner proposed that the federal government confiscate the land of former slaveholding planters and distribute it to former slaves. Sumner was hardly alone in recognizing the consequence of independent landholding for African American families. But the idea was rejected, and most southern blacks were left without the wherewithal to achieve economic independence. Without their own land, African Americans, alongside poor whites, soon turned to sharecropping for the old planter class. The system was corrupt and exploitative. By the late 1870s, the Ku Klux Klan, working as a paramilitary wing of the Democratic Party, ushered in a period of racial terrorism and swept out the Republican Reconstruction state governments. This "Redemption" of the South was marked by systemic racial violence, "Jim Crow" law, and the persistence of a cotton-based economy—all of which led to pervasive black disfranchisement and poverty. Nearly a hundred years would pass before the unfinished revolution of securing African American rights would be resurrected by a cohort of southern ministers led by Dr. Martin Luther King, Jr.

As historian David Blight has shown in his research into Civil War memory, African Americans who lived through Reconstruction and its collapse had very mixed feelings about their slave past and the significance of the war. For some, slavery represented a burden that saddled them with a legacy of poverty and ignorance. For others, the Civil War was a thwarted revolution in which they had participated but that was undermined by violence and lynching in the post-war South. A few African Americans turned toward Africa in search of a usable past. Still others, such as Booker T. Washington, came to believe that reconciliation should be the goal, accompanied by black efforts at self-reliance.[12]

In any event, memories of slavery endured. In 1976, Alex Haley's book *Roots* and the twelve-part television miniseries based on it stunned many white Americans who had assumed that blacks' memories of their origins and of slavery had been for the most part either forgotten or obliterated. Although Haley's work reflected considerable artistic license, the skeleton of the book was the oral tradition transmitted by his family since the capture of his ancestor Kunta Kinte in West Africa in the late eighteenth century. Haley's family remembered its African origins; their stories about slavery had not been lost but rather passed down through the generations.

Since the 1960s and 1970s, folk music, customs, religious practices, stories, and artifacts have continued to attract increasing scholarly attention. In seeking to answer questions about African American history, scholars turned to this rich diversity of sources and employed new approaches to engaging evidence. As a result, historians have been able to reconstruct the lives, thoughts, and feelings of people once considered unknowable. It simply took determination and imagination to let the evidence speak.

12. David W. Blight, "Black Memory and the Progress of the Race," Chapter 9 in *Race and Reunion* (Cambridge, MA: Belknap Press of Harvard University Press, 2001), pp. 300–337.

10

Civil Liberties in Time of War: The Case of Clement Vallandigham

♦

The Problem

Before dawn on the morning of May 5, 1863, a company of United States soldiers commanded by Captain Charles Hutton surrounded a private home at 323 First Street in Dayton, Ohio. Hutton had been ordered by Major General Ambrose Burnside to arrest the owner of the house, former congressman Clement L. Vallandigham, and bring him to Cincinnati for trial before a military court. Vallandigham stood accused of having violated Burnside's General Order Number 38, which stated that "all persons . . . who commit acts for the benefit of the enemies of our country will be tried as spies or traitors and if convicted will suffer death."[1]

Captain Hutton rang the doorbell and Vallandigham appeared at an upstairs window. Instead of surrendering to the soldiers, however, the former congressman

shouted loudly that he had committed no crime, that Burnside had no authority to arrest him, and that he was not dressed. He then cried, "If Burnside wants me, let him come up and take me" and fired three pistol shots in the air. The soldiers then broke down the back door, went upstairs, and crashed through two bedroom doors before they found their quarry. Separated from his almost hysterical wife and sobbing family, Vallandigham was then escorted out of his home to the railroad station, where a special train sped him to Cincinnati for trial.[2]

1. For Burnside's General Order No. 38 see *Official Records of the War of the Rebellion* (Washington: Government Printing Office, 1899), Series 2, vol. 5, p. 480. For the arrest order, see Captain D. R. Larned to Hutton, May 4, 1863 in *ibid.*, p. 555.

2. The best account of Vallandingham's arrest is in Frank L. Klement, *The Limits of Dissent: Clement L. Vallandigham and the Civil War* (Lexington: University Press of Kentucky, 1970), pp. 152–159. Most primary sources are not completely accurate. See *Speeches, Arguments, Addresses, and Letters of Clement L. Vallandigham* (New York: J. Walter & Co., 1864), p. 45; and *The Record of Hon C. L. Vallandigham on Abolition, the Union, and the Civil War* (Columbus, OH: J. Walter & Co., 1863), p. 253. For Burnside's report, see Burnside to Gen. H. W. Halleck, May 7, 1863, in *Official Record*, Series 1, vol. 23, part 2, pp. 315–316.

As soon as he arrived in Cincinnati and was taken to a military prison, Vallandigham wrote a letter to Ohio Democrats:

> I am here in a military Bastille for no other offense than my Political opinions . . . speeches made in the hearing of thousands of you in denunciation of the usurpations of power, infractions of the Constitution and Laws and of Military Despotism, were the sole cause of my arrest and imprisonment. I am a Democrat . . . this is my only crime. . . .[3]

What in fact had Clement Vallandigham done? He claimed, correctly, that he had broken no law passed by Congress. Was he persecuted because he was a prominent Ohio Democrat who was seeking his party's gubernatorial nomination? Had his civil rights, stated specifically in the Bill of Rights, been violated? Had he been arrested and tried for statements critical of the Lincoln administration and of the war itself?

On the other hand, the vast preponderance of legal opinion has stated that civil liberties in times of war may not be absolute. As distinguished jurist Learned Hand put it during the Second World War, "A society in which men recognize no check upon their freedom soon becomes a society where freedom is in the possession of only a savage few." The late Chief Justice of the United States Supreme Court, William H. Rehnquist, has agreed with Hand, stating, "In any civilized society the most important task is achieving a proper balance between freedom and order. In wartime, reason and history both suggest that this balance shifts to some degree in favor of order—in favor of the government's ability to deal with conditions that threaten the national well-being." Did Vallandigham exceed the limits of freedom of speech during wartime?[4]

The evidence in this chapter has been drawn chiefly from selected speeches and writings of Clement Vallandigham and from writings of President Abraham Lincoln. Was Vallandigham a villain, a victim, both, or neither? Think of yourself as a member of a jury or a tribunal in a trial of Clement Vallandigham. What is your verdict? How would you support that verdict?

◆

Background

Soon after the firing on Fort Sumter (April 12, 1861), at a concert performed by the children at the Philadelphia Home for the Blind, ninety-year-old retired merchant and philanthropist Samuel Breck called for three cheers "for the Union and the Constitution, one and indivisible." Following the cheers, Breck stated, "I was a man when they were formed, and God forbid that I should live to witness their downfall." That ringing statement was followed by more cheers,

3. "To the Democracy of Ohio," in *Record*, p. 253.

4. Learned Hand, *The Spirit of Liberty* (New York: Knopf, 1952), p. 191; William H. Rehnquist, *All the Laws but One: Civil Liberties in Wartime* (New York: Knopf, 1998), p. 222.

"three times three, to the great wonderment of the blind pupils."[5]

Although Samuel Breck did not live to see the profound changes the Civil War wrought on the United States, in his nine decades he was able to witness a virtual revolution in the life of nearly every American.

Without doubt the most dramatic change that Breck witnessed was the incredible growth of the United States in both size and population. At the time of the first federal census in 1790, the new nation was approximately 891,364 square miles, already four times the size of France and almost ten times that of Great Britain. Due to six major territorial acquisitions between 1803 and 1853, however, by 1860 the United States had more than tripled its size, to 3,021,296 square miles and had become the dominant, although not the largest, nation in the Western Hemisphere.[6]

As the young republic had more than tripled in size, during the same period its population increased eightfold, from 3,929,214 in 1790 to 31,443,321 in 1860, doubling roughly every 25 years. Not only were large families responsible for this growth (native-born white women gave birth on average of between four and five children throughout the first

half of the nineteenth century), but massive immigration, especially after 1845, added significant numbers to the nation's population (approximately 5.1 million between 1820 and 1860). Immigration increased the ethnic and religious diversity of the young republic, but it also gave rise to anti-immigrant movements, especially in the Northeast.

By 1860, the economy was still largely agricultural. But farming had changed significantly since the days of Samuel Breck's childhood. The opening of new farmlands in the North Central (midwestern) states and the introduction of new technology (steel plows; McCormick reapers; mowing, thrashing, and haying machines; seed drills; and cultivators) created an agricultural revolution in which wheat, corn, potatoes, meat, and dairy products all increased enormously, making it possible to feed the rapidly growing cities but also (thanks to transportation innovations of roads, canals, and railroads) allowed surplus agricultural yields to be sold in foreign markets. In the South, cotton production rose from approximately 100,000 bales in 1801 to almost 5.4 million bales by 1859 (Mississippi and Alabama accounted for roughly 40 percent of the cotton crop).

As agriculture was experiencing its own revolution, the seeds of an industrial revolution were being planted as well, especially in the Northeast. The apprentice system was already fading by the War of 1812, eventually to be replaced by the factory system, at first in textile, clothing, and shoe production and later in cheap furniture and iron products. By 1860, almost

5. Joseph R. Ingersoll, *Samuel Breck, Vice-President of the Historical Society of Pennsylvania, January 12, 1863* (Philadelphia: King and Baird, 1863), p. 73. Breck died on August 31, 1862.

6. The six territorial acquisitions were the Louisiana Purchase (1803), the Floridas (1819), the Red River Basin (1819), the annexation of Texas (1845), the Mexican Cession (1848), and the Gadsden Purchase (1853). Canada and Brazil are the largest and second largest nations in the Western Hemisphere.

50 percent of the North's population was making its living outside of agriculture, as New England and the mid-Atlantic States accounted for over half of the nation's total manufacturing establishments. This emerging industrial revolution created a number of middle-class occupations, such as retail and sales clerks, secretaries, agents and traveling salesmen (called "drummers"), bank employees, and so on.[7]

The dual revolutions in agriculture and industry raised the general living standards of most Americans. In general they ate better, cooked on cast-iron stoves, lived in warmer dwellings, wore store-bought clothes, used kerosene lamps instead of candles, bought and read books and inexpensive newspapers, bathed and washed their clothing more frequently, and enjoyed traveling entertainers and theater troupes. In the cities, many families even had indoor plumbing.

Yet, as profoundly as American life had changed in the nine decades of Samuel Breck's life, the institution that, strangely, appears to have changed the least was the nation's central government. In 1861, there were only 36,672 paid civilian employees of the federal government, 30,269 of whom worked for the U.S. Post Office.[8] Indeed, by the time of the Civil War, most Americans had never met any civilian outside of the post office who worked for the federal government. Order was maintained by county sheriffs and their deputized posses. Roads, such as

they were, were maintained by local or county officials or by individuals who worked on the roads as a substitute for paying their county or town taxes. And while the emerging modern society had many problems (unequal distribution of wealth, exploitive urban working conditions, spotty public health services, instability of banks, agricultural price fluctuations, and economic depressions), almost no one believed that it was the responsibility of the federal government to address or solve these difficulties.[9]

Nor was the nation as unified economically, culturally, and politically as it would become in the decades after the Civil War. The United States was in many ways still very much a decentralized nation. The South relied on a cash crop, plantation, slave-based economy presided over by a small plantation aristocracy which ruled with a kind of genteel arrogance. Even after southern states had extended the vote to most free whites, a significant number were still disfranchised and remained dependent on the planter elite for their livelihoods and for keeping the slave population under control. In Tidewater, Virginia, eastern North Carolina, and other areas in the South, the free white population actually declined as many families abandoned their modest farms and moved west.

As noted earlier, the North was composed of small family farms but also had an emerging commercial and industrial system. At first, nascent

7. By 1860, approximately 2 million Americans worked in factories.
8. *Statistical History of the United States* (Stanford, CT: Fairfield, 1965), p. 710.

9. Between 1772 and 1858, there were ten major economic depressions, lasting for an average of 34.4 months. Richard B. Morris, ed., *Encyclopedia of American History* (New York: Harper & Brothers, 1961), p. 536.

factories recruited young females from surrounding farms but turned to immigrants when the number of females proved insufficient and when the female factory workers proved less docile than factory managers both hoped and expected. Overpopulated New England farm areas witnessed an exodus of single young men and families to seek opportunities westward. Of the nation's four largest cities, three—New York, Boston, and Philadelphia—were in the Northeast.[10]

The newest section of the United States was the Northwest, eventually composed of the states of Ohio, Indiana, Illinois, Michigan, Wisconsin, Iowa, and Minnesota. Comprising roughly one-quarter of the nation's population in 1860, the Northwest's population was a diverse mixture of families fleeing overpopulated New England, yeoman farmers abandoning the plantation South, and immigrants from the German states, Ireland, Britain, and British Canada.[11] Living in small towns or on sizable family farms, the majority of people prospered due to the adoption of new agricultural practices (such as crop rotation of planting corn in the spring and winter wheat in manure-fertilized fields, and using corn stalks and ears to feed dairy

cattle), agricultural technology (which worked best in the large open fields), and transportation facilities (canals and railroads). Basic education was supported, and literacy rates generally were high.

Most people living in the Northwest considered themselves as belonging to a different section, neither North or South but West. Many looked with increasing distaste at the South's plantation aristocracy who sought to extend the institution of slavery. Although few westerners were abolitionists, they feared the expansion of slavery into the West of free farms. Therefore, most westerners were shocked and angered by the Dred Scott Decision of 1857, which held out the theoretical possibility of slavery intruding itself into the states of the West.

At the same time, people of the Northwest also were suspicious of the Northeast, with its growing industrial prowess, its banking and financial power, and its influence in the federal government. Therefore, when the Northwest's economy collapsed in the regional economic depression of 1861–1862, not a few blamed the railroad men, manufacturers, and bankers of the Northeast. The actual causes of the sharp depression were overproduction due to the opening up of new farming regions, the closing of the Mississippi River by the Confederacy (thus preventing crops from being exported through the port of New Orleans), and regional bank failures, especially in Illinois and Wisconsin; but the simultaneous increase in railroad freight rates and the passage of the Morrill Tariff Act of 1861 (which increased duties on iron products and wool) caused many

10. New York was the largest city, with 515,547 people in 1850. The next largest cities, in descending order, were Baltimore, Boston, Philadelphia, New Orleans, Cincinnati, and Brooklyn, (annexed to New York City in 1898). 11. Much of the German population lived in towns and the section's emerging cities, thus giving cities such as Chicago, Cincinnati, St. Louis, and Milwaukee their distinctive characters. For ethnic groups see Wood Gray, *The Hidden Civil War: The Story of the Copperheads* (New York: Viking Press, 1942), pp. 19–26.

people to blame the power brokers of the Northeast.[12]

Politically, therefore, the northwestern states voted their own interests and were not solidly in either of the major party's camps. In 1828, they were unanimously for Andrew Jackson, whereas in 1840 three of the four midwestern states backed William Henry Harrison. In 1856, four of the six states supported Republican nominee John C. Fremont, and in 1860 they voted unanimously for favorite son Abraham Lincoln (giving him 37 percent of his total electoral vote). Yet in state races (for governor, Congress, state legislature, and so on), the parties were evenly balanced.

The secession of South Carolina followed by that of Mississippi, Florida, Alabama, Georgia, Louisiana, and Texas presented Democrats in the Northwest with a serious dilemma. Although most northwestern Democrats advocated compromise in order to avoid disunion, they were deeply divided over what should be done if compromise failed. Western nationalist Stephen A. Douglas stated, "We can never acknowledge the right of a State to secede and cut us off from the Ocean and the world," whereas Illinois congressman John McClernand warned, "If we become entangled with disunionism we will be lost as a party." On the extreme, some northwestern Democrats believed that any civil war was not *their* war, and that they should refuse to become involved. In a much-circulated and published editorial, one Ohio journalist mourned, "A war of conquest would end in a military despotism. . . .and if successful or unsuccessful we shall come out of the conflict . . . with a standing army on our hands, and with military leaders that will have all the power in their own control." And on January 29, 1861, the Detroit *Free Press* threatened that "if troops shall be raised in the North to march against the people of the South, a fire in the rear will be opened upon such troops. . . .there are some sixty-five thousand able-bodied men . . . who will interpose themselves between any troops that may be raised in Michigan and the people of the South."[13]

The firing on Fort Sumter and President Lincoln's call for volunteers caused a temporary wave of patriotism to ripple through the Northwest. But these feelings were short-lived, especially as it appeared that victory would not be quick and relatively painless and as the Union's 1862 casualty figures mounted. Americans had never before experienced such horrific numbers of dead and wounded in any war, and people in the Northwest were beginning to believe that their men and boys were doing the brunt of the fighting while the number of New England volunteers was comparatively anemic. The Militia Act of July 1862 promised that there would be more casualties as President

---

12. For the 1861–1862 depression, see Jennifer L. Weber, *Copperheads: The Rise and Fall of Lincoln's Opponents in the North* (New York: Oxford University Press, 2006), pp. 28–29; and Frank L. Klement, *The Copperheads in the Middle West* (Chicago: University of Chicago Press, 1960), p. 4. New farmlands were opened up in the 1850s, largely in Iowa and Wisconsin. For the Morrill Tariff, see F. W. Taussig, *The Tariff History of the United States* (New York: Capricorn Books, 8th ed. 1964 [orig. pub. 1892]), p. 159.

13. See Gray, *The Hidden Civil War*, pp. 43, 44, 47.

Lincoln was authorized to call up local militia units and required all males between the ages of 18 and 45 to enroll for a possible conscription. As a result, it was reported that Montreal was "brimming with deserters" and that several men reported fake illnesses in order to avoid military service.

In addition to these causes of the draining of support for the war, many northwesterners were increasingly disturbed by what they regarded as the unconstitutional centralization of power in the hands of the federal government. Especially feared were new federal taxes (national income tax, passed in 1861; new direct tax on manufactures, which tended to raise prices); the authorization of $150 million of paper money; the denial of the right of *habeas corpus* to those accused of aiding the rebels, discouraging army enlistments, and resisting enrollments for conscription; and especially President Lincoln's Preliminary Emancipation Proclamation of September 22, 1862.

Many Democrats in the Northwest recognized the political opportunity the waning of support for the federal government offered. Charging that the war was unwinnable, several Democratic leaders called for peace, accused Republicans of having started the war in order to emancipate slaves, and spread fears of an emerging centralized despotism. As one English newspaper correspondent wrote of the Northwest's numerous immigrants, "The jealousy of the low Germans and Irish against the free negro was sufficient to set them against the war which would have brought four million of their black rivals into competition for that hard and dirty work

which American freedom bestows on them."[14]

As a result, the 1862 elections in most of the Northwest were largely swept by antiwar Democrats. In the votes for the federal House of Representatives, Democrats won 14 of 19 seats in Ohio, 7 of 11 in Indiana, and 9 of 14 in Illinois. Democrats also seized control of state legislatures in Indiana and Illinois and several other state races in those states and in Ohio. At the beginning of 1862, President Lincoln, sensing the ill political winds, confided to Massachusetts Senator Charles Sumner, Sumner recalled

> The President tells me that he now fears "the fire in the rear"—meaning the Democracy, especially at the Northwest—more than our military chances.

And after the elections Lincoln wrote to Brigadier-General Carl Schurz

> I have just received, and read, your letter of the 20th. The purport of it is that we lost the late elections, and the administration is failing, because the war is unsuccessful; and that I must not flatter myself that I am not justly to blame for it . . . but I must say I need success more than I need sympathy. . . .[15]

---

14. *London Times*, December 1, 1863, quoted in Klement, *The Limits of Dissent*, p. 108. For opposition to the war, see Weber, *Copperheads*, pp. 51–54; Gray, *The Hidden Civil War*, pp. 63–77.

15. For election results, see Gray, *The Hidden Civil War*, p. 108. For Sumner's recollection of January 17, 1862, see Edward L. Pierce, ed., *Memoir and Letters of Charles Sumner* (Boston: Roberts Brothers, 1893), vol. 4, p. 114. For Lincoln's letter to Schurz of November 24, 1862, see Roy P. Basler, ed., *The Collected Works of Abraham Lincoln* (New Brunswick: Rutgers University Press, 1953), vol. 5, pp. 509–510.

Undoubtedly the most vocal opponent of "a war of coercion"[16] was Ohio congressman Clement L. Vallandigham. A prosperous attorney with political ambitions, Vallandigham served two terms in the Ohio House of Representatives, but then lost three federal congressional elections. He challenged the third election's results, charging that black voters, specifically prohibited by Ohio's constitution, had been allowed to cast ballots. In a straight party vote, the members of the federal House of Representatives seated him. Vallandigham then won two re-election bids (in 1858 and 1860) but lost again in 1862, in large part because his congressional district had been gerrymandered to guarantee his defeat.

Determined to run for the governorship of Ohio in 1863, Vallandigham saw Democratic Party elder statesman Hugh J. Jewett (1816–1898) as his chief obstacle to getting his party's nomination. Trailing Jewett in pledged delegates to the party's state convention, he devised a plan whereby he would purposely disobey General Ambrose Burnside's General Order Number 38 so that he would be arrested and appear as a martyr in the eyes of the Democratic delegates. Therefore, at a speech at Mount Vernon, Ohio, knowing full well that Burnside's observers were in the crowd, Vallandigham delivered a blistering speech in which he virtually dared Burnside to arrest him. Four days later the general obliged.

By examining and analyzing the evidence in this chapter along with discussions with your instructor and classmates, reach a conclusion as to why Clement Vallandigham was arrested. Was his arrest a political persecution? Or had he made public statements that exceeded the limits of freedom of speech during wartime? Imagine yourself as one member of the military court that heard Vallandigham's case. What do you think a proper verdict should have been?

The Method

American orators of the nineteenth century were expected to deliver long and flowery addresses. Daniel Webster, thought by his contemporaries to be the greatest orator of their times, rarely spoke for less than two hours. After his death in 1852, that title passed to Edward Everett, the principal speaker at the dedication of the Gettysburg National Cemetery on November 19, 1863, an address that took over two hours to give.[17] Although certainly not equal to Everett's in

---

16. Anti-war northern Democrats used the phrase "war of coercion" to refer to forcing the southern states back into the Union, a tactic they thought would never work. Vallandigham used the phrase many times.

17. By contrast, President Lincoln's speech at Gettysburg was only 272 words long and was delivered in approximately three minutes. It is considered by many to be one of the most important and best addresses in American history. See Garry Wills, *Lincoln at Gettysburg: The Words that Remade America* (New York: Simon and Schuster, 1992).

quality, the speeches of Clement Vallandigham very often exceeded Everett's in length, as did most of the speeches excerpted in the Evidence section of this chapter (Sources 1 through 10). However, we have tried to make those excerpts as representative of Vallandigham's arguments as possible. To answer the questions in this chapter, you will have to read very carefully each of those excerpts, taking extensive notes on the points that he made. (General Burnside's observers of Vallandigham's May 1, 1863, Mt. Vernon speech took copious notes that, unfortunately, have been lost.) Did Vallandigham say anything that would have been labeled treasonous? Did he exceed what you would judge to be an individual's civil rights in wartime? Did anything he said "give aid and comfort to the enemy"? Discourage enlistments

or enrollment? Urge anyone to break the law? As you take notes, be sure to list points that might have done any of the above.

Vallandigham himself and several other Democrats were convinced that his arrest and trial had *political* motives. Can you find any evidence that Vallandigham's arrest and trial were politically motivated?

By replying to the two sets of pro-Vallandigham resolutions presented to him, President Lincoln stated very clearly (Sources 11 and 12) why Vallandigham had been arrested. How do his points compare with what you have uncovered in Vallandigham's speeches? Who do you think had the stronger argument? Support your hypothesis with evidence from this chapter, your text, and discussions with your fellow students and instructor.

♦

The Evidence

Sources 1 through 9 from *Speeches, Arguments, Addresses, and Letters of Clement L. Vallandigham* (New York: J. Walter & Co., 1864), pp. 208–222, 263–270, 291–300, 315, 318–323, 362–366, 420–430, 458–461, 479–490, 501, 562–563.

1. Speech in the House of Representatives, December 15, 1859.

[The House of Representatives was in the midst of a fierce debate over choosing a Speaker. Some southern congressmen stated that no antislavery congressman should be elected Speaker, while some northern representatives charged that no slaveholder should be Speaker of the House.]

The North and the South stand here arrayed against each other. Upon the one side I behold numerical power; upon the other, the violent, even fierce spirit of resistance. Disunion has been threatened. Sir, in all this controversy, *so far as it is sectional*, I occupy the position of ARMED NEUTRALITY. I am not a Northern man. I have little sympathy with the North, no very good feeling for, and I am bound to her by no tie whatsoever, other than what once were and ought always to be among the strongest of all ties—a common language and common country. Least of all am I that most unseemly and abject object of all political spectacles—"A Northern man with Southern principles;" but, God be thanked, still a United States man with United States principles. When I emigrate to the South, take up my abode there, identify myself with her interests, holding slaves or holding none; then, and not till then, will I have a right, and will it be my duty, and no doubt my pleasure to maintain and support Southern principles and Southern institutions.

Then, sir, I am not a Southern man, either—although, in this unholy and most unconstitutional crusade against the South, in the midst of the invasion, arson, insurrection, and murder to which she has been subject, and with which she is still threatened—with the torch of the incendiary and the dagger of the assassin suspended over her—my most cordial sympathies are wholly with her.

Then, sir, I am not a Northern man, nor yet a Southern man; but I am a WESTERN MAN, by birth, in habit, by education; and although still a United States man with United States principles, yet within, and subordinate to the Constitution, am wholly devoted to Western interests. . . .

[Vallandigham then accused congressmen of both the North and the South of ignoring the West (". . . the Western man was held to be a sort of outside barbarian") while they hurtled the nation toward civil war.]

Sir, in this war of sections, standing here between the living and the dead, we the Democratic representatives of the West, and I, as one of that number, have a duty to perform, which, in all humbleness, but in all faithfulness, shall be fulfilled. But too many of you of the North are striving with might and main to force the South out of this Union; and too many of you of the South are most anxious to be forced out. Do not deny it, either of you. I know it.

Sir, I will not consent that an honest and conscientious opposition to slavery forms any part of the motives of the leaders of the Republican party. In the earlier stages of the Abolition agitation, it may have been otherwise, but not so to-day. This whole controversy has now become but one of mere sectionalism—a war for political domination, in which slavery performs but the part of the letter x in an algebraic equation, and is used now, in the political algebra of the day, only to work out the problem of disunion. It was admitted, in 1820, in the beginning, by Rufus King, who hurled the first thunderbolt in the Missouri controversy, to be but a question of sectional power and control. To-day it exists, and is fostered and maintained, because the North has, or believes that she has the power and numbers and strength and wealth, and every other element which constitutes a State, superior to you of the South. Power has always been arrogant, domineering, wrathful, inexorable, fierce, denying that constitutions and laws were made for it. Power now, and here, is just what power has been everywhere, and in every age. But, gentlemen of the North, you who ignorantly or wittingly are hurrying this Republic to its destruction, you who tell the South to go out of the Union if she dare, and you will bring her back by force, or leave her to languish and to perish under your overshadowing greatness, did it never occur to you that when this most momentous but most disastrous of all the events which history shall ever to the end of time record, shall have been brought about, the West, the great West, which you now coolly reckon yours as a province, yours as a fief of your vast empire, may choose, of her own sovereign good-will and pleasure, in the exercise of a popular sovereignty, which will demand, and will have non-intervention, to set up for herself? Did you never dream of a WESTERN CONFEDERACY? Did that horrid phantom never flit across you in visions of the night, when deep sleep falls upon men? So, we have fed you, we have clothed you, we have paid tribute to, and enriched you, for now these sixty years; we it is who have built up your marts of commerce; we it is who have caused your manufacturing establishments to flourish.

Then, sir I am against disunion. I find no more pleasure in a Southern disunionist than in a Northern or Western disunionist. Do not tell me that you of the South have an apology in the events and developments of the last few months. I know you have. War—irrepressible war, has been proclaimed against your institution of slavery; it has been carried into your own States; arson and murder have been committed upon your own soil; peaceful citizens have been ruthlessly shot down at the threshold of their own doors. You avenged the wrong; you executed the murderer and the felon; but he has risen from the dead a hero and a martyr; and now the apostles of this new Messiah of Abolition, with scrip and purse, armed with the sword, insolent from augmenting numbers, apostles rather of Mahomet, disciples of Peter the Hermit are but gathering strength, and awaiting the hour for a new invasions.[18] Certainly—certainly, in all this you have ample justification for whatsoever of excitement and alarm and indignation pervade now the whole South, from Mason and Dixon's line down to the Gulf of Mexico. But will you secede now? Will you break up the Union of these States? Will you bring down forever, in one promiscuous ruin, the columns and pillars of this magnificent temple of liberty, which our fathers reared at so great cost of blood and of treasure? Wait a little! Wait a little! Let us try again the peaceful, the ordinary, the constitutional means for the redress of grievances. Let us resort once more to the ballot-box. Let us try once again *that weapon, surer set, and better than the bayonet.*

18. Here Vallandigham was referring to John Brown, who was executed 13 days before Vallandigham's speech.

2. Remarks upon Being Called Out at a Serenade to Ohio Senator George E. Pugh, December 22, 1860.

To-night you are here to indorse the great policy of conciliation, not force; peace, not civil war. The desire nearest the heart of every patriot in this crisis, is the preservation of the Union of these States, as our fathers made it. [Applause.] But the Union can be preserved only by maintaining the Constitution, and the constitutional rights, and above all, the perfect equality of every State and every section of this Confederacy. [Cheers.] That Constitution was made in peace; it has, for now more than seventy years, been preserved by the policy of peace at home, and it can alone be maintained for our children, and their children after them, by that same peace policy.

This Union is not to be held together, this Constitution is not be cemented by the blood of our citizens poured out in civil war; and coercion is civil war, and it is folly to attempt to disguise its true character under the name and pretence of "enforcing the laws." The people will in the end demand a bloody reckoning upon the heads of those who may thus deceive them. [Loud cheers.] No; let us negotiate, compromise, concede; let us, if need be, give and receive new guarantees for our respective rights; for this is wisdom and true statesmanship; and in this way only can the Government be preserved or restored. At all events let us have no civil war. [Applause.] And, as one living near the borders of what may be, unhappily, and in an evil hour, a divided Confederacy, I am resolved that by no vote, by no speech, by no act of mine shall any thing be done to plunge this my country, into the horrors of a war among brethren.

I lament profoundly indeed the causes which have led to this most alarming crisis in the midst of which we now are. I have labored faithfully and right manfully for years to correct and to remove them. I regret also the results which naturally and inevitably have followed them. But if we must separate, let it, in God's name, be in peace. Then we shall be able to reconstruct this Government. If we cannot preserve, we can, and we will, restore it, and become thus the second founders of the Republic. That is our mission, inferior only in glory and honor, and in good, to the mission of those who laid its foundation at first. . . . [Applause.]

[Vallandigham then accused Republican abolitionists of forcing the southern states out of the Union. Were the institution of slavery to be guaranteed, he claimed that they would "gladly return."]

Fellow-citizens, I am all over, and altogether, a Union man. I would preserve it in all its integrity and worth. But, I repeat, that this cannot be done by coercion—by the sword. He who would resort to force—military force, is a disunionist, call himself what he may, and disguise it though he may under the pretext of executing the laws and preserving the Union. He is a "disunionist," whether he knows it and means it or not. Hence I am for peace and for compromise, fixed, irrepealable compromise, so that we may secure peace; but I am for peace in any event—peace upon both sides and upon all sides, now and forever.

3. Speech in the House of Representatives, February 20, 1861.[19]

Mr. SPEAKER: It was my purpose, some three months ago, to speak solely upon the question of peace and war between the two great sections of the Union, and to defend at length the position which, in the very beginning of this crisis, and almost alone, I assumed against the employment of military force by the Federal Government to execute its laws and restore its authority within the States which might secede. Subsequent events have rendered this unnecessary. Within the three months or more, since the presidential election, so rapid has been the progress of events, and such the magnitude which the movement in the South has attained, that the country has been forced—as this House and the incoming Administration will at last be forced, in spite of their warlike purposes now—to regard it as no longer a mere casual and temporary rebellion of discontented individuals, but a great and terrible REVOLUTION, which threatens now to result in permanent dissolution of the Union, and division into two or more rival, if not hostile, confederacies. Before this dread reality, the atrocious and fruitless policy of a war of coercion to preserve or to restore the Union has, outside, at least, of these walls and of this capital, rapidly dissolved. The people have taken the subject up, and have reflected upon it, till to-day, in the South, almost as one man, and by a very large majority, as I believe, in the North, and especially in the West, they are resolved that, whatever else of calamity may befall us, that horrible scourge of CIVIL WAR shall be averted. Sir, I rejoice that the hard Anglo-Saxon sense and pious and humane impulses of the American people have rejected the specious disguise of words without wisdom which appealed to them to enforce the laws, collect the revenue, maintain the Union, and restore the Federal authority by the perilous edge of battle, and that thus early in the revolution they are resolved to compel us, their Representatives, belligerent as you of the Republican party here may now be, to the choice of peaceable

19. The speech was titled "The Great American Revolution of 1861," and was published and distributed in pamphlet form. See *Speech of Hon. C. L. Vallandigham, of Ohio, Delivered in the House of Representatives, February 20, 1861* (Washington: Henry Polkinhorn, 1861).

disunion upon the one hand, or Union through adjustment and conciliation upon the other. Born, sir, upon the soil of the United States; attached to my country from earliest boyhood; living and revering her, with some part, at least, of the spirit of Greek and Roman patriotism; between these two alternatives, with all my mind, with all my heart, with all my strength of body and of soul, living or dying at home or in exile, I am for the Union which made it what it is; and therefore I am also for such terms of peace and adjustment as will maintain that Union now and forever.

[Here Vallandigham stated that the cause of the present difficulty resided in the "nature of man" and his unquenchable thirst for power. For their part, the powerful believe that "might makes right." To guard against this inevitable situation, governments are formed.]

Sir, the framers of the Constitution—and I speak it reverently, but with the freedom of history—failed to foresee the strength and centralizing tendencies of the Federal Government. They mistook wholly the real danger to the system. They looked for it in the aggressions of the large States upon the small States, without regard to geographical position, and accordingly guarded jealously in that direction, giving, for this purpose, as I have said, the power of a self-protecting veto in the Senate to the small States, by means of their equal suffrage in that Chamber, and forbidding even amendment of the Constitution, in this particular, without the consent of every State. But, they seem wholly to have overlooked the danger of SECTIONAL COMBINATIONS as against other sections, and to the injury and oppression of other sections, to secure possession of the several departments of the Federal Government, and of the vast powers and influence which belong to them. In like manner, too, they seem to have utterly under-estimated SLAVERY as a disturbing element in the system, possibly because it existed still in almost every State, but chiefly because the growth and manufacture of cotton had scarce yet been commenced in the United States—because cotton was not yet crowned King. The vast extent of the patronage of the Executive, and the immense power and influence which it exerts, seem also to have been altogether under-estimated. And independent of all these, or rather, perhaps, in connection with them, there were inherent defects, incident to the nature of all governments; some of them peculiar to our system, and to the circumstances of the country, and the character of the people over which it was instituted, which no human sagacity could have foreseen, but which have led to evils, mischiefs, and abuses, which time and experience alone have disclosed. The men who made our Government were human; they were *men,* and they made it for men of like passions and infirmities with themselves.

[Vallandigham then spoke of the urge by certain interests to control the federal government, especially the Executive branch, for revenue, patronage, and power to put their programs into practice. Then, as slavery became an issue, former President Thomas Jefferson feared that it would destroy the Union.[20] In Vallandigham's opinion, the Republican Party was using its newly won power in an attempt to destroy slavery.]

I propose then, sir, to do as all others in the Senate and the House have done, so far—to recognize the existence of sections as a fixed fact, which, lamentable as it is, can no longer be denied or suppressed; but, for the reasons I have already stated, I propose to establish four instead of two grand sections of the Union, all of them well known, or easily designated by marked, natural, or geographical lines and boundaries. I propose four sections instead of two; because, if two only are recognized, the natural and inevitable division will be into slaveholding and non-slaveholding sections; and it is this very division, either by constitutional enactment, or by common consent, as hitherto, which, in my deliberate judgment and deepest conviction, it concerns the peace and stability of the Union, should be forever hereafter ignored. Till then, there cannot be, and will not be, perfect union and peace between these United States; because, in the first place, the nature of the question is such that it stirs up, necessarily, as forty years of strife conclusively proves, the strongest and the bitterest passions and antagonism possible among men; and, in the next place, because the non-slaveholding section has now, and will have to the end, a steadily increasing majority, and enormously disproportioned weight and influence in the government; thus combining that which never can be very long resisted in any government—the temptation and the power to aggress . . .

But it is not in legislation alone that the danger, or the temptation to aggress, is to be found. Of the tremendous power and influence of the Executive I have already spoken. And, indeed, the present revolutionary movements are the result of the apprehension of executive usurpation and encroachments, to the injury of the rights of the South. But for secession, because of this apprehended danger, the legislative department would have remained, for the present at least, in other and safer hands. Hence the necessity for equal protection and guarantee against sectional combinations and majorities, to secure the election of the President, and to control him when elected. I propose, therefore, that a concurrent majority of the electors, or Senators, as the case may require, of each section, shall be necessary to the choice of President and Vice-President; and lest, by reason of this increased complexity, there may be a failure of choice oftener than heretofore, I propose also a special election in such case, and an extension of the term, in all cases,

20. For example, see Jefferson to John Holmes, April 22, 1820, in Paul Leisester Ford, ed., *The Writings of Thomas Jefferson* (New York: G.P. Putnam's Sons, 1897) vol. 10, pp. 157–158.

to six years. This is the outline of the plan; the details may be learned in full from the joint resolution itself; and I will not detain the House by any further explanation now.

Sir, the natural and inevitable result of these amendments will be to preclude the possibility to sectional parties and combinations to obtain possession of either the legislative or the executive power and patronage of the Federal Government; and, if not to suppress totally, at least very greatly to diminish the evil results of national caucuses, conventions, and other similar party appliances. It will no longer be possible to elect a President by the votes of a mere dominant and majority section. Sectional issues must cease, as the basis, at least, of large party organizations. Ambition, or lust for power and place, must look no longer to its own section, but to the whole country; and he who would be President, or in any way the foremost among his countrymen, must consult, henceforth, the combined good, and the good-will, too, of all the sections, and in this way, consistently with the Constitution, can the "general welfare" be best attained. Thus, indeed, will the result be, instead of a narrow, illiberal, and sectional policy, an enlarged patriotism and extended public spirit. . . .

[Vallandigham's three proposed amendments to the Constitution would have divided the nation into four sections (North, West, Pacific, South). To elect a president, a majority of electors in each section would be necessary, and the president would serve only one term of six years. Secession of any state would not be permitted unless the legislatures of all the other states in that section approved. The property of all citizens would be protected, even when they moved to another section. As expected, Vallandigham's proposals were doomed, even without the outbreak of war.]

4. Speech in the House of Representatives, July 10, 1861, in Response to President Lincoln's Message to Congress in to Special Session.[21]

[Vallandigham's speech was a broad attack on the President, charging him in instance after instance with gross executive usurpation of power. He charged that Lincoln's inaugural address was written "with the forked tongue and crooked counsel of the New York politician (possibly Secretary of State William Seward), leaving many people in doubt whether it meant peace or war." Vallandigham then attacked Lincoln and his fellow Republicans for the passage of the Morrill Tariff.]

But, whatever may have been the purpose, I assert here, to-day, as a Representative, that every principal act of the Administration since has been

21. For Lincoln's message, see Roy P. Basler, ed., *The Collected Works of Abraham Lincoln* (New Brunswick: Rutgers University Press, 1953), vol. 4, pp. 421–441.

a glaring usurpation of power, and a palpable and dangerous violation of that very Constitution which this civil war is professedly waged to support.

Beginning with this wide breach of the Constitution, this enormous usurpation of the most dangerous of all powers—the power of the sword—other infractions and assumptions were easy; and after public liberty, private right soon fell. The privacy of the telegraph was invaded, in the search after treason and traitors; although it turns out, significantly enough, that the only victim, so far, is one of the appointees and especial pets of the Administration. The telegraphic dispatches, preserved under every pledge of secrecy, for the protection and safety of the telegraph companies; were seized and carried away without search-warrant, without probable cause, without oath, and without description of the places to be searched, or of the things to be seized, and in plain violation of the right of the people to be secure in their houses, persons, *papers,* and effects, against unreasonable searches and seizures. One step more, sir, will bring upon us search and seizure of the public mails.

Sir, the rights of property having been thus wantonly violated, it needed but a little stretch of usurpation to invade the sanctity of the person; and a victim was not long wanting. A private citizen of Maryland, not subject to the rules and articles of war—not in a case arising in the land or naval forces, nor in the militia, when in actual service—is seized in his own house, in the dead hour of night, not by any civil officer, nor upon any civil process, but by a band of armed soldiers, under the verbal orders of a military chief, and is ruthlessly torn from his wife and his children, and hurried off to a fortress of the United States—and that fortress, as if in mockery, the very one over whose ramparts had floated that star-spangled banner, which "in the dawn's early light," gladdened the eyes and inspired the soul of the patriot prisoner, who in the midst of battle, and upon the deck of one of the enemy's ships, made it memorable by the noblest of American national lyrics.

And, sir, when the highest judicial officer of the land, the Chief Justice of the Supreme Court, upon whose shoulders "when the judicial ermine fell, it touched nothing less spotless than itself," the aged, the venerable, the gentle, and pure-minded Taney, who, but a little while before, had administered to the President the oath to support the Constitution, and to execute the laws, issued, as by law it was his sworn duty to issue, the high prerogative writ of *habeas corpus*—that great writ of right, that main bulwark of personal liberty, commanding the body of the accused to be brought before him, that justice and right might be done by due course of law, and without denial or delay, the gates of the fortress, its cannon turned towards, and in plain sight of the city, where the court sat and frowning from the ramparts, were closed against the officer of the law, and the answer returned that the officer in command had, by the authority of the President, *suspended* the writ of *habeas corpus.* And thus it is, sir, that the accused has ever since been held a prisoner without due process of law; without bail; without presentment by a grand jury; without speedy, or public trial by a petit jury, of his own State or district, or any trial at all; without information of the nature and cause of the accusation; without being confronted with the witnesses against him; without compulsory process to obtain witnesses in his favor; and without the assistance of counsel for his defence. And this is our boasted American liberty.[22]

Sir, I am obliged to pass by, for want of time, other grave and dangerous infractions and usurpations of the President since the 4th of March. I only allude casually to the quartering of soldiers in private houses without the consent of the owners, and without any manner having been prescribed by law; to the subversion in a part, at least, of Maryland of her own State Government and of the authorities under it; to the censorship over the telegraph, and the infringement, repeatedly, in one or more of the States, of the right of the people to keep and to bear arms for their defence. But if all these things, I ask, have been done in the first two months after the commencement of this war, and by men not military chieftains, and unused to arbitrary power, what may we not expect to see in three years, and by the successful heroes of the fight? Sir, the power and rights of the States and the people, and of their Representatives, have been usurped; the sanctity of the private house and of private property has been invaded; and the liberty of the person wantonly and wickedly stricken down; free speech, too, has been repeatedly denied; and this under the plea of necessity. Sir, the right of petition will follow next—nay, it has already been shaken; the freedom of the press will soon fall after it; and let me whisper in your ear, that there will be few to mourn over its loss, unless, indeed, its ancient high and honorable character shall be rescued and redeemed from its present reckless mendacity and degradation. Freedom of religion will yield too, at last, amid the exultant shouts of millions, who have seen its holy temples defiled, and its white robes of a former innocency trampled now under the polluting hoofs of an ambitious and faithless or fanatical clergy.

Sir, I have spoken freely and fearlessly to-day, as became an American Representative and an American citizen; one firmly resolved, come what may, not to lose his own Constitutional liberties, nor to surrender his own Constitutional rights in the vain effort to impose these rights and liberties upon ten millions of unwilling people.

---

22. Vallandigham was referring to the federal circuit court decision of *Ex parte Merryman* (1861) in which Chief Justice Roger Taney ruled that only Congress had the right to suspend the writ of *habeas corpus* (in which officials are required to bring arrested people before a court to convince a judge that there are lawful reasons to hold the prisoner; otherwise, he or she must be released). Lincoln ignored the ruling.

5. Speech to the Democratic Party Members of the House of Representatives, May 8, 1862.

FELLOW-CITIZENS:—The perilous condition of the country demands that we should counsel together. Party organization, restricted within proper limits, is a positive good, and indeed essential to the preservation of public liberty. Without it the best government would soon degenerate into the worst of tyrannies. In dispositions the chief use of power is in crushing out party opposition. In our own country the experience of the last twelve months proves, more than any lesson in history, the necessity of party organization. The present Administration was chosen by a party, and in all civil acts and appointments has recognized, and still does, its fealty and obligations to that party. There must and will be an opposition. The public safety and good demand it. Shall it be a new organization or an old one? The Democratic party was founded more than sixty years ago. It has never been disbanded. Today it numbers one million five hundred thousand electors in the States still loyal to the Union. Its recent numerous victories in municipal elections in the Western and Middle States prove its vitality. Within the last ten months it has held State conventions and nominated full Democratic tickets in every free State in the Union. Of no other party opposed to the Republicans can the same be said.

Is the POLICY of the Democratic party wrong that it should be disbanded?

Its policy is consistent with its principles, and may be summed up, from the beginning, as follows: The support of liberty as against power; of the people as against their agents and servants; and of State rights as against consolidation and centralized despotism; a simple Government; no public debt; low taxes; no high protective tariff; no general system of internal improvements by Federal authority; no National Bank; hard money for the Federal public dues; no assumption of State debts; expansion of territory; self-government for the Territories, subject only to the Constitution; the absolute compatibility of a Union of the States, "part slave and part free;" the admission of new States, with or without slavery, as they may elect; noninterference by the Federal Government with slavery in State and Territory, or in the District of Columbia; and finally, as set forth in the Cincinnati Platform, in 1856, and reaffirmed in 1860, absolute and eternal " repudiation of ALL SECTIONAL PARTIES AND PLATFORMS concerning domestic slavery which seek to embroil the States and incite to treason and armed resistance to law in the Territories, *and whose avowed purpose, if consummated, must end in* CIVIL WAR AND DISUNION."

Such was the ancient and the recent policy of the Democratic party, running through a period of sixty years—a policy consistent with the principles of the Constitution, and absolutely essential to the preservation of the Union. . . .

The first step towards a restoration of the Union as it was is to maintain the Constitution as it is. So long as it was maintained in fact, and not threatened with infraction in spirit and in letter, actual or imminent, the Union was unbroken.

To restore the Union, it is essential, first, to give assurance to every State and to the people of every section that their rights and liberties and property will be secure within the Union under the Constitution. What assurance so doubly sure as the restoration to power of that ancient, organized, consolidated Democratic party which for sixty years *did* secure the property, rights, and liberties of the States and of the people; and thus did maintain the Constitution and preserve the Union, and with them the multiplied blessings which distinguished us above all other nations?

To restore the Union is to crush out sectionalism North and South. To begin the great work of restoration through the ballot is to KILL ABOLITION. The bitter waters of secession flowed first and are fed still from the unclean fountain of abolition. That fountain must be dried up. Armies may break down the power of the Confederate Government in the South; but the work of restoration can be carried on only through political organization and the ballot in the North and West. In this great work we cordially invite the co-operation of all men of every party, who are opposed to the fell spirit of abolition, and who, in sincerity, desire the Constitution as it is, and Union as it was.

Let the dead past bury its dead. Rally, lovers of the Union, the Constitution, and of Liberty, to the standard of the Democratic party, already in the field and confident of victory. That party is the natural and persistent enemy of abolition. Upon this question its record as a national organization, however it may have been at times with particular men or in particular States, is clear and unquestionable.

To conclude: Inviting all men; without distinction of State, section, or party, who are for the Constitution as it is, and the Union as it was, to unite with us in this great work upon terms of perfect equality, we insist that—

The restoration of the Union, whether through peace or by war, demands the continued organization and success of the Democratic party;

The preservation of the Constitution demands it;

The maintenance of liberty and free democratical government demands it;

The restoration of a sound system of internal policy demands it;

Economy and honesty in the public expenditures, now at the rate of nearly four millions of dollars a day, demands it;

The rapid accumulation of an enormous and permanent public debt, demand it—a public debt, or liability, already one thousand millions of dollars, and equal, at the present rate, in three years, to England's debt of a century and a half in growth;

The heavy taxation, direct and indirect, State and Federal, already more than two hundred million of dollars a year, eating out the substance of the people, and augmenting every year, demands it;

Reduced wages, low prices, depression of trade, decay of business, scarcity of work, and impending ruin on every side, demands it;

And, finally the restoration of the concord, good feeling, and prosperity of former years, demands that the Democratic party shall be maintained, and made victorious.

6. Resolutions Introduced by Vallandigham in the House of Representatives, December 16, 1862 (postponed and tabled).

"*Resolved*, 1. That the Union as it was must be restored and maintained forever, under the Constitution as it is—the fifth article, providing for amendments, included.

"2. That no final treaty of peace, ending the present civil war, can be permitted to be made *by the Executive, or any other person in the civil or military service of the United States*, on any other basis than the integrity and entirety of the Federal Union, and of the States composing the same as at the beginning of hostilities, and upon that basis peace ought immediately to be made.

"3. That the Government can never permit armed or hostile intervention by any Foreign power, in regard to the present civil war.

"4. That the unhappy civil war in which we are engaged was waged, in the beginning, professedly, "not in any spirit of oppression, or for any purpose of conquest or subjugation or purpose of overthrowing or interfering with the rights or established institutions of the States, but to defend and maintain the supremacy of the Constitution, and to preserve the Union, with all the dignity, equality, and rights of the several States unipaired," and was so understood and accepted by the people, and especially by the army and navy of the United States; and that, therefore, whoever shall pervert, or attempt to prevent, the same to a war of conquest and subjugation, or for the overthrowing or interfering with the rights or established institutions of any of the States, and to abolish slavery therein, or for the purpose of destroying or impairing the dignity, equality or rights of any of the States, will be guilty of a flagrant breach of public faith, and of a high crime against the Constitution and the Union.

"5. That whoever shall propose, by Federal authority, to extinguish any of the States of the Union, or to declare any of them extinguished, and to establish territorial governments, or permanent military governments within the same, will be deserving of the censure of this House and of the country.

"6. That whoever shall attempt to establish a dictatorship in the United States, thereby superseding or suspending the constitutional authorities of the Union, or to clothe the President or any other officer, civil or military, with dictatorial or arbitrary power, will be guilty of a high crime against the Constitution and the Union, and public liberty."

On the 22nd of the same month, Mr. VALLANDIGHAM offered the following, which, also, went over for debate:

"*Resolved*, That, this House earnestly desire that the most speedy and effectual measures be taken for restoring peace in America, and that no time may be lost in proposing an immediate cessation of hostilities, in order to the speedy settlement of the unhappy controversies which brought about this unnecessary and injurious civil war, by just and adequate security against the return of like calamities in time to come; and this House desire to offer the most earnest assurances to the country, that they will in due time cheerfully co-operate with the Executive and the States for the restoration of the Union, by such explicit and most solemn amendments the rights of the several States and sections within the Union, under the Constitution."

7. Speech on the Great Civil War in America, Delivered in the House of Representatives, January 14, 1863.

[Vallandigham began by tracing the history of secession, of Lincoln's inauguration, of the firing on Fort Sumter, and of the initial wave of patriotism in the North and West.]

But the reign of the mob was inaugurated only to be supplanted by the iron domination of arbitrary power. Constitutional limitation was broken down; *habeas corpus* fell; liberty of the press, of speech, of the person, of the mails, of travel, of one's own house, and of religion; the right to bear arms, due process of law, judicial trial, trial by jury, trial at all; every badge and muniment of freedom in republican government or kingly government—all went down at a blow; and the chief law officer of the crown—I beg pardon, sir, but it is easy now to fall into this courtly language—the Attorney-General, first of all men, proclaimed in the United States the maxim of Roman servility: Whatever pleases the President, that is law! Prisoners of state were then first heard of here. Midnight and arbitrary arrests commenced; travel was interdicted; trade embargoed; passports demanded; bastilles were introduced; strange oaths invented; a secret police organized; "piping" began; informers multiplied; spies now first appeared in America. The right to declare war, to raise and support armies, and to provide and maintain a navy was usurped by the Executive; and in a little more than two months a land and naval force of over three hundred thousand men was in the field or upon the sea. An army of public plunderers followed, and corruption struggled with power in friendly strife for the mastery at home.

On the 4th of July Congress met, not to seek peace; not to rebuke usurpation nor to restrain power; not certainly to deliberate; not even to legislate, but to register and ratify the edicts and acts of the Executive; and in your language, sir, upon the first day of the session, to invoke a universal baptism of fire and blood amid the roar of cannon and the din of battle. Free speech was had only at the risk of a prison; possibly of life. Opposition was silenced by the fierce clamor of "disloyalty." All business not of war was voted out of order. Five hundred thousand men, an immense navy, and two hundred and fifty millions of money were speedily granted. In twenty, at most in sixty days, the rebellion was to be crushed out. To doubt it was treason. Abject submission was demanded. Lay down your arms, sue for peace, surrender your leaders—forfeiture, death—this was the only language heard on this floor. The galleries responded; the corridors echoed; and contractors and placemen and other venal patriots everywhere gnashed upon the friends of peace as they passed by. In five weeks seventy-eight public and private acts and joint resolutions, with declaratory resolutions, in the Senate and House, quite as numerous, all full of slaughter, were hurried through without delay and almost without debate.

Thus was CIVIL WAR inaugurated in America. Can any man to-day see the end of it?

[Vallandigham then explained his own position.]

But to return: the country was at war; and I belonged to that school of politics which teaches that when we are at war, the Government—I do not mean the Executive alone, but the Government—is entitled to demand and have, without resistance, such number of men, and such amount of money and supplies generally, as may be necessary for the war, until an appeal can be had to the people. . . .

Sir, I adopt all this as my own position and my defence; though, perhaps, in a civil war I might fairly go further in opposition. I could not, with my convictions, vote men and money for this war, and I would not, as a Representative, vote against them. I meant that, without opposition, the President might take him to a strict accountability before the people for the results. Not believing the soldiers responsible for the war, or its purposes, or its consequences, I have never withheld my vote where their separate interests were concerned. But I have denounced, from the beginning, the usurpations and the infractions, one and all, of law and Constitution, by the President and those under him; their repeated and persistent arbitrary arrests, the suspension of *habeas corpus*, the violation of freedom of the mails, of the private house, of the press and of speech, and all the other multiplied wrongs and outrages upon public liberty and private right, which have made this country one of the worst despotisms on earth for the past twenty months; and I will continue to rebuke and denounce them to the end; and the people, thanks God! have at last heard and heeded, and rebuked them, too. To the record and to time I appeal again for my justification.

And now, sir, I return to the state of Union to-day. What is it? Sir, twenty months have elapsed, but the rebellion is not crushed out; its military power has not been broken; the insurgents have not dispersed. The Union is not restored; nor the Constitution maintained; nor the laws enforced. Twenty, sixty, ninety, three hundred, six hundred days have passed; a thousand millions been expended; and hundred thousand lives lost or bodies mangled; and to-day the Confederate flag is still near the Potomac and the Ohio, and the Confederate Government stronger, many times, than at the beginning. Not a State has been restored, not any part of any State has voluntarily returned to the Union. . . .

Thus, with twenty millions of people, and every element of strength and force at command—power, patronage, influence, unanimity, enthusiasm, confidence, credit, money, men, and Army and a Navy the largest and the noblest ever set in the field, or afloat upon the sea; with the support, almost servile, of every State, country, and municipality in the North and West, with a Congress swift to do the bidding of the Executive; without opposition anywhere at home; and with an arbitrary power which neither the Czar of Russia, nor the Emperor of Austria dare exercise; yet after nearly two years of more vigorous prosecution of war than ever recorded in history; after more skirmishes, combats, and battles than Alexander, Cæsar, or the first Napoleon ever fought in any five years of their military career, you have utterly, signally, disastrously—I will not say ignominiously—failed to subdue ten millions of "rebels," whom you had taught the people of the North and West not only to hate, but to despise. . . .

Sir, in blood she [North and West] has atoned for her credulity; and now there is mourning in every house, and distress and sadness in every heart. Shall she give you any more?

But ought this war to continue? I answer, no—not a day, not an hour. What then? Shall we separate? Again I answer, no, no, no! What then?

But slavery is the cause of the war. Why? Because the South obstinately and wickedly refused to restrict or abolish it at the demand of the philosophers or fanatics and demagogues of the North and West. Then, sir, it was abolition, the purpose to abolish or interfere with and hem in slavery, which caused disunion and war. Slavery is only the subject, but Abolition the cause of this civil war. It was the persistent and determined agitation in the free States of the question of abolishing slavery in the South, because of the alleged "irrepressible conflict" between the forms of labor in the two sections, or, in the false and mischievous cant of the day, between freedom and slavery, that forced a collision of arms at last. Sir, that conflict was not confined to the Territories. It was expressly proclaimed by its apostles, as between the States also—against the institution of domestic slavery everywhere. But, assuming the platforms of the Republican party as a standard, and stating the case most strongly in favor of that party, it was the refusal of the South to consent that slavery agitation, North and South, of that question, and finally to disunion and civil war. Sir, I will not be answered now by the old clamor about "the aggressions of the slave power." That miserable spectre, that unreal mockery, has been exorcised and expelled by debt and taxation and blood. If that power did govern this country for the sixty years preceding this terrible revolution, then sooner this administration and Government return to the principles and policy of Southern statesmanship, the better for the country; and that, sir, is already, or soon will be, the judgment of the people. But I deny that it was the "slave power" that governed for so many years, and so wisely and well. It was the Democratic party, and its principles and policy, moulded and controlled, indeed, largely by Southern statesmen. Neither will I be stopped by that other cry of mingled fanaticism and hypocrisy, about the sin and barbarism of African slavery. Sir, I see more of barbarism and sin, a thousand times, in the continuance of this war, this war, the dissolution of the Union, the breaking up of this Government, and the enslavement of the white race, by debt and taxes and arbitrary power. The day of fanatics and sophists and enthusiasts, thank God, is gone at last; and though the age of chivalry may not, the age of practical statesmanship is about to return. Sir, I accept the language and intent of the Indiana resolution, to the full—"that in considering terms of settlement, we will look only to the welfare, peace, and safety of the white race, without reference to the effect that settlement may have upon the condition of the African." And when we have done this, my word for it, the safety, peace, and welfare of the African will have been best secured. Sir, there is fifty-fold less of anti-slavery sentiment to-day in the West than there was two years ago; and if this war be continued, there will be still less a year hence. The people there begin, at last, to comprehend, that domestic slavery in the South is a question, not of morals, or religion, or humanity, but a form of labor, perfectly compatible with the dignity of free white labor in the same community, and with national vigor, power, and prosperity, and especially with military strength.

Sir, I repeat it, we are in the midst of the very crisis of this revolution. If, to-day, we secure peace, and begin the work of reunion, we shall yet escape; if not, I see nothing before us but universal political and social revolution, anarchy, and bloodshed, compared with which, the Reign of Terror in France was a merciful visitation.

8. Speech on the Conscription Bill, Delivered in the House of Representatives on February 23, 1863.

[Although Vallandigham opposed the bill establishing a draft, he spent most of his time attacking the "tyranny" of the Lincoln administration.]

Sir, I yield to no man in devotion to the Union. I am for maintaining it upon the principles on which it was first formed; and I would have it, at every sacrifice, except of liberty, which is "the life of the nation." I have stood by it in boyhood and in manhood, to this hour; and I will not now consent to yield it up; nor am I to be driven from an earnest and persistent support of the party of the only means by which it can be restored, either by the threats of the party of the Administration here, or because of affected sneers and contemptuous refusals to listen, now, to reunion, by the party of the Administration at Richmond. I never was weak enough to cower before the reign of terror inaugurated by the men in power here, nor vain enough to expect favorable responses now, or terms of settlement, from the men in power, or the presses under their control, in the South. Neither will ever compromise this great quarrel, nor agree to peace on the basis of reunion: but I repeat it—stop fighting, and let time and natural causes operate—uncontrolled by military influences—and the ballot there, as the ballot here, will do its work. I am for the Union of these States; and but for my profound conviction that it can never be restored by force and arms; or, if so restored, could not be maintained, and would not be worth maintaining, I would have united, at first—even now would unite, cordially—in giving, as I have acquiesced, silently, in your taking, all the men and all the money you have demanded. But I did not believe, and do not now believe, that the war could end in any thing but final defeat; and if it should last long enough, then in disunion; or, if successful upon the principles now proclaimed, that it must and would end in the establishment of an imperial military despotism—not only in the South—but in the North and West. And to that I never will submit. No, rather, I am ready first to yield up property, and my own personal liberty—nay, life itself. . . .

[Did the necessity of such legislation mean that the number of volunteers and support for the war were decreasing in the North?]

I repeat it, Sir, this bill is a confession that the people of the country are against this war. It is a solemn admission, upon the record in the legislation of Congress, that they will not voluntarily consent to wage it any longer. And yet, ignoring every principle upon which the Government was founded, this measure is an attempt, by compulsion, to carry it on against the will of the people. Sir, what does all this mean? You were a majority at first, the people were unanimously with you, and they were generous and enthusiastic in your support. You abused your power, and your trust, and you failed to do the work which you promised. You have lost the confidence, lost the hearts of the people. You are now a minority at home. And yet, what a spectacle is exhibited here tonight! You, an accidental, temporary majority in this House, condemned and repudiated by the people, are exhausting the few remaining hours of your political life, in attempting to defeat the popular will, and to compel, by the most desperate and despotic of expedients ever resorted to, the submission of the majority of the people, at home, to the minority, their servants, here. Sir, this experiment has been tried before, in other ages and countries, and its issue always, among a people born free, or fit to be free, has been expulsion or death to the conspirators and tyrants. . . .

9. Speech to the Democratic Union Association of New York City, March 7, 1863.

I am here to speak to-night regardless of all threats; and if there were any disagreeable consequences to follow, regardless of those consequences. (Loud cheers.) But there are none, and I am here to speak just such thing as, in my judgment, a true patriot and a freeman ought to speak. (Enthusiastic cheers.) I accepted the invitation very cordially, to address this Association, and came at no inconsiderable personal sacrifice, because the exigencies of the times which are again upon us, with threatening aspect, not only justify, but, in my judgment, demand of every public man, that all personal considerations should be laid aside for the public good. I know as well as any one, the pressure that is now made upon the Democratic party, with the vain hope of crushing it out. The men who are in power at Washington, extending their agencies out through the cities and States of the Union and threatening to reinaugurate a reign of terror, may as well know that we comprehend precisely their purpose. I beg leave to assure you that it cannot and will not be permitted to succeed. (Applause.) The people of this country indorsed it once because they were told that it was essential to "the speedy suppression or crushing out of the rebellion" and the restoration of the Union; and they so loved the Union of these States, that they would consent even for a little while under the false and now broken promises of the men in power, to surrender those liberties, in order that the great object might, as was promised, be accomplished speedily. They have been deceived; instead of crushing out the rebellion, the effort has been to crush out the spirit of liberty. (Cheers.). . . .

And now no effort, however organized, premeditated, or well concerted to restore those times through which we have passed, and which will stand upon the pages of history as the darkest of all the annals of America, will be permitted to succeed, and the sooner they comprehend this, the better, and the less trouble there will be in the land. (Applause.) We were born to an inheritance of freedom; the Constitution came to us from our fathers; it guaranteed to us rights and liberties older than the instrument itself—God-given, belonging to the people, belonging to men, because God made them free—and we do not mean to surrender one jot or tittle of those rights and liberties. (Loud cheers.)

[Vallandigham attacked Congress for giving the President so much power.]

You have surrendered it—you cannot take it back again. It has gone into the hands of men, of the party of Abolition—men who, base and coward-like, for the sake of appointment when their terms should expire, after the 4th of March, sold out the precious deposit, which you put in their keeping. (A voice—"What can we do?") We will see. We have the ballot-box yet. (Applause.) We can do what we are doing to-night, and we will do it. (Cheers.) We can vote yet, and we mean to vote, and more than that, we mean that the mandate of that ballot-box shall be carried out at all hazards. (Loud applause.) We meet those men fairly under the Constitution and laws of the land, and propose to try this question before the great tribunal of the people. As I have said before, for this is a time for line upon line and precept upon precept, if they beat us we will submit, because we must submit to what is Constitution and law; but if, on the other hand, we conquer them, then, by the Eternal, they must and shall submit. (Loud cheers.) So much for the money—the purse.

And now, as to that other great weapon of government—the sword. What have your "misrepresentatives" done? They gave, and with your consent, ("Never") yes, they did; and I am sorry it is so, my friends. (A voice—"The Republicans.") No, my dear sir, Democrats did it too. I did not. (Cheers.) If I had my way there never would have been a necessity for anything of the kind—the sword never would have been drawn, and we never would have had civil war. . . .

All this, gentlemen, infamous and execrable as it is, is enough to make the blood of the coldest man who has single appreciation in his heart of freedom, to boil with indignation. (Loud applause.) Still, so long as they leave to us free assemblages, free discussion, and a free ballot, I do not want to see, and will not encourage or countenance, any other mode of ridding ourselves of it. ("That's it," and cheers.) We are ready to try these questions in that way; but I have only to repeat what I said a little while ago, that when the attempt is made to take away those other rights, and the only instrumentalities peaceably of reforming and correcting abuses—free assemblages, free speech, free ballot, and free elections—THEN THE HOUR WILL

HAVE ARRIVED WHEN IT WILL BE THE DUTY OF FREEMEN TO FIND SOME OTHER AND EFFICIENT MODE OF DEFENDING THEIR LIBERTIES. (Loud and protracted cheering, the whole audience rising to their feet.) Our fathers did not inaugurate the Revolution of 1776, they did not endure the sufferings and privations of a seven years' war to escape from the mild and moderate control of a constitutional monarchy like that of England, to be at last, in the third generation, subjected to a tyranny equal to that of any upon the face of the globe. (Loud applause.)

But, sir, I repeat that it will not, in my judgment, come to this. I do not believe that this Administration will undertake to deprive us of that right. I do not think it will venture, for one moment, to attempt to prevent, under any pretext whatever, the assembling together of the people for the fair discussion of their measures and policy. I do not believe it, because it seems to me with all the folly and madness which have been manifested in those high places, they must foresee what will inevitably follow. Believing this, and believing that the best way of averting the crisis is to demand inexorably and resolutely, with the firmness and dignity of freemen, these rights, and let them know distinctly that we do not mean to surrender them, I am here to-night to speak it just as I have spoken. (Applause.) There is nothing that will encourage or induce this Administration, for one moment, to attempt any such exercise of despotic power, reaching to assemblages of the people and to elections, except the evidences which they are now seeking for—feeling the public pulse—that the people are terrified and ready to surrender their rights. There never was a tyrant that dared to go one step, if he were a wise tyrant, till he saw his people were ready to submit. It is my duty, therefore, as a freeman in the exercise of these rights, to speak thus to this Administration and to all men of the party in power. I do not speak it in the spirit of a revolutionist; I have already disclaimed that. I desire to see nothing resembling it inaugurated in this country. God knows I have read too much in history, of the horrors of revolutions in ages past and in other countries, to wish one single moment to see these scenes repeated in the land which gave me birth. There is no horror that can enter into the imagination of man, none that has ever been enacted upon this globe since it first came from the hand of God, equal to that of a grand convulsive social revolution among such a people as we are, so descended, of such tempers and such wills, and inheriting all the ferocity of the Anglo-Saxon race. I do not desire to see it, but I will never consent to be made a slave. (Loud cheers.)

I make no threats—no wise man ever did. (Cheers.) I never yield to threats—therefore, I expect no one else to yield; but, in the spirit of warning, as one who would avert the struggle which this people will make to maintain their liberties, I have spoken; and I would that my voice could penetrate that most impenetrable of all recesses, the precincts of the White House, and that the men who are surrounded there by the parasites of power—the flatterers who are the vermin of courts, with that legion of contractors and placemen who speak not the truth, and represent not the people—that, a voice from the people could reach their ears, and that the voice being heard might be heeded. Then shall we escape the convulsions which have visited other countries. . . .

Source 10 from the Reverend James L. Vallandigham, *A Life of Clement L. Vallandigham, by His Brother* (Baltimore: Turnbull Brothers, 1872), pp. 249–253.

10. Vallandigham's Speech at Mount Vernon Ohio, May 1, 1863.[23]

"Although I cannot recollect Mr. Vallandigham's words in his speech to the meeting, I have a distinct impression of the fact that he counseled the people to be firm but temperate in their protests against the unwarrantable proceedings of the men temporarily invested with absolute power, and to trust to the sober second-thought and the might of the people through the ballot-box to vindicate their true principles and outraged representatives.

"Other speakers at the meeting used stronger terms of denunciation than Mr. V., and hence there was much surprise that he was singled out for tyrannic vengeance. From the false allegations of the infamous spies and informers on which he was arrested, the summary trial by a packed military commission, the so-called conviction contrary to the weight of evidence, and the sentence and exile, considered together, the inference was irresistible, in the minds of his friends at least, that his removal from before the people, to prepare the way for the complete intimidation and forcible and fraudulent crushing about of the people's views and votes which followed in the State and Presidential elections of 1863 and 1864, had been deliberately resolved upon as a political necessity."

In the foregoing statement an important fact is developed to which we invite special attention. A prominent reason why the presence of Mr. Vallandigham was especially desired at this meeting was that he might caution certain persons who, becoming restive under the oppressions to which they were subjected, were in danger of breaking out into open resistance. It was supposed that a caution from him who was well known for his firmness and courage

23. No complete transcript of Vallandigham's May 1 speech exists. The former congressman's brother compiled various eyewitness and newspaper accounts. The speech lasted around two hours, right on par for Vallandigham. See also Klement, *The Limits of Dissent,* pp. 153–154.

and determination, would have weight: and the evidence is that such caution was given; that while he exhorted the people to stand firm in defense of their rights, he at the same time counseled them to be patient and forbearing, waiting for the "sober second-thought." And looking to the ballot-box for a redress of their grievances.

(The following account of the meeting we take from the Democratic Banner *of May 9, published in Mount Vernon):*

"Friday, May 1st, 1863, was a proud and glorious day for the faithful and unconquerable Democracy of old Knox, and one that will long be remembered by them with high and patriotic pleasure. Early in the morning the people began to come to town in wagons, carriages, and on horseback. Between ten and eleven o'clock the processions from the several townships arrived, and took the places assigned them by the Marshals. The processions were composed of wagons, carriages, buggies, and filled with people of both sexes and all ages, and of numerous housemen. A remarkably large number of national flags, with all the stars of the Union as it was, on hickory poles, formed a very prominent and pleasing feature in each of these processions. A profusion of butternuts and liberty or copperhead pins, Union badges, and other appropriate emblems of Liberty and Union, were also distinguishable features.

"Between eleven and one o'clock the township processions were united, and the grand procession filed through the principal streets of the city, making a splendid display. It was from four to five miles in length, and was over two hours in passing any one point. About 500 wagons, carriages, etc. came to town in the township processions, a number of which, however, dropped out of line before the grand procession was formed. The Democracy of the city displayed numerous flags on their private residences and places of business, and the processions heartily cheered them as they marched by them. The scene was beautiful and exciting, as well as vast, and caused all the good and true Union men who witnessed it to rejoice in their hearts with the fond hope for the salvation of their country, well knowing that it is by the Democracy that this most desirable object must and can be accomplished. The greatest enthusiasm was manifested throughout the entire line of procession. Cheers upon cheers rent the air in hearty acclaim. The hearts and consciences of those giving them were pure and clear, and the sounds were harmonious, peaceful, and patriotic.

"One of the most noticeable and pleasing incidents of the procession and meeting, was a very large wagon drawn by six ladies representing the thirty-four States of the Union. The wagon was tastefully shaded with evergreens, in which the thirty-four young ladies were embowered.

"The principal stand from which Messrs. Vallandigham, Cox, and Pendleton spoke, was canopied by large and beautiful American flags, and surrounded by various banners and emblems, all betokening the undying principles of the Democratic party.

"The first speaker introduced to the audience was the bold and fearless patriot and statesman, Hon. C. L. Vallandigham, who was received with such a shout of applause as fairly made the welkin ring. He proceeded to deliver one of the ablest and most inspiring true Union addresses ever made, in which he also evinced his unfaltering devotion to Liberty and the Constitution. Manliness, candor, genuine patriotism, and true statesmanship were manifested in the speaker throughout. If any of his lying detractors were present, it must have struck them with overwhelming force, and caused them to wince with a sense of their foul slanders. Mr. V. spoke for about two hours, and was listened to with the greatest attention, accompanied with tremendous shouts of applause."

(A very interesting account of the meeting in a letter from Mount Vernon, dated May 2, was also published in the Columbus Crisis*.) The writer says:*

"In every point of view it was an unparalleled county meeting. Any fair estimate must put its numbers between fifteen and twenty thousand! . . . It being well known that Mr. Vallandigham had come, an immediate and general call was made for him, and he was at once introduced to the vast assembly, which saluted him with three hearty cheers. Mr. Vallandigham addressed the great multitude of people for about two hours, making a most able, eloquent, and truly patriotic speech. It was a noble and glorious effort in behalf of Liberty, Union and the Constitution, and was listened to with wrapt attention, interrupted only by frequent enthusiastic responses and applause. It must have left an ineffaceable impression upon the minds of all who heard it. He showed and established conclusively which the true Union was, and which the disunion party, by tracing the history and proceedings of each from its origin to the present moment. The contrast between the life-long Unionism of the Democratic party, and the original and continuous disunionism of the Abolition party, was so glaring and true, that an Abolitionist with any degree of conscience must have felt confounded and abashed at the recital. . . . Mr. V. spoke in words of burning eloquence of the arbitrary measures and monarchical usurpations of the Administration, the disgraceful surrender of the rights and liberties of the people by the last infamous Congress, and the conversion of the Government into a despotism. No candid man, after hearing Mr. Vallandigham, can for a moment doubt his sincerity and patriotism. These attributes of the man stand out in bold prominence, and are so palpable as not to be drawn in question by any honest man of common sense.

"It being apparent during the delivery of Mr. Vallandigham's speech that it was quite impossible for even his strong and clear voice to reach the edges of the crowd, besides which Main street for several squares below was blocked with people, it was proposed to organize another meeting at the corner of Main and Vine streets, which was gladly accepted. A large meeting was there convened. This second meeting being found insufficient to accommodate the immense number of people, a third large meeting was organized farther down Main street, in front of the Franklin House. In the evening, about eight o'clock, still another large meeting, a considerable proportion of which was composed of Ladies, filled the spacious Court-room."

Source 11 from Lincoln to Erastus Corning and others, June 12, 1863, in Basler, ed., *The Collected Works of Abraham Lincoln*, vol. 6, pp. 260–269.

11. Lincoln's Reply to the Albany Resolutions[24] of May 19, 1863.

[Following Vallandigham's arrest, a public meeting of Democrats was held in Albany, New York that adopted a series of resolutions that were sent to President Lincoln. The resolutions pledged their patriotism and their determination to "secure peace through victory." The meeting, however, denounced the seizure and trial of Vallandigham "for no other reason than words. . . . in criticism of the Administration."]

Ours is a case of rebellion—so called by the resolutions before me—in fact, a clear, flagrant, and gigantic case of Rebellion; and the provision of the constitution that "The privilege of the writ of Habeas Corpus shall not be suspended, unless when in cases of Rebellion or Invasion, the public Safety may require it" is the provision which specially applies to our present case. This provision plainly attests the understanding of those who made the constitution that ordinary courts of justice are inadequate to "cases of Rebellion"—attests their purpose that in such cases, men may be held in custody whom the courts acting on ordinary rules, would discharge. Habeas Corpus, does not discharge men who are proved to be guilty of defined crime; and its suspension is allowed by the constitution on purpose that, men may be arrested and held, who can not be proved to be guilty of defined crime, "when, in cases of Rebellion or Invasion the public Safety may require it." This is precisely our present case—a case of rebellion, wherein the public Safety does require the suspension. Indeed, arrests by process of courts, and arrests in cases of rebellion, do not proceed altogether upon the same basis. The former is directed at the small per centage of ordinary and continuous perpetration of crime; while the latter is directed at sudden and extensive

24. For the Albany Resolutions and Lincoln's reply, see *American Annual Cyclopedia and Register of Important Events of the Year 1863* (New York: D. Appleton & Co., 1864), pp. 799–802.

uprisings against the government, which, at most, will succeed or fail, in no great length of time. In the latter case, arrests are made, not so much for what has been done, as for what probably would be done. The latter is more for the preventive, and less for the vindictive, than the former. In such cases the purposes of men are much more easily understood, than in cases of ordinary crime. The man who stands by and says nothing, when the peril of his government is discussed, can not be misunderstood. If not hindered, he is sure to help the enemy. Much more, if he talks ambiguously—talks for his country with "buts" and "ifs" and "ands." Of how little value the constitutional provision I have quoted will be rendered, if arrests shall never be made until defined crimes shall have been committed, may be illustrated by a few notable examples. Gen. John C. Breckienridge, Gen. Robert E. Lee, Gen. Joseph E. Johnston, Gen. John B. Magruder, Gen. William B. Preston, Gen. Simon B. Buckner, and Comodore [Franklin] Buchanan, now occupying the very highest places in the rebel war service, were all within the power of the government since the rebellion began, and were nearly as well known to be traitors then as now. Unquestionably if we had seized and held them, the insurgent cause would be much weaker. But no one of them had then committed any crime defined in the law. Every one of them if arrested would have been discharged on Habeas Corpus, were the writ allowed to operate. In view of these and similar cases, I think the time not unlikely to come when I shall be blamed for having made too few arrests rather than too many. . . .

Take the particular case mentioned by the meeting. They assert in substance that Mr. Vallandigham was by a military commander, seized and tried "for no other reason than words addressed to a public meeting, in criticism of the course of the administration, and in condemnation of the military orders of that general" Now, if there be no mistake about this—if this assertion is the truth and the whole truth—if there was no other reason for the arrest, then I concede that the arrest was wrong. But the arrest, as I understand, was made for a very different reason. Mr. Vallandigham avows his hostility to the war on the part of the Union; and his arrest was made because he was laboring, with some effect, to prevent the raising of troops, to encourage desertions from the army, and to leave the rebellion without an adequate military force to suppress it. He was not arrested because he was damaging the political prospects of the administration, or the personal interests of the commanding general; but because he was damaging the army, upon the existence, and vigor of which, the life of the nation depends. He was warring upon the military; and this gave the military constitutional jurisdiction to lay hands upon him. If Mr. Vallandigham was not damaging the military power of the country, then his arrest was made on mistake of fact, which I would be glad to correct, on reasonably satisfactory evidence.

I understand the meeting, whose resolutions I am considering, to be in favor of suppressing the rebellion by military force—by armies. Long experience has shown that armies can not be maintained unless desertion shall be punished by the severe penalty of death. The case requires, and the law and the constitution, sanction this punishment. Must I shoot a simple-minded soldier boy who deserts, while I must not touch a hair of a wiley agitator who induces him to desert? This is none the less injurious when effected by getting a father, or brother, or friend, into a public meeting, and there working upon his feelings, till he is persuaded to write the soldier boy, that he is fighting in a bad cause, for a wicked administration of a contemptable government, too weak to arrest and punish him if he shall desert. I think that in such a case, to silence the agitator, and save the boy, is not only constitutional, but withal, a great mercy.

If I be wrong on this question of constitutional power, my error lies in believing that certain proceedings are constitutional when, in cases of rebellion or Invasion, the public Safety requires them, which would not be constitutional when, in absence of rebellion or invasion, the public Safety does not require them—in other words, that the constitution is not in its application in all respects the same, in cases of Rebellion or invasion, involving the public Safety, as it is in times of profound peace and public security. The constitution itself makes the distinction; and I can no more be persuaded that the government can constitutionally take no strong measure in time of rebellion, because it can be shown that the same could not be lawfully taken in time of peace, than I can be persuaded that a particular drug is not good medicine for a sick man, because it can be shown to not be good food for a well one. Nor am I able to appreciate the danger, apprehended by the meeting, that the American people will, by means of military arrests during the rebellion, lose the right of public discussion, the liberty of speech and the press, the law of evidence, trial by jury, and Habeas Corpus, throughout the indefinite peaceful future which I trust lies before them, any more than I am able to believe that a man could contract so strong an appetite for emetics during temporary illness, as to persist in feeding upon them through the remainder of his healthful life.

[Here Lincoln remarked that the authors of the resolutions identified themselves as "Democrats." The President replied that the general who ordered Vallandigham's arrest also was a Democrat, as was the judge who refused to free him. Then Lincoln

wrote of Andrew Jackson, an even more famous Democrat. During the Battle of New Orleans, General Jackson declared martial law and then ordered the arrest of a Louisiana legislator who criticized him in a newspaper article. When U.S. District Judge Dominick Hall issued a writ of habeas corpus *and demanded the man's release, Jackson refused, on the grounds that the United States was being invaded and thus* habeas corpus *was suspended.]*

It may be remarked: First, that we had the same constitution then, as now. Secondly, that we then had a case of Invasion, and that now we have a case of Rebellion, and: Thirdly, that the permanent right of the people to public discussion, the liberty of speech and the press, the trial by jury, the law of evidence, and the Habeas Corpus, suffered no detriment whatever by that conduct of Gen. Jackson, or it's subsequent approval by the American congress.

And yet, let me say that in my own discretion, I do not know whether I would have ordered the arrest of Mr. V. While I can not shift the responsibility from myself, I hold that, as a general rule, the commander in the field is the better judge of the necessity in any particular case. Of course I must practice a general directory and revisory power in the matter.

One of the resolutions expresses the opinion of the meeting that arbitrary arrests will have the effect to divide and distract those who should be united in suppressing the rebellion; and I am specifically called on to discharge Mr. Vallandigham. I regard this as at least, a fair appeal to me, on the expediency of exercising a constitutional power which I think exists. In response to such appeal I have to say it gave me pain when I learned that Mr. V. had been arrested—that is, I was pained that there should have seemed to be necessity for arresting him—and that it will afford me great pleasure to discharge him so soon as I can, by any means, believe the public safety will not suffer by it. I further say, that as the war progresses, it appears to me, opinion, and action, which were in great confusion at first, take shape, and fall into more regular channels; so that the necessity for arbitrary dealing with them gradually decreases. I have every reason to desire that it would cease altogether; and far from the least is my regard for the opinions and wishes of those who, like the meeting at Albany, declare their purpose to sustain the government in every constitutional and lawful measure to suppress the rebellion. Still, I must continue to do so much as may seem to be required by the public safety.

A. LINCOLN.

Source 12 from Lincoln to Matthew Birchard and others, June 29, 1863, in Basler, ed., *The Collected Works of Abraham Lincoln*, vol. 6, pp. 300–306.

12. Lincoln's Reply to the Resolutions Passed by the Ohio State Democratic Convention,[25] June 11, 1863.

[The Ohio Democratic Convention pledged "to co-operate zealously in every constitutional effort to restore the Union." Three of the resolutions, however, protested the "unconstitutional arrest, imprisonment, pretended trial, and actual banishment of" Vallandigham, who by then was a serious candidate for the Democratic nomination for the office of governor—a nomination he ultimately received.]

The earnestness with which you insist that persons can only, in times of rebellion, be lawfully dealt with, in accordance with the rules for criminal trials and punishments in times of peace, induces me to add a word to what I said on that point, in the Albany response. You claim that men may, if they choose, embarrass those who duty it is, to combat a giant rebellion, and then be dealt with in turn, only as if there was no rebellion. The constitution itself rejects this view. The military arrests and detentions, which have been made, including those of Mr. V. which are not different in principle from the others, have been for *prevention,* and not for *punishment*—as injunctions to stay injury, as proceedings to keep the peace—and hence, like proceedings in such cases, and for like reasons, they have not been accompanied with indictments, or trials by juries, nor, in a single case by any punishment whatever, beyond what is purely incidental to the prevention. The original sentence of imprisonment in Mr. V.'s case, was to prevent injury to the Military service only, and the modification of it was made as a less disagreeable mode to him, of securing the same prevention.

I am unable to perceive an insult to Ohio in the case of Mr. V. Quite surely nothing of the sort was or is intended. I was wholly unaware that Mr. V. was at the time of his arrest a candidate for the democratic nomination for Governor until so informed by your reading to me the resolutions of the convention. I am grateful to the State of Ohio for many things, especially for the brave soldiers and officers she has given in the present national trial, to the armies of the Union.

You claim, as I understand, that according to my own position in the Albany response, Mr. V. should be released; and this because, as you claim, he has not damaged the military service, by discouraging enlistments, encouraging desertions, or otherwise; and that if he had, he should have been turned over to the civil authorities under recent acts of congress. I certainly do not *know* that

25. For the resolutions, see *ibid.* pp. 803–806.

Mr. V. has specifically, and by direct language, advised against enlistments, and in favor of desertion, and resistance to drafting. We all know that combinations, armed in some instances, to resist the arrest of deserters, began several months ago; that more recently the like has appeared in resistance to the enrolment [sic] preparatory to a draft; and that quite a number of assassinations have occurred from the same animus. These had to be met by military force, and this again has led to bloodshed and death. And now under a sense of responsibility more weighty and enduring than any which is merely official, I solemnly declare my belief that this hindrance, of the military, including maiming and murder, is due to the course in which Mr. V. has been engaged, in a greater degree than to any other cause; and is due to him personally, in a greater degree than to any other one man. These things have been notorious, known to all, and of course known to Mr. V. Perhaps I would not be wrong to say they originated with his special friends and adherents. With perfect knowledge of them, he has frequently, if not constantly made speeches, in congress, and before popular assemblies; and if it can be shown that, with these things staring him, in the face, he has ever uttered a word of rebuke, or counsel against them, it will be a fact greatly in his favor with me, and one of which, as yet I, am totally ignorant. When it is known that the whole burthen of his speeches has been to stir up men against the prossecution [sic] of the war, and that in the midst of resistance to it, he has not been known, in any instance, to counsel against such resistance, it is next to impossible to repel the inference that he has counseled directly in favor of it. With all this before their eyes the convention you represent have nominated Mr. V. Governor of Ohio; and both they and you, have declared the purpose to sustain the national Union by all constitutional means. But, of course, they and you, in common, reserve to yourselves to decide what are constitutional means; and, unlike the Albany meeting, you omit to state, or intimate, that in your opinion, an army is a constitutional means of saving the Union against a rebellion; or even to intimate that you are conscious of an existing rebellion being in progress with the avowed object of destroying that very Union. At the same time your nominee for Governor, in whose behalf you appeal, is known to you, and to the world, to declare against the use of an army to suppress the rebellion. Your own attitude, therefore, encourages desertion, resistance to the draft and the like, because it teaches those who incline to desert, and to escape the draft, to believe it is your purpose to protect them, and to hope that you will become strong enough to do so. After a short personal intercourse with you gentlemen of the committee, I can not say I think you desire this effect to follow your attitude; but I assure you that both friends and enemies of the Union look upon it in this light. It is a substantial hope, and by consequence, a real strength to the enemy. If it is a false hope, and one which you would willingly dispel, I will make the way exceedingly easy. I send you duplicates of this letter, in order that you, or a majority of you, may if you choose, indorse your names upon one of them, and return it thus indorsed to me, with the understanding that those signing, are thereby committed to the following propositions, and to nothing else. . . .

Still, in regard to Mr. V. and all others, I must hereafter as heretofore, do so much as the public safety may seem to require. I have the honor to be respectfully yours, &c.,

A. LINCOLN.

◆

Questions to Consider

Review the Method section of this chapter, which will suggest a good plan for using the evidence to answer the chapter's central questions.

To begin with, Sources 1 through 3 are excerpts from speeches delivered before the war actually began. Were the arguments Vallandigham made prior to the war similar to or different from the ones he made after the outbreak of hostilities? In Source 1, Vallandigham stated what he considered to be the source of the social conflict that as early as December 1859 appeared to be leading to war. In his view, what was the principal cause of that sectional conflict?

By December 22, 1860, South Carolina had unanimously approved an ordinance of secession, and the five other states of the Deep South (Mississippi, Florida, Alabama, Georgia, and Louisiana) were considering doing the same. In Vallandigham's remarks on December 22, what did he claim was the *wrong way* to restore the Union? What did he suggest? How were these remarks a harbinger (forerunner) of his later speeches? What do you think of his recommendations (in Source 3) for

restoring the Union? Were they helpful? Naïve?

After the war began, Vallandigham's speeches became more like attacks on the federal government in general and on President Lincoln in particular. How would you characterize these assaults? Should they have been protected by the First Amendment, even in wartime? Vallandigham was referred to as "the most unpopular man in America." Why? See Source 4. To what extent were his speeches primarily *political*? See Sources 5 and 6.

By early 1863, not a few people were denouncing Vallandigham as a traitor. In his speech of January 14, 1863 (titled "The Great Civil War in America"), the congressman summarized his opinions on the immediate and long-range causes of the war and his own position. See Source 7. This speech was followed, on February 23, 1863, by an attack on the Conscription Bill (the draft). How did Vallandigham use the Conscription Bill as evidence to prove his own points? What was his opinion of the war itself?

Vallandigham's speech to the Democratic Union Association of New York

City (Source 9) was his sharpest attack on the Lincoln administration and the Republican Party. Not delivered in Congress but instead at a political meeting, can you detect any differences in tone from his speeches in Sources 1, 3, 4, 6, 7, and 8? In your opinion, were there times when Vallandigham crossed the line and exceeded proper civil rights during wartime?

Source 10 is the speech that Vallandigham delivered that purposely dared General Ambrose Burnside to arrest him for violating General Order 38. As you have seen, no transcript of that speech has ever been found. Reread the excerpt from General Order 38 (in the Problem section of this chapter). In your view, had he violated Burnside's order. Was that order constitutional?

Sources 11 and 12 are replies by President Lincoln to resolutions claiming that Vallandigham's arrest had been illegal and urging that the former congressman be freed. What points did the President make in reply to these resolutions? What proof of his arguments did he offer? In your view, which man had the stronger argument, Vallandigham or Lincoln? Now answer the chapter's central questions.

◆

Epilogue

Clement L. Vallandigham's trial in a military court began the day after his arrest, on May 6, 1863. The prosecution charged him with

> Publicly expressing, in violation of General Orders No. 38 . . . sympathy for those in arms against the Government of the United States, and declaring disloyal sentiments and opinions, with the object and purpose of weakening the power of the Government in its efforts to suppress an unlawful rebellion.[26]

In spite of the fact that Vallandigham's only defense witness, Democratic congressman Samuel Cox (1824–1889), testified that he had been in Mount Vernon on May 1, had heard Vallandigham's entire speech, and that the prisoner had not committed the offenses for which he had been charged, the military commission on May 7 found Vallandigham guilty and sentenced him to imprisonment for the remainder of the war.[27]

Back in Washington, President Lincoln was surprised and embarrassed by the whole affair. On one hand, he certainly did not want to make a martyr of Vallandigham. On the other, he didn't want to reverse Burnside's General Orders or his arrest and trial of the former congressman. According to Lincoln's Secretary of the Navy Gideon

---

26. For the charge, see *Vallandigham Speeches*, p. 567. For Vallandigham's protest before the military commission, see *ibid.*, pp. 505–506.

27. Burnside chose Fort Warren in Boston harbor, at the time being used as a Confederate prisoner of war camp. Ironically, Fort Warren had been named for Dr. Joseph Warren (1741–1775), a Revolutionary War hero who was killed at the Battle of Bunker Hill.

Welles (1802–1878), at a Cabinet meeting on May 19, the case of Vallandigham, recently

> arrested by General Burnside, tried by court martial, convicted of something and sentenced to Fort Warren, was before the Cabinet. It was an error on the part of Burnside. All regretted the arrest, but, having been made, every one wished he had been sent over the lines to the Rebels with Whom he sympathized. Until the subject is legitimately before us, and there is a necessity to act, there is no disposition to meddle with the case.[28]

Thus, Lincoln ordered Burnside not to send Vallandigham to Fort Warren but instead to banish him to the Confederacy. Burnside protested the order to Secretary of War Edwin Stanton (1814–1869), to which the president replied, "When I shall wish to supersede you I will let you know. All the cabinet regretted the necessity of arresting . . . Vallandigham, some perhaps, doubting, that there was a real necessity for it—but, being done, all were for seeing you through with it." So Vallandigham was spirited off under heavy guard and left behind the Confederate lines in Tennessee.[29]

The Confederates, however, didn't want him any more than Lincoln did. In a dispatch to Confederate General Braxton Bragg, President Jefferson Davis referred to Vallandigham as "an alien enemy" and ordered that he be taken under guard to Wilmington, North Carolina. From there, ordered Davis, he would be placed on a blockade runner bound for a neutral port (Bermuda, as it turned out) and ultimately to be exiled in Canada. In all, Vallandigham spent 24 days in the Confederacy.[30]

In a rather odd way, Vallandigham's plan worked. His arrest, trial, and banishment had made him a hero and a martyr among many Ohio Democrats, who in a political stampede unanimously nominated him for governor. In an address written on July 15, 1863, that was pure Vallandigham, the nominee expressed his gratitude "for the confidence in my integrity and patriotism" and sounded his campaign's theme of "upon the one side, liberty; on the other, despotism." Determined to campaign from his exile in Canada, Vallandigham decided to make the election a referendum on Lincoln and the war. For their part, the Republicans nominated Cincinnati editor and railroad executive John Brough. Brough received considerable support from outside of Ohio.[31]

---

28. *Diary of Gideon Welles* (Boston: Houghton Mifflin, 1911), vol. 1, pp. 306, 344–345.
29. For Burnside's protest, see *Official Records*, Series 2, vol. 5, pp. 665–666. For Lincoln's May 29 telegram to Burnside, see Basler, *The Collected Works of Abraham L Lincoln*, vol. 6, p. 237.

30. Davis to Bragg, June 2, 1863, in *Official Records*, Series 2, vol. 5, p. 965; Davis to Bragg, June 8, 1863, in *ibid.*, p. 969.
31. See Vallandigham, "Address to the People of Ohio, Upon Arriving in Canada, July 15, 1863": in *Speeches*, pp. 507–510. Lincoln would have preferred it if the Republicans had nominated incumbent Governor David Tod. See Lincoln to Tod, June 18, 1863, in Basler, *Collected Works of Abraham Lincoln*, vol. 6, p. 287. Brough assured Lincoln that he would carry Ohio by "at least 25,000 votes, independent of the soldiers." See John Hay to Lincoln, October 4, 1863, in Michael Burlingame, ed., *At Lincoln's Side: John Hay's Civil War Correspondence and Selected Writings* (Carbondale: Southern Illinois University Press, 2000), p. 65.

The Democrats' campaign was no match for Union victories. In July 1863, Confederate General Robert E. Lee's assault on Union Forces at Gettysburg failed miserably, costing him nearly 25,000 casualties and prevented him from ever leading a major offensive. At the same time, Union General Ulysses Grant's army took Vicksburg and Admiral David Farragut cut the Confederacy in half by seizing control of the Mississippi river. Meanwhile, the Union blockade of rebel ports was beginning to cripple the southern economy and its ability to continue the war.

In the Ohio gubernatorial race, Brough won around 288,000 votes to Vallandigham's 187,000. The Republican carried the civilian vote and approximately 95 percent of the soldiers' ballots. "Glory to God in the highest," Lincoln cabeled to incumbent governor David Tod, "Ohio has saved the Union." The jubilant editor of the *Cleveland Leader* wrote, "The allies of Jeff Davis are overthrown, dispersed, and driven." As for the loser, Vallandigham accepted his defeat gracefully, claiming that "[o]ur defeat will soon be forgotten." Other Democrats, however, blamed the controversial Vallandigham for the routing of the entire party slate.[32]

Confederate leaders realized that their time was running out. In a desperate attempt to force the Union to sue for peace, they fashioned a scheme whereby antiwar men in the Northwest would break into the area's Confederate prisoner of war camps to free and arm the rebel soldiers, then create enough havoc to perhaps drive the northwestern states out of the Union (or at least out of the war) and frighten the federal government to the peace table. In June 1864, a Confederate agent met with Vallandigham in Canada, informing him that he had been chosen as the Supreme Commander of the Sons of Liberty. The plan called for Vallandigham to return to the United States, where his subsequent arrest would be the signal for the rebellion to begin. The exile slipped into the United States in disguise and made a speech on June 15, 1864, in Hamilton, Ohio.[33]

The secret plot, if it ever was an organized conspiracy at all, was hardly a secret. On June 16, Governor Brough telegraphed Stanton, "Vallandigham is in Ohio," and asked the secretary of war whether the former exile should be arrested. But Lincoln was in Philadelphia, where he was scheduled to deliver three speeches and could not be reached. In his stead, Secretary of State Seward ordered that Vallandigham not be arrested until the President could return to make that decision. By that time, the secret—if it ever was a secret—had leaked out. In his diary entry for June 17, 1864, Lincoln's secretary John Hay summarized the entire plot. On June 20, Lincoln

32. Lincoln to Tod, October 14, 1863, quoted in Clement, *The Limits of Dissent*, p. 252. For the *Cleveland Leader* see *ibid*, p. 253. For Vallandigham's reaction, see *ibid.*, p. 255. For the soldiers' reaction to the Democrats, see Sgt. Benjamin Wiley to Sister, February 22, 1863, quoted in Weber, *Copperheads*, pp. 83–84.

33. For the supposed Confederate plot, see Gray, *The Hidden Civil War*, pp. 166–169; and Weber, *Copperheads*, pp. 147–150. For Vallandigham's speech see *Vallandigham Speeches*, pp. 527–531. Later Vallandigham denied any involvement in the Confederate scheme, although some former Confederates claimed that he was fully aware of the plot.

ordered Brough and General Samuel Heintzelman not to arrest Vallandigham but to "watch Vallandigham and others closely." The plot, such as it was, collapsed.[34]

The "Copperheads," as antiwar northerners were called, were often vilified by their neighbors, called traitors by their political foes, and forgotten by later students of Civil War history. Yet, as the most recent scholarship on the Copperheads has shown, "antiwar sentiment was not the peripheral issue that many Civil War histories have made it out to be." While rumors of Copperhead treason abounded, largely spread for political purposes, the vast majority of Copperheads were not traitors, nor did they desire a Confederate victory. Rather, they called (perhaps naïvely) for peace, feared the growth of the power of the federal government in Washington, and yearned for a republic that was rapidly slipping sway. Clement

Vallandigham was the most prominent Copperhead in the nation. In pursuit of his, and other Copperheads', goals, did he step over the line in terms of civil rights in wartime?[35]

Persona non grata in politics, Vallandigham ran unsuccessfully for a seat in the United States Senate, a place in the House of Representatives, and for membership in the Ohio state senate. He then resumed his law practice. His appeals to reverse his convictions by the military tribunal were unsuccessful.

On June 16, 1871, in a Lebanon, Ohio, hotel, he accidentally fatally shot himself with a pistol he believed was not loaded in an attempt to demonstrate to other lawyers how he would prove his client innocent of the charge of murder—because the victim had accidentally shot himself.[36]

The following day the client was acquitted, and Clement L. Vallandigham died.

34. Brough to Stanton, Stanton to Brough, Stanton to Brough, Stanton to Brough, all June 16, 1864 in *Official Records*, Series 2, vol. 7, pp. 371–372; Lincoln to Brough and Heintzelman, June 20, 1864 in Basler, ed., *Collected Works of Abraham Lincoln*, vol. 7, p. 402. For Hay's knowledge see Michael Burlingame and John R. Turner Ettlinger, eds., *Inside Lincoln's White House: The Complete Civil War Diary of John Hay* (Carbondale: Southern Illinois University Press, 1997), pp. 204–205, 207–209.

35. Weber, *Copperheads*, pp. 2, 6.

36. Klement, *The Limits of Dissent*, p. 310.

11

Reconstructing Reconstruction: The Political Cartoonist and Public Opinion

◆

The Problem

The cable that arrived at the U.S. State Department from Guayaquil, Ecuador, on the afternoon of December 7, 1902, was brief: "Nast died today, yellow fever."[1]

Impoverished and nearly forgotten, political cartoonist Thomas Nast had accepted a position as a consular official in out-of-the-way Ecuador as a political favor from President Theodore Roosevelt. The fairly undemanding job paid $4,000, a very nice salary in 1902 but nowhere near his total income in 1879 of $25,000 as America's most well-known and influential political cartoonist, for *Harper's Weekly* in New York City.[2] In that year, Thomas Nast had been at the peak of his career, had been influential in the overthrow of the nation's most powerful political boss (William Marcy Tweed), and had played a major role in every

presidential election since 1864. But by the 1880s, the public had grown tired of his anger, his outrage, and his crusading zeal. And so the cartoonist who had given Americans the first modern depiction of Santa Claus (January 3, 1863), the Democratic donkey (January 15, 1870), the Republican elephant (November 7, 1874),[3] and countless cartoons for *Harper's Weekly* from 1862 to 1886, faded gradually but not quietly from the scene, and in 1902 swallowed his considerable pride and accepted a political favor. Four months later he was dead.

The end of the War of the Rebellion[4] in 1865 left the United States with a

3. All the dates refer to issues of *Harper's Weekly*.
4. Many northerners used the term War of the Rebellion during and immediately after the war. The official records of the conflict, published by the U.S. Government Printing Office from 1880 to 1901 were titled *The Official Records of the War of the Rebellion*. President Lincoln and others, however, preferred the term "Civil War," that was ultimately adopted. During the war, many southerners referred to the War for Southern Independence, and later to the War Between the States.

1. Albert Bigelow Paine, *Th. Nast: His Period and His Pictures* (New York: Macmillan Co., 1904), p. 574.
2. Nast's salary as a customs officer would be comparable to $103,000 in 2009 dollars. His 1879 total income would be $555,000 in 2009 dollars. See http://eh.net.

◆ CHAPTER 11
Reconstructing
Reconstruction:
The Political
Cartoonist and
Public Opinion

host of difficult questions. What should happen to the defeated South? Should the states of the former Confederacy be permitted to take their pre-war places in the Union as quickly and smoothly as possible, with minimum concessions to their northern conquerors? Or should the United States insist on a more drastic reconstruction of the South? Tied to these questions was the thorny constitutional issue of whether the southern states actually had left the Union at all in 1861. But perhaps the most difficult questions the Union's victory raised concerned the status of the former slaves. To be sure, they were no longer in bondage, but should they possess the same rights as whites? Should they be allowed to vote?[5] Should they be assisted in becoming landowners? If not, how would they earn a living? Indeed, while the war settled a number of questions, its conclusion left all Americans with other dilemmas.

In all these questions, public opinion in the victorious North was a critical factor in shaping or altering the federal government's policies designed to reconstruct the South. Earlier democratic reforms (such as universal white male suffrage, rotation in office, the evolution of political campaigns, and so forth) made it unlikely that either the president or Congress could defy public opinion successfully. Yet public opinion can shift with remarkable speed, and political figures forever must be sensitive to its sometimes fickle winds.

Although public opinion is a crucial factor in a democratic republic such as the United States, that same public opinion often can be shaped or manipulated by political figures, interest groups, or the press. In this chapter, you will be examining and analyzing how Thomas Nast, through his cartoons, attempted to influence and shape public opinion in the North. Although Nast certainly was not the only person who sought to do so, many of his contemporaries, friends and foes alike, admitted that his political cartoons ranked among the most powerful opinion shapers during the era of Reconstruction.

What were Nast's views on the controversial issues of the Reconstruction era? How did his cartoons attempt to influence public opinion?

◆

Background

By early 1865, it seemed evident to most northerners and southerners that the Civil War was nearly over. While Grant was hammering at Lee's

5. Until the ratification of the Fifteenth Amendment in 1870, some northern states, most prominently New York, did not grant African Americans the right to vote.

depleted forces in Virginia, Union general William Tecumseh Sherman broke the back of the Confederacy with his devastating march through Georgia and then northward into the Carolinas. Atlanta fell to Sherman's troops in September 1864, Savannah in December, and Charleston and Columbia, South Carolina, in February 1865. Two-thirds of Columbia lay in ashes. Meanwhile, General Philip Sheridan had driven the Confederates out of the Shenandoah Valley of Virginia, thus blocking any escape attempts by Lee and further cutting southern supply routes.

In the South, all but the extreme diehards recognized that defeat was inevitable. One Georgian probably spoke for a majority of southerners when he wrote, "The people are soul-sick and heartily tired of the hateful, hopeless strife. . . . We have had enough of want and woe, of cruelty and carnage, enough of crippling and corpses."[6] As the Confederate government made secret plans to evacuate Richmond, most southerners knew that the end was very near.

The triumph of Union arms had established that the United States was "one nation indivisible," from which no state could secede.[7] And yet, even with victory almost in hand, many northerners had given little thought to what should happen after the war. Would southerners accept the changes that defeat would force on them (especially the end of slavery)? What demands should the victors make on the vanquished? Should the North assist the South in rebuilding after the devastation of war? If so, should the North dictate how that rebuilding, or reconstruction, would take place? What efforts should the North make to ensure that the former slaves were able to exercise the rights of free men and women? During the war, few northerners had seriously considered these questions. Now that victory lay within their grasp, they could not avoid them.

One person who had been wrestling with these questions was Abraham Lincoln. In December 1863, the president announced his own plan for reconstructing the South, a plan that reflected the hope later expressed in his second inaugural address, for "malice toward none; with charity for all; . . . Let us . . . bind up the nation's wounds."[8] In Lincoln's plan, a southern state could resume its normal activities in the Union as soon as 10 percent of the voters of 1860 had taken an oath of loyalty to the United States. High-ranking Confederate leaders would be excluded, and some blacks might gain the right to vote. No mention was made of protecting the civil rights of former slaves; it was presumed that this matter would be left to the slaves' former masters and mistresses.

To many northerners, later known as Radical Republicans, Lincoln's plan seemed much too lenient. In the opinion of these people, a number of whom had been abolitionists, the South, when

6. The letter probably was written by Georgian Herschel V. Walker. See Allan Nevins, *The Organized War to Victory, 1864–1865*, Vol. IV of *The War for the Union* (New York: Charles Scribner's Sons, 1971), p. 221.

7. In response to President Benjamin Harrison's 1892 appeal for schoolchildren to mark Columbus's discovery with patriotic exercises, Bostonian Francis Bellamy (brother of the novelist Edward Bellamy) composed the pledge of allegiance to the American flag, from which the phrase "one nation indivisible" comes. In 1942, Congress made it the official pledge to the flag, and in 1954 added the words "under God" in the middle of Bellamy's phrase.

8. The full text of Lincoln's second inaugural address, delivered on March 4, 1865, can be found in Roy P. Basler, ed., *The Collected Works of Abraham Lincoln*, Vol. VIII (New Brunswick, N. J.: Rutgers University Press, 1953), pp. 332–333.

◆ CHAPTER 11

Reconstructing
Reconstruction:
The Political
Cartoonist and
Public Opinion

conquered, should not be allowed to return to its former ways. Not only should slavery be eradicated, they claimed, but freed blacks should be assisted in their efforts to attain economic, social, and political equity. Most of the Radical Republicans favored education for African Americans, and some advocated carving the South's plantations into small parcels to be given to the freedmen. To implement these reforms, Radical Republicans wanted detachments of the United States Army to remain in the South and favored the appointment of provisional governors to oversee the transitional governments in the southern states. Lincoln approved plans for the Army to stay and supported the idea of provisional governors. But he opposed the more far-reaching reform notions of the Radical Republicans, and as president he was able to block them.

In addition to having diametrically opposed views of Reconstruction, Lincoln and the Radical Republicans differed over the constitutional question of which branch of the federal government would be responsible for the reconstruction of the South. The Constitution made no mention of secession, reunion, or reconstruction. But Radical Republicans, citing passages in the Constitution giving Congress the power to guarantee each state a republican government, insisted that the reconstruction of the South should be carried out by Congress.[9] For his part,

however, Lincoln maintained that as chief enforcer of the law and as commander in chief, the president was the appropriate person to be in charge of Reconstruction. Clearly, a stalemate was in the making, with Radical Republicans calling for a more reform-minded Reconstruction policy and Lincoln continuing to block them.

President Lincoln's death on April 15, 1865 (one week after Lee's surrender at Appomattox Court House),[10] brought Vice President Andrew Johnson to the nation's highest office. At first, Radical Republicans had reason to hope that the new president would follow policies more to their liking. A Tennessean, Johnson had risen to political prominence from humble circumstances, had become a spokesperson for the common white men and women of the South, and had opposed the planter aristocracy. Upon becoming president, he excluded from amnesty all former Confederate political and military leaders as well as all southerners who owned taxable property worth more than $20,000 (an obvious slap at his old planter-aristocrat foes). Moreover, Johnson issued a proclamation setting up provisional military governments in the conquered South and told his cabinet he favored black suffrage, although as a states' rightist he insisted that states adopt the measure voluntarily. At the outset, then, Johnson appeared to be all the Radical Republicans wanted, preferable to the more moderate Lincoln.

9. See Article IV, Section 4, of the Constitution. Later Radical Republicans also justified their position using the Thirteenth Amendment, adopted in 1865, which gave Congress the power to enforce the amendment ending slavery in the South.

10. The last Confederate army to give up, commanded by General Joseph Johnston, surrendered to Sherman at Durham Station, North Carolina, on April 18, 1865.

Yet it did not take Radical Republicans long to realize that President Johnson was not one of them. Although he spoke harshly, he pardoned hundreds of former rebels, who quickly captured control of southern state governments and congressional delegations. Many northerners were shocked to see former Confederate generals and officials, and even former vice president Alexander Stephens, returned to Washington. The new southern state legislatures passed a series of laws, known collectively as black codes, that so severely restricted the rights of freedmen that they were all but slaves again. Moreover, Johnson privately told southerners that he opposed the Fourteenth Amendment to the Constitution, which was intended to confer full civil rights on the newly freed slaves. He also used his veto power to block Radical Republican Reconstruction measures in Congress and seemed to do little to combat the general defiance of the former Confederacy (exhibited in many forms, including insults thrown at U.S. occupation soldiers, the desecration of the United States flag, and the formation of organized resistance groups such as the Ku Klux Klan).

To an increasing number of northerners, the unrepentant spirit of the South and Johnson's acquiescence to it were appalling. Had the Civil War been fought for nothing? Had more than 364,000 federal soldiers died in vain? White southerners were openly defiant, African Americans were being subjugated by white southerners and virtually ignored by President Johnson, and former Confederates were returning to positions of power and prominence. Radical Republicans had

sufficient power in Congress to pass harsher measures, but Johnson kept vetoing them, and the Radicals lacked the votes to override his vetoes.[11] Indeed, the impasse that had existed before Lincoln's death continued.

In such an atmosphere, the congressional elections of 1866 were bitterly fought campaigns, especially in the northern states. President Johnson traveled throughout the North, defending his moderate plan of Reconstruction and viciously attacking his political enemies. However, the Radical Republicans were even more effective. Stirring up the hostilities of wartime, they "waved the bloody shirt" and excited northern voters by charging that the South had never accepted its defeat and that the 364,000 Union dead and 275,000 wounded would be for nothing if the South was permitted to continue its arrogant and stubborn behavior. Increasingly, Johnson was greeted by hostile audiences as the North underwent a major shift in public opinion.

The Radical Republicans won a stunning victory in the congressional elections of 1866 and thus broke the stalemate between Congress and the president. Armed with enough votes to override Johnson's vetoes almost at will, the new Congress proceeded rapidly to implement the Radical Republican vision of Reconstruction. The South was divided into five military districts to be ruled by martial law. Southern states had to ratify the Fourteenth Amendment and institute black suffrage before being allowed to take

11. Congress was able to override Johnson's vetoes of the Civil Rights Act and a revised Freedmen's Bureau bill.

✦ CHAPTER 11

Reconstructing
Reconstruction:
The Political
Cartoonist and
Public Opinion

their formal places in the Union. The Freedmen's Bureau, founded earlier, was given additional federal support to set up schools for African Americans, negotiate labor contracts, and, with the military, help monitor elections. Only the proposal to give land to blacks was rejected, being seen as too extreme even by some Radical Republicans. Congressional Reconstruction had begun.

President Johnson, however, had not been left completely powerless. Determined to undercut the Radical Republicans' Reconstruction policies, he issued orders increasing the powers of civil governments in the South and removed military officers who were enforcing Congress's will, replacing them with commanders less determined to protect black voting rights and more willing to turn the other way when disqualified white southerners voted. Opposed most vigorously by his own secretary of war, Edwin Stanton, Johnson tried to discharge Stanton. To an increasing number of Radicals, it became clear that the president would have to be removed from office.

In 1868, the House of Representatives voted to impeach Andrew Johnson. Charged with violating the Tenure of Office Act and the Command of the Army Act (both of which had been passed over Johnson's vetoes), the president was tried in the Senate, where two-thirds of the senators would have to vote against Johnson for him to be removed.[12] The vast majority of senators disagreed with the president's Reconstruction policies, but they feared that impeachment had become a political tool that, if successful,

threatened to destroy the balance of power between the branches of the federal government. The vote on removal fell one short of the necessary two-thirds, and Johnson was spared the indignity of removal. Nevertheless, the Republican nomination of General Ulysses Grant and his subsequent landslide victory (running as a military hero, Grant carried twenty-six out of thirty-four states) gave Radical Republicans a malleable president, one who, although not a Radical himself, could ensure the continuation of their version of Reconstruction.[13]

The Democratic party, however, was not dead, even though the Republican party dominated national politics in the immediate aftermath of the Civil War. In addition to white farmers and planters in the South and border states, the Democratic party attracted many northerners who favored conservative ("sound money") policies, voters who opposed Radical Reconstruction, and first- and second-generation Irish immigrants who had settled in urban areas and had established powerful political machines such as Tammany Hall in New York City.

By 1872, a renewed Democratic party believed it had a chance to oust Grant and the Republicans. The Grant administration had been rocked by a series of scandals, some involving men quite close to the president. Although honest himself, Grant had lost a good deal of popularity by defending the

12. See Article I, Sections 2 and 3, of the Constitution.

13. In 1868, southern states, where the Democratic party had been strong, either were not in the Union or were under the control of Radical Reconstruction governments. Grant's victory, therefore, was not as sweeping as it may first appear.

culprits and naively aiding in a cover-up of the corruption. These actions, along with some of his other policies, triggered a revolt within the Republican party, in which a group calling themselves Liberal Republicans bolted the party ranks and nominated well-known editor and reformer Horace Greeley to oppose Grant for the presidency. Hoping for a coalition to defeat Grant, the Democrats also nominated the controversial Greeley.

Greeley's platform was designed to attract as many different groups of voters as possible to the Liberal Republican-Democratic fold. He favored civil service reform, the return to a "hard money" fiscal policy, and the reservation of western lands for settlers rather than for large land companies. He vowed an end to corruption in government. But the most dramatic part of Greeley's message was his call for an end to the bitterness of the Civil War, a thinly veiled promise to bring an end to Radical Reconstruction in the South. "Let us," he said, "clasp hands over the bloody chasm."

For their part, Radical Republicans attacked Greeley as the tool of diehard southerners and labeled him as the candidate of white southern bigots and northern Irish immigrants manipulated by political machines. By contrast, Grant was labeled as a great war hero and a friend of blacks and whites alike. The incumbent Grant won easily, capturing 55 percent of the popular vote. Greeley died soon after the exhausting campaign.

Gradually, however, the zeal of Radical Republicanism began to fade. An increasing number of northerners grew tired of the issue. Their commitment to full civil rights for African Americans had never been strong, and they had voted for Radical Republicans more out of anger at southern intransigence than out of any lofty notions of black equality. Thus northerners did not protest when, one by one, southern Democrats returned to power in the states of the former Confederacy.[14] As an indication of how little their own attitudes had changed, white southerners labeled these native Democrats "Redeemers," who were swept back into power by anti-northern rhetoric and violence.

Although much that was fruitful and beneficial was accomplished in the South during the Reconstruction period (most notably black suffrage and public education), some of this was to be temporary, and many opportunities for progress were lost. By the presidential election of 1876, both candidates (Rutherford B. Hayes and Samuel Tilden) promised an end to Reconstruction, and the Radical Republican experiment, for all intents and purposes, was over.

It is clear that northern public opinion from 1865 to 1876 was far from static but was almost constantly shifting. This public opinion was influenced by a number of factors, among them speeches, newspapers, and word of mouth. Especially influential were editorial cartoons, which captured the issues visually, often simplifying them so that virtually everyone could understand them. Perhaps the

14. Southerners regained control of the state governments in Tennessee and Virginia in 1869, North Carolina in 1870, Georgia in 1871, Arkansas and Alabama in 1874, and Mississippi in early 1876. By the presidential election of 1876, only South Carolina, Louisiana, and Florida were still controlled by Reconstruction governments.

✦ CHAPTER 11

Reconstructing
Reconstruction:
The Political
Cartoonist and
Public Opinion

master of this style was Thomas Nast, a political cartoonist whose career, principally with *Harper's Weekly,* spanned the tumultuous years of the Civil War and Reconstruction. Throughout his career, Nast produced more than three thousand cartoons, illustrations for books, and paintings. Congratulating themselves for having hired Nast, the editors of *Harper's Weekly* once exclaimed that each of Nast's drawings was at once "a poem and a speech."

Apparently, Thomas Nast developed his talents early in life. Born in the German Palatinate (one of the German states) in 1840, Nast was the son of a musician in the Ninth Regiment Bavarian Band. The family moved to New York City in 1846, at which time young Thomas was enrolled in school. It seems that art was his only interest. One teacher admonished him, "Go finish your picture. You will never learn to read or figure." After unsuccessfully trying to interest their son in music, his parents eventually encouraged the development of his artistic talent. By the age of fifteen, Thomas Nast was drawing illustrations for *Frank Leslie's Illustrated Newspaper.* He joined *Harper's Weekly* in 1862 (at the age of twenty-two), where he developed the cartoon style that was to win him a national reputation, as well as enemies.[15] He received praise from Abraham Lincoln, Ulysses Grant, and Samuel Clemens (also known as Mark Twain, who in 1872 asked Nast to do

the illustrations for one of his books so that "then I will have good pictures"). In contrast, one of Nast's favorite targets, political boss William Marcy Tweed of New York's Tammany Hall, once shouted, "Let's stop these damn pictures. I don't care so much what the papers say about me—my constituents can't read; but damn it, they can see pictures!"

It is obvious from his work that Nast was a man of strong feelings and emotions. In his eyes, those people whom he admired possessed no flaws. Conversely, those whom he opposed were, to him, capable of every conceivable villainy. As a result, his characterizations often were terribly unfair, gross distortions of reality and more than occasionally libelous. In his view, however, his central purpose was not to entertain but to move his audience, to make them scream out in outrage or anger, to prod them to action. The selection of Nast's cartoons in this chapter is typical of the body of his work for *Harper's Weekly*: artistically inventive and polished, blatantly slanted, and brimming with indignation and emotion.

The evidence in this chapter consists of fourteen cartoons by Thomas Nast that were published in *Harper's Weekly* between August 5, 1865, and December 9, 1876. Your tasks in this chapter are to determine Nast's views on the controversial issues of the Reconstruction era, and how his cartoons attempted to sway public opinion on those issues.

---

15. Nast began to make the transition from artistry to caricature in 1867. Note the differences between Sources 1 and 2 and Sources 3 through 14. As you can see, the transition was more gradual than immediate.

The Method

Although Thomas Nast developed the political cartoon into a true art form, cartoons and caricatures had a long tradition in both Europe and America before Nast. English artists helped bring forth the cartoon style that eventually made *Punch* (founded in 1841) one of the liveliest illustrated periodicals on both sides of the Atlantic. In America, Benjamin Franklin is traditionally credited with publishing the first newspaper cartoon in 1754—the multidivided snake (each part of the snake representing one colony) with the ominous warning "Join or Die." By the time Andrew Jackson sought the presidency, the political cartoon had become a regular and popular feature of American political life. Crude by modern standards, these cartoons influenced some people far more than did the printed word.

As we noted, the political cartoon, like the newspaper editorial, is intended to do more than objectively report events. It is meant to express an opinion, a point of view, approval or disapproval. Political cartoonists want to move people, to make them laugh, to anger them, or to move them to action. In short, political cartoons do not depict exactly what is happening; rather, they portray popular reaction to what is happening and try to persuade people to react in a particular way.

How do you analyze political cartoons? First, using your text and the Problem and Background sections of this chapter, make a list of the most important issues and events (including elections) of the period between 1865 and 1876. As you examine the cartoons in this chapter, try to determine what event or issue is being portrayed. Often a cartoon's caption, dialogue, or date will help you discover its focus.

Next, look closely at each cartoon for clues that will help you understand the message that Nast was trying to convey. People who saw these cartoons more than one hundred years ago did not have to study them so carefully, of course. The individuals and events shown in each cartoon were immediately familiar to them, and the message was obvious. But you are historians, using these cartoons as evidence to help you understand how people were reacting to important events many years ago.

As you can see, Nast was a talented artist. Like many political cartoonists, he often explored the differences between what he believed was the ideal (justice, fairness) and the reality (his view of what was actually happening). To "read" Nast's cartoons, you should identify the issue or event on which the cartoon is based. Then look at the *imagery* Nast used: the situation, the setting, the clothes people are wearing, and the objects in the picture. It is especially important to note how people are portrayed: Do they look handsome and noble, or do they look like animals? Are they happy or sad? Intelligent or stupid?

Political cartoonists often use *symbolism* to make their point, sometimes in the form of an *allegory*. In an

✦ CHAPTER 11

Reconstructing
Reconstruction:
The Political
Cartoonist and
Public Opinion

allegory, familiar figures are shown in a situation or setting that everyone knows—for example, a setting from the Bible, a fairy tale, or another well-known source. For instance, a cartoon showing a tiny president of the United States holding a slingshot, dressed in sandals and rags, and fighting a giant, muscular man labeled "Congress" would remind viewers of the story of David and Goliath. In that story, the small man won. The message of the cartoon is that the president will win in his struggle with Congress.

Other, less complicated symbolism is often used in political cartoons. In Nast's time, as today, the American flag was an important symbol of the ideals of our democratic country, and an olive branch or dove represented the desire for peace. Some symbols have changed, however. Today, the tall, skinny figure we call Uncle Sam represents the United States. In Nast's time, Columbia, a tall woman wearing a long classical dress, represented the United States. Also in Nast's time, an hourglass, rather than a clock, symbolized that time was running out. And military uniforms, regardless of the fact that the Civil War had ended in 1865, were used to indicate whether a person had supported the Union (and, by implication, was a Republican) or the Confederacy (by implication, a Democrat).

As you can see, a political cartoon must be analyzed in detail to get the full meaning the cartoonist was trying to convey. From that analysis, one can discover the message of the cartoon, along with the cartoonist's views on the subject and the ways in which the cartoonist was trying to influence public opinion. Now you are ready to begin your analysis of the Reconstruction era through the cartoons of Thomas Nast.

◆

The Evidence

Sources 1 through 14 from *Harper's Weekly. A Journal of Civilization*, August 5, 1865; June 30, 1866; March 30, 1867; September 5, October 3, 1868; April 13, August 3, September 21, 1872; March 14, September 26, December 5, 1874; September 2, December 9, November 4, 1876.

1. Columbia—"Shall I Trust These Men, And Not This Man?," August 5, 1865.

♦ CHAPTER 11

Reconstructing
Reconstruction:
The Political
Cartoonist and
Public Opinion

2. "The Contrast of Suffering—Andersonville and Fortress Monroe,"
   June 30, 1866.

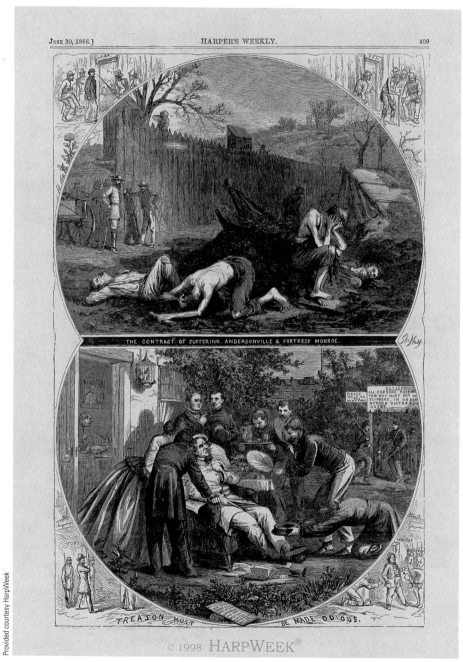

3. Amphitheatrum Johnsonianum—"Massacre of the Innocents At New Orleans," March 30, 1867.

AMPHITHEATRUM JOHNSONIANUM—MASSACRE OF THE INNOCENTS AT NEW ORLEANS, July 30, 1866.

◆ CHAPTER 11

Reconstructing
Reconstruction:
The Political
Cartoonist and
Public Opinion

4. "This Is a White Man's Government," September 5, 1868.

5. "The Modern Samson," October 3, 1868.

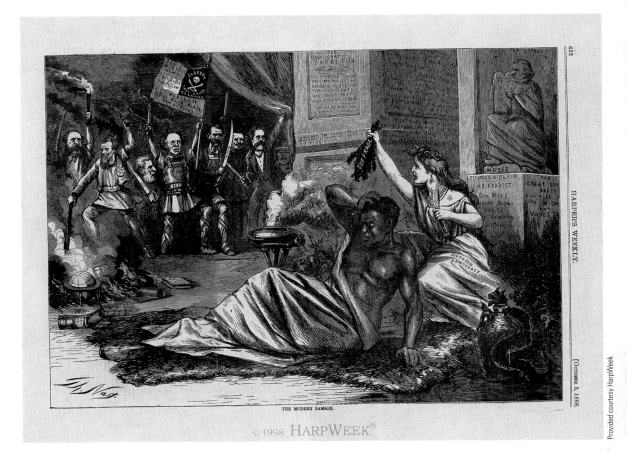

✦ CHAPTER 11

Reconstructing
Reconstruction:
The Political
Cartoonist and
Public Opinion

6. "The Republic Is Not Ungrateful," April 13, 1872.

THE REPUBLIC IS NOT UNGRATEFUL.

"It is not what is *charged* but what is *proved* that damages the party defendant. Any one may be accused of the most heinous offenses; the Saviour of mankind was not only arraigned but convicted; but what of it? Facts alone are decisive."—*New York Tribune, March* 13, 1872.

7. "Baltimore 1861–1872," August 3, 1872.

BALTIMORE 1861–1872.
"Let us Clasp Hands over the Bloody Chasm."

✦ CHAPTER 11

Reconstructing
Reconstruction:
The Political
Cartoonist and
Public Opinion

8. "Let Us Clasp Hands over the Bloody Chasm" (Horace Greeley)
   September 21, 1872.

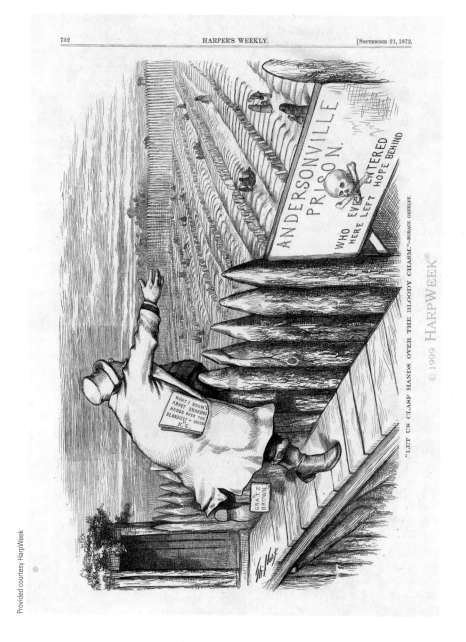

9. "Colored Rule in Reconstructed (?) State," March 14, 1874.

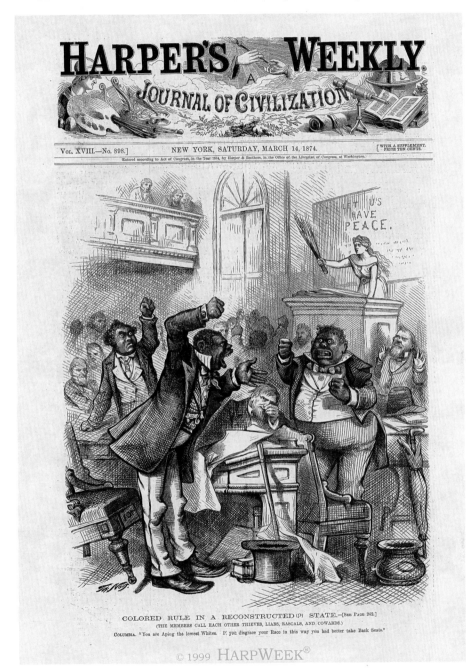

✦ CHAPTER 11

Reconstructing
Reconstruction:
The Political
Cartoonist and
Public Opinion

10. "The Commandments in South Carolina," September 26, 1874.

THE COMMANDMENTS IN SOUTH CAROLINA.
"We've pretty well smashed that; but I suppose, Massa Moses, you can get another one."

11. "Now Gnaw Away!," December 5, 1874.

NOW GNAW AWAY!

◆ CHAPTER 11

Reconstructing
Reconstruction:
The Political
Cartoonist and
Public Opinion

12. "Is This a Republican Form of Government? Is This Protecting Life, Liberty, or Property? Is This the Equal Protection of the Laws?," September 2, 1876.

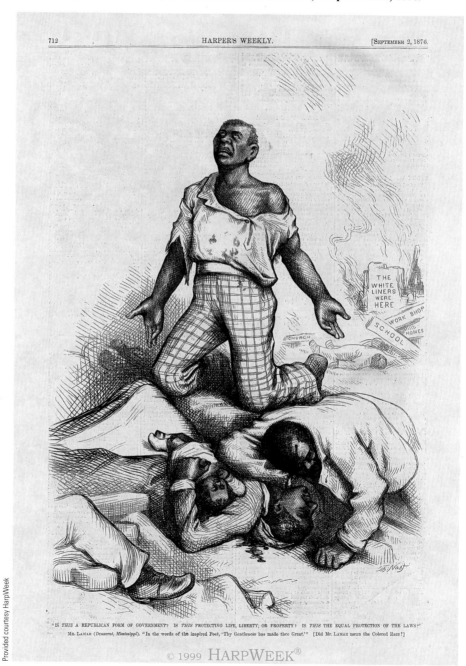

13. "The Ignorant Vote—Honors Are Easy," December 9, 1876.

✦ CHAPTER 11

Reconstructing
Reconstruction:
The Political
Cartoonist and
Public Opinion

14. "The Solid South Against the Union," November 4, 1876.

Questions to Consider

Begin by reviewing your list of the important issues and events of the Reconstruction era. Then systematically examine the cartoons, answering the following questions for each one:

1. What issues or event is represented by this cartoon?
2. Who are the principal figures, and how are they portrayed?
3. What *imagery* is used?
4. Is this cartoon an *allegory*? If so, what is the basis of the allegory?
5. What *symbols* are used?
6. How was Nast trying to influence public opinion through this cartoon?

You may find that making a chart is the easiest way to do this.

Sources 1 through 3 represent Nast's view of Presidential Reconstruction under Andrew Johnson. Who is the woman in Source 1? Who are the men kneeling before her in the left frame? What do they seek? Who does the African American in the right frame represent? Can you formulate one sentence that summarizes Nast's "message" in Source 1?

Source 2 is more complex: two drawings within two other drawings. If you do not already know what purpose Andersonville and Fortress Monroe served, consult a text on this time period, an encyclopedia, or a good Civil War history book. Then look at the upper left and upper right outside drawings. Contrast the appearance of the man entering with the man leaving. Now examine the lower left and lower right outside drawings the same way. What was Nast

trying to tell? The larger inside drawings explain the contrast. What were the conditions like at Andersonville? At Fortress Monroe? What did the cartoonist think were the physical and psychological results?

On July 30, 1866, several blacks attending a Radical Republican convention in New Orleans were shot and killed by white policemen. Who is the emperor in Source 3, and how is he portrayed? What kind of setting is used in this cartoon? Who is the person in the lower left intended to represent? What did Nast think caused this event? What was his own reaction to it?

Each of the three people standing in Source 4 represents part of the Democratic party coalition, and each has something to contribute to the party. Can you identify the groups that the man on the right and the man in the center represent? What do they offer the party? Notice the facial features of the man on the left as well as his dress, particularly the hatband from Five Points (a notorious slum section of New York City). Who is this man supposed to represent, and what does he give the party (see the club in his left hand)? Notice the knife and the belt buckle of the man in the middle. Who does he represent? The man on the right probably is meant to represent Horatio Seymour, the Democratic party's nominee for president to oppose Republican nominee Ulysses Grant. What is the African American U.S. Army veteran reaching for? What is Nast's "message" in Source 4? How does Source 4 relate

[329]

✦ CHAPTER 11

Reconstructing
Reconstruction:
The Political
Cartoonist and
Public Opinion

to Source 5? What is the *allegory* Nast was using? Who are the men on the left of the cartoon? Who does the statue on the right represent? What is Nast's "message" here?

Sources 6 through 8 dealt with the presidential election of 1872, which pitted the incumbent President Grant against the Democratic challenger editor Horace Greeley.[16] Grant is depicted in Source 6, protected by Miss Liberty. What does the bust behind Grant represent? What is Nast's message here? Hoping to finally put an end to what he considered a fruitless Reconstruction, Greeley called for northerners and southerners to "clasp hands over the bloody chasm." How did Nast use (or misuse) Greeley's statement? How would you assess Nast's cartoons in Sources 7 and 8?

Sources 9 through 13 reflect Nast's thinking in the later years of Reconstruction. Sources 9 and 10 portray his opinion of Reconstruction in South Carolina, presided over by Radical Republican governor

Franklin J. Moses (caricatured in Source 10). How are African Americans portrayed in Sources 9, 10, and 13 (compared to portrayals in Sources 1, 4, 5, and 7)? What is the meaning of Source 13? Of Source 11? Source 12?

The last cartoon (Source 14) is Nast's reaction to a bill in Congress to grant amnesty to hundreds of unpardoned former Confederates. What is the *allegory* Nast was using here? What does the fort represent? What is the significance of the African American hiding on the left side of the panel? Who are the men preparing to fire on the fort? What do the two cannons represent? What is Nast's troubling "message" here? Now return to the central questions asked earlier. What significant events took place during Reconstruction? How did Nast try to influence public opinion on the important issues of the era? How did Nast's own views change between 1865 and 1876? Why did Reconstruction finally end?

✦

Epilogue

Undoubtedly, Thomas Nast's work had an important impact on northern opinion of Reconstruction, the Democratic Party, Andrew Johnson, Ulysses Grant, Horace Greeley, Irish-Americans, and a host of other individuals and issues.

16. Angered at the corruption of Grant's administration, several Liberal Republicans bolted their party and supported Greeley.

Yet gradually, northern ardor began to decline as other issues and concerns eased Reconstruction out of the limelight and as it appeared that the crusade to reconstruct the South would be an endless one. Gradually southern Democrats regained control of their state governments, partly through intimidation of black voters and partly through appeals to whites to return the

South to the hands of white southerners.[17] Fearing northern outrage and a potential return to Radical Reconstruction, however, on the surface most southern political leaders claimed to accept emancipation and decried against widespread lynchings and terror against former slaves.

Meanwhile in the North, those Radical Republicans who had insisted on equality for the freedmen either were dying or retiring from politics, replaced by conservative Republicans who spoke for economic expansion, industrialism and commerce, and prosperous farmers. For their part, northern Democrats envisaged a political reunion of northern and southern Democrats that could win control of the federal government. Like their Republican counterparts but for different reasons, northern Democrats had no stomach for assuring freedom and rights to former slaves.

Finally, in the late 1880s, when white southerners realized that the Reconstruction spirit had waned in the North, southern state legislatures began instituting rigid segregation of schools, public transportation and accommodations, parks, restaurants and theaters, elevators, drinking fountains, and so on. Not until the 1950s did those chains begin to be broken.

As the reform spirit waned in the later years of Reconstruction, Nast's popularity suffered. The public appeared to tire of his anger, his self-righteousness, and his relentless crusades. Meanwhile newspaper and magazine technology was changing, and Nast had great difficulty adjusting to the new methodology.[18] Finally, the new publisher of *Harper's Weekly* sought to make the publication less political, and in such an atmosphere there was no place for Thomas Nast. His last cartoon for *Harper's Weekly* appeared on Christmas Day of 1886. He continued to drift from job to job, in 1893 briefly owned his own paper, *Nast's Weekly*, which turned out to be a financial disaster, and by 1901 was deeply in debt. It was then that President Roosevelt came to his aid with a minor consular post in Ecuador, where he died four months after his arrival. He was buried in a quiet ceremony in Woodlawn Cemetery in The Bronx, New York.

Although Nast was only sixty-two years old when he died, most of the famous subjects of his cartoons had long predeceased him. William Marcy Tweed, the political boss of New York's Tammany Hall who Nast had helped to bring down, was sentenced to twelve years in prison in late 1873. But "Boss" Tweed escaped in 1875 and fled to Cuba, where he was apprehended by authorities who identified him with the assistance of a Nast cartoon. He died in prison in 1878.

18. Nast began drawing his cartoons in soft pencil on wooden blocks that were then prepared by engravers. Around 1880 photomechanical reproduction of ink drawings replaced the older and slower method. J. Chal Vinson, *Thomas Nast, Political Cartoonist* (Athens: University of Georgia Press, 1967), p. 35; and Morton Keller, *The Art and Politics of Thomas Nast* (London: Oxford University Press, 1968), p. 327.

17. Conservative Democrats regained control of southern state governments in Tennessee and Virginia (1869); Georgia (1872); Alabama, Arkansas, and Texas (1874); Mississippi (1876); North Carolina, South Carolina, Louisiana, and Florida (1877).

✦ CHAPTER 11

Reconstructing
Reconstruction:
The Political
Cartoonist and
Public Opinion

Nast's hero, Ulysses S. Grant, left the White House in 1877 after an administration marked by corruption and scandal. Not a wealthy man, Grant hurried to finish his memoirs (to provide for his wife Julia) before the throat cancer he had been diagnosed with killed him. He died on July 23, 1885, and was interred in Central Park in New York City, not far from Nast's modest grave. In 1897, a magnificent tomb was dedicated to Grant and his remains were relocated there. When Julia died in 1902, she was laid to rest in what grammatically should be called Grants' Tomb.

Thomas Nast was a pioneer of a tradition and a political art form that remains extremely popular today. As Joel Pett, cartoonist for the Lexington (KY) *Herald-Leader* put it, "If [newspaper publishers] . . . sign on to the quaint but true notion that journalism ought to comfort the afflicted and afflict the comfortable, there's no better way to afflict the comfortable than with editorial cartoons."[19] Nast couldn't have said it better himself.

19. Chris Lamb, *Drawn to Extremes: The Use and Abuse of Editorial Cartoons* (New York: Columbia University Press, 2004), p. 238.